Frontera Madre(hood)

The Feminist Wire Books
Connecting Feminisms, Race, and Social Justice

ALSO IN THE FEMINIST WIRE BOOKS

Black Women and 'da Rona: Community, Consciousness, and Ethics of Care, edited by Julia S. Jordan-Zachery and Shamara Wyllie Alhassan

Lavender Fields: Black Women Experiencing Fear, Agency, and Hope in the Time of COVID-19, edited by Julia S. Jordan-Zachery

A Love Letter to This Bridge Called My Back, edited by gloria j. wilson, Joni B. Acuff, and Amelia M. Kraehe

Black Girl Magic Beyond the Hashtag: Twenty-First-Century Acts of Self-Definition, edited by Julia S. Jordan-Zachery and Duchess Harris

The Chicana M(other)work Anthology, edited by Cecilia Caballero, Yvette Martínez-Vu, Judith Pérez-Torres, Michelle Téllez, and Christine Vega

Them Goon Rules: Fugitive Essays on Radical Black Feminism, by Marquis Bey

FRONTERA MADRE(HOOD)

Brown Mothers Challenging Oppression and Transborder Violence at the U.S.-Mexico Border

EDITED BY CYNTHIA BEJARANO & MARIA CRISTINA MORALES

Foreword by Michelle Téllez | Afterword by Irene Lara

THE UNIVERSITY OF
ARIZONA PRESS
TUCSON

The University of Arizona Press
www.uapress.arizona.edu

We respectfully acknowledge that the University of Arizona is on the land and territories of Indigenous peoples. Today, Arizona is home to twenty-two federally recognized tribes, with Tucson being home to the O'odham and the Yaqui. Committed to diversity and inclusion, the University strives to build sustainable relationships with sovereign Native Nations and Indigenous communities through education offerings, partnerships, and community service.

ISBN-13: 978-0-8165-4668-8 (paperback)
ISBN-13: 978-0-8165-4669-5 (ebook)

Cover design by Leigh McDonald
Cover art by Paola Isabel Nava González
Typeset by Sara Thaxton in 10.5/14 Warnock Pro with Headline Gothic ATF and Atrament

Publication of this book is made possible in part by financial support from the New Mexico State University, College of Arts and Sciences Stan Fulton Endowed Chair.

Library of Congress Cataloging-in-Publication Data
Names: Bejarano, Cynthia L., 1973– editor. | Morales, María Cristina, editor.
Title: Frontera madrehood : brown mothers challenging oppression and transborder violence at
    the U.S.-Mexico border / edited by Cynthia Bejarano and Maria Cristina Morales ; foreword
    by Michelle Téllez ; afterword by Irene Lara.
Other titles: Feminist wire books.
Description: Tucson : University of Arizona Press, 2024. | Series: The feminist wire books |
    Includes bibliographical references and index.
Identifiers: LCCN 2023048962 (print) | LCCN 2023048963 (ebook) | ISBN 9780816546688
    (paperback) | ISBN 9780816546695 (ebook)
Subjects: LCSH: Minority women activists—Mexican-American Border Region. | Mothers—
    Mexican-American Border Region—Social conditions. | Mother and child—Mexican-
    American Border Region. | Transnationalism.
Classification: LCC HQ1236.5.U6 F766 2024 (print) | LCC HQ1236.5.U6 (ebook) |
    DDC 306.874/309721—c23/eng/20231212
LC record available at https://lccn.loc.gov/2023048962
LC ebook record available at https://lccn.loc.gov/2023048963

Printed in the United States of America
♾ This paper meets the requirements of ANSI/NISO Z39.48-1992 (Permanence of Paper).

Para mi hijo, Joaquín Félix, who gives me love and light each day.
—CYNTHIA BEJARANO

For the first madre fronteriza to touch my life—my mother, who crossed the border to provide us a path to future opportunities while keeping us rooted in family and culture on the Mexican side of the border.

Por la primera madre fronteriza que tocó mi vida, mi madre, que cruzó la frontera para brindarnos un camino hacia oportunidades futuras, manteniendo nuestras raíces en familia y cultura del lado mexicano de la frontera.
—CRISTINA MORALES

We dedicate this book to *fronteriza madres, amás, mamás, mámis,* and those who engage in countless forms of mothering that endure the ordinary and the unimaginable. They inspire us with their resilience.
—CYNTHIA AND CRISTINA

CONTENTS

FOREWORD

My daughter was just months old when I saw a video of a woman carrying an infant on her back crossing the Sonoran corridor of the U.S.-Mexico border. She and her group had been detained by the Minutemen, a since-disbanded vigilante group founded in 2004, whose self-proclaimed mission was to monitor and protect the border. The incident was being recorded by human rights observers to ensure the safety of the migrants while they waited for the border patrol to arrive. As I watched the video, I couldn't keep my eyes off the mother; she looked visibly distressed and frustrated but was taking care of her child's needs. Our babies must have been around the same age. As a new mother exhausted from sleepless nights and from caring for my daughter alone, I couldn't imagine how she had traversed hundreds, if not thousands, of miles while carrying her child. I wondered what she had had to endure only to be stopped and deterred from crossing into the United States.

Was someone waiting for them, panicked because they had never arrived? Was she sent back to her country of origin? It never occurred to me that the mother might be separated from her baby. In 2007, the USian public was several years away from witnessing the mass family separations that began in 2018—acts of tremendous violence that have yet to be repaired. To date, hundreds of children have not been returned to their families, their mothers.

This short video provided me a glimpse into a reality I couldn't possibly begin to comprehend otherwise. What does it mean to mother at the intersections of violence, loss, migration, trauma, separation, militarization, and cultural shock? Indeed, the essays in this outstanding volume begin to paint a picture of "a state of being and a condition of Brown mothering, specifically at the U.S.-Mexico border, that is unique, complex, and a departure from other locations" (introduction, this vol.). What the editors have coined *frontera madre(hood)*—a concept that captures the challenges of mothering for Brown women on both sides of the U.S.-Mexico border—will help us, as readers, understand and bear witness to the experiences of mothers as agents of change, who fight for the education and healthcare of their families as they survive in the borderlands. This project is both essential and transformative.

In 2006, I started writing about my own encounters as a Brown Chicana single mother navigating multiple hetero-patriarchal institutions— the medical system, the family court system, academia—because writing was the only way I could both let out my frustrations and name my experiences. I was trying to decipher what it meant to critically navigate care work through the lens of cultural and radical insistence. My contemplations often led me to my own mother, an immigrant woman from a small town in Mexico, and to my childhood of living along the border, navigating the cities of San Diego and Tijuana. Grocery runs into pre-NAFTA-era Mexico to Comercial Mexicana (grocery store) meant eating Fruti Lupis instead of Fruit Loops cereal as a child and long border waits upon our families' return, never sure if we would be sent to secondary inspection for saying the wrong thing or looking too suspect.

Nonetheless, divisive border ideology existed beyond the geopolitical demarcation, and boundaries between neighborhoods and people were a practice of everyday life. I can still feel the sting of my neighbor's words when they told me that my mother sounded like a broken record when she spoke English. Language terrorism was a marker of living in the borderlands.

Writing is cathartic as much as it is an act of resistance; the concept of Chicana m(other)work (Caballero et al. 2019) emerged from my early writings and then expanded into a powerful conceptual framework and model of collectivity through a group of incredible mother-scholars committed to amplifying the experiences of Chicana mothers across multiple spaces and experiences. Our tagline, *Porque sin madres no hay revolución*, recentered the life force of mothers.

This anthology, on the other hand, recenters the voices who must be most urgently listened to as policies are enacted that affect the life experiences—and possibilities—of those most vulnerable to distant powerholders. Mothers are directly affected by policies at the border, as are those they care for. As I've argued elsewhere (Téllez 2021), the border is not simply a space of passage but also one of conviviality, mutuality, and exchange. It is a place where people live. The essays and *testimonios* in this volume bring meaning to frontera madre(hood), stories and theories that allow us to contemplate the role of mothering at this unique location. It is a place where mixed-status families figure out pathways to remain connected to their loved ones, where laboring in transitional spaces starts at a young age, where solidarity with mothers across and between borders is enacted.

Mothers endure pain. Mothers endure surveillance. Mothers (and their children, even if they are now adults) are abused while in detention. Mothers also resist. Mothers build networks of support with and through their *comadres*. Mothers imagine liberation and abolition. Mothers dream.

Frontera mother(hood) is also about the borders of class, sexuality, gender, and race. We are reminded that "papers, please" not only signifies citizenship but also marks the exclusionary tactics of the state by defining who gets to be a mother.

This book changes the narrative of how Brown women, migrant women, border crossers, and border dwellers are perceived. The authors authentically speak and shape their own stories to bring their realities to life for those who are far from the border.

I carry the words of Sagrario's mother, who has experienced great tragedy and survived unimaginable loss. It is through her resilience that I can imagine hope.

The editors of this collection, Cynthia Bejarano and Cristina Morales, have dedicated their lives' work to uplifting borderland communities. Through this project they have helped us understand how location shapes experience and how imperative it is to center *madres fronterizas*. Their collaboration and vision have brought together an authoritative testament that will not be ignored.

I am honored to have been asked to comment on this beautiful offering, and I welcome you to this journey. Edith Treviño states, "La Frontera is who I am," and these essays are a visceral reflection of this sentiment.

Michelle Téllez
University of Arizona, Tucson

REFERENCES

Téllez, Michelle. 2021. *Border Women and the Community of Maclovio Rojas: Autonomy in the Spaces of Neoliberal Neglect*. Tucson: University of Arizona Press.

ACKNOWLEDGMENTS

This book is possible because of the love and sustenance of the people in my orbit. The constellation of stars that have guided me in my life's journey begins with my parents, my northern star, Elvira† and Félix Bejarano† who joined the ancestors when this book was first imagined; their sacrifices and service to community stay with me *siempre*. To my forever starlights, Joaquin Félix and Jeff, your unconditional love and humor anchor me in all the universes. *Gracias* for creating love space and intellectual space for me always. Love to *mi familia* Debbie, Rich, Santana, Daniel, Walt, Sharon, and *mis tias* Elenas for their *cariño* and encouragement. To my protective star lights, Carmen Vaquera, Melissa Lara, Maru Hernández Sánchez, Sylvia Acosta, Margo Tamez, Myla Vicenti Carpio, Karen Leong, Cristina Morales, Martha Estrada, Waded Cruzado, Zulma Toro, Lisa Ramirez, Rachel Stevens, Mary O'Connell, Graciela Unguez, Sonya Cooper, Jean Fulton, and Jack Wright. *Para mis musas*, Paula Flores Bonilla, Eva Arce, Irma Monrreal, Norma Ledezma, Soledad Aguilar†, Lucha Castro, Alma Gómez, Sally Meisenhelder, Gabino Gómez, Víctor Muñoz, Raymundo Lara y Joe Graham, *gracias por el ejemplo de luchar.*

Love to the activists and scholars in this collection and beyond that I have worked with for several years, especially Paula Flores Bonilla, Guillermina Gonzalez Flores, Lucha Castro, Macrina Cárdenas Montaño, Ma. Eugenia Hernández Sánchez, Sandra Gutiérrez, Sylvia Fernández, Ariana

Saludares, Michelle Téllez, Bertha Tapia, Margaret Brown Vega, Cristina Morales, Taide Elena, Ana María Vásquez, and Vicki Gaubeca. Mil gracias also to my beloved NMSU CAMP *familia* and Gender and Sexuality Studies Program.

—*Cynthia Bejarano*

This book owes its existence to the daily inspiration and wisdom I gained from my children, Brianna and Joaquin. Thank you for transforming how I see the world through a mother's eyes. You have made me love deeper, take more risks, be more grounded, and intensify my compassion for mothers and children globally. My deepest gratitude also extends to my husband, Brian Roebuck, for always being there and supporting me through this process.

I am profoundly fortunate to be surrounded by resilient women: my mother, Maria de Jesus Morales; sister, Cindy; sister-in-law, Debbie Ramirez; Tía Doris; Tía Flor, and my abuelas Aurora Garcia† and Emma Martinez†. Their strength fuels my pursuit of independence and resilience. My father, Oscar Morales' unconditional love and lessons in hard work and humor are also cherished. I also want to thank my brother, Oscar Morales, for his support. To my nieces, Alessandra, Andrea, Bella; nephews, Noah and Ivan; and brother-in-law, Andres, thank you for your joyous presence. *También gracias a mis primas/os Silvia, Lilia, Fernando, Norma, y Claudia Retana.*

I sincerely appreciate Cynthia Bejarano for her camaraderie for nearly two decades. I am looking forward to our next venture. I am grateful to all the collaborators in this book for sharing their work and stories. Special thanks to Rogelio Sáenz, Leisy Abrego, and Lorena Murga, whose emotional support has been instrumental. Lastly, thank you to the faculty, students, and staff at the Sociology and Anthropology Department at UTEP; your tenacity is inspirational.

—*Cristina Morales*

We would both like to thank the NMSU College of Arts and Sciences (CoAS) Stan Fulton Endowed funding and Business Center staff, particularly Lucille Casas and Kellie Cooper, and amazing research assistants

Zaira Martin and Fatima Oliveros, and also, GMRS Transcription Services. We express our gratitude to the artist Paola Nava González, for her impactful artwork titled, "Abuela," which portrays her activist grandmother, Paula Flores Bonilla. All our gratitude to Dolores Delgado Bernal and Mako Ward for their support of this collection, and Nora Martinez and Melanie Mallon for their meticulous editorial work. Our immense appreciation goes to the University of Arizona Press team, especially Kristen Buckles and the Feminist Wire Book Series Editorial Board for their collective support in co-creating a beautiful book honoring *madres fronterizas*.

Frontera Madre(hood)

Introduction

Frontera + Madre + Hood = Frontera Madre(hood)

CYNTHIA BEJARANO AND MARIA CRISTINA MORALES

New Mexico State University and The University of Texas at El Paso

At the Texas-Mexico border in El Paso, we often attend a local Thanks-giving parade with our children. In contrast to the past, when this parade was better known for the dancing of matachines from Ciudad Juárez, Chihuahua, and El Paso, Texas, and when local high school bands were a staple, in this post-9/11 world, the parade route is lined with representations of a surveillance society. A plethora of policing units, including Department of Homeland Security (DHS) units, local and state police, and different military departments, saturate the parade lineup. Ironically, these symbols of social control of Brown and borderland communities are celebrated in combination with familiar symbols oriented toward children, like giant inflatable balloons, clown-driven go-karts, and the spectacular, crowd-pleasing charro and charra horse riders on beautifully adorned horses.[1] Surprisingly and equally disconcerting, when we last attended, the parade lineup included youth, primarily boys, from the Department of Homeland Security (DHS) and military junior explorer programs, wearing uniforms and marching in unison. They looked like miniature replicas of the men and womxn agents installed across the U.S.-Mexico borderline.

---

1. *Charros* and *charras* are Mexican horsemen and horsewomxn dressed in elaborate traditional attire who guide their decorated horses through fancy footwork and often perform roping techniques atop their horses for the public.

The indoctrination of Brown children and youth into this surveillance society at the border is intense. The border patrol truck float has a giant inflatable of a young Brown border patrol agent (figure I.1). We attended this same parade with our parents as children, but we do not remember the presence of any law enforcement, especially not the U.S. Customs and Border Protection agents and vehicles, nor the U.S. Border Patrol presence.

On and off for years, we have met at the parade with our children and families, and we both recognize the abundance of enforcement units and the presence of the military-industrial complex in this parade. Hyperpatriarchal and hypermasculine images, including armored vehicles, patrol units, and other tools of securitization, are prominent throughout the two-hour parade route.

After attending the last parade, we asked ourselves, as mothers, Are border patrol inflatables also seen in parades in the U.S. interior? While we entertained this question, we recognized what to outsiders might seem like a paradox: for impoverished, Brown, and immigrant communities, jobs with the U.S. Department of Homeland Security are among the few sources of livable wages with generous healthcare and retirement benefits. Thousands of Latinx families grapple with the ramifications of these

FIGURE I.1 Border patrol parade route with inflatable. Photo by Cynthia Bejarano.

employment decisions by neighbors, friends, and even family members as they become part of the surveillance system. It is well known that Latinx people are the preferred employees for agents on the borderline, given their understanding of the U.S.-Mexico border and their bicultural and bilingual attributes.

As such, the presence of border patrol agents living and working at the border is also typical. Yet, at the parade route, the display of a Brown, even childlike, inflatable agent raises some questions. Do the young Brown agents on the route, in both human and inflatable cartoon-like forms, represent tools to indoctrinate Latinx children into thinking that they, too, can be border control agents? While the intention behind these representations of militarization and policing is unknown, from a critical Brown mother's perspective, such representations raise concerns: Are these images tools to recruit children and youth into a career in policing their people? Or are they tools of social control against immigrant families, mostly mixed-status families? Do these material images work to legitimize the layers of policing that residents of the U.S.-Mexico border are subjected to every day?

Along with the indoctrination of border enforcement, Brown children endure the violent images of seemingly disposable Brown bodies and of people like themselves who are excluded from the United States. Unlike in any other U.S. region, children and youth at the borderlands face the violent consequences of border enforcement that disproportionately targets Brown people like themselves, including migrant deaths, the detention of migrant children, family separations, and masses of asylum seekers, including children, sleeping on the streets. The symbols of militaristic border and immigration control are normalized along the U.S.-Mexico border, and children must process how Brown bodies, including their own, are racially profiled.

For example, in another part of the U.S.-Mexico border, five-year-old Joaquín asked his mother, Cynthia, a difficult question as they visited the ironically named Friendship Park, which overlooks the Pacific Ocean at the border between San Diego and Tijuana (figure I.2). The massive border wall and additionally buttressed wall reinforcements separate the people that gather on Sundays to visit loved ones from Mexico who cannot cross the border. Joaquín watched a man on the U.S. side lean against the wall as he spoke to a woman in Tijuana and asked, "Momma, why

FIGURE I.2 Picture of border wall at the San Diego Friendship Park with Joaquín. Photo by Cynthia Bejarano.

is the border wall keeping us from our antepasados? *Why can't people just swim across or get on a boat and go around the wall?" At his young age, Joaquín questioned the rationale for separating Mexican families and communities at the U.S.-Mexico border and for the heavy metal wall that separates us.*

The vignettes above illustrate the complexities of coming of age along the U.S.-Mexico border, where violence and the exclusion of Brown bodies is normalized and where layers of fencing separate them from their families, friends, and culture on the other side. Mothering at the border entails actively working on empowering our children in a context that actively criminalizes and excludes Brown people like themselves, where even if they are privileged to live on the U.S. side of the border, Brown borderland children must strive not to internalize being perpetual foreigners in their own country and learn that their Latinx co-ethnics in Mexico or elsewhere are not criminals but victims of globalized processes that uprooted them from somewhere else or worked to exploit them in their homeland. Our children can do more than be the enforcers of borderland regimes (Hawthorne and Kelly 2020) that determine who can and cannot move and why. For their own safety, Brown borderland children in Mexico are taught how to avoid Mexican military apparatuses and even police for their own protection, as well as to avoid any proximity to the U.S. border wall for fear of threats of violence from U.S. agents, as described later in this collection.

How This Collection on *Fronteriza* Mothering Came to Life

The opening vignettes catalyze this anthology as we ruminate over the challenges of raising children in the borderlands. We were both born and raised in the Paso del Norte border region. Maria Cristina is a *fronteriza* who has lived a transborder existence most of her life. Her parents, Maria and Oscar, lived in Ciudad Juárez, Chihuahua, Mexico, and Cristina was born across the border in El Paso, Texas. When she reached school age, Cristina, her parents, and her siblings settled on the U.S. side of the border but continued to live a transborder existence, visiting family and friends several times a week in Juárez. Living the life of a *transfronteriza* and coming from a working-class immigrant family, Cristina was very much familiar with the devaluing of voices from the U.S.-Mexico border and intraethnic social fragmentations among a presumably homogeneous Brown community.

Cynthia is also a *fronteriza*, from a southern New Mexico colonia in the Paso del Norte region called Anthony. Her ancestors were tethered to this region for generations. Her great-grandparents were from Ciudad Juárez and across Chihuahua, and her grandparents and parents, Félix and Elvira, were born in southern New Mexican villages along the Rio Grande, except for one born in El Paso's downtown Segundo Barrio. Her ancestors were farmworkers and ranch hands on farms owned by Anglos and affluent "Hispanics." In her colonia, most everyone was working-class poor, like her family, or labeled as "indigent" by the government. Her barrio, her "hood," was notorious for street gangs and vice, which shaped her social justice work. Growing up, her family crossed to Ciudad Juárez for affordable dental care and other necessities, and now, she crosses over to see close friends forged through activism in the antifeminicide movement, migrant advocacy, and creative work inspired by the border and its people. For Cristina and Cynthia, border regions are precious and why this book exists.

Our main impetus for this collection is to include a space for womxn's voices from both sides of the U.S.-Mexico border. *Fronteriza* womxn (womxn from the border) tend to be marginalized as scholars and active participants in formulating border policies that directly affect them and their families. Therefore, all our contributors are from the U.S.-Mexico border, either born or currently residing in this region; this book provides a space for them to tell their own stories. While our contributors vary in terms of racial and ethnic identity, nationality, nativity, citizenship, and gender orientation and sexuality, they are bound by social and cultural categories, such as being womxn and *madres*, in myriad ways. We also have collective and individual connections to the literal, cultural, and social borderlands discussed throughout this book.

At the U.S.-Mexico border, more so than in any other region in the United States, Brown children are experiencing immediate direct or indirect injustices attributed to border and immigration enforcement, persistent poverty, refugee displacement and incarceration, and human and drug trafficking, among other issues. On the northern Mexican side, these issues for children are rampant. All children grow nervous as they cross U.S. border inspection checkpoints, the international ports of entry, or Mexican military *retenes* (roadblocks)—all reasons among others we insist that mothering at the borderlands is unique. Across any border community, the local news features the stories of the day: children and families apprehended or children and others who are injured or die from attempting to cross deserts, waterways, or the border wall. Drug seizures at international ports of entry and human smuggling and trafficking ring members are paraded across television screens; narco violence is gruesomely displayed; and other stories are presented that speak to the heart of this book.

In *Frontera Madre(hood)*, we also reflect on the subjugation of sex and race in the media and in public images that erroneously represent Brown mothers at the borderlands as passive and docile. Here we provide powerful accounts from community activists, feminists, and activist-scholars who strongly advocate for their families and communities along both sides of the U.S.-Mexico border amid structural, systemic, political, sexualized, sexist, homophobic, social, and racialized violence. In this collection, we defy traditional notions regarding "passive" Brown womxn and mothers and instead work to deconstruct what Indigenous, Mexicana, Chicanx, Latinx, and Black forms of madre(hood) represent, as unconventional and, at times, radical forms of loving and mothering in border landscapes. Our contributors, who are also our elders, *colegas*, and *hermanas en solidaridad*, challenge traditional tropes of who can mother and how one can mother, describing the realities of transmothering, and the movement back and forth across militarized and policed international boundaries for many mothers, which is also at the core of *Frontera Madre(hood)*.

Our collection offers a unique opportunity to share the experiences of *mujeres* who mother in numerous life circumstances and who work to undo the social forces that attempt to limit and control our movement, our ideologies, and even our intimate relationships, including how we raise and support children and young people. Various intellectual concepts have contributed to these discussions, like those of Patricia Hill Collins (2002), who developed the term "othermothering" to distinguish biological mothers from womxn who care for children. Collins consequently influenced the creation of *Patricia Hill Collins: Reconceiving Motherhood*, edited by Kaila Adia Story. Elsewhere, Fuentes (2013) identifies Latinx and Black mothers engaged in educational justice struggles for their children. We also recognize that many versions of mothering are not reflected in this collection, and that queer and BIPOC mothering experiences are not fully represented here. It was not an oversight but a limit on book length. We aspire to continue future threads of this work with LGBTQIA+ colleagues and others to include more diverse voices and experiences of nonbinary parenting, queer parenting, transwomxn and transmen who mother/parent, and other forms of mothering.

In future writings, we hope to work with more Indigenous, Black, and Afro-Latinx mothers, scholars, and community leaders and to expand on and work with the numerous Indigenous womxn from both sides of the borderlands, including the Tohono O'odham, Yaqui, Ysleta del Sur, Kickapoo, Nan davi, Apache, Rarámuri, Kumeyaay, and countless other Indigenous mothers who live, labor, and honor their border(ed) homelands and deserve a written space to be heard. Some of our contributors come from these communities, but we acknowledge that much more work must be done. Additionally, Africans and Afro-Latinxs (i.e., Haitians, Cubans, Venezuelans, Brazilians) are increasingly represented in the newest migration wave at the U.S.-Mexico border. Our future work aims to reflect more forms of mothering that take place along these nearly two-thousand-mile-long highly politicized and surveilled borderlands.

Madre(hood) at the borderlands, or the more aptly named frontera madre(hood), teaches Brown children how to navigate or challenge restrictive and regimented structures, images, and ideologies embedded in this context.[2] In this anthology, we seek to deconstruct the realities of living on the border as *fronteriza* feminist mothers / co-mothers / fictive kin mothers and scholars and how we are framing the borderlands for our nonbiological or biological children / fictive kin children / future children / children in our hearts and memories and children in our barrios (Mexican neighborhoods, or hoods) as a space of resistance.

Frontera Madre(hood): Brown Mothers Challenging Oppression and Transborder Violence at the U.S.-Mexico Border is a unique critical feminist anthology that centers on the myriad issues of transborder structural violence and oppression faced by Indigenous, Mexicana, Chicanx, Latinx, and Black womxn and womxn of mixed identities living on both sides of the U.S.-Mexico border and their resistance to these often traumatic and systemically violent experiences. We present a collection of *testimonios*, a methodology rooted in Latin American research and used to document the lived experiences of oppressed groups, including their remarkable resilience (e.g., Caballero et al. 2019; Delgado Bernal, Burciaga, and Flores Guzmán 2012; del Alba Acevedo et al. 2001; Moraga and Anzaldúa 1983). We also include scholarly chapters highlighting the voices of *mujeres*: *mujer* scholars, feminist *mujeres*, and activists from both sides of the U.S.-Mexico borderlands who are rarely heard in U.S. scholarly books. Oftentimes, research by border womxn or their lived

---

2. To our knowledge, the only mention in scholarly print of the term *madrehood* without parenthesis, as we use it, is referenced once in a sentence by linguistic anthropologist Liza Bakewell in *Madre: Perilous Journeys with a Spanish Noun*, where she writes, "With Malinche, La Nación, La Virgin de Guadalupe, and the Liberals' Good Mother, Mexico's Madrehood became a constellation united in name, but not in temperament, obedience, or constitution" (2011, 186).

experiences are misrepresented or interpreted through someone else's optic, such as that of the media or academia.

This collection was designed to create a writing space for womxn laboring at border universities or living in borderlands communities, barrios/hoods, whose visceral border experiences are palpable. We recognize that several important scholars from and beyond the U.S.-Mexico border have contributed key writings about these contested and complex borderland spaces, and we feel that our collection can contribute to this canon of work. *Frontera Madre(hood)* contributors share their diverse lived experiences, advocacy work and scholarly activism, and critical perspectives while living in the U.S.-Mexico transborder regions of California–Baja California, Arizona-Sonora, New Mexico–Chihuahua, Texas-Chihuahua, Texas–Nuevo Leon, and Texas-Tamaulipas. This anthology, then, is genuinely *transfronterizo/a* and represents a cadre of womxn marked, shaped, influenced, and even defined and identified by the spaces and places we inhabit with twenty million other border people from both sides of the nearly two-thousand-mile borderline. As *fronterizas* and *transfronterizas* who personify Indigenous, Latinx, Latina, Mexicana, Chicanx, Black, and mixed identities, our collective voices simultaneously represent resiliency through our various forms of mothering to confront multiple challenges in the U.S.-Mexico geopolitical zone. To our knowledge, no collective work captures the myriad experiences of mothers who resist, struggle, and work to create shelter, safe spaces, and survival for their families, border youth, and overall communities on both sides of the U.S.-Mexico border.

Mothering in Action

Experiences of mothering at the borderlands span topics as diverse as history, theorizing, and popular culture (Anzaldúa 1987; Cantú 2015; Castañeda 2003; Elenes 2010; Saldívar-Hull 2000); mothers' grassroots resistance as intellectuals and community organizers (Bejarano 2002; Morales and Bejarano 2009; Téllez 2021); spirituality and activism (Facio and Lara 2014; Lara 2014); and beyond. Despite stereotypical cultural representations of Latinx mothers as passive and docile, Latina *madres* are strong and resilient. For example, in collaboration with the Children's

Disabilities Information Coalition, Guillermina "Gina" Núñez-Mchiri published *Hopelighting* (2021), which highlights stories of mothers' resiliency at the El Paso–Juárez border as they advocate for their children with disabilities. Rather than feeling defeated, these mostly Latinx mothers are working to create a more inclusive society for children with disabilities.

Chicana feminist theory has challenged these traditional conceptualizations of Latina *madres* and has also been used to help explain Latinx *madres'* politics of motherhood and activism, as well as their work to transform the lives of their children and communities (Velazquez 2017). More than forty years ago, Chicanx feminists Cherríe Moraga and Gloria Anzaldúa inspired generations of womxn with *This Bridge Called My Back* (1981). *This Bridge* was among the first books developed by and written entirely by womxn of color. This collection enlightened us about the marginalized position of Chicanx *mujeres* within a feminist movement dominated by privileged white womxn. It provided a sense of struggle and pain and a catalyst for rebellion. Decades later, *This Bridge* has come to represent a countercultural insurgence into white feminist theory.

Chicana poet and cultural critic Gloria Anzaldúa (1987) went on to create a cultural and academic revolution in feminism and motherhood in *Borderlands / La Frontera*. Rereading Anzaldúa's scholarship with what she calls her "Chicana mami eyes," Irene Lara (2014) developed "serpentine conocimientos." Following Anzaldúa's critical thought, the serpent with the head of a womxn is not the root of all evil portrayed by colonial thought but instinctual knowledge and transformation, leading to Lara's positionality of serpentine mamihood.

This Bridge is also the inspiration for literature on radical mothers of color, including the motivation behind Alexis Pauline Gumbs, China Martens, and Mai'a Williams's *Revolutionary Mothering: Love on the Front Lines* (2016), a literary anthology dedicated to "revolutionary mothers and all the revolutions they've created." Here, we are in solidarity with Gumbs, Martens, and Williams's aim of connecting radical mothering to feminists of color's transformative practices from the fringes of two societies. Adding to these conversations is Yvonne Bynoe's (2009) *Who's Your Mama? The Unsung Voices of Women and Mothers*, which is a collection of everyday people's experiences of motherhood and intersectionality, politics, and personal tragedy, representative of personal narratives on parenting and the social and economic issues affecting womxn and their families in the United States. Complementing this book is Mignon R. Moore's (2011) *Invisible Families: Gay Identities, Relationships, and Motherhood Among Black Women*, which makes visible family life for gay womxn of color, by confronting traditional tropes on racial identity, family formation, and motherhood. In a study on Black lesbian families in New York City, *Invisible Families* examines how race and class structurally shape family formation. Moore's book breaks away from research focusing on white middle-class families to illustrate how the vulnerability of Blackness makes the vulnerability associated with sexual and family intimacy more challenging for African Americans, creating a double jeopardy situation.

A central scholarly focus on motherhood among womxn of color points to the necessity of recognizing culture, race, ethnicity, and other intersectional realities that set their mothering experiences apart. Dorsía Smith Silva's (2011) *Latina/Chicana Mothering* draws from Teresa Arendell's argument in "Mothering and Motherhood: A Decade Review" (1999) that mothering is not experienced the same by all womxn but must account for cultural differences. Silva (2011) pushed the boundaries of what it means to be a Latina/Chicana mother by critically questioning the contrary depictions of Latina/Chicana mothers as powerful but also victims of patriarchal control. Similarly, in the case of Black motherhoods, Dawn Marie Dow's *Mothering While Black* illustrates that "motherhood was not an experience that transcended racial divisions" but, in fact, solidified those racial divisions that exclude Black mothers from the white mothering experience (2019, 2). Here, Dow illustrates how middle-class Black mothers experience parenting differently from their white counterparts, because despite their shared social class, racism continues to jeopardize the well-being of Black mothers and their children. Raising children in a racially unequal world calls for different parenting strategies. In line with Patricia Hill Collins's work on Black motherhood in *Black Feminist Thought* (2002), Black motherhood is dynamic, dialectical, contextual, and not isolated from the intersecting oppressions of race, gender, class, sexuality, and nation.

We also credit *The Chicana M(other)work Anthology*, edited by Cecilia Caballero, Yvette Martínez-Vu, Judith Pérez-Torres, Michelle Téllez, and Christine Vega (2019), who offer a platform to disrupt stereotypical notions of mothering among womxn of color and Chicanas within the

U.S. context of home, workplace, and communities. Chicana m(other) work is a concept and project informed by the authors' shared gendered, classed, and racialized experiences as first-generation Chicana scholars from working-class (im)migrant Mexican families. The Chicana m(other) work framework highlights resistance that makes various forms of feminized labor visible and promotes collective action, holistic healing, and social justice for mother-scholars and activists of color and their children and communities (Caballero et al. 2019, 4).

In our work, we also follow Dolores Delgado Bernal's (2006) explanation that for Latinas, mothering occurs through *consejos* (advice), *cuentos* (stories), and *pláticas* (conversations). Expanding on Delgado Bernal's framework, Latina *madres* use the mothering tools above to socialize their daughters into *"guerra* girls" who induce positive self-agency (Guzmán 2012). The decolonial processes of stories/*cuentos*, advice/*consejos*, and conversations/*pláticas* are also used to challenge the racist discourse that Latinas face daily by creating instances where learning can occur for both mother and daughter (Delgado Bernal 2006; Guzmán 2012).

This decolonial praxis is also clearly present for Indigenous womxn at the U.S.-Mexico border. Political mothering for Indigenous womxn is rooted in care and advocacy for children at the familial and community levels, as well as in claiming Indigenous rights and sovereignty over traditional homelands. Indigenous feminist scholars and activists are at the forefront of continuing to protect their ancestral territories. Lipan Apache scholar Margo Tamez (2020) documents her mother Eloisa Tamez's lawsuit against DHS in the unprecedented case *Tamez vs. Chertoff et al.*, after DHS and the Army Corp of Engineers built the border wall literally in their backyard. This case underscored the bravery mothers exhibit to protect and safeguard not just their families but their ancestral lands from the exercise of eminent domain and concomitant assaults on Indigenous culture and identity. The attack on Lipan land in South Texas mirrored events throughout the borderlands, as in Southern California, where Kumeyaay womxn led protests against constructing the border wall in their homelands (Rivlin-Nadler 2020). Womxn in the Tohono O'odham reservation at the Arizona/Sonora border have also taken on similar struggles.

Indigenous scholars from the borderlands also write about other forms of safeguarding traditional knowledge ways and experiences that affect

Indigenous mothers. An important example is Patrisia Gonzales's (2012) work on Indigenous curative birthing and healing practices and reclaiming these healing systems by Indigenous Mexican and Chicanx peoples. Theresa Gregor (Iipay/Yoéme; 2022) also writes about her "twin journeys" in academia and raising children while remaining committed to her community and recognizing the historical, cultural, and social forces at play during her upbringing in the Santa Ysabel reservation, an hour outside San Diego. Including the scholarship of Indigenous womxn at the border is necessary, as they are often overlooked or categorized as Mexicana or Chicanx *fronterizas*, and yet, their experiences speak to the uniqueness of their demands for sovereignty and self-determination in a context of double scrutiny, surveillance, and settler colonialism at the U.S-Mexico border.

For some Chicanx, Mexicana, Indigenous, and other BIPOC *mamás* at the border, motherhood is more about daily survival than advocacy. Economic hardships have reconstructed Latinx mothers from providing daily care and raising children to being the primary financial providers for their families. For single mothers or mothers who must work to provide for their children economically, a motherhood identity is associated more with meeting the material needs of their children rather than providing daily care and fulfilling children's emotional needs. In a study of womxn incarcerated in Mexico, being physically separated from their children challenged hegemonic motherhood expectations. Reinforcing their motherhood identity, however, provided these womxn a way to help them cope with the stigma of delinquency (Agoff, Sandberg, and Fondevila 2021). In another common phenomenon, as the sole financial providers for their families, mothers often find employment in maquiladoras, as they are economically forced to leave their children for long hours to work (see Quintero Ramírez, this volume), while other mothers revert to transnational migration (Abrego 2014) for their survival, with childrearing usually spread across many generations (i.e., grandmothers) (Agoff, Sandberg, and Fondevila 2021; Abrego 2014). Jessica P. Cerdeña's (2023) *Pressing Onward* highlights Latin American migrant mothers who overcome past traumatic histories and ongoing structural adversities based on racial, economic, and gender-based oppression by enacting resilience and engaging cognitive and social strategies to *seguir adelante* (press onward). Elizabeth Farfán-Santos's (2022) *Undocumented Mother-*

hood: Conversations on Love, Trauma, and Border Crossing narrates how transborder migrants survive and resist systems of power for their children once in the United States, while Mexican scholars Eunice D. Vargas Valle and Marie-Laure Coubès (2017) document the work trends and resistance tactics of certain Mexican womxn to cross into the United States to birth children. Our collection addresses many of these lived realities.

Frontera + Madre + Hood

Frontera Madre(hood) builds on the scholarship above and is deeply inspired by the organic intellectual mothers and activists from northern Mexico. Their social justice and human rights work in their neighborhoods and communities, and their insistence on survival in their everyday lives, anchors this concept. Their work directed us to take note of the motherist activist (Bejarano 2002) work at the border and to develop our analytical and intersectional concept, frontera madre(hood), as a theoretical and methodological tool.

We also want to pay homage to the Latina and feminist border scholars who have brought to light systemic social injustices in *La Frontera* to the forefront. A significant portion of this scholarship has focused on the *feminicidio*, or feminicides, in Ciudad Juárez, where stereotypes and sexism in the transborder capitalist context have exacerbated the killings of hundreds of girls and women (i.e., Fregoso and Bejarano 2010; Lagarde y de los Ríos 2005; Monárrez-Fragoso 2009; Ravelo Blancas 2005; Staudt 2008; Staudt and Coronado 2010; Wright 2011). A related focus is on the violence toward girls and young women on the migration journey (Ravelo Blancas 2017) as well as intimate partner violence (Moya, Chávez-Baray, and Martinez 2014; Paat et al. 2017). The intersections of migration and class have also been explored in studies of migration settlements and class (Zavella 2011), the political ecology of the colonias (unincorporated regions on the outskirts) on the border (Núñez 2015), and the female laborers displaced by NAFTA (Staudt and Coronado 2016). Gender on the border has also been expressed through literary scholarship, such as the work of Sonia Saldívar-Hull (2000) and Norma Elia Cantú ([1995] 2015). We also want to recognize the work of feminist border historians who have highlighted oral history on the border (Martínez and Chávez Leyva

2020), Japanese Mexicans and WWII at the borderlands (Chew 2015), and writing Chicanas into history (Castañeda 2007; Pérez 1999). This body of work was the genesis of scholarship on feminism on the border.

To better understand the approaches to mothering at the U.S.-Mexico border that we discuss in our collection requires a theoretical shift and *concientización* (Anzaldúa 1987). We propose an epistemological shift in researching and writing about the borderlands that emphasizes critical Latinx and Mexican feminist perspectives to address the challenges of Brown motherwork (Caballero et al. 2019) in raising children at the U.S.-Mexico border. To achieve this goal, frontera madre(hood) is a multilayered framework that stems from these three deconstructed concepts: frontera + madre + hood.

We acknowledge here the highly contested landscape that the *frontera* represents. This region is marked by multiple layers of colonization that position womxn as subordinate, as, for example, in Mexico's colonial and colonization history and the controversial story of La Malinche. As the mistress of Cortés, a Spanish conquistador, La Malinche is historically depicted as a medium for conquest and, for some, a symbol of the betrayal and rape of Indigenous people (Elenes 2010). To this day, La Malinche represents a womxn who sold out her people (Elenes 2010; Morales and Bejarano 2009). In recent times, womxn at the *frontera* are still depicted negatively and stereotypically, the intimacies of their lives scrutinized while Mexican and migrant womxn's fertility rates are publicly vilified and shamed through the hateful rhetoric of "anchor babies" and xenophobic debates over birthright citizenship (Hiemstra 2021). Contrary to perceptions of impoverished Mexican mothers crossing the international port of entry to have their children in the United States, middle-upper-class Mexicans with transborder employment are more likely to do so (Vargas Valle and Coubès 2017).

Also perpetuated in this border context, particularly on the Mexican side, are womxn's sexualized bodies woven into the local reputation of red-light districts, like the former Mariscal in the northern Mexican city of Ciudad Juárez, which transcends into other venues and institutions where womxn are sexualized and commoditized (Morales and Bejarano 2009). *Zona rosas* (red-light districts) like the Mariscal have popularized Juárez and other places like Tijuana as lurid places of "whores" (Langley 1988, 32). With such seedy depictions, Juárez continues to unfairly resonate in Mexican (Vila 2000) and U.S. popular cultures as a city of vice (Morales and Bejarano 2009) like several other northern urban Mexican cities. Fighting this perpetuation of violent imagery toward border cities and the womxn who live there are the motherist activists Las Super Madres, the mothers of the murdered and missing womxn and girls in Ciudad Juárez and Chihuahua (Bejarano 2002), who heavily inspired this collection.

In this subsequent section, we deconstruct and interpret frontera madre(hood) and all its parts. We argue that it functions as a tool for understanding and analyzing intersectionality (Crenshaw 1991) along Mexican and U.S. borderlands and describe our vision for this concept's utility as a theoretical and methodological framework.

frontera + madre + hood = frontera madre(hood):

Frontera is Spanish for "border" and commonly refers to the U.S.-Mexico border as well as cultural, social, and psychological boundaries that form insider and outsider relations and relationships. *Fronteras* represent the margins of nation-states, states, or localized geopolitical boundaries that are place based and space based.

Madre is Spanish for mother. The mystic and historical figures of La Malinche and La Llorona not only are symbols of colonization but are recycled into binary mother archetypes of good–bad mothers (Silva 2011). Here, we contest those restricted binaries of motherhood. We use *madre* as an expression not only of individuality and a nonessentializing and nonbiological standpoint, but also of motherhood as a social institution that cannot remain apolitical (Guzmán 2012). We include tenets of *terra madre* (mother earth), *de ser madre* (to be a mother), and *de ser madre del barrio* (to be a mother from Brown neighbor[hoods]). Rather than biological and conventional notions of mothering, we use *madre* to highlight the practice of raising and protecting Latinx children and youth, as well as other children and youth of color. At the *frontera*, BIPOC and Latinx/Latina/Mexicana/Chicanx/*fronteriza* motherwork (Caballero et al. 2019) requires resiliency to stand up to oppressive structures to protect Brown children and youth.

Hood is a complex word used as a suffix and a noun. We follow the work of Black feminists, like Mikki Kendall's *Hood Feminism: Notes from the Women that a Movement Forgot* (2020), and her words: "The hood taught me that feminism isn't just academic theory. . . . Feminism is the work that you do, and the people you do it for who matter more than anything else" (2020, xiii). This work inspired our use and deconstruction of motherhood and the word *hood* as a significant reference to interpret and analyze the spaces and places of the borderlands that mothers call home. We first conceptualized the suffix *-hood*, which means a particular state, condition, quality of being, or period, as in *motherhood*. We also build on *motherhood* by expanding our concept of *madre(hood)* to represent an individual status and a condition of Brown mothering.

Our second understanding of the term *hood* in madre(hood) is the place-based notion of the hood/barrio, where people of color create meaningful spaces based on their sociocultural perceptions and productions as well as the lived realities across the U.S.-Mexico border and Mexico-U.S. border. We want to emphasize that we borrow from and acknowledge our debt to Black scholars, their scholarship, and their intellectual work on the term *hood* (Kendall 2020). As stated earlier, we were raised in the urban and rural settings of the Paso del Norte region, Cristina at the El Paso border with Ciudad Juárez, Chihuahua, and Cynthia at the Anthony, New Mexico, border near El Paso and Ciudad Juárez. The two places we call home were Mexican/Chicanx barrios that we affectionately called our barrio and our hood. Growing up in our barrios/hoods, we experienced poverty, violence, strength, resilience, and community in unique and specific ways, as did most contributors to this collection. Hence, we use the term *hood* here to describe specific spaces across both sides of the borderlands, in communities, neighborhoods, and homes across the two-thousand-mile border span. We also use hood/barrio interchangeably as a metaphor for communities on the U.S.-Mexico border.

In sum, our concept frontera madre(hood) provides a theoretical framework to capture the challenges of mothering for Brown womxn on both sides of the borderlands, and how our collective experiences challenge popular tropes on mothering and motherwork (Caballero et al. 2019). Frontera madre(hood) can help interpret the anxieties and stresses of caring for children and adolescents while mothering others under intense government surveillance tactics, violence, and other forms of injustice. Frontera madre(hood) also works to disrupt traditional notions of Brown motherhood by challenging and denouncing state systems and the tools of those who mother across two heavily paternalistic and patriarchal nation-states.

Frontera Madre(hood) as a Methodology

Frontera madre(hood) also functions as a methodological paradigm that seeks to bridge potential gaps between academics, activists, and other mothers in the community. It aligns with other feminist texts and links academic and community involvement to show their mutual connection through mother/madre(hood). Through *testimonios*, community activists—*madres*—are provided a space to show their struggles and resiliencies in their *own words.* These *testimonios* are in conversations with academic contributors in our book. Bridging the activist *madre* work with the academic *madres* is valuable, given that they share a space in our collection and in our community/ies. As such, our frontera madre-(hood) methodological approach increases relationality across academic and community contexts.

Frontera madre(hood) as a methodological tool also draws from intersectionality and frontera+madre+hood as individual units of analysis. As a methodological tool, if we disaggregate frontera madre(hood) into its individual and intersecting parts as frontera+madre+hood, then each concept operates as a unit of analysis: *frontera* as a site of inquiry; *hood* as a location for examining and engaging in participatory action research, community-based research, or other critical forms of inquiry like critical ethnography, participation observation, and interviews; and *madres* as individuals/participants to intentionally and purposefully engage with, learn from, and create with together.

In our collection, we have worked to incorporate various locations, cities, and barrios/hoods across the borderlands that, on their own, are studied and researched for the benefit of their community. Mothering as a specific unit is also studied to gauge the experiences, struggles, and strategies of survival that mothers use within personal and public spaces.

Hood as a unit of analysis interrogates the role of geopoliticized locations within workplaces, educational spaces, environmentally degraded spaces, and home and barrio/hood spaces.

Frontera madre(hood) offers a paradigm shift in our understanding of mothers and people who mother in their respective communities at the U.S.-Mexico border as agents of change, of resistance, and in action, a shift that recognizes this idea of borders, mothers, and neighborhoods/communities in advocacy, in action, and in activism for positive change. Our contributors touch on these units of analysis in their research and words as *testimonios*, in-depth interviews, secondary data analysis, or a combination of all of the above.

Breaking It Down, Chapter *por* Chapter *y* Testimonio *por* Testimonio

Frontera madre(hood) is then a state of being and a condition of Brown mothering, specifically at the U.S.-Mexico border, that is unique, complex, and a departure from other locations. The idea of madre(hood) also brings us together as a collective to write about what we see as varied and diverse mothering practices at the U.S.-Mexico border. Our book centers on the voices of feminists through *testimonios* and research from the perspectives of Indigenous, Mexicana, Chicanx, Latinx, Black, and mixed-identifying community activists and academic scholars who use antiracist and anti-imperialist approaches, as well as organic intellectuals and community activists who live and work at the border. Our contributors also have diverse relationships to different uses of languages. Some of our contributors feel strongly against providing an English translation to the Spanish or Spanglish text and channel the words of influential Chicanx cultural critic Gloria Anzaldúa (1987), who passionately argued, "as long as I have to accommodate the English speakers rather than having them accommodate me, my tongue will be illegitimate." We, therefore, respect their decision not to offer a translation across some of the chapters and *testimonios* in this collection.

Frontera Madre(hood): Brown Mothers Challenging Oppression and Transborder Violence at the U.S.-Mexico Border opens with a foreword by Tucson Chicanx scholar Michelle Téllez, co-editor of *Chicana*

M(other)work, which served as a guiding force for this anthology. Her affirmation of this project as "both essential and transformative" echoes our sentiment that this anthology offers insightful analyses and beautifully written *testimonios* by womxn whose shared geopolitical experiences are rarely, if ever, in conversation with each other. It centers the north and south of the borderline as neglected regions needing humane and dignified interventions. This book is organized into three sections, each with *testimonios* that complement interspersed scholarly chapters. Together, these amazing womxn guide the reader through heavy but necessary reading. Our readers will viscerally feel pain and love, rage, and reverence, in concert with our contributors—our *hermanas en solidaridad*.

Part I, "Survival in the Face of Violence," begins with an open letter by internationally known human rights defender and Chihuahuense Lucha Castro. In "A Letter Acknowledging Antigone Mothers, Our Desert Mothers," Lucha dedicates her open letter to this collection's authors, particularly the *madre testimonialistas* who share their stories of struggle against state systems. The first *testimonio* of *Frontera Madre(hood)* belongs to Paula Flores Bonilla, cofounder of Voces sin Eco and Fundación Maria Sagrario, named after her daughter, a victim of *feminicidio*. Paula shares her *testimonio* "A Motherist Activist Story of Migration, Community Building, and Femicide." This is accompanied by a drawing of Paula, titled *Abuelita*, by her granddaughter Paola Isabel Nava González. Paula shares her migration story from Durango to Juárez with her children and husband, as well as her resilience in becoming a community activist before and after the feminicide of her daughter, Maria Sagrario.[3] Her bravery and courage in defending her community and in creating meaningful change as a motherist activist (Bejarano 2002) encapsulates the essence of this collection.

We open our chapters with Juárez social anthropologist and art scholar Ma. Eugenia Hernández Sánchez's "*Ellos Matan*?: Visual Autoethnog-

---

3. The terms feminicide and femicide are sometimes used interchangeably in this volume. At times, authors use both terms in their contribution, or use femicide over feminicide as an individual preference. To learn more about these concepts, see Fregoso and Bejarano, *Terrorizing Women: Feminicide in the Americas* (2010), for their genesis and use.

raphy of Motherhood in the Face of the Militarization at the Border."
Through her visual autoethnography, she powerfully details Juárez mothers' challenges in everyday spaces while negotiating the ubiquitous presence of the Mexican military. She juxtaposes her children's fears, concerns,
and tactics to live through these moments while simultaneously asserting
her children's critical thinking and beliefs. Her chapter includes stunning
digital drawings on photographs by Juárez artist Mariana Martinez. Ma.
Eugenia's chapter is followed by that of a Mexicana of Cuban origin, urban planner, and border scholar, Marisol Rodríguez Sosa, whose "Frontera Madre(hood) and Survival Tactics of Urban Life" documents through
street images the dangers for safe movement in certain areas of this urban
border metropolis. Marisol discusses the collective strategies womxn use
for their own and their children's safety, while also sharing her lived experiences of navigating barrios, streets, and the city as a newcomer.

In the *testimonio* "La Frontera: Experiencing Border Violence Through
Different Lenses," West Texas educator Edith Treviño Espinosa offers
her heartbreaking story, chronicling the devastating border spillover
violence that altered her and her children's lives and how in her classroom, she unabashedly validates and confronts her young students' experiences of border violence. We continue with Matamoros sociologist
Cirila Quintero Ramírez's important study on maquiladora workers in
Ciudad Juárez, Tijuana, and Matamoros. Although her chapter "'Yo no
Tengo Derecho a Enfermarme': Conceptions of Madre(hood) in Women
Maquiladora Workers" touches on all three locations, the workers represented in her chapter are from Ciudad Juárez. She discusses maquiladora
mothers' tactics to care for their children while working long hours in
the factories and how they cope with the emotional and physical toll of
this combined labor.

Taide Elena, cofounder of Border Patrol Victims Network from Ambos Nogales, Arizona, and Sonora, offers us her compelling *testimonio*
"'Mi Nieto Tenía Metas. . . . Nos Tenemos Que Reunir Todos': A Grandmother's Fight for Justice Through the Border Patrol Victims Network."[4]
Doña Taide's heart-shattering but profoundly brave *testimonio* details her
grandson's murder by a border patrol agent and the long road demanding
justice that she and her family and supporters have endured for over a

---

4. "My Grandson Had Goals. . . . We All Need to Come Together."

decade. Accompanying her *testimonio* is a photograph of a portrait depicting doña Taide's sixteen-year-old grandson, José Antonio Rodríguez, who was killed.

Part II, "Confronting Caging, Migration, and Deportation," describes in painful detail the toll migration, separation, and deportation have on border communities. This section begins with a two-part *testimonio* by sociologist Bertha A. Bermúdez Tapia, "Women, Family, Border Enforcement, and Humanitarian Work on the Banks of the Rio Grande in Matamoros," based on her activist scholarship in Matamoros, her hometown. She also writes about her collaborative activist and advocacy work and admiration for Felicia Rangel-Samponaro, founder of the Sidewalk School in Matamoros and Reynosa, Tamaulipas. In conversation with Bertha's *testimonio* is Felicia's succinctly titled *testimonio* "The Sidewalk School," in which she candidly shares her struggles with urgent and emergency advocacy work in Tamaulipas, alongside her partner, to help thousands of migrants while simultaneously mothering her young son in Brownsville, Texas. Felicia's *testimonio* is a powerful example of mothers in action who come to the aid of people in desperate need, especially in the ways she dignifies and humanizes them.

Following these paired *testimonios* is the salient work of New Mexico–based anthropologist and migrant advocate Margaret Brown Vega in her chapter "A Different Kind of Motherhood for Liberation: Fictive Kin, Advocacy, and Mothering Adult Migrants in Immigration Detention." Her chapter poignantly captures our collection's efforts to highlight the nonbiological, nonessentializing categories that embody mothering. By weaving together research, analysis, and her lived experiences, Margaret shares how she cares for and foments maternal ties with young adult migrant men in southern New Mexico migrant detention centers.

Another evocative dual *testimonio* is personified in "*Madres De Una Frontera*: A Bilateral Experience," by *hermanas* Coda Rayo-Garza and Shamma Rayo-Gutierrez, who share their mixed-status upbringing in Laredo, Texas, and the lengths that their mother would go to for their survival. Their heart-wrenching and moving *testimonios* juxtapose questions of belonging and status with bureaucratic violence (Heckert 2020), demonstrating how bureaucratic functionality can cause systemic harm.

"Mothering in a Bicultural Border Context," by Sandra Gutiérrez, a licensed clinical social worker based out of Las Cruces, New Mexico, epitomizes transmothering across Ciudad Juárez and the Las Cruces area, as she juggled the birth of her child and raising him across borders after her husband was deported. Her *testimonio* is one of determination and *sobrevivencia* (Galván 2006) to complete her higher education degrees while holding together her young family across international borders. The sacrifices she endured are indicative of what *Frontera Madre(hood)* works to reveal.

Following this *testimonio* is a chapter by Baja Californians Macrina Cárdenas Montaño and Olga Odgers-Ortiz, "Knitting Hope: Conversations with Migrant Women in Tijuana Shelters." Macrina, a lifelong human rights defender and political and migrant activist, and Olga, a sociologist and migrant advocate, intricately weave together the collaborative stories of migrants who arrive at their shelter and how they alleviate their trauma, albeit momentarily, by learning how to knit.

An equally compelling account of migrants and migrant advocacy is that of social worker, longtime migrant advocate, and former director of Casa de Menores Migrantes in Ciudad Juárez Leticia López Manzano, who writes "My Motherhood *Testimonio* in the Service and Defense of Children and Youth at the Border." Lety shares her professional experiences and deep dedication to migrant families, particularly migrant children and youth. She takes us through the labyrinth of transborder migrant protocols across Ciudad Juárez and El Paso, describing how this process passes on to her daughter the gift of caring for humanity.

Part two on migration ends with "Colores United: Mothers Offering Sanctuary and Dignity in Southern New Mexico," by Ariana Saludares, cofounder of Colores United in Deming, New Mexico. Her *testimonio* captures her innate resolve to aid migrants at whatever cost. Ariana went from full-time mothering her children to suddenly coordinating efforts to aid migrant families moving through the New Mexico–Chihuahua border area that had nowhere to go or no one to sponsor them. Hers is another mother-in-action *testimonio*, like Felicia Rangel-Samponaro's, in that she built something from nothing to aid others in need.

Part III, "Asserting Rights and Calling Out Hegemony and Oppression Through a Praxis of Frontera Madre(hood)," offers powerful examples of mothers in action and their fierce commitment to creating meaningful

change for the communities they serve, including the risks and sacrifices
they make to provide additional opportunities for their children. This
section also reveals the daily affronts womxn receive in their workplace
and in life in general, including racialized violence, workplace aggression,
social violence, and homophobia.

This section opens with El Pasoan and pedagogue Claudia Yolanda
Casillas's moving account of raising her beloved child in the El Paso–
Ciudad Juárez region. In her *testimonio* "I AM His Mother: Challenging
Traditional Paradigms of Latina Mothering in the Paso del Norte Region,"
Claudia shares her journey of "queer love," the birth of her and her part-
ner's child, and the painful and hateful hegemonic structures in society
that her family is forced to confront daily.

The first chapter of this part is "On Fronteriza Madre(hood)s: Una
Plática Entre Mujeres Académicas," by Chicanx scholars and pedagogues
Judith Flores Carmona and Brenda Rubio, who reside in Las Cruces, New
Mexico, and Denton, Texas, respectively. Their *testimonios* reveal the
harrowing experiences that professional womxn endure, academics in
this context, to place work before family and to resign themselves to
workplace abuses. Their *testimonios* offer courageous accounts of loss
and perseverance as they share with readers about the children in their
hearts and memories and touch on the experiences that so many womxn
endure alone.

Themes of loss, grief, remembrance, and transition are pronounced
in Yaqui scholar Marisa Elena Duarte's chapter. Rooted in her Yaqui traditions and ties to Arizona and New Mexico's southern borders, "Ma'ala
Meecha Watch Over Me: A Hiaki Interpretation of Frontera Mother+-
hood" is a beautifully written chapter, raw and revealing, as Marisa, like
Claudia, Judith, and Brenda, selflessly shares the intimacies of her life.
Marisa's poignant words anchor the importance of spirituality and relationality for Indigenous Chicanx feminists grieving the loss of a child.

Continuing the theme of loss, mourning, and macroaggressions is
Nan davi Mariela Vásquez Tobon's chapter, "Indigenous Women and
Motherhood Within a Border Context: The Case of the Nan davi in Ciudad Juárez, Chihuahua." This revealing work reaches a wider audience
beyond her Indigenous Nan davi community by exposing the blatantly
ignored racialized violence, structural violence, and oppression that
Indigenous womxn endure in the borderlands. Through her research,

experience as an Indigenous legal scholar, and analysis of Indigenous womxn's *testimonios*, Mariela brings to light the colonial violence that penetrates every fabric of border living in Ciudad Juárez (and across the borderlands), which reflects systemic structures in place that prohibit access to healthcare systems for Indigenous *mujeres*.

In sync with Mariela's chapter on the lack of dignified healthcare for Indigenous womxn in the borderlands are Southern California community-based researchers in public health and psychology Marisa S. Torres, Victoria M. Telles, and Elva M. Arrendondo. Their chapter, "Border Walls and Barriers to Care: Latina Mothers and Access to Care During the COVID-19 Pandemic," offers an empirically based analysis of barriers to healthcare for *fronteriza* womxn in San Diego and Imperial Valley Counties. This chapter delineates the generational practices of border families traversing the border for healthcare purposes. The authors' focus is on Tijuana as a destination for affordable healthcare.

Moving from a concentration on health to education, a natural transition is the mother–daughter *testimonio* "'Ya Vámonos Que Va a Ver Mucha Fila en el Puente': A Mother–Daughter's Reflection on Crossing Borders Using a *Transfronteriza* Intersectional Consciousness," by Sylvia Fernández Quintanilla and Silvia Quintanilla Moreno. Based in Ciudad Juárez–El Paso, Sylvia is a digital humanities scholar who narrates in her *testimonio* her daily routine, crossing the international border to attend public school in El Paso. Her mother, Silvia, describes her transmothering experiences and bravery to cross the border as a monolingual Spanish speaker with only tourist documents to take her children to school. Mother and daughter share their quotidian struggles, the international border inspection they endured for years, and the intense fears and anxieties they lived with. This is a quintessential border experience that *Frontera Madre(hood)* works to articulate.

Switching themes to community organizing and activism, a final *testimonio* comes from La Mujer Obrera and Las Familias Unidas del Chamizal activist and community organizer Hilda Villegas. Her *testimonio*, "Changing the Narrative on How Our Mexican Immigrant Communities Should Be Served Along the Border," tells the story of the iconic institution La Mujer Obrera as a base of activism for womxn factory workers laid off from the Farah jeans factory as jobs moved south across the international border. Hilda writes of her fierce commitment to working-class communities, specifically her historic neighborhood in El Chamizal, one of the closest barrios to the U.S. border wall and securitization complexes in El Paso. Hilda tells the tale of economic, educational, and environmental injustices in her community and the work that Las Familias Unidas del Chamizal engages in daily to assert their rights as border people.

En fin, our collection ends with an afterword from San Diegoan and fellow *fronteriza*, Chicanx scholar and spiritual activist Irene Lara. Her words in "Frontera Madre(hood) and the Path of Conocimiento" on self-healing serve as a bookend reminding us all of the need for continuous motherwork (Caballero et al. 2019), mothering in action, and *auto-cuidado*. We invite you, our reader, to join us in engaging with this collection and the powerful and fierce embodied experiences of frontera madre(hood).

REFERENCES

Abrego, Leisy J. 2014. *Sacrificing Families: Navigating Laws, Labor, and Love Across Borders*. Stanford, Calif.: Stanford University Press.

Agoff, Carolina, Sveinung Sandberg, and Gustavo Fondevila. 2021. "Doing Marginalized Motherhood: Identities and Practices Among Incarcerated Women in Mexico." *International Journal for Crime, Justice and Social Democracy* 10 (1): 15–29.

Anzaldúa, Gloria. 1987. *Borderlands/La Frontera: The New Mestiza*. San Francisco, Calif.: Aunt Lute.

Arendell, Teresa. 1999. "Mothering and Motherhood: A Decade Review." Working Paper 3. Center for Working Families, University of California, Berkeley.

Bakewell, Liza. 2011. *Madre: Perilous Journeys with a Spanish Noun*. Albuquerque: University of New Mexico Press.

Bejarano, Cynthia. 2002. "Las Super Madres de Latino América: Transforming Motherhood by Challenging Violence in Mexico, Argentina, and El Salvador." *Frontiers: A Journal of Women Studies* 23 (1): 126–50.

Bynoe, Yvonne. 2009. *Who's Your Mama? The Unsung Voices of Women and Mothers*. New York: Soft Skull Press.

Caballero, Cecilia, Yvette Martínez-Vu, Judith Pérez-Torres, Michelle Téllez, and Christine Vega, eds. 2019. *The Chicana M(other)work Anthology: Porque Sin Madres No Hay Revolución*. Tucson: University of Arizona Press.

Cantú, Norma Elia. (1995) 2015. *Canícula: Snapshots of a Girlhood en la Frontera*. Updated ed. Albuquerque: University of New Mexico Press.

Castañeda, Antonia. 2003. "Introduction: Gender on the Borderlands." *Frontiers: A Journal of Women Studies* 24 (2–3): xi–xix.

Castañeda, Antonia. 2007. *Gender on the Borderlands: The Frontiers Reader.* Lincoln: University of Nebraska Press.

Cerdeña, Jessica P. 2023. *Pressing Onward: The Imperative Resilience of Latina Migrant Mothers.* Oakland: University of California Press.

Chew, Selfa A. 2015. *Uprooting Community: Japanese Mexicans, World War II, and the U.S.-Mexico Borderlands.* Tucson: University of Arizona Press.

Collins, Patricia Hill. 2002. *Black Feminist Thought: Knowledge, Consciousness, and the Politics of Empowerment.* New York: Routledge.

Crenshaw, Kimberlé. 1991. "Mapping the Margins: Intersectionality, Identity Politics, and Violence Against Women of Color." *Stanford Law Review* 43 (6): 1241–99.

del Alba Acevedo, Luz, Norma Alarcón, Celia Alvarez, Ruth Behar, Rina Benmayor, Norma E. Cantú, Daisy Cocco De Filippis, et al., eds. 2001. *Telling to Live: Latina Feminist Testimonios.* Durham, N.C.: Duke University Press.

Delgado Bernal, Dolores. 2006. "Mujeres in College: Negotiating Identities and Challenging Educational Norms." In *Chicana/Latina Education in Everyday Life: Feminista Perspectives on Pedagogy and Epistemology*, edited by Dolores Delgado Bernal, C. Alejandra Elenes, Francisca E. Godinez, and Sofia A. Villenas, 77–79. Albany: State University of New York Press.

Delgado Bernal, Dolores, Rebeca Burciaga, and Judith Flores Carmona. 2012. "Chicana/Latina *Testimonios*: Mapping the Methodological, Pedagogical, and Political." *Equity and Excellence in Education* 45 (3): 363–72.

Dow, Dawn Marie. 2019. *Mothering While Black: Boundaries and Burdens of Middle-Class Parenthood.* Berkeley: University of California Press.

Elenes, Alejandra C. 2010. *Transforming Borders: Chicana/o Popular Culture and Pedagogy.* Lanham, Md.: Lexington Books.

Facio, Elisa, and Irene Lara, eds. 2014. *Fleshing the Spirit: Spirituality and Activism in Chicana, Latina, and Indigenous Women's Lives.* Tucson: University of Arizona Press.

Farfán-Santos, Elizabeth. 2022. *Undocumented Motherhood: Conversations on Love, Trauma, and Border Crossing.* Austin: University of Texas Press.

Fregoso, Rosa-Linda, and Cynthia Bejarano, eds. *Terrorizing Women: Feminicide in the Américas.* Durham, N.C.: Duke University Press, 2010.

Fuentes, Emma. 2013. "Political Mothering: Latina and African American Mothers in the Struggle for Educational Justice." *Anthropology and Education Quarterly* 44 (3): 304–19.

Galván, Ruth Trinidad. 2006. "Campesina Epistemologies and Pedagogies of the Spirit: Examining Women's Sobrevivencia." In *Chicana/Latina Education in*

Everyday Life: Feminista Perspectives on Pedagogy and Epistemology, edited by Dolores Delgado Bernal, C. Alejandra Elenes, Francisca E. Godinez, and Sofia A. Villenas, 161–80. Albany: State University of New York Press.

Gonzales, Patrisia. 2012. *Red Medicine: Traditional Indigenous Rites of Birthing and Healing*. Tucson: University of Arizona Press.

Gregor, Theresa. 2022. "Kuhkwany Kuchemayo 'Aaknach, an Iipay Mother's/ Teacher's Story." In *Indigenous Motherhood in the Academy*, edited by Robin Zape-tah-hol-ah Minthorn, Christine A. Nelson, and Heather J. Shotton, 169–76. New Brunswick, N.J.: Rutgers University Press.

Gumbs, Alexis Pauline, China Martens, and Mai'a Williams, eds. 2016. *Revolutionary Mothering: Love on the Front Lines*. Oakland, Calif.: PM Press.

Guzmán, Bianca. 2012. "Cultivating a Guerrera Spirit in Latinas: The Praxis of Mothering." *Journal of the Association of Mexican American Educators* 6 (1): 45–51.

Hawthorne, Camilla, and Jennifer Lynn Kelly. 2020. "Borderland Regimes and Resistance in Global Perspective." Special issue, *Critical Ethnic Studies* 6 (2).

Heckert, Carina. 2020. "The Bureaucratic Violence of the Health Care System for Pregnant Immigrants on the United States–Mexico Border." *Human Organization* 79 (1): 33–42.

Hiemstra, Nancy. 2021. "Mothers, Babies, and Abortion at the Border: Contradictory U.S. Policies, or Targeting Fertility?" *Politics and Space* 39 (8): 1692–1710.

Kendall, Mikki. 2020. *Hood Feminism: Notes from the Women that a Movement Forgot*. New York: Viking.

Lagarde y de los Ríos, Marcela. 2005. *Por La Vida y La Libertad de Las Mujeres: Primer Informe Sustantivo de Las Actividades de la Comisión Especial para Conocer y Dar Seguimiento a Las Investigaciones Relacionadas con Los Feminicidios en La República Mexicana y a La Procuración de Justicia Vinculada*. Cámara de Diputados, H. Congreso de la Unión, LIX Legislatura, Mexico City.

Langley, Lester D. 1988. *MexAmerica: Two Countries, One Future*. New York: Crown.

Lara, Irene. 2014. "Sensing the Serpent in the Mother, Dando a Luz la Madre Serpiente: Chicana Spirituality, Sexuality, and Mamihood." In *Fleshing the Spirit: Spirituality and Activism in Chicana, Latina, and Indigenous Women's Lives*, edited by Elisa Facio and Irene Lara, 113–34. Tucson: University of Arizona Press.

Martínez, Angelina T., and Yolanda Chávez Leyva. 2020. "La cultura cura: Oral History on the Border." Notes from the Community. *U.S. Latina and Latino Oral History Journal* 4 (1): 86–92.

Monárrez Fragoso, Julia E. 2009. "Trauma de una Injusticia: Feminicido Sexual Sistémico en Cd. Juárez." Thesis, El Colegio de la Frontera Norte, Tijuana.

Moore, Mignon R. 2011. *Invisible Families: Gay Identities, Relationships, and Motherhood Among Black Women*. Berkeley: University of California Press.

Moraga, Cherríe, and Gloria Anzaldúa. 1983. *This Bridge Called My Back*. New York: Kitchen Table.

Morales, Maria Cristina, and Cynthia Bejarano. 2009. "Transnational Sexual and Gendered Violence: An Application of Border Sexual Conquest at a Mexico–US Border." *Global Networks* 9 (3): 420–39.

Moya, Eva M., Silvia Chávez-Baray, and Omar Martinez. 2014. "Intimate Partner Violence and Sexual Health: Voices and Images of Latina Immigrant Survivors in Southwestern United States." *Health Promotion Practice* 15 (6): 881–93.

Núñez, Guillermina Gina. 2015. "The Political Ecology of Colonias on the US-Mexico Border: Ethnography for Hidden and Hard-to-Reach Communities." In *The International Handbook of Political Ecology*, edited by Raymond L. Bryant, 460–74. Cheltenham: Edward Elgar.

Núñez-Mchiri, Guillermina, and Children's Disabilities Information Coalition. 2021. *Hopelighting: Sus Discapacidades Nos Hacen Más Fuertes*. El Paso, Tex.: Mouthfeel Press.

Paat, Yok-Fong, Trina L. Hope, Thenral Mangadu, Guillermina Gina Núñez-Mchiri, and Silvia M. Chávez-Baray. 2017. "Family- and Community-Related Determinants of Intimate Partner Violence Among Mexican and Puerto Rican Origin Mothers in Fragile Families." *Women's Studies International Forum* 62:136–47.

Pérez, Emma. 1999. *The Decolonial Imaginary: Writing Chicanas into History*. Bloomington: Indiana University Press.

Ravelo Blancas, Patricia. 2005. "La costumbre de matar: Proliferación de la violencia en Ciudad Juárez, Chihuahua, México." *Nueva antropología* 20 (65): 149–66.

Ravelo Blancas, Patricia. 2017. "Cuerpos marcados por la violencia sexual: Niñas y mujeres jóvenes migrantes en la frontera norte." *Sociológica (México)* 32 (91): 317–32.

Rivlin-Nadler, Max. 2020. "Young Kumeyaay Women Lead Protests Against Border Wall." *KPBS*, August 6, 2020. https://www.kpbs.org/news/border-immigration/2020/08/06/young-kumeyaay-women-lead-protests-against-border.

Saldívar-Hull, Sonia. 2000. *Feminism on the Border: Chicana Gender Politics and Literature*. Berkeley: University of California Press.

Silva, Dorsía Smith. 2011. *Latina/Chicana Mothering*. Toronto: Demeter Press.

Staudt, Kathleen. 2008. *Violence and Activism at the Border: Gender, Fear, and Everyday Life in Ciudad Juárez*. Austin: University of Texas Press.

Staudt, Kathleen, and Irasema Coronado. 2010. "Binational Civic Action for Accountability: Antiviolence Organizing in Ciudad Juárez/El Paso." In *Making a Killing: Femicide, Free Trade, and La Frontera*, edited by Alicia Gaspar de Alba and Georgina Guzmán, 157–81. University of Texas Press.

Staudt, Kathleen, and Irasema Coronado. 2016. *Fronteras No Más: Toward Social Justice at the U.S.-Mexico Border*. New York: Palgrave.

Story, Kaila Adia, ed. 2014. *Patricia Hill Collins: Reconceiving Motherhood*. Bradford, Ont.: Demeter Press.

Tamez, Margo. 2020. "Place and Perspective in the Shadow of the Wall: Recovering Ndé Knowledge and Self-Determination in Texas." In *Autobiography Without Apology: The Personal Essay in Chicanx and Latinx Studies*, edited by Chon A. Noriega, Wendy Laura Belcher, and Charlene Villaseñor Black, 357–84. Los Angeles: UCLA Chicano Studies Research Center Press.

Téllez, Michelle. 2021. *Border Women and the Community of Maclovio Rojas: Autonomy in the Spaces of Neoliberal Neglect*. Tucson: University of Arizona Press.

Vargas Valle, Eunice D., and Marie-Laure Coubès. 2017. "Working and Giving Birth in the United States: Changing Strategies of Transborder Life in the North of Mexico." *Journal of Frontera Norte El Colegio de la Frontera Norte AC* 29 (57): 57–82.

Velazquez, Mirelsie. 2017. "Primero Madres: Love and Mothering in the Educational Lives of Latina/os." *Gender and Education* 29 (4): 508–24.

Vila, Pablo. 2000. *Crossing Borders, Reinforcing Borders: Social Categories, Metaphors, and Narrative Identities on the U.S.-Mexico Frontier*. Austin: University of Texas Press.

Wright, Melissa. 2011. "Necropolitics, Narcopolitics, and Femicide: Gendered Violence on the Mexico-U.S. Border." *Signs: Journal of Women in Culture and Society* 36 (3): 707–31.

Zavella, Patricia. 2011. *I'm Neither Here Nor There: Mexicans' Quotidian Struggles with Migration and Poverty*. Durham, N.C.: Duke University Press.

PART I

Survival in the Face of Violence

FIGURE A Photo of Lucha Castro, taken by Cynthia Bejarano, at a border wall protest in 2009.

A Letter Acknowledging Antigone Mothers, Our Desert Mothers

LUCHA CASTRO
Human Rights Defender, Theologian, Feminist Lawyer, and Mother

As I write this for you [womxn represented in this book], the protagonists of stories of courage, love, hope, and dignity, it makes me
recall my thirty-five years as an activist accompanying the victims
[of injustices, femicide, gender-based violence and disappearance in Chi-
huahua].[1] Their faces, names, and shared dreams came to my mind as I
was thinking and writing this letter to you all. I found a character that
symbolizes who they are [as victims of violence] and who you are for me:
the Antigones, mothers of the desert.

The story of Antigone is about a woman condemned to death for
wanting to bury her brother, abandoned to the whim of dogs and ravens
by order of the king.

Antigone, like each of you, is a victim and a heroine. She is the symbol
of struggle and determination and the only one capable of defying the
state to bury the injustices she experienced.

You, like her, transgress the established order. You are guardians of the
blood of your ancestors, defenders of life who raise their voices and with
their actions recover public spaces, to shout to the world what happens,
and to manage to awaken the dormant conscience. It reminds me of the

---

1. This chapter was originally written in Spanish and translated by GMR Transcription Services, Inc.

words of Malala Yousafzai, "When the whole world is silent, even one voice becomes powerful."

You are our Antigones, las doñas, dressed in dignity, humble women with popular wisdom, with a single longing to caress the face of justice. I have read with great emotion and recognition your life stories. None of you have spent your time in vain [fighting for justice]. While thinking about you and imagining the places where you live or survive, the words of poet Eduardo Galeano remind me of your *testimonios* when he says, "Many small people, in small places, doing small things, can change the world."

In your narratives, one can read the state crimes committed by authorities directly or with the approval of a complicit silence.[2]

And there in front of cruelty, standing as Mary the mother of Jesus was, Mary Magdalene and other women, is you, with immense tenderness, you reconstruct the stories of your own, pronouncing the name of your loved ones in an infinite echo. Your stories remind us that they are not just another case file, and that your activism/s are not nostalgic gatherings plagued by vain suffering; they are remembrances of shared collective struggles, they are strength, hope and light in the midst of darkness.[3]

Creativity in the face of adversity is your shield with which you impart everyday lessons of resistance and rebellion against the abuses of power. The dignity of the social struggle is essential in your creed and your walk, teaching, loving, and raising children in the womb or in other ways—all of you extended motherhood to those who needed it.

Those who were abandoned, left by the side of the road to the fate of the desert, buried without love or tears, or those who were dehumanized, the Antigones gave them back their humanity that was denied to them.

You firmly stand with an invisible struggle; your hands are used to mend a sock, to distribute posters or fliers [searching for the missing or to demand justice], to wipe away the tears of those who suffer. We know that your hands were meant to care for your children and others and were not destined to scratch at the desert's surface looking for the remains of sons and daughters, nor reviewing abandoned files for clues. Your broken

---

2. Reflects some *testimonios* in this collection.

3. "Case file" is a reference to victims of femicide, gender-based violence, disappearances, and U.S. and Mexican state and narco violence.

fingernails and hands have aged digging in anonymous graves and giving condolences.

The social and political responses to government indolence lies in the Antigones, the women of the desert, who today share their stories with us. Their fingers point to those state authorities responsible [for their suffering], unable to provide security. They [Antigones] stand and give strength when others need them, and in them, the poetry of Mario Benedetti is made alive when he says, "Their hands are my caresses, my daily chords, I love them because their hands work for justice, and in the street side by side we are many more than two."

The *testimonios* reflected in this collection of Indigenous women discriminated against, the endless journeys of mothers to preserve family ties, of remembering and fighting for victims of gender-based violence and unpunished murders, of the experiences of factory slavery [maquiladora workers], and of mothers adopting refugees from forced displacement, and symbolic motherhood as a shield against the militarization of the border, and other situations [where the women represented in this collection] are in poor health, in mourning or in defiance of injustices— all of them are Antigones.

FIGURE B *Abuelita*, portrait of Paula Flores Bonilla by her granddaughter Paola Isabel Nava González. Ink on paper.

TESTIMONIO

A Motherist Activist Story of Migration, Community Building, and Femicide

PAULA FLORES BONILLA

Cofounder of Voces sin Eco and Fundación Maria Sagrario

M y name is Paula Flores Bonilla, and this is a testimony of my life, including the love of my family, the tragedy of my daughter's murder, and my activism on the Ciudad Juárez–El Paso border.[1] I was born on September 19, 1957, in El Salto, Pueblo Nuevo, Durango. I grew up with my seven siblings, six of whom were girls and one boy. My mother, Monica Bonilla, dedicated herself to domestic work to help us get by after my father died when I was five. She later remarried, and I grew up with a stepfather who abused and beat me and my younger sister. At the age of twelve, I realized that I had to survive, and I began to help a lady make her tortillas and bring her water to feed me. While we were still minors, my mother would "lend" me and my younger sister to ladies so that we could live with them to survive economically.

When I was eighteen years old, I decided to run away from home with my first boyfriend. I only stayed with him for a month because he mistreated me, beat me, and humiliated me a lot in the short time we were together. So, I decided that I didn't want this for myself and left him to go back home to my mom. I started working in a mill where they made nixtamal, and I was in charge of making the dumplings. It was at that stage of my life that I met my husband, Jesús. I met him on June 5, 1975,

---

1. This chapter was originally written in Spanish and translated by GMR Transcription Services, Inc.

and we only dated about three times. This is how on July 5 of the same year we got married in the Catholic Church, having seven children: six daughters and a son. My husband worked cutting wood in the fields in El Salto, and he left and returned every week, so my children and I could only spend the weekends with him in our house in Durango. Most of the time my children were under my care. And as they grew up, they needed to study. I convinced my husband to let me work since there was not enough for all of us with the salary he had. At first, he didn't want to, but I convinced him, and he let me work at home. My daughter Guillermina (Guille)—the oldest—was fifteen years old when she started working with my bosses in a stationery store. That is how we managed to get Chuy, Juana, and Sagrario to finish high school and Guadalupe, Claudia, and Alicia to finish elementary school. My daughter Guille said that for the time being, she was not going to study, even though she was a very intelligent girl who always had good grades. It felt unfair to me that she would leave her studies, because I knew as a mother that it was to support the family economy.

I want to tell you that despite so many shortcomings, we were very happy, always united, with stable communication between parents and children. My husband was always very responsible, since he gave me his salary, and I always managed it. I remember that we used to take my children's shoes on credit at a shoe store where we could pay for them in installments, and we were just finishing paying for them when they needed new ones. That's how we kept them dressed and with good shoes. Thank God they didn't lack anything; that's what I thought.

As time went by, I realized that in elementary school, my daughters Juana and Sagrario would erase pages from their notebooks to write on them again. For that reason, they failed on one occasion. That is how we succeeded in providing them with some studying as we could. I did not want them to experience what I did, a girl with many needs who could not study, because at that time it was more important to get a plate of food than to be in school. I was only able to reach the third grade of elementary school, which I did as a married woman with my husband when we were both adults.

I can't complain, since he always supported me in whatever I decided and tried to give us the best he could. He built us a mud house on the ranch and a wooden house in El Salto. As I mentioned before, he always gave me his salary and only left enough for the gas for the chainsaw and for some spare parts he needed. He always worked with social security to receive medical attention, since I had a midwife for four of my children and insurance for only three. All my children were born with a year's difference between each one.

I was very happy to have them, and I thank God for the husband and children he gave me, because I never received an offense from him, much less a [physical] blow. I always felt protected by him, and I thought that by being with him, nothing else could happen. We ran in the countryside, we played with my children, and I washed in the rivers and streams. Those were happy times, with lots of love. I remember that he always told me, "The family is you, me, and my children; let me make it clear to you," and that is how I learned that only we could protect and take care of them. I think that thanks to God we were able to build a family with a lot of love and values, but above all with good feelings.

It was not until 1995, when my sister-in-law Francisca, my husband's sister, invited us to come to Ciudad Juárez, with the promise that there was a lot of work here and that she already had land for us in a neighborhood that was being formed, called Lomas de Poleo, near the U.S. border. My husband came [to Ciudad Juárez] in September and came for us in November 1995. My sister-in-law sent one of her sons to pick us up in a van with only a single mattress, a tub of dishes, four chairs, and a change of clothes for each of us. We arrived safely, thank God, even though we had not yet left the state of Durango. My daughters Juana and Sagrario got very sick, and we thought they were getting intoxicated since they [sat near] a gallon of gasoline in the truck. They began to fall asleep and did not react, and we had to stop and walk them to get them to react, and they began to vomit. That was the first hardship we went through.

We left at two o'clock in the afternoon and arrived in Ciudad Juárez at 10 p.m. the next day. It was a very drastic change because we came from the mountains to the desert, where there was no water or electricity, so they brought us water in pipes once a week. We had to ration that water to wash clothes, dishes, make food, and bathe. We arrived with my sister-in-law Francisca and her children. She had a piece of land for us with a roofless wall in the upper part of Lomas de Poleo on the way to the dumps in the United States. My husband would bring up scrap wood to roof the wall and make a little kitchen. I started to go with him, and we would collect the [aluminum] cans, and I collected the money, and we would sell it to buy a four-burner grill.

Then he, my children, and I would go to this dump site [located up against the U.S. borderline with Mexico] and collect whatever we could use, such as clothes, dishes, wood, and food. I remember there was a truck that would come with vegetables, meats, and fruits, and the [drivers] would talk to us [to let us know there was fresh food in their dump trucks] before they went to throw the food away in the open trash pit. They would hand it over saying it came from Walmart and it was all clean. Thanks to that person we could eat healthy for the time being. But despite that, I [would spend my time] crying because I had left Guille in Durango with my employers at the stationery store. They asked me for her because the best sales dates were approaching, which were the Christmas season.

My life was terrible in that community; I was forced to work to help my husband, and just seeing myself collecting things from the garbage and in a community with no services made me feel terrible. The only thing that encouraged me was that we were still together and that Guille would soon be coming with us. My husband did not start working soon because my sister-in-law told him that because of his age, they would not give him a job. It wasn't until Guille arrived and got a job at the Capcom maquila [that] Juana and Sagrario and my husband [began working there, and] Chuy, my son, already worked there. Chuy also went to study at the Ciudad Juárez Technological School because it was also in the plans for my son to study. Lupe and Claudia went to Altavista high school and Alicia to Lomas de Poleo elementary school. I was left to take care of the housework and the care of my children.

Soon after, with the wages of those who worked, we were able to buy an Aerostar van so that they could travel from work to home. Chuy had to stop working to be able to study; only my husband, Guille, Juana, and Sagrario were left working together in the afternoon shift, entering at 3 p.m. and leaving at 12:30 at night. That was until they were told that Sagrario could no longer work that shift because she was a minor. She was seventeen years old, and she was five months shy of her eighteenth birthday, which she would have turned eighteen on July 31. According to legal reasons, she was changed to the morning shift, and although my husband and my other daughters claimed that she was safe with them, the change was made in February [of 1998]. I noticed that this change affected her; she became sleepy and got up at three in the morning to take a bath. I asked her if she wanted to stop working until she came of age, but she said that without her salary, they would not have enough.

This lasted until April 16, 1998, when she left for work and never returned. It was a fourteen-day ordeal to find her. Finally, after fourteen days, her body was found in the Valle of Ciudad Juárez in Loma Blanca. During her absence, we were able to distribute about four thousand inquiries throughout Ciudad Juárez. In the investigation file, all the negligence and irregularities [by authorities] were committed in the case of my daughter Sagrario, from a negative DNA to the wrong grave to perform an exhumation. Because of this case, we formed a group of families of murdered girls which was Voces sin Eco, where the black cross with a pink background was created as a protest against the authorities at all levels. Due to a lack of resources, we could not continue as a group, but we never neglected our cases even to this day.

In 1999, my community proposed that I represent them in a neighborhood committee when they saw my way of demanding justice for Sagrario's case. I accepted with the support of my family and with the support of my community, and I was able to make arrangements for basic services [in Lomas de Poleo]. My greatest need was prevention, so I focused on obtaining electricity service. In the lower part of Poleo, we were able to obtain drinking water, public telephones, improvements for primary and secondary schools, and we were able to get the garbage collection truck and numbering for houses and streets. Subsequently, the upper part of Poleo [a mesa hill] was provided with electricity, but in 2002, nineteen children were left without a place in the kindergarten, and I was able to arrange for a rural kindergarten. The neighbors decided to name it after my daughter: Maria Sagrario Kindergarten, which is now an official federal kindergarten located on the bottom level of Lomas de Poleo.

Likewise, in 2002, we had a very serious problem in our community when these lands were being claimed by a very powerful family, the Zaragoza family from Ciudad Juárez. We had a group in a concentration camp, where the families and especially the women were mistreated and harassed.[2] There were evictions, burning of houses with children in-

---

2. A fence was built around the community, with men who would guard the entrance, monitoring who would come and go into the neighborhood.

side, threats, and beatings. They killed a neighbor with blows and sticks. Everything was denounced to the authorities, but as always, justice was conspicuous by its absence. I denounced it to José Luis Soberanes, the president of the national human rights commission, but it all remained a simple report. In May 2003, there were two attempts by the federal commission to take away our electricity, which we were able to stop by burning tires to prevent the police from passing. But in the same month and year, we could no longer stop them. They came with a federal order, according to them, with about 150 patrol cars and riot gear to take away the electrical wiring. I, along with other women, built a human fence to prevent this action, and I was the first one they threw into the patrol car like a dog. My son and husband witnessed this, and they were beaten. [Seven of us were] arrested, and I could not believe that I went to jail. I am not ashamed because it was for a just cause, defending a right like every human being. I remember that while I was behind bars, some Vincentian women arrived and gave me juice and lunch. They asked me if I wanted to pray with them and I shouted no [and asked them] where was God with so much injustice? I was very angry to see everything that was happening to us and how nobody did anything.

Finally, I want to say that all my community work has been like therapy for me, and any achievement I always say and will forever say [is] for Sagrario. Because she, as well as all the girls and women who have been murdered, live in that black cross with the pink background. Sagrario lives in my heart, she lives in that kindergarten, she lives in every child's certificate, she lives in the community of Poleo, and she lives in the whole world and Ciudad Juárez. Forever and ever.

CHAPTER 1

Ellos Matan?

Visual Autoethnography of Motherhood in the Face of the Militarization at the Border

MA. EUGENIA HERNÁNDEZ SÁNCHEZ

Autonomous University of Ciudad Juárez

Nothing is stranger than this business of humans
Observing other humans
In order to write about them.

—RUTH BEHAR, 1996

I have always lived on the border; it is not just a coincidence. This place and I chose each other; we understand each other; we get tired of each other and we meet again. When people ask me, why are you still there? I respond romantically that I believe in her, that this is where the processes of the world begin. This is where the great differences bring out the best and the worst in oneself and others. Borrowing from Bonfil Batalla (1990), the border is where those denied participation in the nation, the "profound Mexico" (9), come to mind. I recognize that my perspective is the result of a generational learning about being here. My mother and father said that they were from Ciudad Juárez when this is not entirely true. Thus, its origin was a choice, and the denial of its roots painfully intentional. I think that at the border, you can partially invent your own story and not be determined by the environment, but every gift has a cost: the cost of daily survival.

In this work, I address motherhood through a visual autoethnography as the axis of survival in a border city with a growing military presence over the last twenty years. The importance of exploring military institutions from the maternal experience is recent; Eloisio Moulin de

Souza (2022) exposes the need for "new studies [that] would provide the problematization and deconstruction of gendered power relations that downgrade mothers and pregnant women, and other expressions of gender identity" (10). With Moulin de Souza in mind, I explore: What kind of negotiations are carried out between family life and the contradictions that survival presents? How are children and youth included as active participants in the elaboration of visual autoethnography? Following Paul Stoller's work (2020), he claims, "[with] an artistic ethnography, we have the ability to show the public sphere a wisdom full of nuances, the very foundation of the anthropological gaze. That wisdom can chart a course that ultimately leads to meaningful change and social justice" (20). Although I can only present my own story as a complicit mother, teacher, and researcher, this autoethnography is crossed by the structures of continuous surveillance presented from the collective self (del Alba Acevedo et al. 2001) with the intention to engage in "reflexive remembering" (Salazar Gutiérrez and Rivero Peña 2014, 106).

Nelly Richard (2002) proposes that "collecting . . . fragments [and] avoiding the forced junction, [symbolizes] delving, rather, into disharmony and conflict, in the hope of their edges, [representing] a question of ethics as well as aesthetics" (192). In this way, the motherhood-militarized relationship is presented, emphasizing the moments that resist being forgotten. I therefore follow the feminist line of betting on subjectivity as a way of making evident the positionality of the researcher. To this extent, the reader can question the present work openly. Finally, I hope not only to continue insisting on questioning the traditional division between what is public and private, but to further accentuate the intimate dimension of encounters that take place in public spaces among strangers.

Theoretical-Methodological Approach: Visual Autoethnography

I propose a theoretical-methodological collaboration between autoethnography and digital drawing. Specifically, a visual autoethnography. Both branches present different angles of reality that are possible, thanks to constant and acute observations. Classical ethnography observes the same space or event for long periods, where the alien ceases to be alien, showing a new panorama from cognition. The challenge in autoethnography, however, is that "the social group that the researcher considers his own is studied" (Blanco 2012, 55). Therefore, belonging is at the core of what is questioned.

Likewise, art allows us to materialize analysis through an intimate dimension, showing a hidden yet shared reality through composition. Therefore, digital drawing is superimposed on photography, where "the research process based on practice is the simultaneous production of knowledge through the artifact" (Carrillo 2015, 223). Therefore, in this work, the autoethnographic narrative is intertwined by weaving text into photographs and digital drawing, thus acknowledging the intentionality of each moment.[1] In this sense, the image is no longer considered only a visualization of the idea expressed in the text, but gives rise to "self-reflexivity" (223) from different forms of knowledge. This allows for contrast in each image and complementarity (among the images). Autoethnography and images are combined to produce a visual autoethnography in this work.

Consequently, both processes, autoethnography and art, focus on showing a dimension that is not expressed in terms of the classical academic text. I share Stoller's (2020) concern: "Let us admit that our apparently consolidated methods and our conventions of representation are no longer in tune with the current state of social, political, environmental or economic upheaval" (19). Going beyond traditional methods is needed to elucidate the experiences of mothers at the border.

Mother-Accomplice

In 2012, the "strong hand" (war against drugs) was established by then-president of Mexico Felipe Calderón, and the city entered a curfew. At that time, statistics revealed there were 5.8 murders per day (Esquivel 2012). In the city, there were more than three thousand soldiers, and life centered on the privacy of the home and the suspicion of those closest to it (Esquivel 2012). Neighborhoods close by gating themselves in for protection. Metal bars and security guards are financed by neighborhood residents themselves, and the surveillance business increases by leaps

---

1. Mariana Martinez is a visual artist who elaborated every image presented in this chapter. Their work focuses on comic strips in which they address how cities fracture.

and bounds. Everyone acquires the equipment they can afford to protect their homes, as if life were only experienced at home. On the television news, the count of daily deaths appears in a corner of the screen, and mistrust floods the city.

On one intensely hot afternoon in northern Mexico in 2012, we reach almost 100 degrees Fahrenheit. I leave work, pick up my youngest child from school, and I don't have dinner ready—nor food to make it with—so we rush to the supermarket. We talk about school and work, the challenges of friendships in the classroom at six years old, the challenges of friendships at work at forty. I'm excited that this could be an important moment between mother and child. We are distracted, looking for *bolillos* to make sandwiches, and we run into three members of the army in the corridor, with their long weapons and their hard (but smiling) faces.[2] They are three young people gathering bags and bags of *bolillo* bread and *teleras*. You would think that they carried almost a hundred *bolillos* in their big transparent bag. The image surprises us, soldiers and *bolillos*; there is a kind of overflow in every sense. We look at each other head on. There are no reactions. Then both groups just avoid looking at each other, especially me. I don't see their eyes, but I don't see my child's either.

But my child does not evade anything; they are honest.[3] They are six years old, and I know that they are a stubborn observer of the surprising little things in the world. My child asks me questions about how the light through the car glass breaks into various colors—rainbows—as they try to catch it. They place snails in the house and soil in a box so that they can live with them. The surprise of our encounter with the soldiers is the beginning of the next inquiry, and I know that my child will not let it pass. My child stops, looks at them, and, pointing to the soldiers, asks me, "Mamá, ellos matan?"[4]

The point here is that weapons are good for only one thing: to kill. The point in this interaction is that my objective is only one: to go unnoticed, my child and I. To be invisible. But it is too late; the question was asked in the precise space where the civilian gaze collides with the

---

2. *Bolillos* are a type of Mexican bread.

3. I use the pronouns they/them as subject identification to address gender-neutral identification.

4. "Mom, do they kill?"

FIGURE 1.1 *Ellos Matan?* Artwork by Mariana Martinez.

military inspection, motherhood clashing with the institution. I like to think that I was honest, that I answered, "Yes, guns kill. They shouldn't be in a supermarket full of people. The army must go!" but it was not like that. Getting out of the situation as soon as possible required navigating between contradictions. My heart racing and my mind cold, I said to my child that there are several activities the army does. My response was filled with ambiguity, a failed attempt not to contradict our family life with soldiers on the city streets, as our parallel lives passed each other. I finished with a "good afternoon," and my child walked away with me, their face questioning. Of course, without doubt, what I said and did on that day contradicted my everyday convictions.

Mother-Teacher

In 2020, during the pandemic, my family and I decide to go out at night to the ice cream shop ten minutes from home. Walking at this time allowed us to maintain social distancing from others. Finally, we can walk together outside. We pass through a narrow street next to a vacant lot, where a military checkpoint surprises us. After almost nine years of military presence, I thought that I could just go through the checkpoint on autopilot and say the obligatory good evening to the soldiers, waiting to see whether there would be any questions or we would be allowed to continue moving on our way. But once again, the acute observation of my children surprises me when I hear one address the soldier directly, telling him, "I also play *Halo*."[5] My heart is fluttering because now there is an interaction and not just an encounter. My stomach hurts, and the last thing I want is ice cream. The soldier, a young man of twenty years or less, responds only with a nod and a few laughs.

What does my child see and think? What are the specific associations between the video game and the reality of the city? In what way should motherhood, as a survival mediation, create or deny access to the symbols needed to uncode these interactions? In the video game, if you kill, you level up, and more weapons and allegiances are formed. As I write this, my child is now a fifteen-year-old teenager, and my anxiety level increases for their future.

As we walked for ice cream, I had hoped that our conversation would be centered on their online school, friendships, a first love disappointment, or even how to pass a level in a video game, but no—the conversation in this scenario was about avoiding the interaction, domesticating the gaze, and just saying hello and leaving the place without attracting attention. In this scenario, what does the maternal message mean of teaching our children "You have the right to always say what you think"? How can you negotiate motherhood as justice at the same time that you interact with a symbol of power? How do we teach our children at the border social justice and yet demonstrate a behavior that contradicts it?

As we walk, we return to the conversation about how to interact with military figures. As a teenager, they have the look of someone who knows everything about life at fifteen, and they answer, "Yo te defiendo."[6] How do I explain to my child that the problem is not that young soldier, nor his group, but the system that confronts us?

---

5. *Halo* is an Xbox video game.

6. "I'll defend you."

FIGURE 1.2 *Ice Cream.* Artwork by Mariana Martinez.

Mother-Researcher

There is a pattern. It is not only the growing militarization in the city, but the reorganization of intimate family life in public spaces related to increasing frequent military encounters. The local newspaper reports: "A total of 300 elements of the Special Forces of the Mexican Army arrived at the border this afternoon to reinforce 'Operation Juárez 2023' and to help with security after the escape of 30 inmates from Social Readaptation Center number 3" (Olmos 2023).

My children have grown up. They are teenagers, and they know perfectly well, as the children of an academic, what ethnography is and how difficult it is for me to document the daily spaces where the Guardia Nacional (GN) is given continuing military powers.[7] Now, we see them everywhere. Just the thought of simply picking up my children from school and seeing or being stopped by the GN makes my stomach ache.

What I did not expect is that my teenagers would be faster than me to document this proliferation of the military. One of my teens rushes

---

7. Guardia Nacional is the Mexican National Guard.

FIGURE 1.3 *Take a Selfie*. Artwork by Mariana Martinez.

home and tells me, "I have something for you." "What?" I answer. With teenagers at home, I do not know what to expect, perhaps a report card or a new drawing. They show me their cell phone with photographs of the GN. "How did you take them?" I asked, trying to appear calm. They answer, "I pretended that I was taking some selfies of myself, and I reversed the camera and took them." I thought, *Who is the mother here and who is the researcher?*

They performed being a teenager while being a teenager. They read the context of what is expected of teens and used it. They imagined how adolescents are expected to be constantly taking photos of themselves, but they demonstrated that they also show awareness of the context around them when taking these images. This is how visual autoethnography becomes collective and merges with the intentional process of generating an image.

Prejudices about youth crumble, and my children show me their own strategy, their methodology, their visual ethnography. I am faced with the fact that "reality continues its march regardless of the scheme proposed on how to put methodological strategies into practice" (Rojas Soriano 2010, 115). I have a mixture of fear and joy. It is not fair that young people in Juárez must navigate safety and protection and always be aware in the current environment of violence they experience. As teens, however, my children also show their knowledge as young people and their own way of contributing to understanding our role in the place we call home.

Conclusion: They Are (Also) My Children

The antagonism between the military institution and motherhood is evident. The historicity of motherhood, associated with the private sphere, now facing the historicity of the military institution, associated with the public sphere, is undeniably an asymmetrical power relation. Thus, "maternal bodies are considered abject bodies in organizations, bodies that destabilize social norms and borders between public and private worlds, harming the status of women at work, and creating subtle forms of exclusion, either implicitly, by social isolation in the organizational space, or explicitly" (Gratell 2013, as cited in Moulin de Souza 2022, 3). I want to reflect in this last section, however, on another equally problematic optic, and that is getting closer to considering the *reflexivity of the encounter*.

In this visual autoethnography, I intend to show intimate moments in the public spaces that generate the rearticulation of the family organization from the viewpoint and experiences of motherhood via encounters with the military. By making the photographic intervention (drawings) evident, I wish to state that the autoethnographic work is collective, from the maternal experience where the "visual imaginary does not represent a window onto the world, but rather a created perspective" (Leavy 2009, 215), which includes the observations and wisdom of my children.

Autoethnography allows us not only to use observation, but also to question it. I allow myself to remember that from a motherhood perspective, when we raise our voice at home to have our children comply with a rule, it indicates that we are losing the battle with our children. In the same way, motherhood from the perspective of visual autoethnography emphasizes that "violent conflict occurs specifically in relatively symmetrical but inconsistent relationships" (Tilly 2005, 17). This argument enables us to ask ourselves, How different are these young soldiers from my children? What conditions bring them to the north of Mexico, mainly from southern Mexico? And how do their mothers care for them at a distance? What does it mean to operate in environments of increasing citizen mistrust? For Tilly, "Transactional accounts take interactions among social sites as their starting points, treating both events at those sites and durable characteristics of those sites as outcomes of interaction. Transactional accounts become relational—another term widely employed in this context—when they focus on persistent features of transactions between specific social sites" (2005, 14).

Finally, my intention is not to erase what Ciudad Juárez has experienced for decades, but to try to take the dialogue toward more analytical horizons than reactive ones, if we want to transform this border landscape one interaction at a time. These narrated encounters are experienced as moments, but they are the result of long-lasting processes. I follow Umberto Eco's proposal that "trying to understand the other means destroying the cliches that surround him, without denying or erasing his otherness" (2013, 22). Thus, this visual autoethnography fights for centering a representation of everyday (maternal) and uncertain life, where the encounter with otherness (the military) is thought of in different ways, such as through visuality and the participation of the youngest of voices.

REFERENCES

Behar, Ruth. 1996. *The Vulnerable Observer: Anthropology That Breaks Your Heart*. Boston, Mass.: Beacon Press.

Blanco, Mercedes. 2012. "Autoetnografía: Una forma narrativa de generación de conocimientos." *Andamios: Revista de Investigación Social* 9 (19): 49–74.

Bonfil Batalla, Guillermo. 1990. *México profundo: Una civilización negada*. Mexico City: Editorial Grijalbo.

Carrillo Quiroga, Perla. 2015. "La investigación basada en la práctica de las artes y los medios audiovisuales." *Revista mexicana de investigación educativa* 20 (64): 219–40.

del Alba Acevedo, Luz, Norma Alarcón, Celia Alvarez, Ruth Behar, Rina Benmayor, Norma E. Cantú, Daisy Cocco De Filippis, et al., eds. 2001. *Telling to Live: Latina Feminist Testimonios*. Durham, N.C.: Duke University Press.

Eco, Umberto. 2013. *Construir al enemigo*. Barcelona: Penguin Random House Grupo Editorial.

Esquivel, J. Jesús. 2012. "Juárez, símbolo de la mortandad." *Proceso*, November 8, 2012. https://www.proceso.com.mx/reportajes/2012/11/8/juarez-simbolo-de-la-mortandad-110555.html.

Leavy, Patricia. 2009. *Method Meets Art: Arts-Based Research Practice*. New York: Guilford.

Moulin de Souza, Eloisio. 2022. "Can Mothers Be Heroes? Maternity and Maternal Body Work in Military Firefighters." Supplement, *Revista de Administração Contemporânea* 26 (S1): 1–13.

Olmos, Javier. 2023. "Arriban 300 militares para reforzar seguridad en Juárez." *Diario de Juarez*, January 3, 2023. https://diario.mx/juarez/arriban-300 -militares-para-reforzar-seguridad-en-juarez-20230103-2009682.html.

Richard, Nelly. 2002. "Crítica de la memoria." *Cuadernos de Literatura* 8 (15): 187–93.

Rojas Soriano, Raúl. 2010. *Metodología en la calle, salud-enfermedad, política, cárcel, escuela . . . .* Mexico City: Plaza y Valdés.

Salazar Gutiérrez, Salvador, and Héctor Rivero Peña. 2014. "Ciudad dramatizada: La erosión de la memoria y el dominio de la eventualidad en el escenario de Ciudad Juárez, México." *Espiral* 10 (59): 89–107.

Stoller, Paul. 2020. "El arte de la etnografía en tiempos turbulentos." *Revista de antropología iberoamericana* 6 (1): 17–36.

Tilly, Charles. 2005. *Identities, Boundaries and Social Ties.* New York: Routledge.

CHAPTER 2

Frontera Madre(hood) and Survival Tactics of Urban Life

MARISOL RODRÍGUEZ SOSA

Universidad Autónoma de Cuidad Juárez

Frontera madre(hood), the central concept of this anthology, argues that the geopolitics of border living/making/crossing/deconstructing generates a form of border motherhood in U.S.-Mexico border cities. This chapter, written from Ciudad Juárez, on the Mexican side of the border, explores and discusses the ideas that resonate from south of the border: How does the geopolitics of border living affect forms of madre(hood) south of the U.S.-Mexico border? How do Mexican mothers and families adapt and define ways of life to survive in a place as hostile as a militarized border city? My narrative unfolds from the *testimonio* of my first years living as a mother in Ciudad Juárez, Chihuahua, where I moved in 2008 for work reasons with my family and a one-year-old baby. Thus, from the perspective of a researcher and a mother who has faced migration processes and lives south of the U.S.-Mexico border, I seek to reveal mothering practices that I had to quickly learn to coexist or adapt to what it means to live at this border.

Living in a northern Mexican border city means living in the territory of two countries, two nationalities, two societies, two cultures, and two power structures, which unfold between the north of Mexico and the south of the United States. This creates a binational territory with cross-border urban life and cross-border risks that arise from this proximity. Thereby, madre(hood) in a border metropolis means being a mother in a dangerous and hostile context, which is the genesis of what we consider in this anthology. "Mothering practices at the U.S.-Mexico border" (Bejarano and Morales, this volume) manifest in everyday urban life tactics and in the way our communities are built—in my case, how Ciudad Juárez is built.

Frontera madre(hood) emphasizes *hood* as a space-time interpretation, which is the genesis of this concept, along with border mothers' experiences, habits, and practices to protect those they love and care for. The natural instinct of any living and sentient being that feels fear or the need for protection is to wrap itself in the fetal position and to seek refuge; it is an innate instinct for self-preservation. This sense is also natural in madre(hood) because every mother knows that the safety and health of their children depends on the care and protection they receive, from the womb and throughout childhood and youth. The need for self-preservation is also manifested in the way we build our living spaces. Cities are the creation of the societies that inhabit them and reflect their dreams, desires, fears, and concerns. When we are afraid or feel unsafe in our homes, we protect ourselves by installing cameras and security bars on doors and windows. In the same way, when the city we live in is hostile and threatening, we also want our neighborhoods to function as a safe space, a refuge for the protection of those we care about, even at the cost of self-confinement. We have all had that experience with the COVID-19 pandemic, when faced with uncertainty and fear of contagion. We all take refuge at home, the safest and most protected space for our family's survival.

The term *fronteriza* refers to a woman who lives in a border city, as the meaning of the word implies: "That is on the border"; "That is in front of something else" ("Que está en la frontera"; "Que está enfrente de otra cosa"; Real Academia Española, n.d., my translation). Living on the border means to inhabit a territory of separations, of extremes, of militarization on both sides—an inside and outside existence. That is what happens at the U.S.-Mexico border, where the militarization of urban space is the most obvious manifestation of fear of the other, as the built environment is designed to supposedly protect U.S. citizens, and every exchange between the two cities must be extremely guarded in the name of security. It is most noticeable in the international division, namely in the border wall built by the U.S. government on a staggering scale; in

FIGURE 2.1 The U.S.-Mexico border in Ciudad Juárez, prominently showing the iconic *La Equis* (*The X*) structure, with a view of the cement canals of the Rio Grande against a row of concertina wire at the U.S. border wall. Photo taken by Arq. Priscilla Pérez, 2024.

Ciudad Juárez, even the Rio Grande (Río Bravo) had to be confined to prevent any natural movement of the water that could alter the international border line, where U.S. helicopters and border patrol agents are commonplace (figures 2.1 and 2.2).

A more worrisome situation occurs inside the cities south of the border, however, where we get the perception that we can be victims of a crime just because we live in this city. What is visible is the Mexican militarization of the public realm in response to fear through the creation of inner borders, gated neighborhoods, and blocked streets. That is why the negative urban effects of border geopolitics and dynamics are more severe in Mexican border cities that have become fighting arenas and militarized urban territories, with the constant presence of military and police personnel and vehicles, as well as law enforcement officers of different levels circulating through the streets and everyday public spaces.

FIGURE 2.2 The view of the U.S.-Mexico border wall from Ciudad Juárez, showing the concertina wire on top and El Paso, Texas, in the backdrop. Photo taken by Arq. Priscilla Pérez, 2024.

Considering all the above, I argue that frontera madre(hood) south of the U.S.-Mexico border implies a double connotation of the border, one that is constructed by international geopolitics, and another at the community level, since border living/crossing/making/deconstructing has complex effects on quotidian urban life and madre(hood). This is precisely what I want to make visible in this chapter, by exploring the "mothering practices at the border" that emerge from this more militarized universe of border urban life, and from the need to protect those we love and need to care for. Thus, from the idea of frontera madre(hood) proposed by the editors of this anthology, my contribution discusses three aspects of urban life that reveal survival tactics built from madre(hood) at the border: (1) use of militarized public space and frontera madre(hood); (2) neighborhood and madre(hood) responses to protect our children; and (3) madre(hood) support networks, childcare, and community resilience. I seek to visualize the strategies and practices developed by mothers and women within these militarized public spaces, to protect their neighborhoods and families, which is born from the need of border inhabitants to feel safe and to rebuild the community in which they were born and in which their families live.

Testimonial Narrative, a Methodological Framework

In this chapter, *testimonio* is used as an epistemic approach to explore perceptions and experiences that are often silenced in the most generalizing or statistically representative ways. Incorporating the *testimonio* of lived experiences opens space to other views, to communicate from the humanities aspects of social life that statistics cannot capture, which transmit what has been lived, what is witnessed, what is felt, and what is perceived. It is an invitation to be in the place of the other, to listen from the perspective of a narrator who was there. It is a witness of events; therefore, *testimonio* is approached as a way of sharing lived, observed, and witnessed experiences.

Testimonio is a "vehicle of social memory," a "space for the reconstruction of collective memory," understood from its "condition of narration of real events" (García 2016, 76, 78, 81, my translation). It is also an essential source for oral history that "recognizes the value of direct testimonies from individual social actors. . . . It is a resource to register the voice and memory of the old, of women, of the marginalized, of the unheard" (Galindo Cáceres 2009, 107, my translation). The *testimonio* goes beyond statistical data because it communicates the complexity of social life: "Positivism does not accept as a principle that an oral testimony is a sufficient element to confirm a reading about something. . . . The defense of the meaning of comprehensive and hermeneutical epistemologies does not accept these rigors and considers that social life already has its own ways of communicating without the need for the apparent rigors and details of positive scientism" (Galindo Cáceres 2009, 109, my translation).

Thus, in this writing, the testimonial narrative is used as an effort to express and visualize the social memory of someone who has been there, in the past, in the present. It is about expressing the experiences of social life on the border, the challenges faced by women and mothers when migrating, what it means to be a mother and what it means to be a child in a militarized borderland. *Testimonio* is a vehicle to understand the silenced and to promote a broadened interpretation of the current situation.

Use of Militarized Public Space and Frontera Madre(hood)

In 2008, Ciudad Juárez was experiencing unprecedented violence due to a long dispute between organized crime groups. The records of femicide of women in Ciudad Juárez counted "833 women murdered from 1993 to 2009" (Fuentes Flores 2011, 18, my translation). In 2008, precisely 1,607 homicides were registered in the city derived from organized crime violence, of which 132 were homicides of women (Monárrez Fragoso 2011, 137). In addition to the local crisis, between 2006 and 2011, there was an accelerated increase in the number of missing persons throughout Mexico. Between 1999 and 2017, a total of 9,327 women were reported missing throughout the country, exactly 25.7 percent of the total number of disappeared during that period (Velasco-Domínguez and Castañeda-Xochitl 2020, 105).

Thus, living in Ciudad Juárez in 2008 meant living in the middle of a war being fought in the streets of the city. To survive in those circumstances, I had to change many of my daily life habits and practices to adapt to the new reality of being a migrant woman and a mother in a border city. A few days after arriving, I had the first experience warning me that living in this border city would be different from my previous living situations. I needed paper to print something for a class, and since I had not yet bought a car, I decided to walk to the nearby Office Depot, about 150 meters from the house in which we were living temporarily. On the way back home, I saw a red truck parking about ten meters in front of me on the same sidewalk I was walking on. At that moment, I just thought someone was parking. But no one got out of the vehicle. I continued walking, passing the truck, and immediately the truck moved and parked again about ten meters in front of me, and then I felt that something was wrong. Still, I went ahead and passed quickly without looking, and the same thing happened again, although luckily this third time, I managed to reach the access door to the private neighborhood where I lived, and so I was able to escape.

When I got home scared, I told my partner what happened to me. For the next hour he went out to the street repeatedly to observe and confirmed that the truck was parked outside the neighborhood, as if waiting for me to come out again. That experience was undoubtedly a great warning for my family and me as newcomers to the border, and from that moment on, at the request of my family and for my own protection, I had to abandon what was a normal practice for me: walking alone to buy something nearby. Since then, I understood that a woman walking alone in Ciudad Juárez is in constant risk, and that I should always drive a car to protect my son and myself.

I also remember that, like all newcomers to a city, I wanted to visit its center, but all my colleagues and people I had just met persuaded me not to. They suggested avoiding the city center, which caused me great consternation. I understood that the public space and urban life of this border city were not the same as those of the Latin American cities I had lived in before, in which women walk alone daily to go to work or do the grocery shopping, or as tourists to visit the city center, its churches and museums, and where it is not at all common to see military cars on the streets.

Another event that stayed in my mind forever happened around a year later. My son and I were on our way to kindergarten, and because of traffic hazards, we ended up waiting at a traffic light just behind a military vehicle, with three soldiers standing in the back holding high-caliber weapons pointed in all directions, including one pointing in our direction. The silence was broken when my son, who was about three years old, asked me from the back seat, "Mom, are we bad?" To which I replied, "No, why do you say that?" He answered, "Because they target us." I remember hating when I had to stop at traffic lights because the newspaper vendors brought copies closer to the car, and the front page was always a carnage. So I put thick children's visors on the back windows so that my son would not see them.

A short time later, I told a close friend about this experience, and she shared some strategies on how to drive around the city to avoid dangerous situations. She suggested that I use only wide streets with at least two or three lanes to avoid being behind or next to a military or police vehicle, which could be targets of attacks. She also recommended that to avoid being in the way of someone who wanted to escape or go at high speed, I should drive in the center lane so I wouldn't interrupt the passage of vehicles traveling fast in the left lane or those that wanted to take an exit in the right lane. In addition, she explained to me that it was important that my car have good tires and that it have its regular mechanical check-ups to avoid getting a flat tire or having to call a tow truck. Regarding the use of polarized glass windows, she said I should use them for sun protection—but not too dark, so I could be identified and not confused with someone else. Another tip was to avoid convenience stores, where you were most likely to be exposed to risk both inside and in the parking lot. Regarding routine journeys from home to work or school, she recommended I avoid doing the same routes every day and instead look for alternate routes to avoid being predictable.

Of course, these tips helped me a lot, and I have always used them ever since. I remember being surprised that the women of this border city had developed a set of tactics and strategies that I was unaware of. These experiences of my first years living in Ciudad Juárez taught me that living on the U.S.-Mexico border requires women and mothers to develop certain tactics and strategies for using public spaces that implies losing certain individual freedoms, such as walking alone, going to the city center alone, or moving freely through the city, and which forces women to drive a car for their self-protection and the protection of their children.

This restricted use of public space by women was confirmed by a 2009 investigation, conducted with a probabilistic survey using a gender perspective, with the purpose of identifying gender differences in the use and perception of public space in the urban area of Ciudad Juárez (Fuentes Flores 2009). The results were presented in the book *Espacio público y género en Ciudad, Chihuahua: Accesibilidad, sociabilidad, participación y seguridad* (Fuentes Flores et al. 2011), which contextualizes the impact of urban insecurity in the abandonment of public spaces by women who live on the border.

I had the opportunity to analyze the survey and write a chapter for that book (Rodríguez Sosa 2011), in which I analyzed whether the use of public spaces was more intense in central urban areas, which consists of more commercial activity and services. Considering that the survey was georeferenced, I compared the sample applied throughout the city with a subsample of surveys applied in a buffer with a radius of two kilometers from the centralities. Less than half of the women surveyed (48.5 percent) stated that they used public spaces in the city, such as parks, squares, and sports fields, and that percentage drops to 40.2 percent of women surveyed in the central areas. Additionally, only 47.6 percent of the women surveyed used neighborhood public spaces, in contrast to 38.1 percent of women surveyed in the central neighborhoods. The two spaces where the surveyed women had the highest perception of insecurity were the city center (31.1 percent) and public transport (28.6 percent). The two spaces with the highest perception of security were shopping centers (35.5 percent) and the streets of their neighborhoods (22.9 percent) (Rodríguez Sosa 2011, 65, 66, 77, 84).

The spaces indicated as the safest or most unsecure confirm the preference of women living in this border city for more confined or delimited spaces, such as malls and neighborhoods, and the avoidance of those perceived to be more unsafe, such as central areas and public transportation. When choosing how to get to work or school, public transportation continues to be seen as insecure for women and as a portal to femicide; and this, of course, exposes the vulnerability of working mothers and their children, who sometimes do not have the option of avoiding the center, remote areas, or public transportation.

The lack of attention for decades to these chronic urban vulnerabilities for women living in this border city, and the constant discourses explaining femicides from a narrative that naturalizes the disappearance and murder of women because they were doing something wrong—besides the little success and effort deployed by the government to investigate and solve these homicides—have led academic women to argue that femicide is used as a form of social control by the government, as stated by Bejarano in "(Re)Living Femicide through Social Control: The Regulation of Life and Bodies through Fear and (In)Formal Social Control": "Women and girls are told indirectly by the State and, by extension, segments of society, that behaviors which transgress gender-conforming roles and spatial boundaries can result in their victimization and even feminicide. Building on these preliminary observations, this article deconstructs the use of manipulation of 'the femicides' as a controlling technology that works to limit the freedom—spatially, temporally, and otherwise—of women and girls in Juárez, Chihuahua, and throughout the borderlands more broadly" (2015, 68). In this regard, it is important to note that in Ciudad Juárez, "some of the murdered women disappeared from the public space during the journey to school or work" (Fuentes Flores 2011, 18, my translation). Many working women, including mothers, work in the well-known *maquilas,* and when they use public transportation and walk through remote and lonely areas, they are not doing anything wrong (they are not going out at night for illicit activities); they are just commuting to and from work, without the resources to buy a car, and they have no other option than to live and work in urban areas with few conditions of urban livability and security.

Industrial production, which is one of the main economic activities of the city, requires many workers and the provision of large urban lands for the location of industries. This creates unattractive, nonwalkable, and lonely urban spaces, designed for the circulation of semitrailer trucks, which are also used in the main avenues (figure 2.3). The urban landscape of the *maquilas* is dangerous and hostile for women because it is made up of large blocks with high fences along lonely sidewalks, creating an environment that is not safe during the day, much less at night. Yet, *maquilas* often work twenty-four hours in a row when they have urgent orders. The workers enter and leave in three shifts of eight hours each: 8:00 a.m. to 3:00 p.m.; 3:00 p.m. to 11:00 p.m.; and 11:00 p.m. to 8:00 a.m. Therefore, working women fall into a situation of vulnerability on the journey to and from home and work, even more so if there are vacant lots, which increase the perception of insecurity in this city according to Monárrez Fragoso (2011): "Women have a socialization about sexual violence that passes directly through their bodies, and these vacant lots—in the memory and experience of women—that make it easier for aggressors committing these crimes against girls, adolescents and women" (159, my translation). Recognizing the risk and cost of transportation from home to work, the industries have proposed offering personnel transportation.

Industrial activity has reduced unemployment, but wages for production workers remain low. The current minimum daily wage for Mexican border cities as of February 2022 is 260.34 Mexican pesos, which is equivalent to $13.10 a day (Comisión Nacional de los Salarios Mínimos 2021), resulting in a monthly wage of approximately 7,918.60 Mexican pesos, or about $398.50 a month. To discuss whether these are livable wages or not, it is important to consider that according to the National

FIGURE 2.3 The urban landscape of the *maquilas* in Ciudad Juárez. Photos taken by Marisol Rodríguez Sosa, 2021.

Council for the Evaluation of Social Development Policy (Consejo Nacional de Evaluación de la Política de Desarrollo Social [CONEVAL]), in Mexico each person needs 3,542.14 Mexican pesos per month, approximately $178, to reach the basic basket of goods used to measure the poverty line, including food and nonfood expenses in urban areas (CONEVAL 2021). The minimum monthly wage would thus be enough to cover the basic expenses of only 2.2 people, which is not enough even for a family with only one child.

These low wages are why industries offer workers transportation to save them the need to take urban public transportation at a cost of ten Mexican pesos per trip, or a minimum daily expense per person of twenty Mexican pesos (one dollar) for commuting to and from work. This may seem inexpensive, but two family members taking public transportation each day of the month would cost $60, which is 15 percent of the monthly minimum wage.

Many of the men and women who work in the *maquilas* are beneficiaries of social housing as a result of their low incomes, causing a significant increase in the demand for social housing in border cities and the consequent creation of large and dense affordable housing neighborhoods in remote urban areas, where urban land is cheaper. Inhabitants of these new social housing neighborhoods built on the outskirts of the city face higher transportation costs, a lack of quality public space, and inadequate coverage of infrastructure and public educational, health, and recreational facilities. So the underlying social problem and its impact on family life remain unaddressed, worsening the urban hostility of public spaces for working mothers, who also, in many cases, lack the educational background and healthcare to guarantee their childcare needs.

Working women simply do not have the option to avoid remote areas and public or workers' transportation buses. Between 3:00 p.m. and 4:00 p.m. the city experiences great vehicular stress due to the long lines of workers' transportation units, which burst onto the streets and generate temporary chaos (figure 2.4). In those minutes, working women of all ages are seen leaving the *maquilas*. Some opt for personnel transportation buses, even though they do not have the best security conditions since they are old American school buses (figure 2.5). Other women call someone on the phone as soon as they leave and walk to a nearby place, where perhaps a family member will pick them up, avoiding worker transportation (figure 2.6). An hour later, the urban space outside these industries returns to its characteristic emptiness and solitude.

Neighborhoods and Madre(hood): Responses to Protect the Children

Another manifestation of fear and the abandonment of public spaces in cities south of the U.S.-Mexico border is the proliferation of gated

FIGURE 2.4 Long lines of *maquila* transportation units, Ciudad Juárez. Photos taken by Marisol Rodríguez Sosa, May 31, 2022, between 3:20 and 3:25 p.m.; forms of identification removed by digital pixelation.

FIGURE 2.5 Working women head toward the *maquila* transportation units, Ciudad Juárez. Photos taken by Marisol Rodríguez Sosa, May 31, 2022, between 3:20 and 3:25 p.m.; forms of identification removed by digital pixelation.

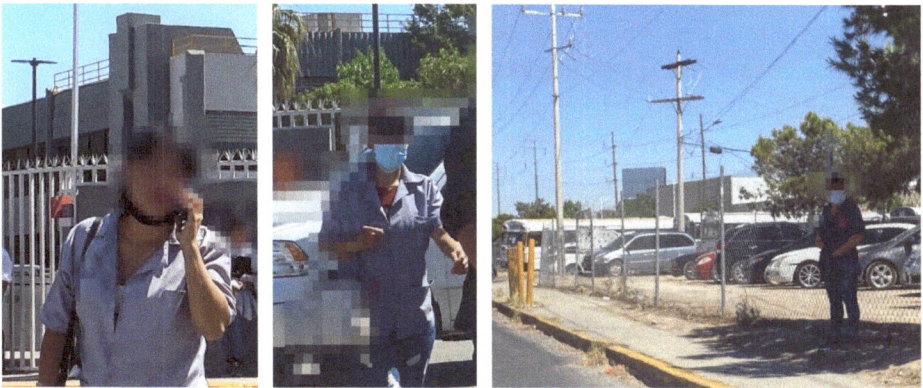

FIGURE 2.6 Working women calling and walking outside the *maquilas*, Ciudad Juárez. Photos taken by Marisol Rodríguez Sosa, May 31, 2022, between 3:20 and 3:25 p.m.; forms of identification removed by digital pixelation.

communities, which causes urban ostracism and isolation. The need for protection has led to an increase in closed and guarded streets, squares, parks, neighborhoods, and shopping centers, through the construction of inner walls and borders that privatize public space in the hope of offering more security. Paradoxically, the more the public space gets closed, the more insecure it becomes, because "natural surveillance" is lost, a concept proposed in Crime Prevention Through Environmental Design (CPTED), a methodology focused on reducing crime, urban insecurity, and the fear of being victimized, using an urban design approach that promotes the ability to observe surrounding territory (ICA 2022).

As an urban planner, I am aware that gated communities mean the death of urban street life as a basic scale of social association and interaction, but the experiences of my first year living in Ciudad Juárez forced me to rethink and reconsider these theoretical positions. Like all who move to a new city for work reasons, in June 2008, we needed to rent a house. As we had done before when we thought about choosing a place to live, we looked for a familiar neighborhood as close as possible to the workplace, thinking that the short distance would be most important for our safety and comfort. We chose a house in a normal open middle-class neighborhood because we were looking for the social interaction of a traditional neighborhood. Reality quickly showed me, however, that theory should never be imposed on context. We had lived in the new house for barely fifteen days when on our way back from work, and with a baby in our arms, we found the doors open. The house had been robbed. That night I remember I did not sleep; I watched all the windows, spending the night moving from one window to the other. I was very afraid for my baby and for all of us. That day they stole what little we had, since as migrants you arrive with only two suitcases. But what affected me the most was that they stole our peace of mind, and I learned that as a woman and mother living on the U.S.-Mexico border, I needed to prioritize security. It was then that we decided to move to a gated neighborhood.

Since then, I have lived in a closed neighborhood, where my son and his friends, both boys and girls, can go out alone to play in the park. As a professional, I do not feel comfortable demanding or suggesting to other families and mothers that they do something that I did not dare do for the safety of my family in this city. It was then that I understood that although closed and gated communities are not well received in urban planning theories, perhaps these ideas cannot be rigidly applied to cities with constant violence.

Before the security crisis in Ciudad Juárez, it was normal for families to buy their houses in open neighborhoods, that is, traditional residential urban blocks, with permeable public streets where all people could walk. In the face of extreme violence, however, many neighbors agreed

FIGURE 2.7 Closure and privatization of neighborhood streets that were previously open. Photos taken by Marisol Rodríguez Sosa, 2021.

to install security doors and to privatize the neighborhood streets that until then were open. This is a collective neighborhood defense tactic (figure 2.7) born out of fear and the need to protect the family and children.

Cities are the result of historical and cultural processes of societies, and therefore, we must learn from the context and the practices that arise from the need of mothers and families to survive circumstances of sustained urban insecurity over time. The proliferation of gated communities is the result of our collective experiences of living on the border. The preference for this form of living space must be understood as responses of middle-class families and mothers trying to keep their children safe. Yet, families with lower incomes or with informal jobs cannot make this decision, which is dependent on having the necessary resources and access to credit. In Ciudad Juárez and in many border cities, however, the increasing number of gated communities in recent decades is unique in that they are not, as we might imagine, exceptions associated with the luxurious lifestyles of very few wealthy people. Instead, the gated community is a response of everyday inhabitants, of medium and medium-low income, for the defense of their homes, families, and groups of neighbors.

Currently, the new middle-class housing developments in Ciudad Juárez are gated communities, which are the preferred housing option for middle-class sectors. Legally, they constitute subdivisions (*fraccionamientos*) in which the municipality authorizes construction companies to design and build a neighborhood with perimeter walls, access doors, and the presence of a security guard who controls access into the communities. Thereby, the urban space is transformed from urban insecurity to urban ostracism, leading even more to the isolation and desolation of sidewalks and streets. This development has also allowed for the use of highly militarized defense elements, such as concertina wire, electrified mesh, security cameras, intercoms, and panic buttons (figure 2.8). To access these communities, neighbors have remote controls, smart cards, or other encoded options, and they must help pay for the maintenance of the security automated access control and surveillance systems, as well as for the care of parks, gardens, and cleaning.

Note, however, that these real estate products are not available to all economic segments. In the last few decades, Ciudad Juárez has experienced soaring land values, largely as a consequence of the profitability of renting large plots of land to industries and building shopping centers and gated communities for the upper and middle classes in locations close to the international crossing bridges. The change in economic dynamics generated by the introduction of industrial activity has had a profound impact on urban land occupation strategies and, consequently, on land value. Industry preference for locations close to the border—with good accessibility to the three public international bridges to transport products from both sides—causes an increase in the value of the most centrally located urban lands.

Market demand for these activities and uses has expelled social housing to neighborhoods in the urban periphery, where land is cheaper, although there is no good coverage of health and educational access for the adequate development of families and the autonomy of working mothers. Despite these issues, housing developers concentrate the supply of social housing in these remote urban areas, with the approval of municipal and state authorities. These are open high-density neighborhoods with very

FIGURE 2.8 Defensive devices in gated communities in Ciudad Juárez.
Photos taken by Marisol Rodríguez Sosa, 2021.

small one- or two-bedroom homes, where public safety depends on every individual.

Unsafe social housing is also a consequence of living on the border, and although locating it on the periphery is a problem in many Mexican cities, it is even more severe in border cities. Industrial activity demands a large number of workers, but since they receive low incomes, the demand for social housing increases in parallel, especially with many migrating from other states of Mexico. Having personnel transportation from home to the *maquilas* has been the excuse to justify municipal authorization for construction companies to build social housing in remote locations, where urban land is cheaper. But the decision makers (municipal government, construction companies, industries) forget the families, mothers and children who stay at home when the father or mother goes to work. They forget that public transportation does not reach many of these neighborhoods, or is too expensive, which leaves families in a situation of helplessness. This is undoubtedly an example of the negative effects of rational urban planning when the point of view of women and families is not integrated into the city. Thus, self-confinement and spatial segregation at the community and urban levels combine to generate a hostile city.

The destruction of public life as a side effect of the militarization of urban space has already been pointed out by Mike Davis (1992) in the book *City of Quartz: Excavating the Future in Los Angeles*, which uses the term "Fortress L.A." to describe the configuration of Los Angeles's Westside in the 1990s and the new forms of repression associated with the proliferation of "ominous little signs warning: 'Armed Response!'" (223). Whether as a result of a security crisis or as a defense of luxury lifestyles, the militarization of public spaces results from the effort to make cities safer, but it causes the abandonment of the public realm, urban ostracism, and the segregation of the other, especially of the poorest, who cannot access that urban security.

Madre(hood) Support Networks, Childcare, and Community Resilience

Again going back to my first year living in Ciudad Juárez and being an immigrant mother, whose son was also an immigrant, one of my most urgent needs as a working mother was to find a nursery for my baby, considering that my family life had to be organized to attend to my professional responsibilities. I then realized that having access to childcare is not so easy for migrant mothers or those who work in informal jobs, since they do not have access to the Mexican public system. Working mothers with formal jobs and work visas (if migrants) can enroll their children in childcare provided by the Mexican Institute of Social Security (Instituto Mexicano del Seguro Social, or IMSS), which is available to insured workers for children under four years of age. Working mothers who do not have access to an IMSS nursery usually enroll their children in private nurseries, which often consists of converting a private family home into a nursery, where the owner and some women in her family offer these services, so that other working mothers can have access to childcare.

These formulas, born from women, are forms of madre(hood) that exist within support networks among women. Of course, these activities require safety standards that are not discussed in this text, but the practice has been essential for working mothers south of the border so that they can work to provide for their children and make sure that they at least are not alone and receive the care they need. These mothers' support networks are an example of collectively shared mothering practices and a manifestation of the social resilience of the community, even in situations of extreme violence.

The support network between mothers, neighbors, and friends to protect families is a way of rebuilding community and hope for border inhabitants who long to return to the times when they lived in peace. This cannot be overemphasized, as it is characteristic of border life and families in recent decades. Community support networks were born out of the desolation of inhabitants in the face of violence with impunity and the inability of law enforcement to control that violence. In the most violent years, due to the increase in crimes such as kidnapping, extortion, and robbery, many private businesses, even childcare, closed their doors but continued working covertly, limiting their services to networks of acquaintances. From then on, urban social life in Ciudad Juárez disappeared from the public domain and took refuge in the networks of family, friends, colleagues, and neighbors.

Consulting our support networks for referrals became an obligatory practice and a protection mechanism that we maintain to this day, which is also mothers' responses to protect their children. Border women and mothers consult their support networks for references related to the well-being of the family and those they care for, such as where to live, schools for children, restaurants, medical services, trusted technicians for repair and maintenance of the house, and other areas, including safety and protection. This practice has strengthened the bonds of friendship and community.

An important and valued support group is a mother's school network. Establishing these networks is a practice that we do collectively as mothers through participation in school celebrations, parents' meetings, birthday parties at school and at home, Mother's Day parties, and WhatsApp groups. These social networks and interactions strengthen the bonds of trust and friendship between mothers and children. We support each other to improve the school environment, to notify each other if there is an accident or event that we must avoid on the streets on the way to school or in its vicinity, and to carpool or even take care of another child if a working mother has had an emergency at her job.

In Juárez, the neighborhood network is also highly valued, something that is built through respect and tolerance, despite the differences that may exist. Living in a closed community does not guarantee complete security, but despite the exterior roughness of the defensive physical characteristics of gated communities, the very separation from the urban public space forces residents to agree to take care of the community. As in any neighborhood, it is possible to find very sociable neighbors and others who are not interested in participating in any activity. Nonetheless, the presence of community spaces such as playgrounds, gardens, and sports fields promotes closeness among children, youths, mothers, fathers, and families. Thus, the desire to have a safe community for our children and families is what unites us all to improve our community.

Ties of trust between neighbors, although not always easy, are built above all through the union between mothers, who are more active and present in community meetings and WhatsApp groups, in promoting the care of children's areas and organizing community activities to improve green spaces, birthday parties, and fundraising events. An interesting example of a neighborhood network that has transcended the limits of the gated communities is the Asociación Civil Red de Vecinos de Juárez (Juárez Neighbors Network Civil Association). Initiated from the voluntary union of neighborhood groups from several gated communities east of the city, it has now become an ever-present voice in town hall meetings to influence decision making on urban improvement (Plan Estratégico de Juárez, Asociación Civil, n.d.). In this group, women's voices and opinions are strongly expressed, demanding improvement to roads and infrastructure, the creation of schools and spaces for recreation, and strengthened community participation channels. The purpose of this association is to encourage activism and citizen participation to evaluate the performance of municipal administration and to demand improvements in areas such as lighting, garbage collection, cleaning and caring for parks, urban forestry, road paving, access to water supply, participatory budgets for public works, among other topics.

Conclusion

Madre(hood) in the U.S.-Mexico border means adapting daily to how the geopolitics of the border affects community life. Living south of the border implies living in a doubly militarized environment: first, at the territorial level due to the geopolitics of the international border; and second, at the community level due to the fear and violence that arises from legal and illegal economic forces seeking to cross and deconstruct the border.

Living at the border has a direct influence on the configuration of urban space and on the dynamics of urban social life. Public space has a double connotation as a delimited physical environment and as a sociocultural realm where public life takes place. Thus, it is important to remember that any change in the physical urban dimension has implications on social life and vice versa. The dynamics of fear related to the border multiply within the city, leading to new strategies and tactics of separation from the other, such as self-confinement, which ends up leading to an international and community sociospatial segregation on both sides of the border and inside the city.

Madre(hood) in a circumstance of extreme violence, separation, and segregation leads women and mothers to adopt practices and tactics of self-confinement, in the use of both urban public space and the livable space of the neighborhood. Faced with fear, our self-preservation reproduces more confinement, and this in turn exacerbates the abandonment of public space, which remains at the mercy of the operators of violence, creating the ideal scenario to further promote urban ostracism and sociospatial segregation.

Women and mothers in this border city, to avoid disappearing from this world, have almost disappeared from the city, from the sidewalks, public squares, parks, the city center, and public transportation. But removing themselves from these public spaces and using cars as a safety device are not solutions or options for all women; thus, we need to continue developing practices and tactics that enable us to appropriate public space in other ways.

Community support networks are a form of appropriation through which women raise their voice and engage in public life. These collective tactics built through women's sociability are defense and survival mechanisms born in the face of fear. Somehow, even in the most severe public insecurity, women have found a way to defend their individuality and freedom, to continue being women and mothers, and to strengthen our madre(hood) to protect and care for our children, demonstrating that the role of women and mothers is essential for the transformation of the communities we inhabit.

REFERENCES

Bejarano, Cynthia. 2015. "(Re)Living Femicide through Social Control: The Regulation of Life and Bodies through Fear and (In)Formal Social Control." *FIAR* 8 (2): 67–91.

Comisión Nacional de los Salarios Mínimos. 2021. "Incremento a los Salarios Mínimos para 2022." Comisión Nacional de los Salarios Mínimos blog, December 1, 2021. https://www.gob.mx/conasami/articulos/incremento-a-los -salarios-minimos-para-2022?idiom=es.

CONEVAL. 2021. "Medición de la pobreza 2021." CONEVAL. Last modified December 2021. https://www.coneval.org.mx/Medicion/MP/Paginas/Lineas -de-bienestar-y-canasta-basica.aspx.

Davis, Mike. 1992. *City of Quartz: Excavating the Future in Los Angeles.* New York: Vintage.

Fuentes Flores, César. 2009. "Ciudad, espacio público y género, Ciudad Juárez, Chih. [encuesta]." El COLEF, CONACYT, Gobierno del Estado de Chihuahua.

Fuentes Flores, César. 2011. "Introducción." In *Espacio público y género en Ciudad Juárez, Chihuahua: accesibilidad, sociabilidad, participación y seguridad,* edited by César Fuentes Flores, Luis Ernesto Cervera Gómez, Julia Estela Monárrez Fragoso, and Sergio Peña Medina, 15–24. Juárez: El Colegio de la Frontera Norte; Universidad Autónoma de Ciudad Juárez.

Fuentes Flores, César, Luis Ernesto Cervera Gómez, Julia Estela Monárrez Fragoso, and Sergio Peña Medina, eds. 2011. *Espacio público y género en Ciudad Juárez, Chihuahua: accesibilidad, sociabilidad, participación y seguridad.* Juárez: El Colegio de la Frontera Norte; Universidad Autónoma de Ciudad Juárez.

Galindo Cáceres, Luis Jesús. 2009. "Ingeniería social, comunicología e historia oral: Contextos posibles para el desarrollo de un oficio emergente." *Estudios sobre las Culturas Contemporáneas* 2 (30): 105–22.

García, Victoria. 2016. "*Testimonio* y ficción en la Argentina de la postdictadura: Los relatos del sobreviviente-testigo." *Revista chilena de literatura,* no. 93, 73–100.

ICA (International CPTED Association). 2022. "Primer in CPTED—What Is CPTED?" ICA. Last modified January 3, 2022. https://www.cpted.net/Primer -in-CPTED.

Monárrez Fragoso, Julia Estela. 2011. "Uso y recuperación del espacio público y los lugares de esparcimiento para las mujeres y los hombres en Ciudad Juárez, Chihuahua." In *Espacio público y género en Ciudad Juárez, Chihuahua: accesibilidad, sociabilidad, participación y seguridad,* edited by César Fuentes Flores, Luis Ernesto Cervera Gómez, Julia Estela Monárrez Fragoso, and Sergio Peña Medina, 135–72. Juárez: El Colegio de la Frontera Norte; Universidad Autónoma de Ciudad Juárez.

Plan Estratégico de Juárez, Asociación Civil. n.d. "Red de Vecinos de Juárez." Nuestros Proyectos, Plan Estratégico de Juárez, Asociación Civil. Accessed December 31, 2022. https://planjuarez.org/red-de-vecinos-de-juarez/?doing _wp_cron=1672522989.5942380428314208984375.

Real Academia Española. n.d. *Diccionario de la lengua Española,* s.v., "fronterizo, za." Accessed November 4, 2023. https://dle.rae.es/fronterizo?m=form.

Rodríguez Sosa, Marisol. 2011. "Espacio público, centralidades y experiencias de género: Desafíos actuales para 'hacer ciudad' en Ciudad Juárez, Chihuahua." In *Espacio público y género en Ciudad Juárez, Chihuahua: accesibilidad, sociabilidad, participación y seguridad,* edited by César Fuentes Flores, Luis Ernesto Cervera Gómez, Julia Estela Monárrez Fragoso, and Sergio Peña Medina, 63–89. Juárez: El Colegio de la Frontera Norte; Universidad Autónoma de Ciudad Juárez.

Velasco-Domínguez, María de Lourdes, and Salomé Castañeda-Xochitl. 2020. "Desaparición de mujeres y niñas en México: Aportes desde los feminismos para entender procesos macrosociales." *Revista de Ciencias Sociales,* no. 67, 95–117.

TESTIMONIO

La Frontera

Experiencing Border Violence Through Different Lenses

EDITH TREVIÑO ESPINOSA

Daughter, Mother, and Educator: La Frontera and Me

My name is Edith Treviño Espinosa, and I live in Weslaco, Texas. I am an educator, a daughter, and the mother of five. I am originally from the border of Del Rio, Texas, and Ciudad Acuña, Coahuila. I have lived in La Frontera all my life. I was raised on the border of Del Rio and Ciudad Acuña. Life later took me to the El Paso, Texas, border with Ciudad Juárez, Chihuahua, and then to the Brownsville border with Matamoros. The only time I have lived away from the border was during my days in the U.S. Army Reserves, which took me to Ft. Leonard Wood, Missouri, and Ft. Lee, Virginia. I have also lived in Edinboro, Pennsylvania, during my college years, but life always brought me back to La Frontera.

La Frontera is a place where the role of a mother takes on new meanings. My role as a mother has been one of courage, fearlessness, strength, and forgiveness. As [Gloria] Anzaldúa says, "Borders are set up to define the places that are safe and unsafe. . . . A border is a dividing line. . . . It is in a constant state of transition" (1991, 3). La Frontera can be viewed as a crossroads to many different perspectives, which include pain and suffering but also resilience. La Frontera is such a unique place and has a life of its own. How people feel about La Frontera really has to do with how they experience it. My Frontera is my home, and in this complicated place, with a combination of suffering, tragedy, loss, grace, resilience, and compassion—all of which I embrace—La Frontera is who I am.

La Frontera and Violence

It is important to understand the geographical location of La Frontera with Mexico. Mexico is situated in what some may interpret as an ideal location in comparison to other Latin American countries. It is right in the middle of North and South America. Due to this location, La Frontera turns into "the largest corridor in the world" (Infante et al. 2012, 449) for the movement of people and many things. The Texas-Mexico frontera is made up of 1,254 miles (Aguirre and Simmers 2009).

It is in this space that I experienced border violence, but I understand that we are caught in a real crossfire of escalating violence. While this is a controversial point, the violence I experienced in La Frontera is occurring mainly due to the spillover of border wars. This same Frontera that we call home has also been a burial ground for people who attempt to cross into the United States without documents (Aguirre and Simmers 2009). Many of these border crossers die from dehydration, drowning, thirst, lack of food, violence, or snake bites. Unaccompanied minors arrive at my Frontera in search for a life free from violence.

Since 2009 my family and I have lived on the border in Weslaco, Texas. We moved from one border to another leaving Del Rio, Texas, for the Rio Grande Valley after my father's murder on U.S. soil. I experience La Frontera through different lenses, all based on my lived experiences. At times, La Frontera is a dangerous place, because that is my truth. I am very aware that this might send the wrong message, as I am constantly "reminded" that I need to stop portraying La Frontera as a horrible place. That is never my intent. I love La Frontera. I have lived here my entire life, from Brownsville to El Paso to Del Rio. There is a lot of good that comes from La Frontera. However, what happened to my father, children, and me is not something that I can sugarcoat or ignore. Ignoring the lived experience of our people is a form of oppression, which demonstrates that what happens here does not matter.

My Father's Murder at La Frontera

For several years after our relocation, I would not share my lived experience of border violence with anyone. While [I lived] in the Rio Grande Valley, people would constantly ask me why we had moved here. During that time, I was failing to share my family's reality with border violence in La Frontera. I was not ready to face the backlash of sharing our tragedy with others. This is not a topic of conversation that goes well at the water cooler. Now, I no longer respond this way, but it is interesting to consider how many of us who have experienced border violence hide our tragedy.

In an effort to share my story, in 2018, I wrote my dissertation about my family's experience with border violence. The following is an excerpt from my dissertation:

> What brings you to The Valley? This is a question I hear much too often when making basic conversations with people I meet. The question immediately takes me back to September 19, 2007. As I am transcended back to this day, I quickly and simultaneously brainstorm the different responses I could give, depending on who is asking the question. I resort back to "we love the beach," or "there are more job opportunities here." Regardless of the evasive reason I offer my innocent inquisitioners, I feel my transparency is visible. I am embarrassed to confess the truth of why we moved here. I fear being misjudged as somehow contributing to Mexico's growing violence problem which has crossed our borders. I feel my response is not the type of information I can share with a total stranger or is appropriate to discuss in social conversations. But it is a question I am always asked. I often overhear people discuss the violence in Mexico, and how it has infiltrated into the United States. During these conversations, I wish I had the courage to interject and exclaim, "My family experienced that same border violence you mention, and it changed our lives forever." (Treviño 2018, 2)

Through my doctoral studies, I learned about the power of *testimonio*, and as a mother and teacher, I realized that my pain was my power. I no longer hid my story as many others do. My paradigm changed, and now when people ask me about why we moved here, I share the truth in detail. *Testimonio* allows me to gain power from my pain and allows me to help others find their own. My doctoral research stems from my family's own lived experience with border violence and trauma. When I share with people my experience, the question is always, "Did this happen in Mexico?" As if Mexico is the only place where murders happen. My response is always, "It happened here in La Frontera, on the U.S. side." People's eyes always get larger, as they are shocked beyond belief.

My father was murdered in Del Rio, Texas, at approximately 3:30 p.m. on a Wednesday afternoon. According to the sheriff, who I met with a day later, he was shot twice in the head—in his temple. From the police reports, there was a struggle as he fought for his life. It was apparent in the beating he took and the markings on his body and hands. Writing or talking about this is incredibly difficult, as it has taken me years of therapy to not think about this on a daily basis. For a long time, I would think of his last minutes on earth at every moment. My therapist taught me to tell myself, "It is what it is." And she also taught me to wear a tight *liga* rubber band on my wrist, and whenever I had a negative thought about the day my dad died, to pull the rubber band and let it go. That would cause pain to my wrist but would also remind me that I needed to shift my thinking. As I was going through this, all I could think about was my own children, who had seen way more than I ever saw.

As a reader, I am sure you are wondering what exactly happened, and I will share that with my heart on my sleeve. It is always difficult to write or even speak about it. Below are some painful details from my dissertation:

On September 19, 2007, my father became a border violence statistic of La Frontera. He was shot twice in the head, in his temple to be exact. He was shot as he fought for his life after he exited his truck outside of his South Texas home. His body showed signs of a scuffle, according to the Sheriff. The lens of a grieving daughter has been a painful one. . . . My father's murder can be described as spillover violence. Yes, just like the literature discusses, border violence and spillover violence are real. I lived through it. My family experienced border violence. After this tragic and life changing event, I became a displaced daughter. Not only had I lost the pillar to my family, [but] I also had to disenfranchise my family from everything they knew and moved them some 600 miles south. My children's therapist suggested that being "out of mind and out of sight" would make for a better life for them. I left everything I knew behind, my childhood home, my job, my friends, and my life as I knew it. But even more painful than being uprooted from my own home was watching my own children deal with their own displacement. Reading the literature of displacement always pokes at my wounds, which only helps me determine that I am not healed. (Treviño 2018, 4)

What I have failed to mention in this narrative is that my children walked into this murder scene by accident. They arrived from school in my mom's vehicle. My mother parked her car in the driveway, and they jumped out to see their grandfather. They believed their grandfather was checking the oil under his truck. Instead, what they found was a pool of blood and his lifeless body. I wrote about their discovery in my dissertation, which was painful to write:

The pain of witnessing my children grieve in hopelessness has been crippling. As my older son shared with me the other day, "I learned to block things out." My children walked into the crime scene on accident, thinking their beloved grandfather was checking his truck tires. My mother had put "two and two together" and warned them to stay inside the vehicle. Not listening to Guelita, they jumped out of the SUV excited to see their grandfather. To their shocking surprise, their happy visit became their worst nightmare in seconds. My children found their beloved grandfather in a pool of blood. Imagine the scene. Imagine the crying, imagine the running, the screaming, and the panic. My father's dog tore the blinds from inside the house in trying to get out. I still remember the frantic phone call from my oldest son, and the screams in the background. Although I feel much sadness as I write this, I know nothing compares to what my children experienced that day. And on that day, my children lost part of their innocence, and learned that this world is not always kind. And I became a mother of three children [at the time] who had experienced border violence. (Treviño 2018, 4)

The mother in me wanted so desperately to turn back time and erase the experience my children had lived. I wanted to erase what they saw. During that time, I spoke to different psychologists only to be told, "Children are resilient; they always bounce back." Even though I was not a therapist, I knew it would only be a matter of time before this lived experience would come back to haunt my children. To shield them from these painful memories, we decided to uproot our family to another city. We went from the central Texas part of the Frontera to the southern tip of it, and even though we moved, we were never able to escape our experiences with spillover violence.

Mothering at La Frontera After Trauma

The shock and fear that went through my children's little bodies sent them all running. It was difficult for my mom to gather them all back into the car. On that day, my children experienced La Frontera as an unwelcoming beast that does not give you a choice at life. This day changed the way they viewed the world, while at the same time taking their most precious gift: their grandfather. When I feel that life here is too painful, I look at my children and their own resilience. The backlash of this life experience set me on a trail of seeking support for my children, especially one of them. This experience would haunt him for years to follow and therefore impact his learning in school.

I love La Frontera, even though it has taught me many life lessons that I never signed up to learn. Some of those life lessons have left scars in my heart and soul. When I share my family's lived experience with border violence in La Frontera, the responses are always the same Participants share, "You are so strong." Meanwhile, inside I am thinking to myself that we had no other choice but to be strong. No one asked if I wanted to be strong or weak. It just happened. La Frontera does not always give us a choice. It finds us, and then we must accept our fate. This is why the people of La Frontera are so resilient. Many have overcome tremendous obstacles, especially children. La Frontera, together with its historical trauma, adds insult to injury to the lived experience of our children.

During the time of my doctoral research, I sought support from a medical therapist. As mothers, we also find ourselves in deep pain as we try to navigate this terrain of mothering on our own. My therapist asked me why I was so detailed and blunt when I shared my lived experiences. She would say to me, "Why don't you say that your father died in a tragic way. Why do you do this to yourself? Reliving every detail? Being so blunt?" I would explain to her that there was a reason for my madness.

This is my truth, this is my reality, as [it] is the reality of my children and many other students and teachers in La Frontera. I am graphic; not as much as I could be. But this is my truth.

In La Frontera you will find mothers who continuously advocate for the well-being and safety of all children. The word *mother* takes on many different roles, as we all become fierce advocates, defenders, and protectors against violence. As mothers, we are also aware of the historical trauma of our region and the constant stereotypes that come from speaking Spanish, and the basic right of being Mexican. Whether we gave birth to our children or met them in our classroom, we are all mothers. We all share an understanding of the struggles that come with living on the border, *la vida en* La Frontera.

La Frontera and Teaching

Mothering in La Frontera takes on different roles. Living and teaching in La Frontera has allowed me to experience motherhood through different lenses and through different roles. As a mother of five children who have been raised in La Frontera, I have learned to relentlessly fight for them. It is almost impossible to understand La Frontera unless you have lived here. Allow me to reframe what I just wrote: Even people who live in La Frontera might not understand the phenomenon that is taking place unless they experience it. There are some who live here but are not fully aware of what goes on, either because they are shut down mentally to the needs of students in this area, or they are too privileged to figure it out. If you have taught here, then you can identify with what I am sharing.

How do teachers know what happens in La Frontera? If a teacher has a connection with his or her students, the students will share their *testimonios*. Unless you have experienced it, you cannot get a full grasp of life here. In La Frontera, our children are not only invisible, but they also stand out. As Anzaldúa states, "we are *atravesados*" (1991, 3). The pain, suffering, and lived experiences of our children is downplayed and ignored by many, which is why bringing light to this topic is crucial. As an educator, I have learned to become an advocate for children who don't have a voice and have no one to speak on their behalf. Living on the U.S. border is not like living anywhere else in the United States. Here, we navigate through so many experiences that are unknown to others who are not from this area.

As a mother and as a teacher, I found many correlations that exist in this region. When I was a young teacher in La Frontera, I began to witness the discrepancies of how children of color were treated, especially those coming from low-income families. As a young teacher, I would advocate for them, only to be told that, "You can't save these kids." I soon found out firsthand that my students and children were seen with a lens of negativity and a lack of compassion.

My son began exhibiting a great deal of trauma during his early elementary years. He would wake up thinking of what he saw the day my father was murdered. He began sharing his feelings at school, only to be reprimanded. That is where the journey started for me: recognizing how a counselor and an assistant principal would ignore my child's trauma. Those were some very dark days for me as a mother, not being able to help my son. I could not believe how the educational system was not responsive or compassionate enough to care. In class, stressors would set him off, maybe a lesson having to do with something that triggered his trauma. It was during that time that I became a researcher and found help for my son on my own. I remember feeling completely alone and devastated for my child, yet at the same time thinking to myself, if no one cares about my own children, and I am an educator, what is happening with the children who do not have someone to represent them?

As a teacher, I could only do so much, which in my eyes was never enough. I know that I speak for countless teachers who shed a tear for their students as they desperately try to figure out how to help their students through an educational system that does not validate students' lived experiences. To understand our students, we need to first understand their lived experiences. For me, my lens as a mother and the loss we experienced in losing my father and my children's grandfather influenced my role as a teacher.

I am immersed in the words of Gloria Anzaldúa (1991), who described the U.S. and Mexico border as an "open wound where the Third World grates against the First World and bleeds" (3). Our children, our students, are impacted by border violence, and most of us are just watching from afar—or from up close. Watching this *herida* bleed itself out, while no one does anything to help, is painful.

Every day we see the faces of children, yet we have no idea what is going on beyond the surface. Life in La Frontera impacts a child's life in ways which are incomprehensible. Lived experiences should be validated, and student pain and suffering should be addressed with a plan and a map before we can begin to teach. La Frontera is a complicated place, one which we love to despise and cannot live without. Our children are experiencing some difficult times, some incomprehensible experiences.

Conclusion

The mother in me offers some questions that come to mind as my thoughts come to an end. Should we continue to blatantly ignore the lived experiences of our children on the Texas-Mexico border and look the other way? By doing this, we are contributing to oppressing our children and ourselves. By ignoring our students' lived experiences, we are only adding to inequality in education along the border region. How can educational systems focus on a lived and learned curriculum? Those are the questions we need to continue to ask ourselves and others. Those are the questions we need to work tirelessly to answer.

REFERENCES

Aguirre, Adalberto, Jr., and Jennifer K. Simmers. 2009. "Mexican Border Crossers: The Mexican Body in Immigration Discourse." *Social Justice* 35 (4): 99–106. http://www.jstor.org/stable/29768517.

Anzaldúa, Gloria E. 1991. *Borderlands / La Frontera: The New Mestiza*. San Francisco: Aunt Lute.

Infante, César, Alvaro J. Idrovo, Mario S. Sánchez-Domínguez, Stéphane Vinhas, and Tonatiuh González-Vázquez. 2012. "Violence Committed Against Migrants in Transit: Experiences on the Northern Mexican Border." *Journal of Immigrant and Minority Health* 14 (3): 449–59.

Treviño, Edith. 2018. "Teaching and Living in La Frontera: Teacher Perceptions of Mexican Immigrant Students' Lived Experiences with Border Violence." PhD diss., University of Texas Rio Grande Valley.

CHAPTER 3

"Yo no Tengo Derecho a Enfermarme"

*Conceptions of Madre(hood) in Women
Maquiladora Workers*

CIRILA QUINTERO RAMÍREZ

El Colegio de la Frontera Norte, Matamoros, Tamaulipas

This study of women maquiladora workers highlights both the economic impact of their labor force participation and the poor labor conditions inside the maquiladoras located at the northern Mexican border.[1] This chapter also analyzes the maternity and maternal experiences and frontera madre(hood) of women workers beyond a simple reproductive aspect by also focusing on the social and spatial perspectives of maternity and maquiladora employment. I build on the concept of frontera madre(hood) as a social construction in which individual decisions, labor characteristics, and the social context where women are living and working intersect to shape experiences widely seen at the northern Mexico border, where the international maquiladora industry is prevalent.

This chapter also shows the tools that women maquiladora workers use as heads of their family to economically survive, and how they make decisions to care for and educate their children, while resolving, for instance, the lack of public services available to them, like transportation. In this qualitative study, I present the voices and experiences of fifteen

---

1. This chapter was originally written in Spanish and translated by GMR Transcription Services, Inc.

women workers from Ciudad Juárez by centering their voices, their feelings, and the fears they experience as maquiladora mothers.

Women in Maquiladoras

A significantly important percentage of women at the U.S.-Mexico border entered the labor market during the midsixties, especially in the maquiladoras. Most early studies from the 1970s and 1980s focused on labor exploitation, low wages, and poor labor conditions in the maquiladoras where women worked (Arenal 1986; Fernández 1980). Later studies explored how the maquiladora industry transformed border spaces and how cities changed the status of women working in maquiladoras (Carrillo and Hernández 1985; Iglesias 1985; Kopinak 1997). The mid-1980s and 1990s were characterized by the modernization and flexibility of maquiladoras, and a period marking the decrease of women workers, which was called the *defeminización* of maquiladoras (de la O Martínez 2006). Midway through the next decade, in 2006, men had increased their presence as workers and accounted for 51 percent of the labor force (INEGI 2007).

These shifts in the workforce prompted new considerations and studies about women working in maquiladoras. Different scholars wrote about the importance of meaning and gender in the industry (Salzinger 2003), the complexity of the world of women workers (Quintero and Dragustinovis 2006), and the mobilizations and protests inside maquiladoras, in which the participation of women was central (Hennessy 2013; Pequeño 2015; Plankey-Videla 2012). Significant attention was also placed on women in maquiladoras who confronted enormous insecurities on city streets, despite the modernization and sophistication of maquiladoras within cities like Ciudad Juárez, where hundreds of mostly young women—several of whom worked in the maquiladoras—have been killed since the 1990s (Fregoso and Bejarano 2010; González Rodríguez 2002; Ronquillo 2004).

Recent studies have opened new perspectives for considering constructed stereotypes about women working in maquiladoras. Initially, women were depicted as young, single migrants and as docile workers with no familial responsibilities (Arenal 1986; Iglesias 1985). Current analyses, however, examine the prevalence of workers as disposable for companies, women's roles as heads of households, the importance of considering intersectionality, and other social aspects like race and complex relationships in addition to gender (Bachour 2015). Others emphasize the agency of women maquiladora workers instead of their victimization (Quintero 2020).

Since the 1980s, most women working in maquiladoras have been the principal income providers for their households. Women are also overwhelmingly the problem solvers in their colonias (neighborhoods/barrios), working to address a lack of quality housing and public services (Reygadas 1992). Most of these women have traditionally been migrants, but several are women native to the cities of the northeastern border, where they worked in Ciudad Juárez, Tijuana, and Matamoros (Quintero 2010).

This chapter gives other perspectives about what it means to be a mother working in maquiladoras, emphasizing the parallel stresses of work and production demands, and their daily concerns about caring for their children to the best of their abilities. Women maquiladora workers carry out their work to avoid being fired because of their economic dependence on this job. It is important because women maquiladora workers in Ciudad Juárez have been studied regarding the violence against them on the streets (Monárrez 2009), but there are few studies in the domestic space and even less about their feelings and concerns as mothers.

Motherhood in Maquiladoras

Motherhood is a social category, while frontera madre(hood) is a social and cultural concept rooted in time, space, and place (Bejarano and Morales, this volume). Some of the first studies on motherhood and maquiladora workers were conducted in Nogales, Sonora, by Catalina Denman (1988), considering a mother's health, including reproductive health, and the effects on their newborn babies, especially low birth weight. Denman found that women remained unaware of their rights to healthcare during pregnancy and did not understand that their babies' low birth weight would negatively affect their growth and health. In the mid-1990s, Norma Ojeda de la Peña (1995b) showed the relationship between the health of a mother and child and the available labor and health services for women workers in Tijuana, especially for users of public services through the Instituto Mexicano del Seguro Social (IMSS). Both Denman (1988) and Ojeda de la Peña (1995a) revealed the complex landscape that women confronted in border cities, with a lack of public services and social marginalization. Ojeda de la Peña (1995b) analyzed the demographic characteristics of women workers who used IMSS services and found that they were younger in reproductive age and had a secondary school education, and that 50 percent were migrants, while 39 percent were single women. Several had different problems during their pregnancies, including 20 percent who had a miscarriage, while some women died during childbirth or during their pregnancy.

Galia Carolina Ladino (1999) also made important findings and contributions to the understanding of motherhood in maquiladoras. She interviewed different women workers of varying ages in low-income households in Ciudad Juárez and found that motherhood was related not only to taking care of children at home, but also to earning wages to provide for them. In Ladino's words: "Motherhood will be understood as a socially and historically constructed concept, which is not biologically determined, but a constantly changing concept that allocates women the role of caring for and nurturing their offspring" (1999, 219). This is to say that women workers not only have continued to engage with domestic tasks and childcare, but have also become family breadwinners, as both form a part of motherhood. Therefore, they are disrupting traditional gender binaries of who "mothers" are and who is considered the breadwinner. A similar trend has been noted among Salvadoran mothers who migrated to provide a better living and future for their children, who remained in their homeland (Terrón-Caro and Monreal-Gimeno 2014).

While the primary importance for women workers is childcare (Quintero and Dragustinovis 2006), there are some differences across generations of women maquiladora laborers. In earlier years of the maquiladora industry, Fernando Cortés and Rosa María Ruvalcaba (1993) found, women working in Matamoro's maquiladoras, mainly migrants, were without social networks or familial support, so they left their children, including adolescents, alone at home. Conversely, women in Reynosa who recently migrated, from 2000 on, preferred to bring a family member with them to take care of their children. A common and traditional idea among women was perpetuated, that the care and education of their children are their responsibility alone, even though women were critical of the conservative ideas of the state and the Catholic Church about their femininity (Ladino 1999).

In Ladino's (1999) literature review, she mentions that the most important question linked with motherhood for maquiladora workers was the compatibility between being a worker in an industry with strong international requirements—where production time is continuous and difficult to stop—with also caring for their children. According to Ladino (1999), in this discussion are two groups of mothers: one that does maquiladora work compatible with child caretaking, and another that considers income the most important aspect of motherhood but sometimes struggles with carrying out mothering responsibilities. For this second group, prioritizing income is necessary to support their families as breadwinners, and family or friendship support is very important in resolving the care of children in different ways, which allows these women to fulfill their work obligations (Ladino 1999).

Other authors (Quintero and Dragustinovis 2006) have shown, however, that this compatibility is superficial, because even when women workers receive support in caring for their offspring, they experience uneasy feelings of not having time to take care of their children or for their self-care. This feeling is a result of dominant patriarchal ideologies that place the responsibility for caregiving solely on women. Therefore, to not be with your children full time implies being a bad mother. It is common in maquiladora cities to hear this sentiment expressed. It perpetuates the view that all manner of social problems—from adolescent pregnancy to drug use in young people—are the result of the carelessness of mothers working in maquiladoras, rather than questioning the state or international companies for not having strategies to collaborate in caring for the children of their women workers. Ladino (1999) mentions that women who do not work outside their home are proud to provide full-time care to their children and are critical of working mothers for not dedicating sufficient time to their children. This moral sanction is repeated by the government, churches, and the media.

Motherhood as a social category is related not only to their work, but also to their marital status, migratory origin, and age. In foundational studies on maquiladoras (Fernández 1980; Iglesias 1985), both women's youth and the absence of children are mentioned. By the eighties, however, most women were married and with children. Different scholars (Ladino 1999; Hernández 2010) have shown that in homes with spouses or partners, childcare is mostly the responsibility of women, or it is a constantly negotiated struggle with partners about how to share childcare responsibilities. As a result, single mothers who have roles as both father and mother have often left domestic violence situations or lazy partners.

In a study of women workers in maquiladoras in Ciudad Acuña, Coahuila, Mexico, Hortencia Hernández Méndez (2010) shows that the increasing participation of women's contribution to the family income is not guaranteed to increase the participation of women in decision making about childcare, the home, or the distribution of the family budget. The prevalence of traditional attitudes and behaviors toward women, despite their financial contributions, kept them disempowered when it came to their homes. Some local governments, including cities like Tijuana, are conservative in their thinking and perpetuate images of women as mothers and responsible for the home (Veloz 2017).

Frontera Madre(hood) and Maquiladoras

In established maquiladora cities such as Matamoros and Ciudad Juárez, the ideas of frontera madre(hood) presented in this collection are also revealed through the second generation of women workers. A significant portion of women workers are the daughters or even the granddaughters of the first generation of maquiladora workers. As such, the lure of maquiladoras continues attracting women, especially to border cities with a recent boom in maquiladoras, like Reynosa in northeastern Mexico, which has attracted hundreds of Veracruzanos to work in its companies since 2000 (Petros 2006). Frontera madre(hood) offers a lens to analyze how space, place, migration, work exploitation, and generational maquiladora work intersect with racism, classism, and sexism, as well as strategies that women use to provide financially and care for their children at the U.S.-Mexico border.

In Reynosa, Petros (2007) found that motherhood was very different on the border from that experienced in the women workers' towns of origin, especially for those employed in maquiladoras. Women in their hometowns dedicated themselves to childcare full time, and men were the principal breadwinners. When working at the Reynosa border, women approached motherhood by bringing parents or siblings to Reynosa to help them in childcare or involved their partners in caring for their children more; when both parents were working, mothers would pay for nursery services. Frontera madre(hood) represents these practices predominant in border cities, more so than in women's cities of origin. Moreover, men, especially those who are younger, exhibited flexible gender roles by sharing childcare responsibilities (Petros 2007). Mothers were also proud that working in maquiladoras provided them with a legacy for their children, such as providing a house that their children could inherit (Petros 2007). They were also pleased that they could give their children quality clothes, toys, and other items that were impossible to provide in their towns of origin. In other words, although maquiladora work is fraught with stress and work-related problems, mothering practices are reflected in the ideas of frontera madre(hood) in that women use strategies of migrating and assuming the head of household not only to draw a better income for their families, but also to provide a legacy for their offspring.

The first generation of workers and later generations have different perceptions of labor and frontera madre(hood). The first generation of maquiladora workers considered themselves to be good mothers and workers (Ladino 1999). Subsequent generations of women maquiladora workers considered it a privilege to work over being a mother. Some of the first generations of mothers even pressured their daughters to leave work to take care of their children, although they did recognize that leaving work was not easy given their daughters were the primary providers in their families. The newer generation of women workers experienced the social opprobrium of working and being labeled "a bad mother," despite sustaining their children and the entire family. Several of these earlier findings are reflected in my research, along with new insights that my study offers.

Data and Methods

Qualitative methodologies are the best approach to study the meanings and feelings associated with ideas reflected in the framework of frontera madre(hood). At any given time, women cope with daily economic stresses and a lack of family resources to care for their children and to attend to their work. They receive no support from the Mexican government or the companies they work for. Frontera madre(hood), as it relates to this study, is shaped by several characteristics, including age, marital status, migratory status, economic disparities, traditional gendered and patriarchal norms, and sexism, among others. These factors are shaped by the regional and historical issues where women are living and working, as well as the period when maquiladoras were established in their border region.

This study is based on in-depth interviews conducted between 2017 and 2018 with fifteen women in Ciudad Juárez. Each interview lasted approximately forty-five minutes and was transcribed.[2] In these semistructured life and labor history interviews, I focus on maquiladora mothers' domestic lives and the relationships women have with their children and partners.[3] These women worked in various maquiladoras, especially in the electronics sector, and were *obreras* who worked on production lines. The interviews I conducted were done not in their homes, but in public spaces like markets, parks, and commercial centers, since it was impossible to interview them close to the maquiladoras. Some maquiladoras prohibit workers to discuss their work experiences and environments. If workers denounce any labor problem or participate in a labor protest movement, as in Ciudad Juárez in 2015, companies fire those workers. The control is not only inside the company but throughout the entire maquiladora industry (Mayorga 2015).

These interviews are part of a larger archive consisting of forty-five interviews with women workers from Tijuana, Matamoros, and Ciudad Juárez—cities known for their maquiladora industries. These women of

---

2. These fifteen interviews have not been published.

3. These interviews are part of a larger project, "The Maquila: An Ideal Workplace for Women?," in which the main objective is to reconstruct the history of maquiladoras from the voices of women workers representing different generations from Tijuana, Ciudad Juárez, and Matamoros, who have lengthy histories working in maquiladoras. The questionnaire used was divided into sections focusing on worker characteristics, development and interactions in the labor space, the domestic sphere, and participation in labor organizations. Fifteen interviews were conducted within each city.

different ages speak about work, family, and their social environment. The main objective for this larger study is to create a historical archive about maquiladoras from the perspective of women workers. In each city, my assistant and I conducted the interviews and contacted women in different ways. In Matamoros, I reached women through trade unions. In Tijuana and Ciudad Juárez, I contacted NGOs (nongovernmental organizations) working with women workers. I also looked for women workers in the public spaces they would visit during their free time. Within each city, it was important to contact local people I had previously contacted for other studies.

Frontera Madre(hood) in Ciudad Juárez: Assuming the Industrial and Social Costs of Maquiladoras and Building New Meaning

Most research on motherhood considers the difficulty of reconciling work and childcare and the strategies mothers use for resolving these issues (Denman 1988; Ladino 1999; Petros 2007). Despite the strategies maquiladora workers use, they still feel that they do not have sufficient time to take care of their children. Although previous studies of motherhood have called attention to the effects of the social aspects of motherhood on these women, studies have not provided an in-depth analysis of how these factors are influencing motherhood; nor have they distinguished the particular aspects that are affecting motherhood and the meaning these women assign to motherhood. In this section, I address these concerns and use the concept frontera madre(hood) as it applies to maquiladora workers, who assume the costs of urban deficiencies, like the lack of public lighting, drinkable water, and paved streets in border cities like Ciudad Juárez (Reygadas 1992; Fuentes Flores et al. 2011).

Living on the Outskirts and Its Impact on Labor and Frontera Madre(hood)

The fifteen women maquiladora workers I interviewed mostly live in colonias, or unincorporated neighborhoods, in the outskirts of Ciudad Juárez. These colonias are far from services like public transportation and paved and illuminated streets. Despite these urban deficiencies, women needed to be punctual in their employment. Companies do not care if it is raining, snowing, or even flooding. Workers needed to be on the production line working on time, so they were responsible for resolving how to do so despite any obstacles.[4]

The problem with public transportation is not only the inefficiency and remoteness of the routes but its exposure of women to violence. For instance, some bus drivers were accused of murdering women workers in the 1990s (Bejarano 2002). Although the state government of Chihuahua, where Ciudad Juárez is located, captured the alleged men, who were later considered scapegoats (Fregoso and Bejarano 2010), the femicides have continued, along with the fear women experience when going to and from work, especially in the early morning or late at night. These fears when maquiladora women leave for work are also transmitted to their children: "Lo más difícil para mí fue salir y dejar a mis hijos solos en la casa, cuando yo salía a trabajar, 'ellos me preguntaban: ¿mamá, porque siempre nos das la bendición cuando te vas a trabajar?,' yo les respondía: 'Mis amores, porque solo Dios sabe si regresaré a casa'" (Ana María, *trabajadora*, April 2017).[5]

This woman's *testimonio* is related to the violence against women that characterized Ciudad Juárez during the 1990s and continues even today in the 2020s. Women in this city continue to be fearful. In Ciudad Juárez, both as a response to social pressures to protect women workers and as a labor incentive to attract workers, a significant percentage of maquiladoras in the midnineties began to offer transportation services as a benefit, although these services were erratic and at times were suspended without notice. Oftentimes, bus routes were remotely located from where workers lived, and workers needed to walk home alone. The most popular means of transport, the *ruteras* (minivans that take work-

---

4. Some companies offer transportation to their employee but have only a few bus stops, far from the colonias' entrances, so workers need to walk long distances to take a bus.

5. "The most difficult thing for me was going out and leaving my children alone at home. When I went to work, they would ask me, 'Mom, why do you always give us a blessing when you go to work?' I would respond, 'Because God only knows if I'll be coming home.'"

ers to industrial parks) would arrive to *rutera* depots, but workers needed to walk long distances early in the morning, or in the darkness when they were returning home. María, for example, said, "Cuando comencé a trabajar en la maquiladora (en los setentas) necesitaba salir de mi casa a las 5 a.m. y caminar sola casi un kilómetro a la parada de las ruteras, porque ellas no entraban a mi colonia así que necesitaba caminar para tomarla. . . . Yo la esperaba junto con otras trabajadoras, nosotras estábamos esperando todos los días, en la lluvia, con nieve, o relampagueando porque necesitábamos llegar a la empresa" (April 2017).[6] To be at the *ruteras* stop by 5 a.m. means that women begin their working day at 4 a.m. or earlier to prepare their lunch and their children's food before leaving home. Their return home took an hour of travel time, which represented lost time for women, affecting their activities as mothers and their time in the home. This lost travel time from work and their time dedicated to childcare meant fewer hours of sleep for these workers. Societies are unaware of these women's sleep deprivation and other sacrifices women make to create internationally made products. Society owes these workers a debt. The commute to work is made more complex when women must leave their children in nurseries or with family or friends, because they will need to leave home even earlier, as Silvia describes: "Yo veía a las jovencitas temprano, quizá a las 5 o 4:30 a.m., como iban con sus hijos a las guarderías o a dejarlos con su familia. Para ellas no importaba si estaba lloviendo o helando, lo más importante era dejar a sus hijos con alguien. . . . Eso es lo malo como la economía está mal, la mujer necesita trabaja para alimentar y criar a sus hijos, pero también los sacrifican a ellos cuando salen con ellos temprano de sus casas" (March 2017).[7]

---

6. "When I began to work in maquiladoras (in the seventies), I needed to leave my home at 5 a.m. and walk alone almost one kilometer to the *ruteras* station, because they did not go up to my colonia so I needed to walk to reach it. . . . I waited for the *rutera* with other women workers, where we would wait for it every day, in the rain, snow, or lightning because we needed to go to the company."

7. "I saw young girls earlier, at maybe 5 or 4:30 a.m., going with their children to the nurseries or to leave them with their families. It doesn't matter for them if it's raining or freezing, the important thing is leaving their children with somebody. . . . It's bad that the economy is bad, that women need to work to feed and nurture their children, but they also sacrifice the children because they leave them home early."

This *testimonio* shows how a lack of public services, like transportation, and the absence of an integral system for caring for children of women workers creates a daily struggle to find support for childcare and to arrive punctually to work. Some resolve these problems individually, but ideally, maquiladoras and the government should share the responsibility for maquiladora workers and their childcare needs and address the social costs and added stress they experience with, at minimum, adequate compensation. These transportation problems and other urban deficiencies and work demands unfairly burden these women workers who are mothers because they need to leave earlier from their home or arrive later to their homes, which means less time with their children.

Maquiladora Employment and Women's Well-Being

In other cities, forms of frontera madre(hood) are seen in strategies to care for children when women are working, which are different from what my research found in Ciudad Juárez. For instance, in Matamoros in the late seventies and eighties, women workers brought women from their hometowns or family members to help them care for their children: "Mis hijos . . . siempre fueron cuidados por mi madre y mi hermana. . . . Ellas los cuidaron muy bien; ellas me ayudaron mucho [mientras yo trabajaba] . . . Ellas educaron muy bien a mis hijos; yo no tengo queja de ellos" (Magdalena, maquiladora worker in Matamoros, May 2017).[8]

A common strategy Matamoros women maquiladora workers used was to choose the first shift from 7 a.m. to 3 p.m., when the children might be in school, and then women could care for their children in the evenings and at bedtime. But all the women wanted to work this day shift. Nowadays, there are different shifts that are more flexible, so women have more options to fix their schedules to care for their children. For example, Rebeca from Tijuana shared: "Hoy los turnos para trabajar son varios . . . Hay en el fin de semana, en la noche, hay muchos turnos para las madres solteras . . . Ellas pueden trabajar y cuidar a sus hijos sin problema. . . . Antes no había turnos en la noche, hoy hay más libertad para

---

8. "My children . . . were always cared for by my mother and my sister. . . . They took care of my children very well; they helped me a lot [while I worked]. . . . They educated my children very well; I have no complaints about them."

trabajar [y cuidar a los hijos]" (May 2017).[9] This *testimonio* emphasizes the advantage that a flexible maquiladora work schedule now offers.

At work, industrial requirements also placed additional responsibilities on workers, which could affect their madre(hood) activities. If the maquiladoras had a quick turnaround deadline, they "asked" laborers to work overtime. Although overtime work should be voluntary, for some companies, overtime seems to be in essence a condition for workers to keep their jobs. In turn, the domestic care activities of women workers and their needs are secondary to maquiladora production.

In the dwindling sleeping hours of women workers, the production demands of multinational companies took precedence. Maquiladoras took advantage of women workers with children because companies knew that these women required more money to cover their needs, so they were dependent on the overtime that companies offered. The women paid heavily, however, with their lack of sleep and time to rest to receive this extra income. María's *testimonio* explains how these women integrated their daily routines as workers—some assuming the roles of both mother and father, as they put it—with other family responsibilities:

> Cuando estuve trabajando en la tarde, yo salía a las 6 a.m., porque algunas veces yo tenía doble turno para ganar más. . . . Cuando llegaba a mi casa, levantaba a mis hijos y los preparaba para la escuela, yo les daba de desayunar y los llevaba a la escuela, regresaba, preparaba a la casa, dormía un poco porque a las 12:30 p.m., cuando mis hijos regresaban, yo necesitaba preparar la comida. . . . Cuando ellos terminaban de comer yo les ayudaba a hacer sus tareas y salía para trabajar. Necesitaba tomar el autobús a las 2:30 p.m. para estar en la maquiladora a las 3:30 p.m. Esta era mi rutina al menos tres veces a la semana. Yo dormía solo 4 horas al día. (April 2017)[10]

---

9. "Today the time of work is more varied. . . . There are weekend and night shifts, and there are more times available for single mothers. . . . They can work and take care of their children without problem. . . . Before there were no night shifts available, but today there is more freedom to work [and care for the children]."

10. "When I was working in the afternoon, I left work at 6 a.m., because sometimes I took double shifts to earn more. . . . When I arrived home, I woke my children up, I prepared them for school, I gave them breakfast and took them to school, returned home, slept a little because at 12:30 p.m., when my children returned, I

Frontera madre(hood) for these women depended not only on the income they earned to care for and raise their children, but also on sacrificing sleep and leisure time. For thousands of women in maquiladoras, overtime work has been a necessity for their family income. Women like Dulce recognize that working for this extra money affects their health and the quality of time with their children: "El tiempo que trabaje mucho, no estuve conviviendo con mis hijos porque yo quería solo dormir, la mayor parte del día, yo dormía y esta perdida para mis hijos, entonces yo decidí no trabajar más horas extras porque trabajas mucho tu pareces zombie, tú solo quieres dormir el sábado y domingo pero tus hijos quieren divertirse . . . así que yo decidí trabajar solo mi turno normal" (April 2017).[11]

Maquiladoras responded to different international production commitments with overtime and double or triple work shifts for women. When production demands increased, maquiladoras would resort to creating new labor shifts at night or whenever the company needed them, offering the possibility for workers to earn more money with no concern for the deterioration of their health or the lack of care for their children. Maquiladoras need to address their hyperexploitation of women workers and how this affects their mothering. This is a common phenomenon when Mexican women and mothers work for U.S. industries or even U.S. families as domestic workers, but their wages do not reflect U.S. wages, and workers have no one to report their exploitation to. This is another aspect of madre(hood) at the U.S.-Mexico border that is very common.

Despite the effects on their health and their reduction of leisure time, women did not complain about the strenuous work situations, because the extra money they made helped to feed and raise their children. They would do everything necessary to not only work overtime, but also maintain a perfect record in their weekly labor performance. Perfect

---

needed to have the lunch prepared. . . . When they finished eating I had them do their homework and left for work. I needed to take the bus at 2:30 p.m. to be in the maquiladora at 3:30 p.m. It was my routine at least three times per week. In this time, I slept only four hours per day."

11. "The time that I worked a lot, I was not living with my children because I only wanted to sleep, most of the day I slept, and I was losing out on my children, and I made the decision to no longer do any overtime because when you work a lot you seem like a zombie, you only want to sleep on Saturday and Sunday, but your children want to have leisure time . . . so I made the decision to only work my normal labor time."

work attendance would guarantee that they received their full wages without deductions, including company bonuses for workers who had perfect attendance, were punctual, exhibited excellent behavior inside the maquiladoras, and were always available for any needs the company had, as explained by Lucía: "Yo le digo a mis hijos, 'yo no tengo derecho a enfermarme porque yo debo trabajar, así ustedes pueden comer,' y también porque necesito dinero para cuidar a mi hija que está enferma de sus riñones" (March 2017).[12] Women maquiladora workers' madre(-hood) practices prioritize their children at all costs. Sometimes they are unable to work long hours, such as when they have babies. In these instances, their maternal rights are protected by Mexican labor codes, or they leave the maquiladora for a year to take care of their newborns. Women also leave work when their children are sick, even if it means losing out on bonuses or having their wages cut. The main reason for leaving work temporarily or permanently, however, comes when children question their mother's time at work and the women realize the cost their employment is having on their children. For example, Silvia explains, "Un día cuando me estaba preparando para ir a trabajar, mi hijo pequeño despertó y me dijo, 'Mamá, no vayas a trabajar.' Yo le dije, 'No, mi hijo, eso es imposible. Necesito trabajar porque si no no tenemos dinero para comprar tus juguetes,' y él me contestó, 'No me compres juguetes, pero quédate conmigo.' Me dolió el corazón" (March 2017).[13] The feelings Silvia had when she considered her son's words were powerful enough to make her question the time she dedicated to work, even more so than her own exhaustion. At the time Silvia shared her *testimonio*, she had not decided whether she would stay or not, but a few days later, the maquiladora she worked for closed, and she received her final compensation. She went on to spend more time with her children, but weeks later, she returned to work at a maquiladora, given she needed money to feed her children.

---

12. "I tell my children, 'I don't have the right to get sick because I must work so you can eat,' and because I need money to care for my daughter who is sick from her kidneys."

13. "One day when I was preparing to go to work, my little child woke up and told me, 'Mama, don't go to work.' I told him, 'No, my son, it's impossible. I need to work because if I don't, I won't have money to buy your toys,' and he told me, 'It doesn't matter, don't buy me toys, but stay with me.' My heart ached."

Children can also affect the labor mobility of women workers. Maquiladoras define the perfect worker as someone who practically lives in their work facilities and who responds to production requirements or labor requests at any time. Women's commitments to their children, however, jeopardize their commitments to the maquiladora. Lucía, a supervisor, commented:

> En una ocasión, cuando yo estaba trabajando mucho, mi hija fue junto a mi cama y yo estaba adormilada, y ella estaba comiendo una tortilla dura y me dijo, "Mamá, tengo hambre ¿a qué hora te vas a levantar?" En ese momento, sus palabras me golpearon y me dije: "¡Basta! Esto necesita cambiar." Hice cambios en mi turno, hablé con mis compañeros y reduje las horas extras. Ahora, aunque tengo mucho trabajo, yo me aseguro de que lo primero sea que mis hijos tienen comida preparada. (March 2017)[14]

For mothers employed in the maquiladora industry, frontera madre(-hood) crosses different axes that involve financially providing for their children while also considering their work for an international industry and their own performance as mothers. Women are judged by Mexican and U.S. standards and societal norms. Maquiladora workers find themselves concerned with labor, spatial concerns like transportation and remote living, and familial and social tensions as they grapple with caring for their children.

Frontera Madre(hood) as a Collective

Two important themes surface in this work about frontera madre(hood) and maquiladoras. First, madre(hood) is a collective condition. Interviews with women workers in Ciudad Juárez show that childcare is a col-

---

14. "On one occasion, when I was working a lot, my daughter was next to my bed and I was asleep, and she was eating a tortilla *dura* [stale tortilla] and she told me, 'Mama, I'm hungry, what time are you waking up?' In this moment, her words shook me, and I told myself, 'Enough! This needs to change.' I made changes in my labor time, spoke with my coworkers, and reduced the overtime. Nowadays, although I have a lot of work, I make sure that the first thing is that my children have food prepared."

lective activity undertaken by women members of maquiladora workers' families including older daughters, aunts, grandmothers, sisters, nieces, but also friends. Even single and childless women working at the maquiladoras mentioned how they contributed with money and care work, such as caring for their siblings or their nieces and nephews. The amount of care work for single and childless women is extensive enough that they are proud that the children they care for refer to them as "mother" or "adoptive mother."

This also indicates that frontera madre(hood) reaches beyond biological mothering, as other chapters demonstrate. In these cases, frontera madre(hood) is more than solely giving birth but a social construction of care work built on shared practices, behaviors, and meanings through a particular shared space and time, where women workers' personal and social contexts intersect as they collectively negotiate the travails of their complex work, social, and spatial realities. Women heavily rely on the networking systems available to them within their barrios (hoods) and the common bonds they share as maquiladora workers. Work stresses for workers traverse the international border, as they work in Mexico for international industries with added work standards and forms of supervision and protocols beyond Mexico.

Frontera madre(hood) is also represented through the support that older women give to their daughters in caring for their grandchildren. This is especially true when older maquiladora women reach retirement, which is more common since the nineties. This also speaks to the reliance on familial ties overwhelmingly seen in border communities, where multigenerational households are commonplace. Claudia, a retired worker, said, "Aquí en Juárez, hay muchas maquiladoras donde las mujeres trabajan. Las mujeres necesitan trabajar porque necesitan dinero para trabajar. Yo tengo una hija que está trabajando en una maquiladora y yo le ayudo con mi nieta. Yo también ayude a mi hijo a cuidar a mi nieto, él bebe tiene dos años, porque mi hijo y su esposa están trabajando. . . . Entonces mis hijos son trabajadores y necesitan que les ayude" (April 2017).[15]

---

15. "Here in Juárez, there are a lot of maquiladoras where the women work. Women need to work because they need money to live. I have a daughter that is working in a maquiladora, and I help her to care for my granddaughter. I also help my son by caring for my grandson, the baby is two years old, because my son and his wife are working. . . . So my children are workers and I need to support them."

Frontera madre(hood) is also expressed through the emotional support that women workers give to younger workers who have problems. Aracely, for example, describes:

> Cuando yo estaba trabajando, yo tenía mucha experiencia con jóvenes, algunos de ellos se casaron jóvenes, otros usaban drogas . . . ellos tenían problemas. . . . Yo pensaba que era importante . . . ayudarlos. . . . Les decía cuando llegue a trabajar, olviden sus problemas, disfruten su trabajo, concéntrense en él (entonces) tu trabajo será menos cansado. Entonces cuando ellos necesitan un consejo vienen a mí, algunas veces, y yo les digo, "No, eso no está bien." Somos compañeros, necesitamos ayudarnos y hacer menos difícil el trabajo, porque la tristeza o el enojo puede afectar todo. Cuando me jubilé, muchos jóvenes vinieron a decirme, "¡gracias!, eso fue muy bonito." (March 2017)[16]

The feeling of maternal protection that these women felt for younger workers, independent of their age, may have been because they reminded them of their own children. The young workers often needed this care and would establish an emotional relationship with the older women like Ana María: "En mi línea de producción, estábamos produciendo lavadoras y refrigeradores, mi compañero los ensamblaba, y yo checaba la calidad. En una línea teníamos una joven de 17 años, ella vino de Veracruz, yo le dije a mi compañero que era muy joven, que le ayudáramos, si ella necesitaba, y yo le dije a ella 'tú serás mi hija,' entonces, ella respondió: 'si, ma, tú serás mi mama adoptiva.' Ella era la única chavalita en la línea porque todos éramos grandes" (April 2017).[17] Although these types of

---

16. "When I was working, I had a lot of experiences with young workers, some of them married young, others used drugs . . . they had problems. . . . I thought that it was important . . . to help them. . . . I told them when you arrive to work, forget your problems, enjoy your work, concentrate on it, your work will be less tiring. Then when they needed advice, they came to me sometimes, and I told them, 'No, it's not good.' We are coworkers, we need to help to make the work less difficult, because their sadness or anger would affect everything. When I retired, a lot of these young people that I helped came to say, 'thanks, it was very nice.'"

17. "On my production line, we were producing washing machines and refrigerators, my coworkers assembling them, and I was the quality checker. On the line we

relationships are visible in other work settings, maquiladora work reflects the migratory, generational, and social collectives that women forge to provide for their families within these border cities, where multigenerational families live, along with families forged from common work and migratory experiences.

Some Final Remarks

Women maquiladora workers grapple with how to simultaneously be a good worker and a good mother. Their entrance into the labor market does not liberate them from either the obligations of feeding and raising children or their housework. While this can be the case in many industries, what is different about maquiladoras at the border is that women's labor force is attempting to resolve the social problems they experience, due to the lack of infrastructure in terms of transportation and childcare, while also being women proletariats for the many consumer goods enjoyed across the globe. Little to no thought is given to the work that these mothers are engaged in to make our lives more comfortable.

This chapter also highlights the work experiences of women workers, and how work benefited or affected their children. These experiences are complicated. Women workers recognized some liberation that maquiladoras could offer from the oppression of men, especially in earning their own money. Mothers interviewed also recognized that their maquiladora employment allowed them to provide food, clothes, social security, and health services for their children. Despite these advantages, however, childcare continued to be their responsibility. This complicated the feelings that women maquiladora workers had. Women commonly felt that their maquiladora employment prevented them from having better relationships with their children. This can turn into bitterness toward the maquiladora and even self-hatred when working deprives them of enjoying raising their children.

---

have a girl of 17, she came from Veracruz, I told my coworkers that she was younger and to help her when it was needed, then I told her, 'You will be my daughter,' then she answered me, 'Yes, Ma, you will be my adopted mom.' She was the only *chavalita* on the line because we were all older."

Although women have asked for nurseries from the companies they work for, they continue to assume childcare as their responsibility, especially when they are heads of the family, acting as both mother and father. Compounded with the physical stress and exposure to occupational hazards they experience is how their children feel about their work, and how they are to blame if their children choose a *bad path* and find themselves in trouble.

Particularly problematic is the lack of childcare. Women workers need transnational corporations to take some responsibility in attending to their madre(hood) needs by constructing nurseries. The Mexican and U.S. governments and other countries who have maquiladoras in Mexico must also establish public policies that allow their employees to live as mothers and laborers. While this chapter highlights the case of Ciudad Juárez, the strategies to balance work demands and childcare as productive workers living in urban cities with poor infrastructure are also reflected across other northern Mexico cities like Tijuana and Matamoros, where forms of frontera madre(hood) are also witnessed.

REFERENCES

Arenal, Sandra. 1986. *Sangre joven: Las maquiladoras por dentro*. Mexico City: Editorial Nuestro Tiempo.

Bachour, Mary-Kay. 2015. "Disrupting the Myth of Maquila Disposability: Sites of Reproduction and Resistance in Juárez." *Women Studies International Forum* 48 (January–February): 174–84.

Bejarano, Cynthia L. 2002. "Las Super Madres de Latino America: Transforming Motherhood by Challenging Violence in Mexico, Argentina, and El Salvador." *Frontiers: A Journal of Women Studies* 23 (1): 126–50.

Carrillo V., Jorge, and Alberto Hernández. 1985. *Mujeres fronterizas en la industria maquiladora*. Mexico City: CEFNOMEX.

Cortés, Fernando, and Rosa María Ruvalcaba. 1993. "Desocupados precoces: ¿Otra cara de la maquila?" *Estudios Sociológicos* 11 (35): 695–723.

de la O Martínez, María Eugenia. 2006. "Geografía del Trabajo femenino en maquiladoras." *Papeles de Población* 12 (49). https://www.scielo.org.mx/scielo.php?script=sci_arttext&pid=S1405-74252006000300005.

Denman, Catalina. 1988. "Las repercusiones de la industria maquiladora de exportación en la salud: El peso al nacer de hijos de obreras en Nogales." Master's thesis, El Colegio de Sonora.

Fernández, María Patricia. 1980. "'Chavalas de Maquiladora': A Study of the Female Labor Force in Ciudad Juarez' Offshore Production Plants." PhD diss., Rutgers University.

Fregoso, Rosa-Linda, and Cynthia Bejarano. 2010. "Introduction: A Cartography of Feminicide in the Americas." In *Terrorizing Women: Feminicide in the Americas*, edited by Rosa-Linda Fregoso and Cynthia Bejarano, 1–44. Durham, N.C.: Duke University Press.

Fuentes Flores, César, Luis Ernesto Cervera Gómez, Julia Estela Monárrez Fragoso, and Sergio Peña Medina, eds. 2011. *Espacio público y género en Ciudad Juárez, Chihuahua: Accesibilidad, sociabilidad, participación y seguridad.* Juárez: El Colegio de la Frontera Norte; Universidad Autónoma de Ciudad Juárez.

González Rodríguez, Sergio. 2002. *Huesos en el desierto*. Barcelona: Anagrama.

Hennessy, Rosemary. 2013. *Fires on the Border: The Passionate Politics of Labor Organizing on the Mexican Frontera*. Minneapolis: University of Minnesota Press.

Hernández Méndez, Hortencia. 2010. "Las relaciones de poder en el hogar y el espacio laboral: La experiencia de los hombres y mujeres de la industria maquiladora en Ciudad Acuña." Master's thesis, Universidad Autónoma de Coahuila, Saltillo.

Iglesias Prieto, Norma. 1985. *La flor más bella de la maquiladora*. Mexico City: CEFNOMEX.

INEGI (Instituto Nacional de Estadística, Geografía e Informática). 2007. *Industria Maquiladora de Exportación, Estadística Económicas*. February. Aguascalientes: INEGI.

Kopinak, Kathryn. 1997. *Desert Capitalism: What Are the Maquiladoras?* Montreal: Black Rose.

Ladino, Galia Carolina. 1999. "Maquiladora Employment, Low-Income Households and Gender Dynamics: A Case Study in Ciudad Juárez, México." PhD diss., London School of Economics and Political Science, University of London.

Mayorga, Patricia. 2015. "Obreros exhiben la explotación laboral de maquiladoras en Chihuahua." *Proceso*, December 15, 2015. https://www.proceso .com.mx/reportajes/2015/12/15/obreros-exhiben-la-explotacion-laboral-de -maquiladoras-en-chihuahua-156468.html.

Monárrez Fragoso, Julia Estela. 2009. *Trama de una injusticia: Feminicidio sexual sistémico en Ciudad Juárez*. Mexico City: El Colegio de la Frontera Norte.

Ojeda de la Peña, Norma. 1995a. "Salud materno-infantil entre la población trabajadora en Tijuana: Un estudio de caso." *Estudios Demográficos y Urbanos* 10 (3): 651–86.

Ojeda de la Peña, Norma. 1995b. "Uso de los servicios en salud reproductiva y perfil sociodemográfíco de las mujeres: El caso del IMSS en Tijuana." *Frontera Norte* 7 (13): 93–107.

Pequeño Rodríguez, Consuelo. 2015. *Mujeres en movimiento: Organización y resistencia en la industria maquiladora de Ciudad Juárez.* Juárez: Autonomous University of Ciudad Juárez.

Petros, Kristen. 2006. *Motherhood, Mobility, and the Maquiladora in Mexico: Women's Migration from Veracruz to Reynosa.* Summer Funds Research Report, Center for Latin American Social Policy, University of Texas at Austin.

Petros, Kristen. 2007. "Women on the Border, Migration, Maquiladoras, and the Making of Reynosa, Veracruz, Mexico." Master's thesis, University of Texas at Austin.

Plankey-Videla, Nancy. 2012. *We Are in This Dance Together: Gender, Power, and Globalization at a Mexican Garment Firm.* Piscataway, N.J.: Rutgers University Press.

Quintero, Cirila, and Javier Dragustinovis. 2006. *Soy más que mis manos: Los diferentes mundos de la mujer en la maquiladora.* Mexico City: Fundación Friedrich Ebert Stiftung/SJOIIM.

Quintero Ramírez, Cirila. 2010. "Estereotipos femeninos en la maquiladora de México: De prostitutas y sirvientas a jefas de familia: El caso de las primeras mujeres trabajadoras de la maquiladora." In *Islas de la locura: Normatividad y marginalización en América Latina / Islands of Madness: Normativity and Marginalization in Latin America,* edited by Minna Opas, Pirjo Kristiina Virtanen, and Sarri Vuorisalo-Tiitinen. Series Hispano America 10. Madrid: Acta Ibero-Americana Fennica.

Quintero Ramírez, Cirila. 2020. "La primera generación de las trabajadoras en maquiladoras de Ciudad Juárez: Aprendiendo a trabajar y protestar (1965–1979)." *Nuestra historia,* no. 10, 85–104.

Reygadas, Luis. 1992. *Un rostro moderno de la pobreza: Problemática social de las trabajadoras de las maquiladoras de Chihuahua.* Chihuahua: Ediciones Gobierno del Estado de Chihuahua.

Ronquillo, Víctor. 2004. *Las muertas de Juárez: Crónica de una larga pesadilla.* Madrid: Ediciones Temas de Hoy.

Salzinger, Leslie. 2003. *Genders in Production: Making Workers in Mexico's Global Factories.* Berkeley: University of California Press.

Terrón-Caro, Teresa, and María Carmen Monreal-Gimeno. 2014. "Mujeres migrantes en tránsito en la Frontera Norte de México: Motivaciones y expectativas socioeducativas ante el sueño americano." *Papeles de población* 20 (82): 138–66.

Tiano, Susan, and Carolina Ladino. 1999. "Dating, Mating, and Motherhood: Identity Construction Among Mexican Maquila Workers." *Environment and Planning A* 31 (2): 305–25.

Veloz, Areli. 2017. "El sentido común sobre el género y los sentidos del trabajo y la familia para los trabajadores de maquiladoras en Tijuana." *La ventana* 5 (45).

Interviews

Ana María, April 2017

Aracely, March 2017

Claudia, April 2017

Dulce, April 2017

Elena, April 2017

Lucía, March 2017

Magdalena, May 2017

María, April 2017

Martha, April 2017

Rebeca, May 2017

Silvia, March 2017

FIGURE C Portrait of José Antonio Rodríguez in Nogales, Sonora, near the Mexican-U.S. border wall where he was shot and killed by a border patrol agent in 2010. Photo by Cynthia Bejarano in 2021.

TESTIMONIO

"Mi Nieto Tenía Metas. . . . Nos Tenemos Que Reunir Todos"

A Grandmother's Fight for Justice Through the Border Patrol Victims Network

TAIDE ELENA

Cofounder of Border Patrol Victims Network

My name is Taide Elena.[1] I'm the grandmother of José Antonio Elena Rodríguez, a child who was assassinated on the border of Nogales, Sonora, and Nogales, Arizona, near the fence [the border wall]. This child, my grandson, was passing by a bench in front of the border when the U.S. Border Patrol agent Lonnie Swartz stuck his hand through the fence and fired thirty shots into Mexico. Ten hit José Antonio's body: eight in the back and two in the head. [Swartz] cowardly killed [José Antonio] because the child—they say that [Swartz shot José Antonio] because he was throwing rocks, but the wall is so tall in that part that there was no way that a rock would make it there, that it would pass through. If it were the case, that didn't give him the right to take his life, because he was going home. He was two blocks from making it home. And I think that [Swartz] had the need to kill, and that's why he shot so many bullets towards Mexico. The building ended up being filled with holes, and [José Antonio] was face down on the ground under the bench next to the building. So, [José Antonio] didn't have the chance at life at all because [Swartz] could have shot rubber bullets if he was doing what they said he

---

1. This chapter was originally audio recorded in Spanish and transcribed and translated by GMR Transcription Services, Inc. The footnotes were added by the editors for clarification after confirming information with Taide.

was. There were many ways not to kill [José Antonio], but [Swartz] just killed him. [Swartz] was reckless with how many bullets he shot.

José Antonio was a polite little boy. He was very serious. If someone said to him, if they said "Hi" to him, from the family or whoever, his favorite thing to say was, "Everything is good." Two days prior, I had seen him, and he took me to the border [the international port of entry area to cross into Nogales, Arizona, from Nogales, Sonora], and from there, he went back [to his home], and the next day I didn't have him anymore. When they told me about his death, I couldn't believe it. I started to yell, and I started to ask, "Where? How? Why?" And there weren't any answers for me during that time, until later when they told me it had been U.S. Border Patrol.

So it was harder for me to understand because they [Taide's grandsons] never got close to the border, because we would tell them to never get close to the border because we're going [to petition for U.S. residency], and they're going to take them away, and we don't want them to have a record.[2] So they respected that. He was studying open [public] high school because he wanted to finish high school, turn eighteen years old, and go into the military. So I would say to him, "My son, why do you want to be a soldier?"

And [José Antonio] would answer me with another question: "Grandma, why don't you like soldiers?"

I would say, "My son, because soldiers are trained to kill."

"No, Grandma," he said, "not all of them. There are good ones as well." He had friends that had entered the military, and [he would say], "I want to go to the military. Not because I want to go to fight. I want to make a career out of the military for you to be able to rest and not have to pay for my schooling." Because I was paying for the university for the oldest in the UVM—the most expensive university, but where he wanted to study and if he wanted to go there, I wanted him to go there because that's the way he would study. Children are like that. They study what they like and where they're going to study.

So that was his goal, and what he wanted was to get on a plane. So I said, "My son," I said, "Listen, next Saturday, you all are going to start to

---

2. Taide's grandsons are from Nogales, Sonora, on the Mexico side of the border wall.

go with Yolinda," since she was a part of the church.³ They hadn't had their first communion, so she would prepare children for their communion. I said, "But next Saturday, you all are going to Yolinda's house, both of you [José Antonio and Diego, his brother], and she's going to prepare you for your first communion, and you all are going to do it in Guadalajara."

"In Guadalajara?" he said.

"Yes, my son."

"And what are we going in?"

"We're going on a plane."

And his eyes opened wide because he wanted to ride on a plane. "And when are we going to go?"

"In March," I said, "because that's when you all are going to be ready for communion, and it's the month that your cousin is going to turn fifteen years old." I told him, "And that way, we can do both things."

"Oh, Grandma." Every time he would see me, he would say, "Grandma, what does the plane look like? And what does the plane look like up there? Can you see the clouds?"

"Yes, my son." He was very innocent. "Yes, my son," I told him, "You're going to be up in the clouds, and you're going to see them, and you'll see how beautiful it is."

"And am I going to be able to stand up?"

"Well, you're going to be able to stand up to go to the bathroom, so you'll know what it's like to walk on a plane."

Well, he had a bunch of questions all the time. And well, he was excited about that. They didn't get to go to religious formation because that week they—that week would have been like this one because they were on break here, and the man [Swartz] killed him.

And he went by there.⁴ The newspaper said that it was 11:00 at night, but no, it was 9:30 at night. After 11:00 was when they picked him up from there [authorities recovered José Antonio's body]. There was a witness that was walking twenty feet behind him [José Antonio], a trustworthy man. He [the witness] just speaks with a bit of an impediment—

---

3. Taide's neighbor Yolinda passed away before this *testimonio* was written.

4. Referencing José Antonio walking near the Nogales border wall the day he was killed.

his tongue gets stuck. So it was him, and he offered himself as a witness and everything. They never called him to testify—never. He was one of the main witnesses.

Well, [when José Antonio's funeral took place at Colinas del Buen Pastor] I went down [to Nogales, Sonora]. I have diabetes and many things. His mom wanted to go, and I said, "How are you going to leave? What about Diego? Where is Diego going to stay?" I said, "I'm there, and I can't leave because I can't stand in those big lines to go work." At that time, I worked full time. I said, "Well, Lourdes has to come as well because the kids are at school. One day I'm going to come and find Diego having hung himself in a room because [the brothers] were so close."

Diego worked at OXXO, and Toñito's [José Antonio] routine was to wake up, go to school, and then come back when it was later to play baseball.[5] He was the catcher, a field that now the hitmen have.[6] There aren't kids playing there anymore, but during that time, there weren't things like hitmen on the corners. So [José Antonio] would do that, and then he would come and take a shower, and he would help his brother [Diego] close the store because the other son [Diego] closed shop at 12:00. So, [José Antonio] would help [Diego] to close, and then they would come back together. And on the way back, there was a man who still sells hot dogs. They would eat a hot dog and would come up. That was his routine. But that day, Diego got out of work early, and he didn't call [José Antonio] to tell him that he had gotten out early. [Diego] went with his girlfriend. He was older—he was eighteen, two years older than Toño.[7] So [José Antonio] went, and he didn't find [Diego], and [Diego] went back through the same route they always went, because the hill where my house is has different ways to go up.[8] You can go up many ways, and I don't know why they liked going up that way.

I don't know. It's a question of life, destiny, who knows what because I don't understand. I felt that my world ended, and activists and all of that started to come, and I started connecting with the activists. Tere Leal

---

5. OXXO is a convenience store, and Toñito is a nickname for José Antonio.

6. The hitmen are known cartel assassins.

7. Another nickname for José Antonio.

8. Taide's house, which she is referencing, is in Mexico.

was one of them.[9] She died, and then they came from Tucson, and we began with the wake. We did marches. We did a Mass for her. Actually, we had an outdoor Mass with the bishop. We did all of that, and that's how I ended up getting in with them. I was the one who could most miss work and be there. Aside from that, my daughter-in-law, José Antonio's mother, didn't have a passport, so I was always the one who showed my face. After that, the consulate got her a passport, and when the trial happened, she crossed the border. The Tucson community was a beautiful thing. I am grateful to them from the bottom of my heart because they found us a place to stay during the trial. They—we would go out to eat—and they already had food for us there at the courthouse. No, it was amazing. They were good people. The same activists, they would get—each of them would take a different day. We were very grateful, and it was just the two of us [Taide and her daughter-in-law].

So [U.S. authorities in court] lied, many, many lies. I've always said the judge was paid off because the crime was so clear that they didn't need that much. [U.S. authorities] paid off witnesses. We didn't. We had the faith that we were going to win because the crime was so clear. But we didn't [win the case]; they said that the death was in Mexico. It couldn't go to civil court because we went to San Francisco [California], because the civil case was in San Francisco. So, my daughter-in-law and I went to San Francisco. The consul sent us. [The Mexican Consul from Tucson] paid for us that time. I don't know how we made it to San Francisco because neither of us knew English, [me or] my daughter-in-law. And then we had a layover in Los Angeles, from here to there, and then there to here. Well, my daughter-in-law was asking, "Madam, do you speak Spanish?" And "Madam, do you speak Spanish?"[10] But, well, we made it to San Francisco, and we won the civil case there. An activist representing us named—I don't remember what his name was, but he was an activist who is all over the United States. They have offices everywhere. They came, and they asked for our permission, and well, yes—that lawyer whose name I don't remember right now represented us. He is the only lawyer that

9. Teresa "Tere" Leal was an iconic Indigenous historian and environmental activist from Ambos Nogales.

10. Speaking to the people around them as they traveled.

I saw made the defense attorney stutter. He made him feel so little that he [defense attorney for Swartz] had to talk. You couldn't hear what he was saying. So, there are three judges that go out, and the one that talks is the one in the middle, and he said to [the defense attorney], "I can't understand you. I can't hear you. Are you talking to yourself?" And there, people laughed [at the judge's comments].

For example, if one of the two of us had spoken English, we could stand up and talk, but neither of us knew English. And the Mexican consul was translating for us. And [the family attorney] said [to Swartz], "Why did you kill him?"

And [Swartz] said, "Because he was throwing rocks."

"That didn't give you the right to kill him," [the attorney] said.

"What right did you have to kill him?" the judge said. "No one has the right to kill someone like that," he told him. And we won there, and we were very happy because after that, he said he was going to send the case to Washington because there was a similar case.

It's similar because they killed a fifteen-year-old boy [from Ciudad Juárez, killed by an El Paso border patrol agent], but with one shot. And mine had ten, and all three from behind. And I have an image in my mind of the [videos] they showed there in court where [José Antonio] is lying down, and he hasn't died yet, and he raises his left hand, because he was a lefty, and he raises it. I think like he was trying to get out of there, and then he lowers it. And the other shots sound because [Swartz] fired two shots—shot one and reloaded—and you can see in what they put there, because it was the only thing they put because they made the video disappear—the one from the border. But there was a man from the border [patrol] who saw the video and spoke to one of the lawyers and told him: "This video is so clear that you can see even the color of his eyes, and it just has the death of a child, and I am willing to testify. If they call me, I am willing to testify." That would have been the end of [Swartz], but the judge did not let them. He did not allow our defense to call those witnesses.

[There was one person] who saw the video [who] was from the [U.S.] government, but he was willing to testify because he had already left [his position with the government].[11] He wasn't [scared]. Because they took

---

11. This witness from the U.S. government resigned from his position but was never called to testify; they had three total witnesses who were never called.

many months to make the case, and during that time, he had already left, and so he spoke up. This man who killed José Antonio has a record that the judge wouldn't let the jury see either. But they didn't say anything— our defense team. They told us all of that when the last trial finished. So the court doesn't let you talk. If you stand up and want to talk, they'll take you out. At least that's how it was in Tucson. Because Richard, Ana Maria's husband, when they gave the ruling, he stood up, and he said a bunch of things in English, speaking to the judge.[12] They fined him for that, and he left. But that was my son's death; that was my son's death.[13] He didn't deserve that death.

[U.S. Border Patrol authorities during the court hearing] had done it: [they acted] as though they didn't have the video [showing when José Antonio was killed]. [Instead] they had made [a video] like a few monkeys playing Nintendo.[14] Of course, there were many [boys mentioned by U.S. authorities who threw rocks]. [U.S. authorities] would put [figures of boys reflected in the simulacra], and all of them were throwing rocks, but with their right hand. [U.S. authorities during the court hearing] didn't know that José Antonio was a leftie until I got up and testified. But I just had to answer what they asked me, and I said that he was a leftie, and that none of those children were José Antonio [in the video], that that was like playing a video game. That's what I said because I couldn't say any more. They had already told me [to only answer what was asked]. I was very, very disappointed by our defense team. The judge we got at the beginning was very . . .[15] I saw that he was in our favor, but when the criminal attorney went and spoke to the judge, not with the words that I'm going to say—they are words that [a lawyer would use], you know what I mean, right? But in any case, it's like he said to him, "If you allow for this man to be sentenced, you're going to open a Pandora's box." And the judge thought about it and turned back. We noticed. They thought

---

12. Ana Maria is an activist with the Border Patrol Victims Network.

13. Meaning her grandson José Antonio.

14. A digital simulacrum of the shooting was made showing animated figures, one portraying José Antonio wearing a hat and throwing rocks with his right hand. José Antonio never used hats, and he was left-handed, but that is how they portrayed him according to Taide.

15. Taide does not finish her thought.

we were ignorant or people who didn't know anything. Of course we did, and it was so obvious that anyone would have noticed.

During the last trial [second court trial], they didn't let us enter because they were choosing the jury. So, that woman, Susana Manzana, fought with the one who let the people in and said—she speaks Spanish very well.[16] She's American, but she speaks very good Spanish. And she said, "They have a right to be here. They have the right. Why can't they enter? You're not going to come and tell me how to do my job." She said, "I have the order to take them down there," so we could see the trial on the screen. Another one of the activists came. Her name is Mayra. She also fought with the girl [court employee] because they hadn't let us in. In the end, they didn't let us enter. We entered later, but [after] when they did everything they had to do. But we were very nervous. We were very . . . we weren't thinking clearly. We had a lot on our minds. We had seen photographs. I mean, all of that took away from us knowing how to do things, because afterward, we said that we should have said [to the bailiff], "Look, let's see who you have to [take out of the courtroom so others can be let in], but we're going in." But we didn't. We didn't think of it.

Well, that was it. It was done. I didn't even want to see the defense attorneys. I didn't even want to see them. I went to the bathroom to cry, and I didn't want to see them because thirty shots at a sixteen-year-old boy is horrible—to see those photographs. I had seen some photographs from the district attorney when he [José Antonio] was on the table [at the coroner's office]. They still hadn't done the autopsy. No, they didn't let us defend ourselves. They treated us like the criminal; [Swartz] ended up as the greatest, like the innocent one, and we ended up like criminals. That's why I say they humiliated us by saying what they said about our family. They didn't even know [us] and seeing our child laid out. . . .[17]

If you go to Nogales [Sonora], and if you go to La Cruz, you're going to see the bench in line with where the cross is.[18] But when he died,

---

16. A Tucson activist accompanying Taide and her daughter-in-law.

17. Taide was able to see José Antonio's clothes at the attorney general's office, but she states they were not the clothes first sent to Arizona; she saw his clothes on the television screen.

18. La Cruz is where José Antonio was shot and killed. A white cross now marks the location.

the bench wasn't straight. It was like a small ditch, and his body just fit there. He was walking there, inside of the *bardita*.[19] He bled all the way out right there. He came up [during the autopsy] free of drugs, alcohol, everything. He was a clean kid. So how could they say that he was going to Sinaloa for drugs? How? I mean, that lawyer died already [Swartz's defense attorney]. In those times, he was very sick. He had cancer, and he was close to dying, and he was still lying and saying things he knew weren't true.

Now, the rocks that they presented there, there on the street where the child died—that street has never had rocks. It has never been a rocky road [it is a paved road]. Next to the United States [on the U.S. side of the border wall], yes, it was a road filled with rocks, but not anymore. They cleaned it up. It was very easy for anyone to go and make a circle.[20] I wanted to tell them, Look, well, the only thing they didn't do was take a kilo because you're going to see how high that is there [looking up at the border wall and how it would have been impossible for José Antonio to hurl a heavy stone over it], and if you go to where José Antonio's thing [memorial plaque] is, all of his story is there. All of his story is there. The other day, one of the women where I work was saying that she had seen it and that [the border wall where he was shot] is so high that it was impossible for a rock to reach there.

In the end, we lost the trial, and my *mijo* ended up without justice. So now we want to try to make it to the Pope and ask for his help—not just me, many victims—to make it to [the U.S.] Congress to ask for a change in the law because the death [of José Antonio] happened in Mexico. Yes, and where else would they want it to happen if they were killing him in their own country? Where did the shots come from? From the United States. Where is the criminal? In the United States, so here is where the trial should be. We went to Washington. We went to Mexico, to D.F. [Mexico City]. The pandemic began, and we couldn't go back to Mexico, D.F., and we had to stop everything.[21]

---

19. A narrow cement walkway.

20. Taide clarified that rocks were circled with some paint or ink on the U.S. side of the wall, part of the U.S. claim that those were the rocks José Antonio threw across the wall at the border patrol agent.

21. They had to stop their advocacy.

And we have fought a lot, and we're going to continue fighting to see how far we can go. We're also going to come back to Mexico, D.F., but Mexico always is in the red a lot, and we're afraid because of the pandemic.[22] We have a lawyer from Mexico who is a very nice lawyer. We have known him for a very long time, and when I spoke to the lawyer from here, we were supposed to meet in Fray Marcos [a hotel in Nogales, Sonora]. They came from the consul—two lawyers from here arrived. He arrived. He saw my daughter-in-law and me standing outside Fray Marcos waiting for the lawyers, and he said, "What are you doing here at this time of day?" He said it was very early. He said, "And looking so sad." I spoke to him, and that's when the lawyers came, and he came with us, and he offered to help, and he said, "I can help you all with everything on the Mexican side, without charging you anything at all." He said, "Without charging anything, I offer my services." And yes, we went with him to Mexico. We went all over [to Mexican government offices], but as I said, the pandemic began, and that was it.[23]

[José Antonio's case] made it to the Supreme Court, to Washington, D.C., but the one with Hernández Güereca [from Ciudad Juárez] was there as well. They killed that little boy as well in Mexico, also through the fence. He was fifteen years old, and it had already gone to the Supreme Court, but they rejected it, and they sent it back. So his parents fought again, and they sent it back to Washington, D.C. So José Antonio's was last when the other [case] had made it first. The other one [the Hernández Güereca case] was very simple. There weren't as many activists around it. There weren't as many people around [at the U.S. Supreme Court building]. José Antonio had people outside the court. There was a band playing his name, "José lives, José lives, long live José." And they went with us to Washington, D.C. They are university students. Well, there were a lot—the other lawyer asked the judge for the last court to be in Phoenix, and the judge asked why. He said because José Antonio had a big name in Tucson, and the bishop of Tucson would say his name and speak about the case at every Mass, so they wanted to go to Phoenix, where he wasn't as well known, and the Supreme Court did the same thing [rejected the case]. They didn't even see José Antonio's case

---

22. Mexico lacks funds to advocate for victims.

23. At the time, José Antonio's family had a binational legal team helping them.

because they already knew it, and Güereca's was easier. So, if Güereca's case failed, ours failed to go to San Francisco [again], and that's how it was. In Güereca's, four judges came to an agreement, and the others did not, so the case was finished.

I think when he [José Antonio] was there [lying in the coffin] during the wake, it was an incredible thing. And I'll tell you with all honesty, I'm not crazy. I got there, and I saw him. I touched him, and it was like I was touching cardboard. He was frozen, and then they had given him a beard because his mouth was all messed up. When he fell, he broke his mouth open. So, I went down and kissed him on the forehead, and I grabbed his hands, and I played with his hands, and maybe you'll think that during that time I was out of my mind, but his hands, this part here, his fingertips were soft and warm. So, I didn't say anything, and I kept that in my head, and I cried because of that. What did he want to tell me? I went to a priest, and I said—I told him about it—and I said, "Father, I don't think I'm crazy. I felt it." I said, "And how could it be possible if he was icy cold?" And he said, "Look, we can't understand God's design. I can't explain it." And I had to see three different psychologists to be able to continue on because of his death. His life was a good life, and he had many good thoughts, and he would be twenty-five years old now, and he would be in the military.

PART II

Confronting Caging, Migration,
and Deportation

TESTIMONIO

Women, Family, Border Enforcement, and Humanitarian Work on the Banks of the Rio Grande in Matamoros

BERTHA A. BERMÚDEZ TAPIA
New Mexico State University

was born in Matamoros. I went to an elementary school a few blocks away from El Bordo, a small community, where my grandma was a teacher. After school, my grandpa and I always went to the levee to wait until my grandma was done with her classes. I grew up flying handmade kites made of sticks my grandpa and I collected from the levee. My grandpa and I always prepared thread, scissors, paper, and glue. We were always ready to run along the levee, feeling the rise of the kites in our hands, feeling the sensation of lightness and freedom that gives you the idea of flying. That is how my infant self remembers Matamoros, how I remember El Bordo. As a place where the family came together, one of the happiest places in the world.

However, this memory of my childhood has changed dramatically in the last thirty years in terms of border enforcement, violence, and security. And the levee has changed as well, due to a long history of restrictive immigration policies and border enforcement, but both were heightened after 2019, when asylum seekers were forcibly required to wait in Mexico until their asylum petitions were processed due to a policy named the Migrant Protection Protocols (MPP). The great majority of these asylum seekers lived in tents, in a migrant camp located on the levee where I used to play as a child, on the Rio Grande banks. Under MPP, the waiting time in Mexico was supposed to be limited to the duration of the asylum process. Yet, in 2020, COVID-19 radically changed the asylum procedures and the humanitarian crisis across the U.S.-Mexico border. Due to the pandemic, all asylum hearings were suspended indefinitely, and migrants started being expelled under a new policy called Title 42, which prevents people from applying for asylum altogether because they are perceived to pose a health risk during the pandemic. In the end, Title 42 turned waiting times and temporary camps into a more permanent form.

From 2018, through its dismantling in 2021, I conducted fieldwork in the Matamoros camp. I observed camp life from the arrival of the first disoriented families through to its closure. While conducting this research, I learned invaluable lessons on violence, vulnerability, and human strength. People living and working in the camps were constantly fluctuating. The situation and needs inside the camp were constantly changing at a speed that was some days hard to follow. Additionally, even though I was born in Matamoros, it was hard for me to feel like an insider.

Indeed, I felt like a newcomer inside the Matamoros camp for a long time. Most of those providing aid inside the camp belonged to white American NGOs, and only a few were Spanish speakers. I was one of the few bilingual Mexican people working inside the camp. Being Mexican placed me in an ambivalent position between an outsider and an insider.

Nevertheless, even when there was no language barrier between the asylum seekers and myself, I needed to examine other parts of my identity and bring it to balance to have a more egalitarian relationship. For example, the simple fact that after a journey of work, I could come back home safely. And more importantly, the place I called home when I was doing my research was on the U.S. side. Hence, a fundamental part of my ethnographic approach was a continuous recognition of the substantial power differentials and the multiplicity of privileges I embody (in terms of race, class, and legal status). I was both an insider and an outsider. That feeling was always inside me because I was born in Matamoros, and I thought I was doing fieldwork in a place that I knew. However, I rapidly realized I knew the physical area where the camp was established and the city's social context where the camp was formed, but I had no previous knowledge of what it means to be in and to do research work on a migrant camp. For several months, I was a newcomer in my hometown. I imagined I would be working as an insider in my hometown, but that was not always the case. The camp was in Matamoros, but it was undoubtedly not Matamoros. This is something I genuinely worked [on] by talking to NGO volunteers and reading the literature on egalitarian ethnographic approaches. And it is during this part of my journey that meeting Felicia [Rangel-Samponaro] was so important for me and my research inside the camp.

I met Felicia on an afternoon when I was heading out from the camp. She was walking with Victor, her partner. I remember I abruptly stopped my car when I saw their Sidewalk School (SWS) T-shirts. I had never met them in person, but I was aware of their work in the camp and that they were some of the few nonwhite Americans working there. I interviewed Felicia and Victor on several occasions, and we have worked together as well, both in Matamoros and Reynosa. In one of the conversations we had, they told me how they met at the plaza back in 2018, serving dinner to asylum seekers. Separately, Victor was a volunteer with Team Brownsville, and Felicia used to cross the border to bring food, medicines, and other donations. After a month, they started getting closer and talking about how to gather better donations or improve the distribution system. That is how, after a while, they decided it was a good idea to work together.

Later, because Felicia was crossing more often than Victor and she does not speak Spanish, she needed a translator to help her communicate with asylum seekers. That is how someone in the camp introduced her to Andres (pseudonym), who volunteered to support her as a translator. For a few weeks, she thought he was an American volunteer, until one day she was serving food and saw him in the line to take food, then Felicia grabbed his arm and told him, "Andres! What are you doing in line? The food is for asylum seekers. You can't take their food!" And that is how Felicia learned Andres was an asylum seeker living in a nearby abandoned building close to the camp. Later, the group grew, and they started having lunch together and having conversations about what to do next to support the camp. They decided the camp needed a school since the kids had nothing to do all day. Felicia says, "And we thought it would be a good idea to open a school for the kids, and that the project would be better if we only hired asylum seekers as teachers. That is how the Sidewalk School was born, with a conversation on the sidewalk of the plaza." Today, the SWS has evolved in so many ways. They now offer not only educational services but legal counsel. They also supervise a shelter in Reynosa, and provide medical services.

The tenacity of Felicia and Victor is invaluable. They work, day and night, to provide for all asylum seekers in Matamoros and Reynosa. Sometimes I joke with them and ask if they ever sleep. The moment I treasure the most about my relationship with Felicia is when in March 2021, the camp was about to be closed, but still a few people with "complicated cases" remained in the camp. It was a very complex situation because by that time, all access to local NGOs and donations [was] restrained from the camp. The Mexican government had already decided that that day was going to be the last day of the camp, but the few people who were still there refused to leave, out of fear of being forgotten and not getting a chance to cross. Then Felicia asked me to translate for her, so she could convince one of the SWS teachers to leave the camp for his own safety. I am not repeating their conversation, since it was private, but I do want to say that on that day, Felicia was not talking to a teacher or an asylum seeker she met [at] a camp. She was talking to family.

When Cynthia Bejarano and Cristina Morales told me about this project and their concept frontera madre(hood), and how they wanted Felicia to be part of it, I thought there was no better person in the Matamoros camp to be part of it. And this is not only because I am sure Felicia is a great mother for her child, but because after getting to know her better, I am convinced that she embodies perfectly the framework Bejarano and Morales (Bejarano and Morales, this volume) crafted. Felicia mothers her community at the Texas-Tamaulipas border as an agent of change, of resistance, and in action.

Lo que sigue . . .
Bertha A. Bermúdez Tapia in conversation and
in action with Felicia Rangel-Samponaro

TESTIMONIO

The Sidewalk School

FELICIA RANGEL-SAMPONARO

Cofounder of the Sidewalk School

O n December 27, 2021, we, Cynthia Bejarano and Cristina Morales, *saw the headline "The Woman Defending Black Lives on the Border, Including Her Own," published in the* Los Angeles Times, *and it immediately caught our eye. The story documented the work of border activist Felicia Rangel-Samponaro, who founded the nonprofit Sidewalk School—focused on education and other services—and her migrant advocacy in Reynosa and Matamoros, Mexico. This news story also highlighted features of frontera madre(hood), as it focused on her personal journey from stay-at-home mom to migrant activist, all the while balancing her Black racial identity in the mostly Latinx borderlands. Felicia is a fierce advocate for refugee seekers, which made it difficult for her to carve out time to write her testimonio. Here we honor Felicia's voice and her work by highlighting points from a few conversations with her.*[1]

Felicia described the urgency in starting her NGO, the Sidewalk School:

> The work here, what it started out as, was education and bringing education to children, asylum seekers who were stuck in Matamoros because

---

1. We appreciate Bertha A. Bermúdez Tapia's efforts in facilitating our conversation with Felicia.

of Migrant Protection Protocols. That's what the work started out as. The Sidewalk School evolved into adding a clinic, supporting the shelters surrounding us and the NGOs surrounding us. So it grew into providing food, shelter, water, basic necessities, medical, and eventually education. That's what our work is now, as we speak. And we're now in two cities. We're now in Reynosa and Matamoros, Mexico.

So it has been, it's been wonderful and then at times breathtaking. Especially when I think we can't go on any longer, and then someone always comes in and says you all are doing great work. I want to support it. And then we're safe once again, and we can always continue on. That's always—it sometimes makes me cry that people recognize the work that we do and how important it is for them to come in each time and save us when we're almost at the end of it.

Felicia further highlighted the grassroots nature of the Sidewalk School as led by people of color for people of color:

So, in this region, I am the only Black director of an NGO on the border. Farther up Tijuana, that's Guerline Jozef with the Haitian Bridge Alliance, and on the border, it is just me and Guerline Jozef. The two Black directors of NGOs that work on the border. It's just her and I. So, it's a very small club. And then Victor, I believe, is the only male Native American director on the border as well. I think he's the only one. So when we started, no one was trying to give us money. No one was trying to support us. Nobody, nobody. That's why it took so much of our own personal stuff to start the Sidewalk School. And Victor and I worked for free for like two years even though we did have children. We still worked for free. So it's just nice to see all of our hard work finally being acknowledged by our peers. That's always nice. And we have—and we did start off as a school, and now, you know, we built a shelter from the ground up in Reynosa. And we support shelters—all these shelters in Reynosa. And we ended up supporting some of the NGOs in Reynosa as well. We—it's just, we've come really far.

When discussing her motherwork (Caballero et al. 2019), Felicia described the difficulty in life-work balance as a mother of four:

So usually, it's Victor [her partner] that pulls me out of work to spend more time with our children, especially on the weekends. And then, you know, during the week with my son, I have to consciously make a decision to put my work down and spend time with my son because he is just as important. And I try to do that—I try to do that often. I don't know if it's very successful because this work is really demanding and it's all-consuming. But I do go to my son's, you know, award ceremonies and anything that he feels is important. I show up, and I spend time with him as well. It's a tricky balance doing this work and raising a child.

When asked to consider whether her motherhood duties at home carry over into the Sidewalk School through educating and serving Brown and Black migrant children, she initially did not see the connection between her motherwork (Caballero et al. 2019) at home and her frontera madre(hood) advocacy in her professional life.

I don't know if I ever equated being a mother with doing this type of work. Even though it is caring for other people, clearly, it is the same thing; it just never occurred to me to put those two things together. So this is how I put in the work, and then this is how I put being a mother. The work is treating people as people, just having humanity towards others, and recognizing that and doing something about it. Because what is happening to this group of people (refugees and asylum seekers) is awful. And then taking care of my son is usually over here in another space because I have to love and take care of my kid because I want him to be okay and grow up to be a wonderful adult. How the two come together I guess would be me caring for others the way I do for my son. With the same love and compassion. Obviously, because this takes up a lot of my time, this work, I care about it. I care about my work like I care about my son, or I wouldn't put so much time into it. I don't know, because then I think about Victor doing the same thing. So is that a mother? Or is that just having compassion and caring about other people?

At the time of her *testimonio* Felicia was front and center to the refugee crisis at the border and felt the importance of making a call to action

So because we've morphed into what we are today, like right now, when people ask, "What do we need to keep going?" To date, we've crossed almost ten thousand asylum seekers legally into the U.S., just the Sidewalk School. So in order for that to go on seven days a week, we have to pay staff. So when people ask what do you need, it's like, please donate money to us because you are paying our staff so they can continue on seven days a week. So they can continue to get asylum seekers out of Mexico and legally into the U.S. So I would say that's the first thing. Also, [this] all takes electronics. We've got to buy laptops and cell phones for everyone.

Then the second thing I would say is, Victor and I still go out into the communities every day because we help—we still help asylum seekers face to face. But also we need to see what's going on as the community ebbs and flows in both cities. So, like right now, we're trying to find blankets because both cities need blankets. Both cities, especially Reynosa, [have] a huge homeless population as we speak. Matamoros also has a homeless population, but unlike Reynosa, Matamoros has very little resources. So, we do need, like, blankets and coats and jackets and shoes. And if you donate to us, know that it is going out to the community. It doesn't just sit with us.

Felicia also discussed the development of the refugee camps:

When we were in Reynosa, every day we watch as the camps began. Everyone was like, no way; we were like, yeah, we think camp is starting. Then, you know, now we have four. Because we do need to tell everybody else this is what's really going on now, you all need to do something. Like, get ready and do something now. Which is what we're trying to get in the Reynosa group. I'm trying to get people to do something now because an encampment is about to start. It's about to start on its own as people are sleeping outside of Casa Migrante, outside of the original Matamoros encampment, outside Gladys, and this building we just saw, even though it's connected to a shelter, it's still an abandoned building.

In this anthology, it is important to highlight the work of women, like Felicia, that are so deep in the trenches. Felicia places her own safety on the line daily to help migrants and asylum seekers gain legal passage through the international ports of entry in Reynosa and Matamoros, despite harassment by Mexican and U.S. authorities, as well as other challenges.

REFERENCES

Caballero, Cecilia, Yvette Martínez-Vu, Judith Pérez-Torres, Michelle Téllez, and Christine Vega, eds. 2019. *The Chicana Motherwork Anthology: Porque Sin Madres No Hay Revolución.* Tucson: University of Arizona Press.

REFERENCES

CHAPTER 4

A Different Kind of Motherhood for Liberation

Fictive Kin, Advocacy, and Mothering Adult
Migrants in Immigration Detention

MARGARET BROWN VEGA

Community Activist and Anthropologist

"Feliz 10 de mayo, de parte de todos los que somos tus hijos."
—A MESSAGE RECEIVED ON MOTHER'S DAY FROM ONE OF MY FORMERLY
DETAINED COLLEAGUES WHO WAS DEPORTED TO MEXICO

"Happy Mother's Day with love. Your caring n lovely attitude as a mom
should continue to showcase in all children be it biological or not."
—A MESSAGE RECEIVED ON MOTHER'S DAY FROM ONE OF MY FORMERLY
DETAINED SONS WHO WAS DEPORTED TO CAMEROON

am not a mother—that is, I have no biological children and have not
formally adopted any children. So to be called, and treated as, a mother
is something that causes me much reflection.

An anthropologist by training, I teach about the varied ways the people in the world configure their families. I also teach about migration,
nation-states and borders, identity, belief systems, and how we can understand different perspectives from our own. I encourage my students
to question what they view to be normal and to mitigate their ethno-
centrism and seek to understand others without judgment. There is no
one right way to be, or one right way to view the world. To return this
discussion back from abstraction to motherhood: there is not one way
to be a mother. Knowing this as an anthropologist informs how I think
of my own motherly experience.

In 2015 I left a tenure-track job at a small Midwest school because I felt academia sucking my soul away. Being from south-central Texas, with deep roots there and in southern New Mexico and at the U.S.–Mexico border, I decided to come home to my roots. I gave up seeking jobs in my discipline at institutions near my home, because I saw jobs routinely go to outsiders. But I also wanted to do more engaged, activist work related broadly to border issues, and to put my skills to use serving the communities from which I had too long been estranged.

After years of marginalization, of being made invisible, of being exploited and treated as a token, I left academia only to return to contingent work at a local institution to pay the bills. I worked for three and a half years as a part-time adjunct instructor, and was part of the working poor, until last year. I made enough money to live but spent most of my time engaged in volunteer-based community work, especially coordinating an abolitionist group called Advocate Visitors with Immigrants in Detention. I now work full time for a social services organization while juggling the community and antidetention work to which I am still deeply committed. My position on the margins—in terms of my history and my current position—very much informs the advocacy work that I do.

I am an advocate, activist, abolitionist, and aspiring organizer. These pursuits shape my view of the work that I do and how my work links to mothering. In this context, I see the common pattern of outsiders who think they know better coming in to try to lead the charge on social change. There are thus, for me, layers of colonial mentality that shape my experience and are a dominant frame for much of the social justice work I see along the border. It is in this context that I see connections to problematic conceptions of mothering. I seek to navigate these issues through a different kind of mothering, rooted in who I am, what I work to end, and what I hope to build.

In this most recent chapter of my life—postacademic and committed to working with others toward social justice—I encountered abolitionist literature, written largely by black feminists (Davis 2003; Gilmore 2007; Kaba 2021), and more recently, in the context of this writing project, literature on "motherwork," written by Chicana feminists (Caballero et al. 2019). This chapter gives me the opportunity to bring these strands together to highlight what I have come to see and appreciate: the role of local mothers, however unconventional, in leading efforts to bring about much-needed social change and liberation (both real and existential). Despite criticisms of "new maternalism" that push for broader conceptions of parenting (Mezey and Pillard 2012), in my experience doing antidetention work, the role of local mothers and mother figures has been most prominent.

I first briefly discuss kinship, touching on its relationship to migration. Then I coarsely outline the context of immigration detention, which is the context in which I work on both social justice and mothering. I discuss some of the problems that arise in efforts to support migrants in detention, especially in facilities along the Mexico-U.S. border. Such efforts, often plagued by pa/maternalism, can be countered by thinking about antidetention work as mothering.[1] I advocate for a positive notion of kinship and mothering as a critical component of antidetention work, while coupling it within an abolitionist framework that seeks liberation for all of us.

Fictive Kin and Migration

In anthropology and sociology, kinship is a concept with a long history; it is difficult to do it justice here. Throughout that history, scholars have acknowledged that, cross-culturally, people consider themselves related to each other even if they are not related by marriage or by blood. Marshall Sahlins (2013) explains that kinspeople "belong to one another . . . are part of one another, who are co-present in each other, whose lives are joined and interdependent" (21). They do not need to be biologically related, nor related by marriage for that matter. This way of thinking about relatedness and family is very different from dominant ways, and even different sometimes from legal definitions of family structures in the United States. The state-sanctioned way of defining the family, and thus who belongs to a family, is often in opposition to how people everywhere create meaningful family relationships. It is worth mentioning some of the formal ways in which the U.S. government recognizes and validates family relatedness, especially in the context of immigration.

---

1. By pa/maternalism, I refer to both paternalism and maternalism as processes in which individuals seek to create relationships of dependency with others whom they are supporting or helping.

Perhaps surprisingly, family reunification is indeed at the core of much U.S. immigration law (Gubernskaya and Dreby 2017). Yet family reunification is not a straightforward issue when, cross-culturally, there are different definitions of the family. The United States generally views the family as a "nuclear family," that is, as parents and nonadult children. Extended families that include other generations, uncles and aunts, cousins, adult children, let alone fictive kin do not fit conventional, or even legal, definitions of the family. The recent "zero tolerance" policy received deserved attention for cruelly separating nonadult children from parents who were migrating together (U.S. House Judiciary Committee 2020), although family separation is common in the context of migration, with painful effects (Abrego 2014; Boehm 2012). In the U.S. immigration system, even when extended kin arrive together or seek to join kin already here, it is common to separate family members who are not part of a narrow view of the nuclear family (Williams 2019).

Why does this matter for this exploration of mothering? Because in addition to discussing my own experience as a fictive family member, I want to call attention to the fact that migration policies fail to address the valid and meaningful kin relations that are becoming increasingly common in our current world—a world marked by unprecedented displacement and migration, but also characterized by a long history of the creation of new and vibrant fictive relationships that help people cope as family. This sentiment becomes especially acute for those incarcerated in immigration detention.[2]

The two individuals I quote in this chapter's epigraph are two sons with whom I engage as a mother but have never had the opportunity to hug. We developed close bonds despite being constantly separated by physical barriers. Both men were deported, and one of their deportations was especially traumatic for both of us. During the months of weekly visits, of exchanged letters, and of collaborative strategizing on their respective campaigns for their release, we became family, and those bonds persist. Not only do we communicate during major holidays and birthdays, as many family members do, but we stay in touch regularly as

---

2. Note that kinship in the context of migration is not always a positive relationship, and there is a "dark side" to kinship. See the discussion in Andrikopoulos and Duyvendak (2020).

our lives continue to unfold. Our lives remain intertwined despite the detention and deportation apparatus that is designed to isolate, harm, and separate families.

Detention of Immigrants Under ICE: Inhumane Conditions and Torture

The United States has the largest immigration detention system on planet Earth. At its peak in the summer of 2019, Immigration and Customs Enforcement (ICE) detained more than fifty thousand people on any given day, with nearly half a million people booked into ICE detention facilities in FY 2020 (Kassie 2019). The number of people in immigration detention has climbed since 1996, when the Clinton administration passed a series of laws that further criminalized immigrants, funneling more of them into detention for deportation from the United States (Kerwin 2018). Beginning in 2017 with the Trump administration, the intensity with which the United States detained not only those who were in-country and undocumented, but those recently arriving to the Mexico-U.S. border was unprecedented (Cho, Tidwell Cullen, and Long 2020). Under the new Biden administration, advocates are disappointed, but not surprised, that immigration detention continues and that the numbers of people being detained is slowly creeping back up (Loweree and Reichlin-Melnick 2021).

People in immigration detention are held in a nationwide network of facilities to await the outcomes of their civil immigration proceedings. Based on my experience, the general public does not understand the conditions in which people in immigration detention live. Despite several high-profile cases of extreme abuse, neglect, and death, there is insufficient moral outrage about adults in ICE detention to change the situation. To better appreciate what is at stake in antidetention and abolition work, it is important to understand the nature of conditions in ICE detention facilities and what those in detention face.

Despite mythical stories that continue to hold significant meaning for national identity, immigration detention in the United States begins at the purported beacon of welcoming immigrants: Ellis Island (Silverman 2010). But the modern immigration detention system, now the most massive in the world, came into being around 1980 when large numbers of

Haitians, Cubans, and some Central Americans were detained as they fled their countries to enter the United States (Lindskoog 2018). From its inception, abuses and poor conditions have plagued this system. Its very existence allows for the deprivation of freedom for civil legal proceedings. Though in theory, immigration detention is supposed to be nonpunitive, it in fact is punishment by design—a way of deterring individuals from even attempting to migrate to the United States (Hernández et al. 2018). Recent assessments of the U.S. immigration detention system even characterize it as torture (Craig et al. 2021; Koehler 2021). The detained individuals I support are in fact going through an incredibly difficult situation. They are subjected to harmful and deadly conditions, making outside support critical and requiring a commitment to liberation by advocates.

Family Separation

Since we are discussing motherhood and family, it is important to emphasize that incarceration of any kind, including immigration detention, is family separation. Individuals are removed from their family networks, from their homes, and placed in confined and sometimes solitary settings. In ICE detention, individuals are held with other adults, typically in dorms, pods, or "bunkers" rather than in individual confinement cells. Just as in prisons and jails, movement is highly restricted in ICE detention facilities, with prescribed meal, outdoor/recreation, and religious services time. Correctional officers engage in twenty-four-hour guard watch or surveillance of all those held in ICE custody. Though people held by ICE are guaranteed certain rights and "services" guided by government-mandated detention standards, in practice, there are no guarantees.

Social visitation was permitted at ICE facilities until March 13, 2020, when the COVID-19 pandemic prompted ICE to cease all social visitations. Throughout the writing of this chapter, visitation remained suspended at nearly all facilities until it was permitted again in May 2022 under new guidelines. Prior to this suspension, people in detention could receive visits from family and friends. Because people are often detained far away from family, however, many do not receive visits. For undocumented families, visitation is simply not possible. This is the reason that I began to visit people in ICE detention.

There is abundant literature on how migrants who leave their homes and families rebuild fictive families and networks in new places (Ebaugh and Curry 2000). These connections provide much-needed support when family is not close. This dynamic can be especially acute when migrants are detained, especially for long periods. The need to build a family in such a restricted situation is critical yet challenging. While I cannot speak directly to the familial relationships that develop between those who are held in detention, I focus on the more extended family relationships that occur with those who visit migrants in detention, especially with "moms."

Visitation, Advocacy, and Abolition

In 2017, I began visiting people incarcerated in immigration detention, first in Eloy, Arizona, and then in Chaparral, New Mexico, and El Paso, Texas. The facilities in these three locations are all facilities along or very close to the southern U.S.-Mexico border.

Visitation programs in the United States vary widely. Some are faith based, some are charity based, and some are linked with abolitionist organizations, which seek to end the situation of detention entirely. I began visiting people held by ICE with a faith-based organization in Arizona. Five of us visited groups of about fifteen people, both men and women. It was a new initiative negotiated between the organization and the detention facility, with the aim of accompanying and supporting people ICE first encountered when they presented themselves for asylum at the port of entry in Nogales. We divided into small groups, being sure to visit everyone, engaging in conversation, treating people to snacks from the vending machines, gauging a little bit the status of someone's court case, and bookending the whole visit with collective prayer. A few visits with several individuals and the novelty of the experience afforded me only a small opportunity to fathom the cruelty of the whole situation.

When I relocated to New Mexico, I continued visiting people in detention through a charity organization that sought to end people's feeling of isolation in detention. As a volunteer with this organization, I was paired with two individuals whom I would visit weekly during their time in detention. My partner was also paired with two individuals, and we occasionally spoke to the people the other was visiting. For the next two months, I came to know four young gay men who had fled their home countries due to persecution for their identity, all of whom suffered intensely in the facility for being gay. Two of them gave up seeking asylum and asked to be deported. Another experienced such intense verbal and psychological abuse that he was placed in solitary confinement for his "protection." He ultimately was transferred to a facility in another part of the country in an attempt to remove him from the situation. I visited the fourth man until he was released after being granted asylum, a process that had required him to spend about six months in detention.

Through listening to the experiences of those in detention, I found those first months of visitation eye-opening on many levels. Visiting people in detention requires passing through security checks; this involves either walking through metal detectors or placing your hands above your head as a security guard runs a wand down the length of your body on both sides. Visitors speak to their family members through a glass barrier, seated on either side, with only a small circular grate through which they can speak. Sometimes a phone is used, and often the quality of the phone is so bad that it is difficult to hear the other person despite being a few feet away. Detention visitation is designed to keep individuals as distant from each other as possible—at least physically. In my visits, we sometimes placed our hands on each side of the glass as a way of trying to physically connect despite the barrier. Through conversations with people in detention, I learned that if they engaged in touching of any kind, such as hugging a pod mate, they could be punished. Sitting to speak with a fellow detained friend on their bed was not permitted. For everyone inside, their behavior is severely prescribed. And those prescriptions extend to family and friends who visit.

In one particularly revealing experience of the levels of control and intimidation exerted on families and those visiting people in detention, I was nearly banned from visiting people in the Otero County Processing Center. As I was speaking to a friend—a brother—in the general visitation area, I used a pencil and piece of paper to jot down details. He was asking me to relay some information to his wife and two daughters. Though no rules in the ICE detention standards prohibit bringing in paper and pen or pencil to write during visitation, I was approached by two guards who demanded my piece of paper. I refused and put the paper away and tucked the pencil into my hair. But the guards insisted

I give them the piece of paper. When I asked them to show me the rule against having pen or pencil and paper in visitation, they proceeded to shut down visitation for everyone and called me into a separate room. Once inside, the door was shut, and I was surrounded by five guards. For what felt like an eternity, I defended myself with the guards. I was told by one particularly belligerent officer that the captain said if I did not like their rules, I could leave. The repression I experienced for writing information I did not want to forget on a piece of paper is only one expression of the force exerted on those in detention and on their loved ones by the government and their contractors. Shortly after this incident, the facility installed security cameras in the visitation area to surveil more intensely not only those in detention, but those visiting.

By far, the chronic abuse experienced by those who are forced to live in detention is worse. The abuse is mostly verbal, psychological, sexual, and sometimes physical. And while we, as volunteers, were there to alleviate loneliness, we had no coordinated effort to address the abuses or complaints. Prompted by one individual who simply asked us why no one investigated the facility, we began to change the direction of the organization. My partner and I began work on the first advocacy report we wrote, regarding the Otero County Processing Center (Craig and Brown Vega 2018). We called for its closure and an end to immigration detention.

It did not take long to align my participation in visitation with the goals of abolition, with liberation. I came to know many of the people I visited as brothers and sons, although some remain friends or simply acquaintances. Yet moving beyond simply visiting a person heightened my own outrage, grief, and desperation about their imprisonment, and led me to immigration detention abolition. This is an important point, because it is through envisioning a "mutuality of being" (Sahlins 2013, 2, 19) with those in detention that I came to this stance. That is, by viewing those I visited as my family or as *me*, it became urgent to move beyond harm reduction and social support to abolitionist advocacy.

Ma/Paternalism

Not everyone who visits people in detention holds my position. In fact, disagreements have been the source of tremendous conflict with others who also visit detained individuals yet do not seek to end detention. That includes people who may be referred to with familiar terms by those they visit, including "mom" or "mother."

In advocacy circles there are cautionary tales about, and even rules to minimize, paternalism. Examples of paternalism might be telling someone that they are better off in detention rather than pursuing a bond for release, because in detention they have access to healthcare. Or to attempt to get someone to appreciate that they have a bed and food to eat, even if they are detained. To ask someone to accept their deprivation of freedom while being held in inhumane conditions requires a high degree of distance and detachment from that person. Paternalism can also simply be treating adults in detention as children who have no agency. This is particularly dangerous as, given that they are in detention, they are already stripped of much of their agency.

But paternalism is not the only issue. Maternalism, a term with wide and varied usage, but also ascribed to white settler-colonial women, sees women seeking to create relationships of dependency, especially with nonwhite women and children (Jacobs 2009). Adult migrants, men or women, who are subjected to the torment of immigration detention are often treated as children or childlike by facility staff and guards. Unfortunately, they are also often treated this way by charity-driven people who visit them to help uplift them.

While immigration detention exists all over the United States, those facilities along the border are perhaps where issues of ma/paternalism toward immigrants are most acute. The Mexico-U.S. border and border cities like El Paso/Juárez are viewed from other corners of the country as places to go to save people. White saviorism as part of humanitarian aid efforts in this area is pervasive. And the history of colonialism and racism here has also shaped the mentalities of white saviors who live and even have roots here, whose social justice efforts are characterized more by charity than by solidarity. In my view, charity-driven efforts are aimed at the well-being of those giving the charity, not those receiving it. Because if one were truly concerned with the well-being of an individual in detention, one would recognize this profoundly unjust, unethical, and immoral situation for what it is and seek to change it.

In the organization that I now coordinate, volunteers are recruited and trained with explicit expectations that no one should be in immigration detention. The organization is now explicitly abolitionist toward immigration detention. Several of us strive to be prison-industrial complex abolitionists by challenging the need to incarcerate anyone and seeking to strengthen ties with antiprison work (Loyd, Mitchelson, and Burridge 2012). On more than one occasion, however, I have had to address volunteers who do not feel comfortable visiting or writing letters to someone who has a criminal record, who prefer to visit asylum seekers who are viewed to be poor and in need of saving. Good immigrant / bad immigrant narratives and tropes are widespread among immigrant advocacy groups (Lara, Greene, and Bejarano 2009). Those who view their efforts as helping refugees or asylum seekers, and not necessarily other immigrants who do not meet these categories, are solely interested in supporting those immigrants who are, in their minds, deemed to be "good."

Individuals come to the work of supporting people in detention with various motivations. I have encountered people who seek to have a multicultural experience, to practice foreign language skills, to "welcome the stranger" or to "visit and comfort the captive," to bring hope, or to accompany people through their situation. I also work with people, though, who are abolitionists, deeply committed to both ending the prison-industrial complex and to liberation. Class division is a major structuring variable that shapes who makes up the "social justice" volunteers in southern New Mexico and in the border area generally. Those divisions intersect with racial ones. Nearly all people incarcerated in immigration detention are people of color. Yet it is predominantly white activists, retirees, and mostly women who come to the aid of poor migrants with charitable, colonial, and "motherly" mindsets.

Without seeing the possibility of your liberation being tied to that of people in detention, and without being enraged at the injustice experienced by those in detention, you cannot be in solidarity with those in detention (Kendall 2020). To stop at "offering hope," while encouraging people to be patient with their situation and resigning yourself to someone else's deportation without being angry, is problematic. What if we viewed those in detention as, and deeply felt that those in detention were in fact, our family? Might we act differently? Indeed, many people in the United States have family members languishing in detention. For the rest of us, would we take bolder steps to end the situation if our loved ones were detained? It is important not to romanticize the family. I have encountered families who have no interest in helping or supporting their relatives who are in detention. And white maternalism is present and very harmful. But I want to advocate for the positive aspects of kinship that are central to my own experience of mothering, especially as someone who seeks to combat colonialism and detention in my community. As a counter to ma/paternalism—which are undeniably colonial—mothering might be generally thought of as building a close relationship with someone not related by marriage or blood in a way that emphasizes solidarity.

Mothering and Liberation

Viewing kinship as a "mutuality of being" (Sahlins 2013) dovetails with principles that come from both nonviolence and abolition, as well as with Black and Chicana feminist experiences of mothering. In the oft-quoted words of James Baldwin, "We must fight for your life as though it were our own—which it is—and render impassable with our bodies the corridor to the gas chamber. For, if they take you in the morning, they will be coming for us that night" (Baldwin 1971). As Ana Castillo pointed out in her foreword to *The Chicana Motherwork Anthology*, relationships of unconditional love are central to a "Mother Awareness," one in which we see ourselves as close (not distant) and bonded to others (Caballero et al. 2019, xii).

Not everyone that I support in detention considers me a mother. I have many brothers and many friends; but in several instances, I developed close relationships while visiting people in detention that extend beyond their release or deportation. I never initiate the mother-child relationship. Yet without exception, all of the adults, mostly men, who call me "mom," "mother," or "mommy" used the term first. They hail from different home countries: Cameroon, Cuba, Honduras, India, Mexico, and Nepal. Some are a bit too old to actually be a child of mine. But as a colleague of mine expressed to me, often siblings and relatives of similar ages take on motherly roles out of necessity after families have been broken up.

As I mentioned, I have no direct experience raising children, but in some ways, this may have helped me not to view, or treat, the people whom I meet in detention as children. The heartbreak I feel knowing that thousands of people, and especially people I know and consider family, are in detention is visceral and sometimes unbearable. While I view them as close to me, I carefully try to see myself not as a nurturer or guardian, but as an accomplice. I give people information, connect them to resources, and work with them to gain their freedom. I know I cannot save them. I often strategize with people about securing release, acting more as a thought partner. And when they are released, we stay in touch, and those bonds and that support continues. I view all of this as solidarity, as antidetention, abolitionist work—and as motherwork.

The mothering aspect of my solidarity is what prompts me to answer my phone when I know someone from detention is calling. Making phone calls from detention is hard, and I know attorneys and others do not always answer their phones. It is the mothering practice that prompts me to run after senators and representatives in Congress during visits to their home districts because someone in detention is counting on me to convey their story to them. Mothering prompts me to contact the state health department because people inside have told me they are not being protected against the spread of COVID-19. Mothering is what motivates me to struggle through severe language barriers to let someone know that I not only hear them, but I will also take action. It is a blend of nurturing and solidarity—not guardianship, but rather struggling along with my family. Motherwork is an antidote to the dehumanization that underpins our society's—and sometimes our families'—normalization of incarceration (Gilmore 2007). Bonds of motherhood not only help us be there for those in detention but move us to assert that detention of any kind simply cannot be.

It is also this mothering that sometimes does not let me sleep at night. I bring the concerns of those in detention to spaces where they are often not welcome (such as to spaces of congressional visits), and I do it unapologetically. Perhaps that resonates with definitions of Chicana m(other)work that see us resisting from within institutions that try to marginalize us (Caballero et al. 2019). The institution in this case—our very government that has historically marginalized us and continues to do so—must change.

Prison-industrial complex abolition does not just emphasize an end to policing, incarceration, and surveillance; it is hopeful work about building a new society that does not rely on the same racist, capitalist, and classist systems that generations of activists have tried to change (Davis 2016; Kaba 2021). Central to these projects is anticolonial work as well. In the colonized and occupied space of the Mexico-U.S. border, these issues converge and thread together in antidetention work. I want to highlight a different strand of social justice work than what tends to dominate here, usually led by middle-class or upper-class privileged activists. Social justice work is stronger and more transformative when done by accomplices whose work is informed by feminisms derived from women of color. That kind of necessary and much-needed social justice work is unapologetic about abolition and about ending unjust systems to build new ones. Rather than continuing to ask people to be patient and hope for the best, liberation requires us to recognize that we are fighting with and for our family and loved ones—for all of us to be free.

REFERENCES

Abrego, Leisy. 2014. *Sacrificing Families: Navigating Laws, Labor, and Love Across Borders*. Stanford, Calif.: Stanford University Press.

Andrikopoulos, Apostolos, and Jan Willem Duyvendak. 2020. "Migration, Mobility and the Dynamics of Kinship: New Barriers, New Assemblages." *Ethnography* 21 (3): 299–318.

Baldwin, James. 1971. "Open Letter to My Sister, Miss Angela Davis, in Care of the Silent Majority." Schomburg Center for Research in Black Culture, Manuscripts, Archives and Rare Books Division, The New York Public Library. https://digitalcollections.nypl.org/items/5038df00-c284-0135-5e22-13f81637 db93.

Boehm, Deborah A. 2012. *Intimate Migrations: Gender, Family, and Illegality Among Transnational Mexicans*. New York: New York University Press.

Caballero, Cecilia, Yvette Martínez-Vu, Judith Pérez-Torres, Michelle Téllez, and Christine Vega, eds. 2019. *The Chicana Motherwork Anthology: Porque Sin Madres No Hay Revolución*. Tucson: University of Arizona Press.

Cho, Eunice Hyunhye, Tara Tidwell Cullen, and Clara Long. 2020. *Justice-Free Zones: U.S. Immigration Detention Under the Trump Administration*. ACLU Research Report. New York: American Civil Liberties Union, Human Rights Watch, and National Immigrant Justice Center.

Craig, Nathan, and Margaret Brown Vega. 2018. *"Why Doesn't Anyone Investigate This Place": Complaints Made by Migrants Detained at the Otero County Processing Center, Chaparral, NM Compared to Department of Homeland*

Security Inspections and Reports. El Paso, Tex.: Detained Migrant Solidarity Committee and Freedom for Immigrants, July.

Craig, Nathan, AnaKaren Ortiz Varela, Marissa C. Núñez, Margaret Brown Vega, Ian Philabaum, and P. J. Podesta. 2021. *Process by Torment: Immigration Experiences of Persons Detained at the Otero County Processing Center*. El Paso: Innovation Law Lab and Advocate Visitors with Immigrants in Detention, January.

Davis, Angela Y. 2003. *Are Prisons Obsolete?* New York: Seven Stories Press.

Davis, Angela Y. 2016. *Freedom Is a Constant Struggle: Ferguson, Palestine, and the Foundations of a Movement*. Chicago, Ill.: Haymarket.

Ebaugh, Helen Rose, and Mary Curry. 2000. "Fictive Kin as Social Capital in New Immigrant Communities." *Sociological Perspectives* 43 (2): 189–209.

Gilmore, Ruth Wilson. 2007. *Golden Gulag: Prisons, Surplus, Crisis, and Opposition in Globalizing California*. Berkeley: University of California Press.

Gubernskaya, Zoya, and Joanna Dreby. 2017. "U.S. Immigration Policy and the Case for Family Unity." *Journal on Migration and Human Security* 5 (2): 417–30.

Hernández, David, John M. Eason, Pat Rubio Goldsmith, Richard D. Abel, and Andrew McNeely. 2018. "With Mass Deportation Comes Mass Punishment: Punitive Capacity, Health, and Standards in U.S. Immigrant Detention." In *Routledge Handbook on Immigration and Crime*, edited by Holly Ventura Miller and Anthony Peguero, 260–69. New York: Routledge.

Jacobs, Margaret D. 2009. *White Mother to a Dark Race: Settler Colonialism, Maternalism, and the Removal of Indigenous Children in the American West and Australia, 1880–1940*. Lincoln: University of Nebraska Press.

Kaba, Mariame. 2021. *We Do This 'Til We Free Us: Abolitionist Organizing and Transforming Justice*. Chicago, Ill.: Haymarket.

Kassie, Emily. 2019. "Detained: How the U.S. Built the World's Largest Immigrant Detention System." *Guardian* (London), September 24, 2019. https://www.theguardian.com/us-news/2019/sep/24/detained-us-largest-immigrant-detention-trump.

Kendall, Mikki. 2020. *Hood Feminism: Notes from the Women That a Movement Forgot*. New York: Viking.

Kerwin, Donald. 2018. "From IIRIRA to Trump: Connecting the Dots to the Current US Immigration Policy Crisis." *Journal on Migration and Human Security* 6 (3): 192–204.

Koehler, Taylor. 2021. *Arbitrary and Cruel: How U.S. Immigration Detention Violates the Convention Against Torture and Other International Obligations*. St. Paul, Minn.: Center for Victims of Torture.

Lara, Dulcinea, Dana Greene, and Cynthia Bejarano. 2009. "A Critical Analysis of Immigrant Advocacy Tropes: How Popular Discourse Weakens Solidarity and Prevents Broad, Sustainable Justice." *Social Justice* 36 (2): 21–37.

Lindskoog, Carl. 2018. *Detain and Punish: Haitian Refugees and the Rise of the World's Largest Immigration Detention System.* Gainesville: University of Florida Press.

Loweree, Jorge, and Aaron Reichlin-Melnick. 2021. *Tracking the Biden Agenda on Immigration Enforcement.* Special Report. Washington, D.C.: American Immigration Council.

Loyd, Jenna M., Matt Mitchelson, and Andrew Burridge. 2012. *Beyond Walls and Cages: Prisons, Borders, and Global Crisis.* Athens: University of Georgia Press.

Mezey, Naomi, and Cornelia T. L. Pillard. 2012. "Against the New Maternalism." *Michigan Journal of Gender and Law* 18 (2): 229–96.

Sahlins, Marshall. 2013. *What Kinship Is—And Is Not.* Chicago, Ill.: University of Chicago Press.

Silverman, Stephanie J. 2010. "Immigration Detention in America: A History of Its Expansion and a Study of Its Significance." Centre on Migration, Policy and Society Working Paper No. 80, University of Oxford.

U.S. House Judiciary Committee. 2020. *The Trump Administration's Family Separation Policy: Trauma, Destruction, and Chaos.* Majority Staff Report. Washington D.C.: U.S. House of Representatives.

Williams, Alysa. 2019. "The Forgotten Relatives in the Fight Against Family Separation: A Constitutional Analysis of the Statutory Definition of Unaccompanied Minors in Immigration Detention." *William and Mary Journal of Race, Gender, and Social Justice* 26 (1): 191–223.

CHAPTER 5

Madres De Una Frontera

A Bilateral Experience

CODA RAYO-GARZA AND SHAMMA RAYO-GUTIERREZ

The University of Texas at San Antonio, PhD Candidate, and Mamá Fronteriza

In this chapter, we share our *testimonios* and dual experiences of growing up in a mixed-status family along the Texas-Mexico border. Our *testimonios* reflect, even within the same *familia*, the different intersectionalities that each of the women in the household operated under. Our *mamá* was a first-generation Mexican American, raising two daughters with different forms of status (irregular status and U.S. citizen). Her experiences and the pain she suffered alongside us are shared in the form of our *testimonios*. We feel they are the best way to translate our emotions and experiences as well as hers. From our *testimonios*, we hope to bring light to how women and mothers are treated in the process of naturalization, the unequal opportunities for undocumented women, and the barriers that only women and girls from the borderlands could experience. We are two sisters—*hermanas*—two years apart. We grew up, side by side, experiencing life from two different intersections, one of us born in the United States with the privilege of citizenship, and the other born in Nuevo Laredo, Mexico, remaining undocumented for the larger part of her young womanhood. We are the *hijas* of Maria Santos Rayo. Our mother raised us in a colonia alongside the Rio Grande River in Laredo, Texas. *Nuestra historia de madre(hood), les compartimos.*

You will find in our *testimonios* how the three of us (Shamma, Coda, and our *mamá*, Maria) practice(d) frontera madre(hood) primarily through resistance. Shamma, with the support of our *mamá*, pushed against the U.S. legal system and its cold, often unjust, process for obtaining citizenship. We see our existence as a multistatus family unit as an act of resistance itself, because even while on paper, the United States didn't recognize Shamma, we as her *familia* did. Our barrio recognized her through the connections we made and our neighbors simply viewing her as being from the barrio. Our *mamá*, Maria, practiced frontera madre(hood) through her labor. While we often think of a supportive mother as one who attends parent-teacher meetings, sports games, and extracurricular activities, Maria's madre(hood) was working hard, heavy, and intensely so that her daughters had food to eat, a place to sleep at night, and the energy to fight for more. For Coda, the experiences of Maria's work and Shamma's resistance led her to fight for academic achievements not easily attainable for low-income brown girls from the barrio.

Shamma's *Testimonio*

I can still hear the ringing of the bells as the *eloteros* made their very welcomed return. We would beg our parents for pesos and chase our daily evening vendors down our street. I felt safe. I was home. I was born to an immigrant father and a Mexican American mother in the city of Nuevo Laredo, in the state of Tamaulipas, which is in northeastern Mexico. There I lived until the age of seven. I remember walking hand in hand with my father to the *lucha libre* matches, and when the circus would come into town, he would take my sister and me to see the animals outside in their cages, waiting for their turn in the spotlight. One day, everything changed. I remember packing; we were not given a reason or explanation. All we needed to know was that we were leaving Nuevo Laredo. It was my home, the only place I had ever known and loved so profoundly.

There were six of us packed into our small gray sedan: my two brothers, Mauricio and Sergio; my little sister, Coda; my mother, father, and of course, me. My siblings were all fortunate enough to have been born in the United States. Circumstances would not allow that to be in my favor. When we arrived in Laredo, Texas, we were taken in by my father's sister.

It wasn't too long before my father purchased a small piece of land and started the construction of our home. Most nights we slept there, the smell of pine surrounding us, and with no roof above us, under the stars, we were happy. The future seemed hopeful.

Summers were excruciating, and winters were difficult. We boiled water for our showers and sat next to space heaters for warmth. My parents poured every ounce of energy into that home. Little by little those bare walls became our shelter, our protection from danger. We lived on the far west side of Laredo. We lived in what most consider a low-income and gang-ridden neighborhood. Drug deals and drive-by shootings were regular occurrences. The Rio Grande was walking distance from our home, so it was not a surprise to have border patrol units constantly driving up and down our streets. We were not allowed to leave our yard. My sister and I watched the neighborhood kids play together from the safety of our home. I was eager to start school here in the States. The possibility of making friends was stirring, but it wouldn't come so easily.

My kindergarten teacher was kind and patient, often encouraging me to make friends with the other kids in class. Language was a huge barrier for me, and it kept me from making the friends I longed for. I was assigned a dual-language teacher, an older woman with little to no patience. I dreaded every day I spent with her. She repeatedly mocked the way I mispronounced words before correcting me. One day, as the class napped, I started to feel ill. I ended up throwing up. She was in charge of the class that day, and while everyone went out to recess, she made me stay behind and pick up my own vomit. She sat there on her desk watching me. She never moved a finger. Thankfully, another teacher walked in, saw what was happening, and instructed me to stop.

Our financial struggles were very evident. In school, we were given canned foods during the holidays and shoes from donations received from other students for programs like "Pennies for Tennies." My mother worked endlessly to provide for our family, oftentimes picking up a second job selling home decor to make ends meet. I watched her sell the few quality pieces of clothing and jewelry she owned to put food on the table. She made the impossible possible for her children.

At a very young age I learned what I did not want in a partner. I watched my father abuse my mother. Machismo is very prevalent in our community, as Hispanics, even more so back then. *Machistas* are males who feel empowered by their gender and most times will be aggressive, forceful, and abusive to feel a sense of control and to dominate their spouse. My father worked odd jobs here and there, but he was consistently denied anything stable because of his lack of education and inability to speak English. His pursuit of a better life in the States languished. The lack of opportunity made him angry and hostile toward my mother, with him often saying that he longed to move back to Mexico, where "La vida es más fácil" (life is easier). This experience helped shape my future tremendously and what I wanted for my children. It became necessary that they never bear witness to the traumatic things I saw as a child. I would learn how to be fiercely protective of them just as my mother was with us.

It was not until middle school when I found out I was living here illegally. My mother had to register me for the school year, and they asked for my social security number, to which she simply replied that I did not have one. I knew exactly what that meant. I was what other kids called a "mojada," or in English, "wetback," a derogatory slang term used to describe illegal immigrants in the United States. Learning of my illegal status brought great pressure to hide this secret that could bear so many terrible consequences.

In high school, my immigration status took front and center stage. My classmates were filling out college applications and getting summer jobs, but I was lost. I had no direction, and I did not have anybody to ask for guidance. I was stagnant in the whirlwind of young adulthood. I went through the motions and graduated. I watched everyone around me enthusiastically move on to the next chapter of their life. Being a spectator was difficult; I watched my younger sister get a job, learn how to drive, and eventually pack her things and go off to college.

The urgency for independence gnawed at my heart more than ever. It was then that I decided to venture out in search of work. For years, people would talk about downtown shops that would hire undocumented help. I got dressed and hitched a ride downtown. I walked through the downtown streets of Laredo until I finally saw a "help wanted'" sign. With my heart pounding and with sweaty palms, I walked in and asked the lady at the register if they were still looking for help. She said yes and then asked me if I had a social security number. My heart sank as I responded that I did not. To my surprise, she said that it was okay and asked me when I could start. I left that shop with a job that day, my first ever—and I was elated.

Border patrol units were at practically every corner of the downtown streets close to my place of employment. The city of Laredo has five ports of entry, two of which are located downtown. Back then, the *centro* was buzzing with activity. On my lunch break, I would walk over a couple of streets to a nearby snack shop. Frequently I would witness agents walk into shops, ask for verification of legal status, and walk out with individuals that were unable to provide that. They were taken away. It terrified me to think that one day that could be me. My mother and father worried for me; they knew that if I kept working this way, getting caught would be inevitable.

Our first attempt at naturalization was in 2005 with the help of a *notario*, or notary, a person who is authorized in the United States to perform certain legal actions, specifically as a witness to signatures on important documents, such as deeds and contracts. It is often a misconception that these individuals carry the legal right to advise and prepare documents for individuals seeking immigration. They will fraudulently charge anywhere from three to five thousand dollars, exploiting oblivious individuals. Unfortunately, our family fell victim to this hoax. My mother had saved up enough money to pay for my application process. She prepared our file and soon after made an appointment in Ciudad Juárez, Chihuahua, Mexico, with the U.S. Citizenship and Immigration Services (USCIS).

That day, bright and early, we started the ten-hour ride to the El Paso border. The next day we walked to the immigration center and took a seat in a room teeming with people who, like me, waited for their file number to be called. At last, I was called and led into a tiny room lined with blood-drawing chairs. We all got our blood drawn at the same time and were escorted out to individual evaluation rooms. We never asked why things were done as they were, and they didn't care to explain. All we knew was that they held my passage to U.S. citizenship, so we did what they said, no questions asked. The rooms were tiny, dirty, run-down, and had no door, only a curtain. As I walked in, I was handed a paper robe and told to take everything off. I waited nervously for someone to come in, and when she finally did, I was told to lift my robe to expose my body, asked to turn around and bend over, exposing my backside. I felt violated. We were told to come back a few hours later, which we did and waited until my file had been revised. My name was called, and I felt a sense of relief: it would all soon be over. When we approached the immigration officer, she told us my naturalization had been denied. She proceeded to tell us that the person who had filed my application did not do it correctly, and we were missing many important documents. I saw my mother's heart break that day.

With heavy hearts, we made the drive back from the U.S. consulate in Ciudad Juárez to the international bridge. It was a risk that we were willing to take, a chance that could quite literally rip our family apart, but one we had to make. We were cleared and drove back home, defeated. I cried most of the way. My father, a man born into the Mexican ideology that "los hombres no lloran" (men don't cry), broke down that day. I saw as he wiped his tears in silence and with his voice weakened said, "Tu no te preocupes, nosotros haremos lo que tengamos que hacer para que tu salgas adelante." In English, "Don't worry, we will do everything in our power so that you may prosper." His words soothed me. They calmed my soul and, in that moment, gave me peace and reassurance that everything was going to be all right.

Back in Laredo, my parents tried to get in contact with the notary. Their calls went unanswered, and in fear of being reported, my mother decided it was better that we do not make a fuss of what had happened. We had learned our lesson and decided that our next attempt would be through an immigration lawyer.

A couple of months passed until we met our immigration lawyer. He explained that we would need to go through the whole process once again but assured us that we would not have to go through the same experience. I trusted him, oftentimes feeling like I was in the presence of a superhero. It sounds silly to me now, but the feeling was so real then. And so began the endless list of prerequisites we had to provide. We checked the requirements off our list, one by one. After what seemed like an eternity, we finally had a set date and were scheduled to travel just a few hours away to the city of San Antonio, where we were to meet and interview with a USCIS officer. The wait was not awful. We were called in rather quickly after arriving. My mother and I were ushered into an office where a young gentleman sat behind a desk. He introduced himself and began our interview.

I was a nervous wreck. He was cocky and standoffish. He asked my mother why she had birthed me over in Mexico and went on to tell her that it is because of people like her that there is such an immigration problem. He told her that if she would have been more responsible, we wouldn't be in this situation. My mother sat there looking down like a scolded child and did not say a single word. She was terrified. What could she have possibly said in her defense to this officer who held my future in his hands? But I did. I spoke up because I knew that no matter what, I would forever vindicate my mother's actions, as I had many times before. Her fifth-grade education and lack of comprehension would make her extremely vulnerable to many things in life, and this was one of them.

I told him, "Excuse me, but this is not my mother's fault. It's not her fault that I find myself in this situation. Our circumstances then were something that we didn't have the power to change. And it took us so long and so much persistence from my mother's part to get to this point. So, we are here now, and we are ready to make things right."

He looked me dead in the eyes and said he would be denying my naturalization. He did not give us a reason.

As I walked out of his office, my throat started to close, and my eyes started to swell, but I held it in. I could not and did not want him to see me cry as I later learned that he had done to so many others. I swung open the doors of that building and ran into my father's arms. He held me tight. Without having to say a word, he knew what had happened. The next day we met with our lawyer, and he knew exactly who we had been interviewed by. He mentioned that that certain individual had already been reported and that his denial had no base. He said that he was going to fight for us, and so he did.

Two weeks later, we got that phone call we had eagerly been waiting for. "Congratulations, your request for naturalization has been granted. You will be receiving your naturalization form in a couple of days," said the person on the other end of the line. My heart was overjoyed, and tears of relief streamed down my face. I received a letter in the mail a couple of days later with my name on it! My first letter *ever*. That letter held my freedom, my sense of belonging. It held the beginning to the rest of my life.

I have children now, three to be exact. The things I have been through have taught me so much. I saw how beautiful—and how absolutely unfair—life can be. I make sure to remind them where their mommy came from and what she went through. That they are free! Free to roam without fear, free to pursue an education, and how incredible it is to chase after your dreams. Because they can—because unlike mommy, nothing can hold them back. They also understand that their *mami* was not as lucky, and that I fought to get to where I am now. I assure them that with their voice and actions, they can do the same for others. I teach them to be strong, or in Spanish, *chingonas*, because we are not granted happiness. Sometimes we have to smile through the pain and keep on pushing.

I tell them stories about their grandma and how she never, not once, gave up on us. She and my father did their best with what life handed them. And that woman I get to call Mom is the pinnacle of perseverance and grit. I use my sister, Coda, as an example to follow. I set her up on a pedestal because she has overcome so much with so little. She is a leader—always has been and always will be. I still get to watch her rise, but it is no longer from the sidelines.

Most importantly, I teach my children that we are not on the same boat, but all sail the same sea. I instill compassion and empathy because we will never fully understand everyone's story no matter how hard they smile, just like mommy did. I push them to do whatever it is they love; it changes very often, but that is quite okay. My story is one of pain and persistence, of defeat and conquest. "Echame tierra y verás como floresco" (Frida Kahlo).

Coda's *Testimonio*

I grew up on the literal fringes of los Estados Unidos in the town of Laredo, Tejas. I am a *fronteriza*. Ontologies tied to growing up in a border town form a part of who I am, as a woman, a mother, a daughter, and of living in this world. I grew up with two older brothers and one older sister. Before Laredo, we lived in Nuevo Laredo, Tamaulipas, in the country of Mexico. We immigrated to the United States, where I was born. My older sister was born in Mexico and remained undocumented for much of her young adult years. Growing up in a mixed-status family was an added layer to the difficulties we faced as a family and as young women. Laredo, Texas, is a border town whose demographics show us a place different from the rest of the country. Literally, border towns are positioned at the fringes of our country's physical border. Yet, unlike the northern border, along the southern border is an ecosystem whose narratives are dominated by those outside. Ninety-five percent of the people in Laredo are of Hispanic or Latinx race and origin.

Some of my youngest memories take me back to the house where I grew up, in a colonia nestled about half a mile away from the Rio Grande itself. I remember summers in Laredo. They were scorching hot. Our house didn't have an air-conditioning or heating system to keep us cool in the summer or warm in the winter. We relied on open windows for the cool night air in the summer and portable heaters and our gas-fired stove to keep us warm in the winter. We had running water, but no boiler to warm the water. Winters were difficult without warm water. I remember my sister and I waiting for my mom to boil water for us in a small pot on the stove. Once the water was hot enough, my mom would then pour the boiling water into a construction bucket and mix cold water in to bring the water to a tepid temperature that we could use to shower. We would take our showers in that construction bucket and do so quickly to minimize the time spent exposed to the cold winter air.

I also have memories of my mother. In most of my memories, she is tired from work. She would come home and sit down on the couch or lay on the floor, exhausted. While we had both parents, it was our mother who provided the consistent flow of income. Neither of them had a high school education. My mother barely finished middle school, but she was our provider. My mother worked at a nursing home in Laredo for most of her life. It is really the only occupation I have known her to have had. She often told us stories of a time in her life when, as a young woman, she moved to Chicago and worked at a manufacturing plant with many other immigrants and women of color. Now, at age seventy-two, she is still working at a nursing home. With no savings to retire, she has no other option. Her body is tired. Her knees are injured. Her fingers are arthritic. Yet, she still works. When we were little girls, she earned minimum wage, and today she still doesn't earn much more. But she provided for us.

There is one memory I have of my mother's love for us. She hadn't gotten paid yet, and most of the money went to paying bills, as it usually did. There was no bread, no eggs, no food in our refrigerator. Taking one of the few valuable pieces of jewelry she owned, we went to the pawn shop, and she sold it for cash. I will always remember her words, "¿Como voy a dejar que no coman mis hijas?" (How am I going to let my daughters go without food?). We drove to the grocery store right after. That night, we had food. Some nights, we didn't have electricity or water, but my mother was always there to comfort us.

My father worked odd jobs in the United States and Mexico. When he worked *al otro lado,* he would sometimes come back home with Mexican treats: *conchas, penguinos, galletas, dulces de tamarindo.* Those were some of our riches. It was my experience of poverty that was more dominant in my early childhood memories. I remember in elementary school my kinder teacher always sneaking an extra lollipop my way. She was kind and compassionate, but I realize now that she was especially empathetic to us because of how poor we were. One day, my sister and I got home to a huge black plastic garbage bag sitting on the living room floor. My kinder teacher had donated a bag filled with used clothes for us. We were excited and overjoyed. I remember one special sweater that was in that bag: it had donuts on it. I think my sister and I took turns wearing it. As I think back on that memory, I cannot help but recall that there was no shame in wearing used clothes. We were just grateful we would have sweaters to wear in the winter.

In the barrio, my sister and I often took walks in the evenings with my mother, and one of my brothers sometimes joined us. The sunset was so beautiful in our colonia. I remember a clear picture of the orange-pink sky, unfettered by tall buildings. Only warehouses surrounded our neighborhood. In between our neighborhood and the Rio Grande, there was a swath of empty undeveloped land that oftentimes became a dump site for old tractor tires. We would walk down that road sometimes too. The homes in our barrio were of all shapes and sizes. Some had exposed sheetrock, like ours, that were never fully built out. Other homes were mobile homes of all different colors: pink, green, blue. I remember one lady made a *tiendita* (store) out of her mobile home, and she would sell Mexican candies to the kids from the bus stop. This was our hood. We grew up in a place different from any urban core I have ever visited, a place only available in variation along the borders of our countries. I cannot imagine being shaped by any other neighborhood. Even as an adult now, I think of some of the conversations we heard growing up connected to things we could only experience in our barrio along the border.

One time, when our school bus drove down the street along the Rio Grande near the empty land, we saw people crossing the river, but that was not unusual for us. It was our normal. Occasionally during our visits to the park nestled along the *río*, we would see people crossing too. Sometimes we saw traces of people who had recently crossed. "¿Porqué se cruzan?" (Why do they cross?) I would ask. "Porque quieren trabajar" (Because they want to work), my parents would tell me. The reality is that some of these people who crossed were women—women who were hoping to get jobs to send money back to their children, women who were working hard to provide for their children, just like my mother, save her legal status. But how different were we really from families in my barrio? The reality was that they were crossing a river to a different nation but similar culture. Laredo has a sizable Mexican immigrant population. How different are the Mexicans on one side of the border from each other?

I experienced poverty heavily, but as we got a little older, my sister's status as undocumented became more evidently a factor in our everyday decisions. We would not go often to Nuevo Laredo. There was always the fear that my sister would not successfully pass the litmus test at the port of entry back to the United States. This consisted of us repeating a phrase in English—"American"—and demonstrating understanding of what was being asked. My father always showed his residency papers. My mother, as a U.S. citizen, never had to. We, as little girls, just behaved our best at the *puente* (international port of entry) and repeated the phrase we knew would get us back home to the United States. Every year, when the *feria* came around, we begged our parents to take us. It was the food, the culture, the people—it was all of it that made us feel whole. Our family was not perfect in so many ways, but there were certainly times when belonging to two different homes was the most privilege I felt. Other times, it was not.

By chance—and only by chance—I was born last in my family. I benefited from the privilege of having U.S. citizenship. I found a job when I was fifteen years old as a server at a local eatery. I needed to provide for myself. I needed money to buy myself clothes. It felt so good when I got my first paycheck. I bought myself some sandals from Walmart, and I wore those sandals with pride. My sister, on the other hand, was forced to rely on others even into early adulthood because of her citizenship status. This is when the contradictions between my sister's and my experiences were the most pronounced for me. It was knowing that I had access to opportunities that she did not that hurt me the most.

I wish I would have had more knowledge, power, and resources to have made a stronger contribution to helping her get her status as a resident, but I was also a kid. As a teenager, I was also learning about myself and my place in an unjust world. I was learning about what it meant to grow up as a Latina girl from the barrio in a white and male-dominated world. I do have regrets. I wish I would have learned quicker, because I would have done more for my sister. The road to citizenship for my sister is something that only she can speak to. I was there for her through it, but it was her experience and hers alone to share in her words.

It was when I left Laredo to move to Austin for college that I stepped outside of my beloved borderlands. I experienced the hate of white supremacy, the xenophobia of classism, and the anger of sexism. It was difficult for me to call my mom and tell her everything that was happening, mostly because I did not want to worry her, but I always wondered if she or my sister would understand what I was going through. It was the loneliest feeling, being physically separated from family, but I knew I was doing this for my future self. I also kept reminding myself that I was also doing this for them: my mother, father, sister, and brothers. My roots, firmly planted in the borderlands, grew branches of knowledge and understanding through the experiences of being away from my home base. I worked a minimum-wage job at a daycare, and I also worked as a nanny to get myself through college. I got good grades in college and kept my eyes on the end goal: I would earn a degree, get a good job, and make money to support myself and at least try to support my mom, too.

Meanwhile, I learned that my sister had started working and was creating a pathway for herself. Looking back, I think about how powerful and determined she was to find her independence. By the time we had both found life partners, citizenship status was no longer the looming cloud over our lives that it had been for us as children. We were both in our twenties and ready to form families of our own. I watched my sister get married and birth a beautiful baby girl. I watched her build a home with her partner and find her career. However, I cannot emphasize enough that the road to where we both are now was riddled with tears, hunger, depression, hurt, and so much more that did not have to be a part of our story.

As grown women, my sister, mother, and I talk about injustices in our world in a way that we could not when we were younger. My mom talks to me about racism, sexism, mental health, and so many topics, that she feels a whole different person to me. Yet again, the woman in my memories is almost always an exhausted, hard-working *ama*. The truth is my sister was also like a second mother to me. When my mother was working, Shamma took care of me. At school, she looked out for me. Shamma was a *madre* to me too. In elementary and middle school, I was shy and nervous, but in those institutions, Shamma created a safe space for me with her presence, despite her precarious citizenship status as being undocumented. *Eso es amor*. That is love. I also see that as an act of resistance. Sisters can practice frontera madre(hood). My mother was always there for us too, but forever tired—too tired from work to be present in the ways that I try to be for my children now. My life without my sister would have been incomplete, and I would have known in my soul, without knowing in my brain, that something was missing.

We are more connected now than ever as women, *mujeres, madres,* and *hijas*. We reminisce about our childhood, growing up marginalized, poor, hungry, wanting more for our lives. We think about all the other dynamics in our household that scarred us for life, because there were many more, but that is a story for another time. For us, it was not just the dualism of growing up Mexican American that singularly affected us, but the dualism of citizenship status also played a role in developing our perspectives on life, on mothering, and on being in the world.

Now, as I raise my own children, I want them to have the perseverance of my mother and sister. I make sure that they understand that even we have a privilege that their own family and blood did not. I also tell my children stories about their *tía* and I as little girls in the colonia. I tell them both the good and the not so good. I tell my children that when Shamma and I were little girls, we didn't have a lot of toys, but there was a lot of *tierra* outside our house, and we played with dirt, rocks, and our *mangera*. I also tell them the stories about how much I loved my sister and that the love between siblings is so powerful, it can make the coldest days in winter just a little bit warmer by having our sister or brother next to us. I want my children to remember that their grandmother is not just a regular mother. She is a Spanish-speaking *fronteriza* warrior, who with all her shortcomings never stopped finding the strength to make sure her kids had food to eat. The advantages my children have, like access to a doctor, were something my sister and I did not. I relay this message to them, because they need to grow up knowing that our world isn't equal for everyone. My sister and I can speak to this from experience, from the inside looking out. As a mother, I carry the great responsibility of raising my two children with the compassion the world forced me to have for others through the exposure of lived injustice. Carlitos and Grace, my children, represent a whole different dualism. I am their buffer from the experiences of my sister and me. I am also their primary source, along with my partner, for what to expect from our world. And this one thing I know—I couldn't be teaching them the life lessons I know without having grown up the way I did and where I did, in a colonia nestled along the Rio Grande with Shamma and the rest of my family.

Final Reflections

Laredo is a borderland that embodies two dominating cultures from its two host countries: the United States and Mexico. While a physical boundary may signify that Laredo is hosted by the United States, its demographic profile and its culture are born from Mexico. It is in this setting that we explore the concept of mixed-status families and what the implications are for sisters and mothers who grow up in these circumstances. Our *testimonios* reflect a dimension of frontera madre-(hood) where *la frontera* is not only an international boundary between our homeland and our new home, but a border that extended into our home, where one sister had U.S. citizenship and the other lived a life in the shadows as undocumented. This extension of the border into our homes shaped several aspects of our lives beyond access to resources, including our relationship to each other, living with the trauma and hardship in seeking citizenship, and how these experiences have formed us as *madres*.

TESTIMONIO

Mothering in a Bicultural Border Context

SANDRA GUTIÉRREZ

Licensed Clinical Social Worker

My name is Sandra Gutiérrez, and I am originally from Aguascalientes, Mexico. I entered the United States legally at the age of twelve years old and understand this as a huge privilege. I am currently in my late thirties and have tried to make sure that the expectations based on gender (female at birth), intricately imposed at a young age through sociocultural norms, do not affect me to the level they could have affected me should I have stayed in my country of origin. I have attempted to avoid the impact of these sociocultural norms through my formal higher education experiences. I cannot say, however, that these gender-based expectations no longer affected me after receiving my formal education. The larger reality is much more complex.

My formal education, though, has been a great tool to help me navigate my reality as a Latina woman, mother, wife, and professional. I currently serve as a licensed clinical social worker in New Mexico and Colorado. Formal education is something I have enjoyed since a very young age. Luckily, learning has come easily to me despite the linguistic challenges I faced at age twelve, when my father decided to uproot our family from central Mexico and transplant us, so to speak, to the state of New Mexico. As an adult, I am now aware that the idea behind that life-altering move (decided by my parents) was for a better future, a parental decision that has yielded both positive and unexpected results. For that,

I am thankful to both of my parents, as I understand I can thrive today because of the sacrifices made many generations before me.

Context Matters

There is something to be said about mothering through a bicultural lens. Living in a dichotomous context matters. Mothers within the border region are unique in the way they make these choices, and in how they experience them. At least this was the case for me. As a mother of two children, a seventeen-year-old and an eight-year-old, the mothering decisions I made at different life stages look very different, mainly because the context was very different when my children were younger. Clearly, both sets of decisions came from a place of love for each child; however, they were experienced during different personal developmental stages and different contextual realities.

The First Mothering Experience

My first mothering stage or experience—and emotionally the most impactful—was when I gave birth to my oldest son while my husband was undocumented and residing out of state. My husband was deported when he stopped to render aid at a car accident. He was asked for his identification by a state trooper, and when he could not produce it, the trooper called the border patrol, and he was apprehended and deported. My spouse's undocumented status colored various experiences I had at that time. This included driving ten-plus hours during a medically considered full-term pregnancy in order to have somewhat of a normal childbirth experience, one in which my husband, father to my son, could be present. The two contrasting mothering realities cannot be negated, as the birth certificates document each birthing site. One reads Aurora, Colorado (oldest son's birthplace), and another reads Las Cruces, New Mexico (youngest son's birthplace).

In the five years following my first son's birth, many other decisions would be made around how to parent our son in a divided and nontraditional manner—divided by geographical location and not by love. My oldest child was raised by a community of uncles, aunts, in-laws, grandparents, and, of course, by both of his parents. The upbringing was not ideal developmentally; I chose to become a mother prior to graduating from college, and while my husband did not possess legal status to reside in the United States, I clearly did not understand the implications of such a decision. I do today.

Despite this reality, we (the familial community) made it happen. My son was showered with love by each and every member that supported us in his care. Most times, he was by either my side or his father's side. But this was not easy or concern-free, as my husband was residing in Ciudad Juárez during a time in which this border city was extremely violent. At times, my son was with both of us, and at one point, he was not with either parent, as one parent was undocumented, and the other parent (me) was pursuing a master's degree in Michigan. How must this have influenced my son's perception of life? That is something we are still finding out to date. In a clinical setting, this type of disruption is classified as an attachment disruption and, at times, classified as attachment trauma. I know this now but did not know at that time. I honestly think or choose to see this as being saved from this information, as God's way to keep me on a journey that would be collectively beneficial.

Culture and Mothering

I must say I learned how to mother way before becoming a mother. Instinctively, I knew becoming a parent was the formal graduation into adulthood, even though many would agree that there is no such graduation. Today, I would disagree with my own past adulthood graduation framework, as mothering does not equate nor is it necessary to navigate adulthood. I would like to think that I embraced the adulthood experience in a somewhat graceful manner. I do not mean to suggest that adult life has been a breeze—it has not. I also do not think I would navigate adulthood in the same manner had my culture been different. Marrying young and mothering in a single-mother-mimicking way had its challenges. Traveling between Las Cruces, New Mexico, and Ciudad Juárez, Chihuahua, to ensure that a father-son bond and a family bond were established was a conscious choice. At that time, it was not perceived as a challenge, aside from it being financially difficult. Sustaining two households, one in the United States and one in Mexico, while being a broke undergraduate student was challenging. At times this required holding two jobs. Being a female doing this defied every cultural paradigm I had learned growing up; so did deciding to pursue a master's degree far from home while my mother helped care for my oldest son for sixteen months—sixteen crucial months in which contact with him consisted of daily phone calls and monthly visits, with the culmination of this long-distance parenting being that my son (who was two and a half years old at that time) and my sister attended my master's graduation at the University of Michigan. This did not happen without them missing the flight and showing up at the airport a day later, but that is another story. They did make it to my graduation, and we drove back to southern New Mexico before the Michigan snow settled.

Time, Quality of Life, and Family

The reality is that time did not stop, despite my spouse's immigration status. I was very aware of that. Thus, the decision to advance my studies at the University of Michigan came from understanding that my parents had made a sacrifice for a better life and my understanding of a better life being higher education. There was no doubt that pursuing the degree was the choice I had to make, given the full tuition offered. There is a level of loyalty that extends beyond words. For me, that was understood as improving the quality of life of the next generation through education. Raising the bar. I was the first from my family to graduate from college, and soon after, my siblings followed. I do not mean to take credit for their accomplishments; I am simply speaking of the order in which this happened—an order that matters when we speak in gender-expectation terms. I was not supposed to attend high school. Yet, here I was graduating from college and aiming at a master's degree in one of the best universities nationwide, even worldwide. I soon learned that parents would save for years to send their kids to this specific school. My parents could not afford to do that. Their joint salary was almost equitable to my U of M yearly tuition. I can only say I was blessed, had the right academic support during high school and college, and definitely had the best mentorship during my undergraduate studies. In other words, I had an academic mother that guided me through projects that I felt passionate about. Most importantly, I had another female believing I could do it and telling me I could. For this, I am forever grateful.

Not "the" Way

Now, I am certain that my introduction to motherhood was not the only way to experience motherhood or adulthood, but it is one way. And this was the way I was afforded to experience it, through a combination of life circumstances, various sources of support, and academic opportunities. I do not regret the decision, yet I know that at thirty-eight years old, I could not make the same choice and leave a young child of mine behind with his grandmother to go pursue a degree away from my child. What changed? I am not certain; I just know that decisions in my early twenties were shaped by the overall context I was living in at the border, with my husband forced to live in Juárez, Mexico, and me living in Southern New Mexico. I did not have a university degree or career at that time, but I do now. The context in which I now live does not permit me to even fathom the thought of being away from my children. Has the decision served my family well? Absolutely! My professional career and success are based on the studies I pursued and completed at U of M. The person I have become is shaped by the hardships I have endured throughout life and the energy channeled into academics—all experiences lived through a gendered filter that cannot be ignored within our culture. It simply cannot be ignored. Especially when one decides to travel far from home and experience a different reality for women as I did, choosing to embrace that reality, regardless of whether that makes sense to others or not.

Mothering Stage Two

Mothering the second time around, meaning birthing and raising my second child, came during a point in my life when financial pressures were not as present. I was already practicing as a clinical social worker, and my husband had been granted permanent resident status (after five years of waiting and many letters written to immigration officials). My husband is now a U.S. citizen and a civil engineer. During this second pregnancy, I was able to leave work close to a month prior to giving birth, as well as stay home for another two months after giving birth, and being paid during that time. I have never been separated from my second son for more than a couple of nights. There have been no border crossings to half live in Ciudad Juárez and half live in Las Cruces. Now, most of our trips to Ciudad Juárez are a way to continue to experience the richness of our culture, our food, and for family events (I now have a nephew who resides there), or to take a flight somewhere.

As I write this, I become even more aware of the night and day mothering experiences I lived through. The young twenty-one-year-old was a fearless mother, determined student, and a highly driven individual. The thirty-year-old mother was still fearless, determined, and highly driven yet made academics and motherhood work in a different manner. I was still able to attend New York University while my husband supported me by staying back home with our youngest son during the weekends of travel for classes. I did not, however, have to go an entire month at a time, for sixteen months, being away from my sons. I have also had many celebrations during this second mothering stage. The first mothering stage was one to sow, and the second mothering experience was one filled with the fruits of hard labor. It is fair to say that the youngest child owes a lot to the oldest son's experiences and unchosen sacrifices.

Coming Full Circle

In closing, I would like to say that experiencing motherhood, academics, and the professional world has allowed me to grow tremendously. I have learned a lot from others. I have shed a little bit of my perfectionistic tendencies, yet I have maintained my thirst for knowledge. I have become incredibly grateful for all experiences, instead of just the good. I have learned the value of ethnic and gender representation. This means I cannot and will not stay quiet in the face of injustices, especially when these involve gender. This also means I must have aged, since I have been honored to sit at the mentoring seat for several Latinas and have learned that what they seem to value the most within the mentorship experience is the humanness relayed through the mentorship dynamic. To all who have crossed my path, I can only say thank you for coinciding, for supporting or challenging my perspective, and for opening doorways I could not have imagined crossing. Today, I know there are many more doorways to cross, many goals to achieve, and a varied way to savor life within the U.S.-Mexico bicultural border context.

CHAPTER 6

Knitting Hope

Conversations with Migrant Women in Tijuana Shelters

MACRINA CÁRDENAS MONTAÑO AND OLGA ODGERS-ORTIZ

Casa del Migrante de Tijuana Volunteer and El Colegio de la Frontera Norte

International migration is perhaps the most disruptive social process of the traditional family.[1] The presence of mothers, fathers, children, and other relatives living under the same roof, under any type of family arrangement, is called into question when one or more of its members emigrate to another country. Family separation affects everyone differently when the absent person is the mother who seeks to cross borders irregularly to reach the desired destination country. Traveling as a family, on the other hand, allows people to maintain unity, but it requires facing many obstacles, defining family projects, and developing joint strategies.

In the process of emigration, mothers carry out their motherhood in various ways. They can be distant mothers when they seek to reach another country to get a job to support their children, whom they leave at home, usually under the care of other women. In other cases, the mothers bring their children with them, facing dangers and vicissitudes along the way. Others travel accompanied by children and their partners, fulfilling the role of mothers and wives while moving. There are also those who exercise motherhood on the move, traveling while pregnant, or even giving birth on the way.

---

1. This chapter was originally written in Spanish and translated by GMR Transcription Services, Inc.

The largest presence of migrant mothers and minors became visible in the cities of Mexico's northern border beginning in 2014, with the emergence of the so-called crisis of unaccompanied minors (Canizales 2015). In 2016, Haitian citizens arrived en masse to Tijuana, leaving mainly from Brazil. In addition to Haitian migrants, the shelter Casa del Migrante in Tijuana reported that from May to August 2016, it received more than a thousand people from the following twenty-seven countries: Armenia, Benin, Brazil, Burkina Faso, Cameroon, Congo, Ivory Coast, Cuba, El Salvador, Eritrea, Ethiopia, Ghana, Guatemala, Guinea, Haiti, Honduras, India, Nicaragua, Nigeria, Pakistan, Romania, Russia, Senegal, Syria, Sudan, Togo, and Ukraine. Most of these migrants arrived in Tijuana to apply for asylum in the United States (Alarcón and Ortiz 2017).

Later, in 2017, caravans of migrants left Central America to make that dangerous journey, protected by accompanying a large number of people (Odgers-Ortiz and Olivas-Hernández 2019). It is estimated that in November 2018, more than six thousand Central American migrants, members of the so-called migrant caravan, arrived in Tijuana. In the surveys carried out in different shelters by El Colegio de la Frontera Norte, it was found that between 75 and 82 percent of the interviewees were born in Honduras, followed by Salvadorans and Guatemalans (Albicker et al. 2021). Less well known is the movement of Mexican citizens from states like Michoacán and Guerrero who have also traveled to cities from the Mexico's northern border in search of humanitarian protection from the U.S. government.

For the people of Tijuana, the passage of migrants through the city was not new; for many decades, the city has received migrants from both directions. What was new for its residents and the social organizations that host them were the large numbers of migrants arriving at the same time, especially through the caravans. As a result, the city's migrant shelters, overstretched, had to redouble their efforts to house all asylum seekers in what turned out to be an uncertain and lengthy wait. These long periods of forced waiting within migration systems can be conceptualized as places where migrants are immobilized, without the possibility of advancing further and without any desire to return to their place of origin (Odgers-Ortiz and Olivas-Hernández 2019).

Periods of migratory entrapment are a challenge for those who move, not only because of the difficulty obtaining shelter and sustenance as foreigners in a foreign land, but also because of the need to carry out countless confusing administrative procedures. In addition, having to wait in precarious conditions for an indefinite amount of time, without any certainty about the outcome of their migratory project, produces an overwhelming emotional drain.

In this chapter, we analyze the experience of motherhood that Central American women experienced in their journey to the United States. To this end, we recorded conversations with mothers from El Salvador, Honduras, and Guatemala that were carried out in a knitting group organized in migrant shelters in Tijuana between January 2019 and March 2020.

Following the initiative of one of the authors of this article, we wanted to put our knowledge of knitting to the service of migrants. The idea of taking this ancestral activity to migrant shelters was that knitting in a group would serve as occupational therapy, to reduce their anguish while waiting for an interview with a U.S. immigration officer, who would decide their final destination. It was also an activity that women could perform while taking care of their children and, in some cases, incorporating them into this activity. Additionally, the workshop would allow them to create some garments to keep children warm, such as hats and scarves, during that cold winter.

Initially, we thought that only women would attend the knitting group, but to our surprise, some sessions also involved adult men and teenagers. Some came to learn how to knit, and others to apply the knowledge they had already acquired from their mothers or grandmothers.

Contrary to the perception of knitting as a passive and static activity, there was a great dynamism within the group of weavers; the time dedicated to knitting was used by members to exchange information about migratory experiences, motherhood, destinations in the United States, and plans for the future. In the same way, it was a space to express and settle some problems of coexistence within the shelters. Some issues, such as health conditions or future plans, were recurrent, so over several weeks we could see how they were being resolved.

The narratives we use in this chapter come from our direct participation in the knitting group. Therefore, the titles of each section are metaphorically related to this ancestral activity and describe the experiences of the mothers who participated in the knitting group.[2]

Alma's Blanket

At the beginning of the knitting session, we had Daniela, a five- or six-year-old girl, with big black eyes that shine with intelligence and curiosity. She asked if she could make a pompom with the other children from the shelter. While rolling up a deep pink yarn, she told us in great detail about the journey from El Salvador to Tijuana in the company of her father and her mother, who was traveling while pregnant. After Daniela came, Alma, the mother, appeared, still showing visible signs of fatigue from traveling with the second caravan. This caravan covered more than 2,500 miles between Tijuana and El Sonsonate, El Salvador, Alma's place of origin.

Alma was in her fourth month of pregnancy, and she decided to join the workshop to knit a blanket for the baby on the way. To make her garment, she opted for a cream color because, given the uncertainty of the sex of her baby, she preferred to leave the options open. Then, she told us, once the ultrasound shows whether the baby is a boy or a girl, she will adorn her blanket with blue or pink and purple ribbons. In the early knitting sessions, uncertainty is indeed what best seemed to describe Alma's experience.

She and her husband, Oscar, had decided to try their luck with the second caravan, given the lack of opportunities in El Salvador. The north was calling them powerfully because Alma's sister had migrated a few years earlier to marry and settle in California. Oscar had already had the experience emigrating and working in the United States. That was before he returned to El Salvador, met Alma, and married her.

As with so many other families, the passage of the caravan was seen as a call, as an opportunity that would not be repeated. So, far from carefully planning the trip, they decided to take the opportunity and leave at that moment. But once in Tijuana, and arriving at the U.S. border, things did not go so well. In November 2018, with the arrival of the first large caravan from Central America, the U.S. government imposed a drop-on

---

2. Pseudonyms are used for each person described within these narratives.

entry system for asylum seekers, so that those arriving at the border had to register on an informal list and wait their turn for months before being called to present their case (Odgers-Ortiz and Olivas-Hernández 2019).[3] This situation would be aggravated with the establishment of the Migrant Protection Protocols (MPP) in 2019, forcing asylum seekers to remain in Mexico throughout the process of resolving their case, while able to cross the border only to attend their appointments before an immigration officer. The uncertainty of the wait, and of what would happen once having crossed, generated a feeling of anxiety palpable in all the shelter's residents.

As Alma knitted, she heard the other women say, "To apply for asylum, you need to have proof."

"What proof?" Alma asked the others.

"Proof that the government is persecuting you . . . proof that the *maras* are looking for you . . . proof that you have a serious health problem," they replied. Alma continued weaving, and she felt she could only prove that she missed her sister in California, and that she would like to give her children a better future.

While knitting they also talked about the alternative of crossing the border clandestinely. Listening to her knitting partners, Alma thought, *Tomorrow I could be on the other side.* But she also listened to what was being said about apprehensions at the border, the separation of families in detention, and the children whom the Trump administration took away from their parents without anyone knowing how to reunite them (Edyburn and Meek 2021).

Alma knitted but then unwove, because the stitches did not come out even and she wanted her blanket to be perfect for her baby. She went back to knitting and unknitting because the fabric was too tight, and she wanted a soft smooth blanket. As she wove, Alma thought about her

---

3. We argue the idea of drop-on entry, which better reflects the situation of migrants waiting for asylum on the Mexican side of the border. Metering is an informal system, a list for people requesting asylum as they wait their summons to enter the United States to see an immigration judge. Metering suggests an organized and functional system that allows for an orderly flow, while drop-on entry, the term we prefer, better reflects the idea of containment, like a drip system, where trickles of people are allowed to enter the United States to seek asylum.

past, her present, her future, sometimes out loud. She wanted to see her sister, she wanted to have a job, she wanted to have a safe place to give birth to the baby who was increasingly moving in her womb and would not wait for the interview deadlines. She wanted a school for Daniela, who had quickly befriended all the children in the shelter but spent too much time glued to the phone screen. Sometimes, Alma wove silently, self-absorbed, concentrating on one stitch, and the next, and the next. One stitch at a time.

Finally, one day she welcomed us with a radiant smile. She told us that everything was decided. They were not going to cross over. Her husband had found work in Tijuana, and she had the promise of an activist midwife to deliver her baby at no cost in a small newly built clinic. Giving birth to her baby in Tijuana would allow the family to regularize migration in Mexico. Legally settling in this city was Alma's new project. She started saving up so she could furnish the small house her husband had found for rent and knitted now without mistakes or setbacks. A new ultrasound revealed a girl on the way, so Alma adorned her newly finished blanket with large pink, lilac, and purple ribbons. She was ready to receive her baby and settle in Tijuana.

A Hat for Nadia

At sixteen years old, Karla was one of the youngest mothers in our knitting group. She arrived from Honduras to seek asylum in the United States with her young partner and their seven-month-old daughter, Nadia. Since she said she did not know how to knit, we suggested she start with a small project. Our experience taught us that weavers get more excited about knitting when they see their finished garment. Karla chose to knit a hat for her daughter. When she arrived at the group with her little girl, we took turns taking care of her while she struggled with the hook to achieve the stitch required for her hat. Sometimes, when Jonatan, her partner, arrived early from work, he would join the group. They both took turns taking care of their little girl and knitting.

For Karla, traveling from Honduras to Tijuana with a baby in her arms was exhausting. She faced many dangers. In addition to the abuses of authorities, there were people who preyed on migrants passing through

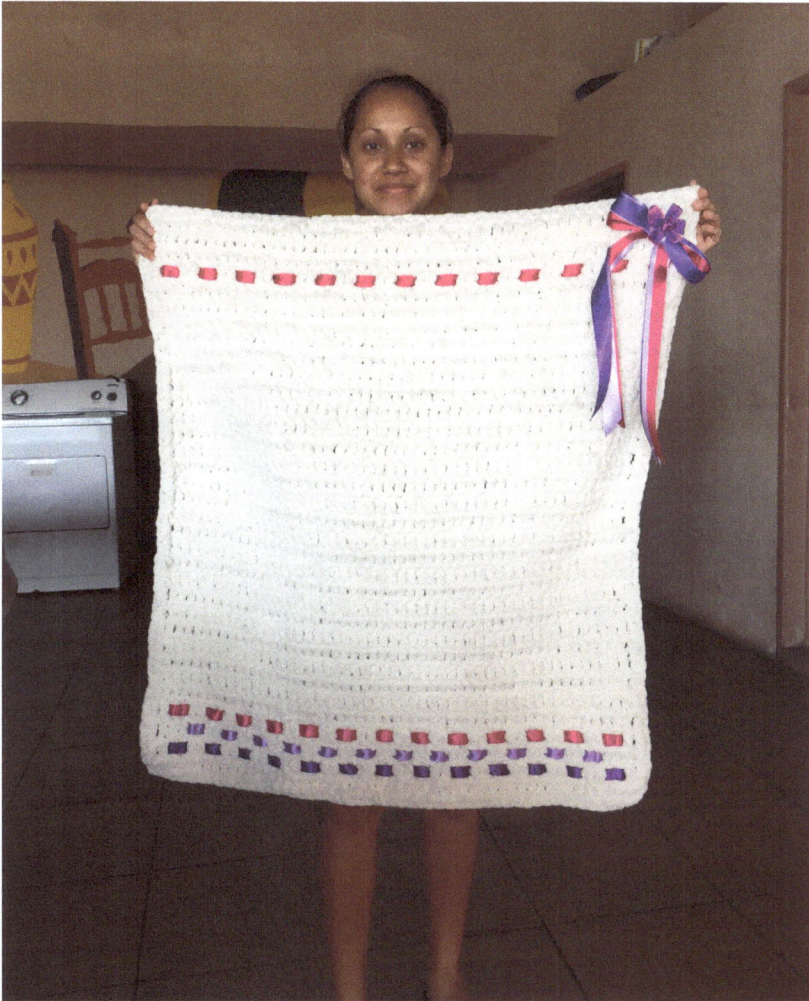

FIGURE 6.1 Alma with the blanket she knitted for her new baby while at a migrant shelter. Photo by Olga Odgers-Ortiz.

Mexico. However, they also received solidarity from many people inside and outside the shelters they encountered along the way. The exercise of her motherhood was facilitated on the trip because Jonatan already knew the way and knew how to travel through safer places, since he had done this journey before. The practice of breastfeeding helped protect the little girl from many diseases, considering the conditions in which they traveled, especially during that long bus ride between Guadalajara and Tijuana that for Karla seemed eternal.

The knitting group was a space conducive to untangling the threads of life. In her short life, Karla had experienced different types of migration. As a daughter, she had a relationship with her mother from a distance; she had been under the care of her paternal grandmother from a very young age, when her parents decided to emigrate to the United States. As a mother, she became an undocumented migrant when she crossed the border into Mexico, then became an asylum seeker at the Tijuana border with San Diego. Jonatan had crossed before but had been deported. Being a partner of an experienced migrant placed her in a different position from those who, for the first time, cross into the world of transnational mobility. Thus, Karla was an undocumented migrant in Mexico, an asylum seeker in the United States, the daughter of migrants, and the partner of a deported migrant.

In the first sessions of knitting, while learning the first stitches and initiating the hat for Nadia, Karla narrated her project to cross the border with her partner and her baby to request asylum in the United States. During these conversations, they eventually discovered difficulties that they had not contemplated. One of them, which was hardly alluded to, was the legal position in which Jonatan would find himself in, since he was already of age and in a relationship with a minor. The other, which was constantly talked about, was the requirement of being included on a long list and then waiting for an opportunity to apply for asylum. Turns were given through a number granted by Beta Group officers at the entrance to the United States. These officers belong to the Mexican National Institute of Migration. The wait time was indefinite and could be extended for weeks or months. Within the knitting group, it was said that there was no order, since those who controlled the list sold a spot in line for a thousand dollars. It was rumored that it was "a lady" who brought the notebook with the list, or that it was the Beta Group itself who sold the places. In any case, an amount was given that Karla and her family could not afford.

When the pale pink hat was halfway done, Karla tried it on Nadia and found that it was too narrow. First, she tried to pull it a little to make it bigger and fit her head, but after a couple of attempts, she decided to unweave and start all over with a cap of a larger size.

Within weeks, Karla told us that they had found a way for her family to go to the United States to apply for asylum. This would be possible, according to the lawyer they had consulted, if they crossed separately. Karla would cross alone and apply as an unaccompanied minor. Little Nadia and her father, Jonatan, would cross through another border town to make their request. They believed that Jonatan, despite having been deported before, could cross if he took little Nadia with him. It was decided that Jonatan and Nadia would apply first, and if they were admitted, Karla would do so later. If for some reason one of the parties was rejected, the agreement was that everyone would return to Honduras.

The shelter where they stayed offered a series of recreational and cultural activities for the children while they waited for their appointment date, such as English classes, drawing, visits to museums, and outings to the cinema. Unlike other mothers, however, Karla's experience of motherhood was more difficult because of Nadia's young age; she could not participate in any of these activities.

One day we arrived at the knitting class, and Karla told us with great sadness that Jonatan and Nadia had left to try to apply for asylum. She was very depressed and felt sick, because by abruptly stopping the breastfeeding, the milk had accumulated in her breasts, causing a fever and immense discomfort. She sat in a chair and wondered, *For whom am I going to knit now?* The hat had been completed just in time, and Nadia had taken it with her.

The weavers comforted her and advised her on how to ease the discomfort in her breasts. They encouraged her to keep knitting so that she would be distracted. She slowly smiled and asked for yarn to start knitting a hat for the baby of one of her companions who was pregnant. She said, "I'm going to knit this hat for your baby because I hold you in high esteem for everything we've been through together." Thus, Karla, at her young age, while knitting strengthened ties with the other mothers, who, in the shelter, understood the need to support and stay together.

The hat was left unfinished. When we arrived at the next knitting session, her companions gave us the good news that Karla had been notified that Nadia and Jonatan had been admitted as asylum seekers; Karla immediately crossed the border. The last we heard was that Karla was in one of the juvenile detention centers in Texas, waiting for her father, who was a permanent resident in the United States, to come and pick her up.

"The Knit Got Screwed"

Julia had arrived at the shelter weeks ago, accompanied by her husband and their two children, Laura and José. Also traveling with them was their brother-in-law Lorenzo, sister-in-law Yamileth, and their three children. Traveling as a family had brought them some advantages on the long journey with the caravan from Guatemala to Tijuana. But upon arriving at the border, being part of a large group was also an inconvenience. Due to the high number of migrants who came in the caravan, the shelters were overcrowded, and it was difficult to find a place that could accommodate them all. They did not want to be separated, so they had to go through several shelters until they found one that welcomed them all.

Once settled, both families began the waiting period after being registered on the list to apply for asylum. For Julia and her family, as for the rest of the migrants waiting, it was frustrating not to have an understanding of how the list worked.

Julia and Yamileth joined the knitting group with the intention of making hats for the children. While knitting, the children ran, played, and talked endlessly—all except Laura, who despite having already turned seven, still did not speak and had difficulty relating to other children. She stood close to the knitting table, sometimes hiding under it, shyly watching as Julia and Yamileth knitted.

While knitting, Julia recounted the difficulties her family had gone through on their journey from Guatemala to Tijuana in one of the caravans to escape the violence in their country. Like other families, violence and poverty had motivated their departure. But the main reason for their departure was their daughter, Laura. For Julia, the American dream meant getting medical treatment for her daughter. When Laura was a few months old, she was diagnosed with a rare neurological problem. As she grew older, that diagnosis was brought up every time Julia went to see the doctors about her daughter's hearing problems, language difficulties, and learning problems in general. As much as Julia sought treatment in Guatemala, the diagnosis remained ambiguous, and Laura's progress was limited. Julia was convinced that Laura's condition was treatable, but not in Guatemala. Therefore, the hope that her daughter could have medical care and a better life in the United States was the main motivation to overcome her difficulties.

Traveling in a large group allowed Julia's family to develop solidarity strategies in their journey. The lack of economic resources, their limited schooling, and the absence of social networks along the way, however, led them to face numerous adversities, turning their trip into a true *via crucis*. This story evoked in us the images that John Steinbeck (1939) captured in *The Grapes of Wrath*. In this famous novel, Joad and his relatives, who are poor farmers, leave Oklahoma to try desperately to reach California, where they are promised that their lives will improve.

Knitting, Julia told us, released the tension caused by living in an environment with such little privacy. She complained that not all parents in the shelter took care of their children, and there was a lot of friction because of this. Sometimes children fought with one another, and the parents, as Julia explained, always tended to blame each other's children. She was also uncomfortable that she perceived preferences in the treatment of some of the residents of the shelter. She thought the manager, who was of a different nationality from her own, distributed food and donations favoring her fellow citizens. "This makes me so angry," she said, "but knitting reassures me, because when I see the injustices against us, I knit even faster."

One day, in the knitting group, we were undoing a hat because Julia had made a mistake. The boys and girls were grouped around the table, watching carefully as we pulled the thread again and again, trying to find the mistake to redo the knit. One of Julia's nephews, watching closely as the yarn came and went, suddenly asked, "Why are you unweaving?" When there was no response, he hastened to say, "I know, it had to be unknit when the fabric got screwed." And everyone laughed.

The situation for Julia's family became more complicated. In the shelter, coexistence was increasingly more difficult, and news of an appointment for the interview would not come. Julia and Yamileth's husbands could not find jobs that would allow them to rent an apartment and leave the shelter, and the women could not work because they had to take care of their children. One of the international organizations that arrived at the border city to support humanitarian tasks offered to help them return to Guatemala. Although they had not thought about that option, they began to consider the offer, but Julia was getting the chills just thinking about having to do the same long journey again, but this time without a dream.

One day we arrived at the shelter to find Julia and her family gone. They had left—not to the United States, but back to Guatemala. Her daughter was left without the medical treatment Julia had hoped to get in the United States. In the same way that the clever seven-year-old boy had watched the knit come apart, this knit—seeking asylum—also got screwed. Julia and her family members decided to repeat the path, disappointed. Perhaps in the near future, they will decide to knit their dream again.

Final Thoughts

The mothers of the knitting group who joined the caravan of migrants bound for the United States and arriving in Tijuana began their motherhood in movement when they decided to leave their countries in Central America. While holding their children's hands, these women crossed not only the borders that defined the territories of nation-states, but also the borders that unfold within national territories, designed to impede their mobility. In the passage of the migrant caravan through Mexico, these internal borders began to play out among other actors, such as the federal army, the National Institute of Migration, the then so-called federal police, and the state and municipal police.

These internal borders were also disguised as government programs to discourage migrants from entering Mexico in the direction of the northern border. In October 2018, during the presidency of Enrique Peña Nieto, the *Estás en tu casa* (You are home) program was implemented, which consisted of offering to regularize the migratory status of caravan members, through a visitor card for humanitarian reasons, which provided work permits and access to medical services and education. The "only" condition was that this "benefit" would be granted to migrants if they stayed in the states of Chiapas or Oaxaca (Frank-Vitale and Núñez-Chaim 2020). This measure clearly shows the pressure of the U.S. government on Mexico to prevent the arrival of Central American and other migrants to the southern border of the United States. It is absurd to ask regularized migrants to remain in regions of greater marginalization, higher unemployment, and worse conditions concerning access to health and education.

The experiences of Alma, Nadia, and Julia, as well as of all those mothers who raise their children in this context of multiple geographical, social, economic, and cultural borders, lie at the intersection of gender, race, class, and migratory status (Bejarano and Morales, this volume). The mothers who participated in our knitting group joined the migrant caravan because it was the only way, as women, to travel with some degree of safety. In the past, some of the women who passed through the migration corridor between Central America and the border to the United States prepared themselves with contraceptives in the face of the threat of being assaulted.

A census conducted by the Municipality of Suchiate, Chiapas, shows that the relative security offered by the caravan explains the high number of women with children who traveled within it. The census was taken in October 2018, just after migrants crossed the Guatemala-Mexico border. The count of migrants participating in the caravan came to 7,237 people, of which 36 percent were adult men and 31 percent adult women. Of the remainder, 18 percent were boys and 15 percent were girls. The antecedent that the mothers had in mind when joining the caravan occurred in 2011, when other Central American mothers decided to travel by caravan to Mexico to look for their children, who had disappeared on the long journey to the United States (Frank-Vitale and Núñez-Chain 2020). This way of traveling gave them some sense of security; they were protected by members of human rights organizations, who accompanied them when crossing dangerous territory dominated by criminal organizations.

The borders created by belonging to different socioeconomic statuses and by different access to social networks also played an important role in differentiating the participants in the caravans. Not all members of the caravans remained cohesive along the way. Those who had more economic resources and social support left the group in some sections of the road. Some were able to buy false visitor cards for humanitarian reasons from government officials, who greatly facilitated transit through Mexican territory in a safer way. Some migrants were even able to travel by plane. The poorest migrants, however, as was the case with Julia's family, had no choice but to walk the entire journey with the caravanners.

But for the migrant mothers who participated in the knitting group, even more than the journey itself, the real obstacle to overcome was migratory entrapment in Tijuana. This migratory entrapment was expressed in the uncertainty of waiting, the lack of clarity in immigration procedures, and the precarious conditions they had to endure for a certain time. Each change in the procedures to request asylum in the United States required these families to rethink a new migratory plan and a new life project. Thus, the migrant mothers who participated in our knitting group collectively developed the ability to unknit and reknit dreams.

REFERENCES

Alarcón Acosta, Rafael, and Cecilia Ortiz Esquivel. 2017. "Los haitianos solicitantes de asilo a Estados Unidos en su paso por Tijuana." *Frontera Norte* 29 (58): 171–79. https://doi.org/10.17428/rfn.v29i58.949.

Albicker, Sandra, Ietza Bojórquez, Oscar F. Contreras, Marie-Laure Coubés, Alberto Hernández, Rafael Alonso Hernández, Dolores París, Gabriel H. Pérez, Olivia Ruíz, and Laura Velasco. 2021. "La caravana de migrantes centroamericanos en Tijuana 2018–2019 (Segunda etapa)." *Documento de Coyuntura Colef* (blog), March 25, 2021. https://www.colef.mx/estudiosdeelcolef/la-caravana-de-migrantes-centroamericanos-en-tijuana-2018-2019-segunda-etapa/.

Canizales, Stephanie L. 2015. "Unaccompanied Migrant Children: A Humanitarian Crisis at the U.S. Border and Beyond." *Policy Brief: Center for Poverty Research* 3 (4). https://poverty.ucdavis.edu/sites/main/files/file-attachments/canizales_migrant_youth_brief.pdf.

Edyburn, Kelly L., and Shantel Meek. 2021. "Seeking Safety and Humanity in the Harshest Immigration Climate in a Generation: A Review of the Literature on the Effects of Separation and Detention on Migrant and Asylum-Seeking Children and Families in the United States During the Trump Administration." *Social Policy Report* 34 (1): 1–46. https://doi.org/10.1002/sop2.12.

Frank-Vitale, Amelia, and Margarita Núñez-Chaim. 2020. "'Lady Frijoles': Las Caravanas centroamericanas y el poder de la hípervisibilidad de la migración indocumentada." *Entre Diversidades* 7 (1): 37–61. https://doi.org/10.31644/ED.V7.N1.2020.A02.

Odgers-Ortiz, Olga, and Olga Olivas-Hernández. 2019. "Les 'caravanes de migrants': Figées dans la mobilité." *La Lettre de l'IHEAL-CREDA*, no. 27 (March).

Steinbeck, John. 1939. *The Grapes of Wrath*. New York: Viking.

TESTIMONIO

My Motherhood *Testimonio* in the Service and Defense of Children and Youth at the Border

LETICIA LÓPEZ MANZANO

Social Worker and Former Director of the Casa de Menores Migrantes

My name is Lety López, and I worked in Casa de Menores Migrantes (CDMM) for twenty-two years.[1] I am mom to Marisol, who, from her birth until she was eighteen years old, accompanied me in all my activities at the shelter. In this way, together, we learned to love migrants, and we realized the lack of love, justice, and respect that existed for their human rights as people. We are both originally from Ciudad Juárez, Chihuahua, Mexico.

Marisol was always the little sister of migrant children at the shelter that I directed. My daughter grew up in the shelter and always engaged with children and young people. She knew the suffering of migrants; she was a very committed volunteer, and now she is a defender of the human rights of migrants. Thank you to my daughter, Marisol, for all your support that you gave me and for being in solidarity with the people who have less. I have always said, "La palabra educa pero el ejemplo arrastra" (The word educates but the example drags on),[2] a Mexican saying that holds great truth.

---

1. This chapter was originally written in Spanish and translated by GMR Transcription Services, Inc. The footnotes were added by the editors for clarification.

2. This saying's literal translation reflects the idea of "lead by example and not by words."

Without a doubt, my daughter, Marisol, has been an engine and support, to help contain so many stories of pain that we live through with migrant children and young people. In my role as a mother, I feel that for Marisol it was very easy to adapt to the situation of each of the children, especially during one of the essential parts of their care, which was when they were fed at the shelter. Regardless of whether we/they were from different cities and countries with different cultures, we all felt like family. The daily coexistence that Marisol had with children and adolescents helped her to form a bond of love and respect. The availability and acceptance of both my daughter and my immediate boss, in allowing me to have Marisol in my work area, eased and allowed me to continue developing in this area [migrant advocacy] by supporting the strong migration problem, where *niñas, niños y adolescentes* (NNAs) were the protagonists, many of whom traveled alone without the company of relatives or only traveled with their traffickers. This paved the way for us to continue learning [about migration] by researching, forming networks, and proclaiming respect for human rights, and for NNAs to know that we are always willing to guide them, support them, and defend them.

I remember that the children would call me Lety, their social mom, teacher, director, and fortune teller because when interviewing them, in some cases, they did not want to talk.[3] I would look at the palm of their hands, and if they were a yellowish color, it made me think that they had been in very closed spaces where they did not get sun, and they told me, "You are a fortune teller; I was locked up for a long time." Some of the young people were locked up for long periods of time in the places where the smugglers took them to move them from one place to another like homes [stash houses] and hotels. They were places where they could not even [be seen by anyone] for any reason, so that they would not be discovered [rescued].

Being a mother at the border has been difficult because of all the large-scale violence that we experienced throughout the city, where children were limited to even freely going outside, and [the reality] that a mother does not have the certainty that her children will be okay. Children living in shelters, including unaccompanied migrant children, gave me the

---

3. The NNAs would call Lety "social mom" as a reference to her being a social worker.

strength and hope to face these challenges and to improve the mechanisms of attention for [migrant] NNAs with dignity during these twenty-two years of my service.

The Arrival

I came knocking on the door of Casa de Menores Migrantes on January 12, 1996, and I was greeted by the director, named Dr. Abel Lerma Talamante, founder of Casa de Menores Migrantes in Ciudad Juárez. Upon entering the house, I took a look around, and I saw an old house in poor condition. It was gloomy with very little office furniture, just a large antique desk and a small typewriter, a ruler, pencils, and pens, and that was everything.

But something that was very important and gratifying was the dialogue we had between Mr. Abel Lerma Talamantes and me. He was very gracious, giving me all the trust and recommendations about the work and the mission for what I was being hired for as a social worker. I would be working with the children and adolescents who were crossing the border of Juárez–El Paso, Texas, and would work to address the problem of migration. At that time, I accepted the challenge to take care of the integrity and human rights of the NNAs, and to grab the bull by the horns and join the work of the corresponding authorities responsible for their care. My position also required me to begin forming networks and to look for other organizations related to the work that needed to begin, with the purpose of together responding to this sensitive problem concerning migration.

The first thing I had to do was to help transform that old farm into a beautiful and cozy house, where the shelter and services offered would be more like what a home could offer. A couple was hired that would be the host family. The main intention was that when the NNA arrived, they really felt at home, since the boys, girls, and adolescents that arrived had been interviewed by authorities who were so cold to them. Authorities often did not detect that the minors came beaten, wet, hungry, anguished, and very scared. It was at this moment that I felt compelled to be part of their [migrant children] family and to be like a mother to them.

I would start each day not knowing what time I would return to my house; sometimes I would have twelve- to sixteen-hour days. I had very emotionally heavy work days due to the stories I heard. Some were very terrifying and sad, while there were other stories where they transmitted their bravery, courage, and anger that they felt. To me, it did not matter [why they were there]. You fall in love with your work for them, and you leave your grain of sand to improve the situation that migrants and their families live through. These moments lasted twenty-two years, where I personally interviewed and tended to thousands of children with a team of people and volunteers. I had to learn the history of—and everything related to—migration, especially as it related to children and adolescents.

In the 1990s, the socioeconomic and demographic dynamics [affecting] global, regional, national, and local dimensions had a profound impact on human development for large populations. These issues manifested into macro-social phenomena related to migration, such as poverty, family disintegration, transculturation, unemployment, and other issues. These in turn led children, young people, and families to increasingly migrate from their place of origin in search of better alternatives in another country, or to reunite with their families in the [United States]. This created "sending" and "receiving" countries, as in the case of Mexico and the [United States], causing serious and irreversible consequences, specifically as they affected children.

At the beginning of the twenty-first century, like other nations of the world, Mexico was in one of the most determining periods of its history as it dealt with youth migration. At the time, there were 100 million people living there. Prior to this, the nineties brought moments of consternation and economic difficulties that were complicated by the effects caused by the massive migration of families attempting to make it to the [United States]. The population that most drew attention on both sides of the border, however, was the . . . young Mexicans [increasingly] willing to risk their lives to try to cross the border. These young people, mostly vulnerable teenagers, left their homes in search of possible solutions to the serious problems they and their families faced. At the shelter, we were also faced with the fact that the very authorities that were responsible for resolving and watching over the NNAs did not have shelters, guidelines, or protocols; and even if they did, they did not carry them out. We wondered how to start to face this issue as a civil society organization (CSO). It was a problem that hurt us a lot, so we fought for unaccompanied migrant children, even those who attempted to cross to the [United States] and who lost their lives.

Open Doors

At that time, from 1996 to 2000, the house had an open-door policy and was in a very strategic place, where young people arrived in two ways. They were either referred through the National Institute of Migration or other authorities, or they arrived alone. There were 9,600 minors interviewed by me, my co-workers, and a volunteer team. We received migrants of all ages from infants in their mothers' arms to young people between twelve and seventeen years of age, twenty-four hours a day. If they arrived during the day, they were interviewed to verify their data and to know the emotional situation in which they arrived. If they were referred to us at night, they were left to rest. They were only asked if they felt in bad health, since there were several cases where the children were asthmatic or were allergic to something or to food. If any type of illness was detected, they were immediately taken to receive medical attention and to ensure a good state of health before reintegrating with the family. If any abuse was detected, the procedure was carried out by the Office of the Attorney for the Defense of Children and the Family, currently the Office of the Attorney for the Care of Boys, Girls, and Adolescents of Bravos Chihuahua District. As you can see, each administration changes its name per the attorney general's office, but the attention placed on children has not changed much. They [the government] continue to have too many deficiencies, and the attention [on most] unaccompanied minors continues to [come from] CSOs and the churches.

At that time, there was no follow-up by any authority or mechanism to know how many minors were received, what their places of origin were or their ages, or what projects existed to serve them so they would not try to cross again. Each minor who was received was offered company, food, lodging, clothing, and telephone calls to any part of the Mexican republic or anywhere in the world. The CDMM was an open door, where no minor was allowed to remain by force. They were granted our services if they agreed to them, and during the first four years of the CDMM's existence, we never had a minor flee from our house. Most of the time before interviewing them, they were immediately offered food. They were always hungry, but in the house, there was always food prepared. When the children talked to their family, this helped the child and the young person to feel safe emotionally. Young people could go out to nearby places such as the Monumento [Benito Juárez monument, a public park], the Plaza de Armas [downtown square], the city center, or they would go in search of their traffickers or friends, or some NNAs were just looking for work each day. These young people could leave the shelter and come back. Our task was to respect their human rights and the decisions they and their families made for them to migrate.

At that time, migrant youth were leaving from the states of Zacatecas, Durango, Chihuahua, and Veracruz, and little by little, each state of the republic was included. Therefore, it was necessary to work more and to join efforts with the authorities and networks that could work hand-in-hand with CDMM to improve actions and to establish mechanisms to protect the integrity of migrants. We managed to coordinate with the following government institutions, civil society organizations, universities, health institutions, and the private sector.

Coordination for Monitoring Migrant NNAs
Type of relationship by services

Civil sector
- General Consulate with El Paso, Texas: Legal advice, coordination in reference to migrant minors, and sometimes economic support for the transfer of minors to their places of origin.
- Attorney General's Office for the Defense of Children and the Family: Legal advice support and referral of minors.

Government sector
- National Institute of Migration: Legal advice, coordination, and referral of minors.
- Municipal System for the Integral Development of the Family (DIF): Support as an official institution of the municipality, referral of migrant minors, and medical care, at times.

- State Human Rights Commission: Legal advice on events that happen to [NNAs] and violations of their human rights by the same authorities.
- Central Bus Station of Juárez: Coordination with the company for the discount of passages for migrant minors.

Education sector
- Autonomous University of Ciudad Juárez (UACJ): Social service providers, research, and health fairs.
- University of Texas at El Paso (UTEP): Social service providers and professional practices.

Private sector
- Casa del Migrante: Formed a network to coordinate migratory awareness activities and referred cases.
- Youth Integration Center: Medical and psychological support for minor drug users, working in coordination with preventive programs in the community.
- Shelter Desk: Referring cases according to the situation.

Service vs. Commitment

Although government institutions are mentioned in this list, none offered a place where migrants could rest, spend the night, and locate their family. The attention [paid to] minors by authorities during these first four years was in providing referrals to migrant minors. They were government institutions that kept statistics, which always varied from one government institution to another. There were no care protocols, or at least we never knew of them. During this time, the CDMM typically did the decision making for minors and the situations they were in.

The press also played a very important role, which made competent authorities react and reflect [to the situation of migrants] when migration statistics were offered by an association such as the CDMM, and not by authorities or by the state or municipality where this migration problem existed. In 2001, a new form of care began. We could see the light at the end of the tunnel when an Advisory Council on Migration was established to address migration, and guidelines were offered. The

CDMM formed part of the council, mainly as it related to unaccompanied children.

In its first five years of work, the CCDM managed to take charge of Ciudad Juárez and bear fruits to this community with the following achievements. We became a member of the Inter-Institutional Advisory Council of the INM [National Migration Institute] for the protection of unaccompanied migrant minors. We gave the CDMM's certification to the city for having met the requirements for an official recognition relating to Article 12 of the regulations for the operation of shelters for minors according to the municipality of Ciudad Juárez, Chihuahua. Also, on February 18, 2000, the first four foot races were held to begin the activities on par with the community's youth activities and our coordination with the Youth Integration Center for preventive programs in the community. We carried these out during periods of school visits in the community. We also coordinated internship programs with the Autonomous University of Ciudad Juárez (UACJ) and the University of Texas at El Paso (UTEP) in the Praxis and Community Partnerships programs. We also collaborated in forums, conferences, and prevention campaigns concerning the human rights of children.

[Despite all these accomplishments], these children continue to be at permanent risk of being forced to commit crimes that can lead to their death. Violence followed this vulnerable group very closely. Unaccompanied migrant minors' human rights were constantly violated. It is important to know and reflect on how this violence arises and is generated. Its roots are in authoritarian and vertical cultural systems that are reproduced in all kinds of institutions, such as the family, with partners, and in companies. Today, it manifests from adults to children, from men to women, from the powerful to the weak, and most of the time, it is exercised against those who are socially considered more vulnerable, such as the elderly, children, people with disabilities, and migrants.

This panorama not only contradicts and overwhelms systems in place, but also deeply questions the approach and philosophical vision of government agencies and institutions, who are responsible for seeking and creating mechanisms, strategies, and actions that consistently address this problem, as defined by international and national organizations. Sometimes, addressing these problems is not clearly articulated, while other times it is completely ignored, as we experienced in the first four years (1996–2000) of CDMM, where we began to provide care for repatriated or unaccompanied migrant children.

Closed Doors

During what I call the second stage of the CDMM, we continue to consistently work together with others, looking out for the welfare of children, and joining authorities in meetings, in training, and in searching for volunteers and networks. When my daughter said to me, "Mom, I love migrants," I always knew [then] that I was doing my job well with these children. My daughter, Marisol, and God were my compass, my engine, my star. Although at times everything went wrong, they continued to illuminate my life and my path, and gave me strength to continue rowing against the strong and murky waters I experienced.

As time passed, a wave of violence in our community began and forced the CDMM to rethink how to continue working. Because of guidelines issued by the Office of the Attorney for the Defense of Children and the Family, our shelter was closed [during] the wave of violence that occurred between 2008 and 2012. As Juarenses, we lived through this violence, where our families were broken apart, where our children were orphaned, and we had a graveyard in the streets of our beloved Juárez of men, women, and families. This violence taught us to work differently, so we had to work with the entire population and not just with migrant children. At that time, children were referred to us by the attorney general's office, and they were placed under our care at the CDMM. They were the only authority that could allow migrant minors to leave our shelter.

At the time, we had a heavier and more frustrating and very exhausting workload. The children waited extremely long periods of time due to the very bureaucratic and slow processes of the authority, but no mother abandoned her children even though they were far away—even if they were back in their place of origin or were already in the [United States]. They always looked for a way to be aware of their children's whereabouts and communicate with them by telephone. Families sold their plots of land or their animals for what was needed [for their child migrants], until they were left with nothing. If they had other children, they could not accompany [their older children] because they could not separate themselves from the smallest children. When they came as a family, the parents were also victims of the traffickers who robbed them, and if they traveled alone, then the girls and mothers were victims of harassment from the traffickers. The whole family suffered. If children were held by traffickers behind closed doors, the children escaped in many ways and put themselves in even more danger. These urgent problems had to be addressed.

I always recommended to authorities that unaccompanied migrant children had to be separated according to their profile, since some of these young people were already involved with traffickers. It was necessary that they . . . receive another type of care and more support and work with their families. Some of the local children worked as circuit children, who lived in the city.[4] There were also those who were from outside of the area, who came from other Mexican states including Central American children. Once these children realized that they were cut off from their freedom, they felt imprisoned, and many of them managed to escape the shelter. These were difficult times. Authorities were overwhelmed by this situation, since young people from nearby areas such as Puerto Anapra, adjacent to the border with El Paso, Texas, and Sunland Park, New Mexico, began working with traffickers by crossing people and drugs.[5]

At that time, I worked with Gilberto Solís, one of the most outstanding professionals who had an extensive career working on this subject. He initiated the program Rescue of Circuit Minors and worked with and for migrants for many years. I worked with him to safeguard the human rights of unaccompanied migrant children and youth. This kind of interinstitutional coordination required the joint participation of individuals, groups, associations, and institutions through the establishment of agreements that would make it possible to join, complement, and develop programs to optimize resources and to multiply our actions. In this regard, consultations were established at the local level with the health and education sectors, municipal and state governments, social and private labor sectors, as well as nongovernmental and decentralized

---

4. Circuit children are border children who are involved in the trafficking business on both sides of the U.S.-Mexico border, a common practice for young people to earn money illicitly.

5. Puerto Anapra is a northern region of Ciudad Juárez.

organizations. For example, the Centro de Integración Juvenil (Center for Juvenile Integration) and the Casa de Migrante, in coordination with the CDMM, worked every year to carry out joint preventive work in the community and to defend migrants' human rights.

In 2012, I received some of the saddest news I have ever heard. I was notified by the authorities, the municipal Desarrollo Integral de la Familia (DIF), and the Attorney General's Office for the Defense of Minors and the Family that the CDMM would stop participating in the Program of Unaccompanied Migrant Minors. It was an erroneous and unfair decision by incompetent authorities.

One Cycle Closes and Another Begins

At that time, the CDMM had to rethink what its activities would be for the future. With a new building that had sufficient space, Dr. Delia Puga, an outstanding researcher from UACJ, immediately assembled a team that worked with us to prioritize the needs we had to most improve the quality of life of the inhabitants of Chaveña, a colonia located in the center of the city, where we were located. We began to develop programs and projects aimed at the community that others had initiated, like recreation, education, health, and community services. No one could stop my work, now that I had more courage, strength, and extensive experience, and the same dedication as always.

The first change took place where the CDMM was founded. It had been a garbage dump, so there was a necessary fundamental change to make in this place, a neighborhood with a lot of history, with resilient people who had experienced so much loss. It was the love of the mothers that opened its doors to their new history, with hopes of changing the lives of the families that decided to accept our work in the Chaveña, one of the oldest colonias, but also one of the most dangerous. We had a new challenge, where the founders of the shelter gladly accepted to take over the work of the shelter and took possession of it [but no longer focused on migrants]. They took care of the workers and the building, and they attended and participated in all the activities. Despite these changes in focus, a phenomenon occurred in which migrant families, like women with children, would still knock on the center's doors daily, so we continued our task of supporting them during 2012 and 2013. We continued to attend isolated cases of mothers with their children and worked with the new project hand in hand until at the end of 2013, when we ended the work with migrants in the CDMM. But we never stopped proclaiming respect for the human rights of migrants.

Reflection on Work with Migrant Children

This complex problem [of migration] affected family dynamics in all aspects, but at the border [these problems] multiplied. Without a doubt, the most affected migrants were children and adolescents. They are the ones who suffered the serious consequences in terms of their health, social development, personal security, education, their economic situation, and the violation of their human rights. It was necessary for the state to remain conscious and aware of the problem [holistically], and not only the aspects that they already knew about. It was/is urgent and a priority to defend the life and dignity of migrants. There must be a strong cooperation and coordination of the highest authorities of the two countries, so that together they seek migration policies and mechanisms that favor a more humane economy that leads to the reduction of causes of this phenomenon [of migration].

Community Border Work

We continued working in the shelter, and I volunteered as a member of La Mesa de Albergues (The Advisory Board of Shelters), comprising thirty legally constituted shelters who contributed to guaranteeing the fundamental rights of children and adolescents. It remains a very rewarding personal experience, supporting the places where children of single mothers are cared for and protected, as well as those who are under the tutelage of the office of the attorney general attending to children. My volunteering with La Mesa de Albergues has always been to contribute to the strengthening and professionalization of the shelters that seek advice, support, and management for compliance with the regulations and laws that regulate these social assistance centers to improve the quality of life of these children. We will continue to generate intervention models that promote actions where children benefit.

La Mesa de Albergues is necessary because there have been cases where migrant children were hurt and even died. One of the saddest events that hurt all of Juárez society [and] that came to represent our city as a symbol of what happens to migrant children took place on March 11, 2014. This case was known worldwide. It was that of an indigenous Ecuadorian migrant girl, Noemí, a twelve-year-old who traveled more than 10,000 kilometers to reunite with her family, who reside in the U.S., but she never arrived. She died in a shelter in Ciudad Juárez. Her case was very manipulated by different authorities. The community was never satisfied with the results of authorities' investigations because of how they were dealing with the case. Authorities did not even carry out a protocol of attention for the girl at the time of her interviews, including the lack of attention by the person in charge of migrant children, the deputy attorney general for the protection of NNA. What was revealed was a lack of support [and lack of protocols] in the shelter where the child had been placed. This was again an alert, a red light, a bucket of cold water for the authorities, who were not using the protocols of attention toward unaccompanied migrant children. It showed the inefficiency and violation of human rights by some authorities.

In October 2020, the government of Chihuahua, in collaboration with UNICEF, started the Center for Integral Care for migrant children and adolescents in Ciudad Juárez, and in good time, since for many years only the shelter Mexico Mi Hogar, a shelter of the municipality of Ciudad Juárez and the CSOs (among them CDMM), were tending to the NNAs. This center now bears Noemí's name; however, naming the shelter after her is revictimizing her and cannot be a tribute to her when she died in such a tragic way. So much pain is felt every time we remember her case and her name. I cannot imagine how much pain, anguish, and loneliness this girl suffered, because finally what happened is evident [she died]. It would be more appropriate to address her case and [those of] many other children and women, with more strategic actions to carry out, to modify laws, and to improve budgets attending to safeguarding the rights of children, so that no more cases like this heartfelt tragedy happen, because the state is still indebted to [her] and to all those families who are still waiting for justice. I will always firmly and openly oppose injustice and defend with the truth the human rights of all those who do not have a voice, like children.

There is a newspaper library with clippings that follow up on the activities carried out during the years we were at the head of CDMM. It recognizes authorities and other CSOs, as well as colleagues and other professionals from different careers, who worked hand in hand with me, endorsing my work and to whom I thank for their unconditional support, feedback, and trust, so that this work was done with a framework of love, justice, and respect for the children who were served.

With all due respect, I hope that my experience serves as a guideline to not continue making mistakes anymore. I appreciate the opportunity to express my *testimonio* that I lived hand in hand with those who do not have a voice, the children and young migrants, but also with all those children who have been mistreated, abused, and forgotten by authorities, family, and society, and who are growing up with a deep imprint of pain.

My sincere thanks and recognition to all the migrants, to the people who always accompanied me, like Dr. Abel Lerma, Uriel González, Dr. María Eugenia Hernández, and Gilberto Solís, and to my family, especially to my daughter, Marisol, and the volunteers, friends, and neighbors who supported [me] and who together rowed this boat with me. All my admiration and gratitude to them from the depths of my heart.

WHEN MIGRATION MOVES, THE HISTORY OF MAN MOVES
AQUEL MIGRANTE, AQUEL MORRAL / THAT MIGRANT,
THAT BACKPACK

LETICIA LÓPEZ, 2009

Lleva una lata, un vaso de agua
poco de pan
lleva una virgen para rezar

Con valentía sigue sus pasos
que ni la muerte podrá para
el, su destino quiere cambiar
sus ilusiones y su familia quedan atrás
son presa fácil de todo el mundo
a donde van, a donde van

Aquel migrante, aquel morral
el, va buscando con humildad
lo que no encuentra en su ciudad
busca trabajo, se busca el pan
y muchos niños a su mama.

Aquel migrante, aquel morral
es confundido por criminal
y cuando logra cruzar fronteras
enormes muros y grandes mallas
por los vagones, por la garita o por el río
se encuentra al miedo
es otro idioma, otra cultura
y está muy lejos de su mamá
es el destino que entró a buscar

Y lo reciben con grandes armas, muy poderosas
es el racismo, humillaciones y falsedad
aquel migrante, el solo lleva en su morral
un vaso de agua, sus ilusiones, poco de pan.

—CD. JUÁREZ, CHIH. 27 DE ABRIL DE 2021

Bring a can, a glass of water
a bit of bread
bring a virgin to pray

courageously follow his footsteps
that not even death can stop
him, his destiny he wants to change
his hopes and his family are left behind
they are easy prey from all over the world
where they're going, where they're going

that migrant, that backpack
he goes looking with humility
what he can't find in his city

Looking for work, looking for bread
and many children for their mother.

That migrant, that backpack
is mistaken for criminal
and when he manages to cross borders
Huge walls and large meshes
by the wagons, by the checkpoint or by the river
meets fear
It's another language, another culture
and is very far from his mom
It is the destination he went looking for

And they greet him with big, very powerful weapons.
It is racism, humiliation, and falsehood
That migrant, he alone carries in his backpack
A glass of water, his illusions, a bit of bread.

TESTIMONIO

Colores United

Mothers Offering Sanctuary and Dignity in Southern New Mexico

ARIANA SALUDARES
Cofounder of Colores United

I am Ariana Jaime Saludares. I am a wife, a mother, and the cofounder of Colores United, a nonprofit organization working with migrant families in Deming, New Mexico. There are many days that have been "the day" my life changed forever. Like a tree growing towards the sky, each day of my life shows the tree bending a little from its original path. In curves and twists, the tree keeps growing towards the sun. Many such days are burned into my memory, but one in particular is special. It was Mother's Day several years back, and I was standing at the old butcher block island in my kitchen. My husband told me lovingly, "This is your day to do whatever you want." I started with making breakfast for my family. My phone interrupted my prep, and I heard the voice of a panicky friend say, "Bring your shoes. Bring them all."

She was referring to the shoes I had collected to give to our community. It was a small project to honor the gift of a pair of shoes that my father had received as a child—changing his life forever. I could feel my heart pounding deep inside me as I calmly put down my chopping knife and walked over to my husband. I said to him, "Hey. You remember how you said today was my day and I could do anything I wanted?"

His eyes shifted nervously from the television to me. He knows I am the spontaneous one between us, and that one of my "great ideas" could be anything from a six-hundred-mile afternoon drive to taking in an entire litter of kittens. "Yes?" he replied suspiciously.

I swallowed and rambled like a skilled auctioneer: "Immigrants were left in the middle of the night, and now they are at our fairgrounds, and they all need help, and they have no food, and they have no shoes, and they are all starving, and there are children, and it is utter chaos, and so I would like to go to the store and go buy them some things and take the extra shoes we have to try and help. Okay?"

He just stared at me as if I had spoken in tongues. I repeated the request, with pauses this time, and gave him even more information. He was in disbelief. "I thought you were just going to say you wanted to go shopping or something. But this is your day, and we will spend it however you wish."

The trucks and cars trailed in a line out of the fairgrounds gate and along the road. There were dozens of vehicles coming in and out. Just as many vehicles were unloading items. People were everywhere, and the atmosphere was thick with angst. "Wait here until I figure out what to do," I told my husband as I hopped out of the truck. Our two children peered out the truck window with wide eyes. As I walked through the open bay door, there were many helpers sitting at tables on phones. Other helpers were writing on huge papers taped to the wall. There were hundreds of people sitting on green cots, each looking as if they had just survived a rollover accident and were in shock. Some were sleeping. Some were minding children playing quietly on the floor or had them suckling their exposed breasts. The noise level was like the hum of a hive, as hundreds of voices spoke at the same time.

I remember the stale smell in the air. In the five seconds I had to assess the situation, I had a million thoughts. I found a face I knew, and I pulled her aside. Rapid words came out as she pressed her hands against her cheeks—overwhelmed. "Here is what I can do. We brought some things for families, and I'll have my husband unload the truck. You let me know what else we can do, and we will try."

There were the cold nights staring at my own child asleep on our cot amongst the others. If you had to try to pick her out of the rest of the sleeping babies, it would be impossible. I told myself if it were me, I too would do anything for my child. I smile to myself, remembering the babies that would quietly wake in the middle of the night. They would sit up from their comfy bed and peer around silently like baby alligators. Deep curious eyes staring back at a stranger. I would smile at them and tell them to lay back down. They could easily talk me out of a late night snack and milk. Afterwards, I would bring them a stuffed animal and pull the blankets up to their chin. "Sleep now; we will play tomorrow," I would say as their deep round eyes blinked back at me.

Sometimes when I close my eyes in the middle of the night, I can still hear the children's screams from the night terrors they had. Unaware of their own cries, they would call out for their mama. If they were little, the parents would just scoop them in closer to stop the tears. When they were older, the cries had become so normal, others would just sleep through it. I had to remind myself their pain was not normal. Their pain is not normal.

Some people want to argue politics and label me with cruel names. My reply to them is always, "I've been called worse." I stand proud and root my words in the strength given to me by my ancestors. I dream for a day that this work is no longer needed. I dream that those seeking freedom from the "wolves" wishing to devour their souls can safely feel the earth of their homeland between their toes. Until then, we will share our soil with them. Some believe this worn road is one propped up by naivety and unattainable expectations. History tells us that if you turn over enough rocks along the way, you will eventually find what you are looking for. If you do not know what you are looking for, you will find everything. I am not alone in this mission. You see, I have them, I have my family, my friends, and of course—I have you. We will continue to walk alongside one another on this mission of advocacy, love, and change until the day we return to Her.

Since the first day we served under Colores United, my life forever changed. We did not want to form Colores United; we *needed* what Colores United could stand for and could evolve into becoming. Our community needed to have their pain validated and a path to healing defined. Our community needed a familiar hand reaching out to theirs to simply help them along. Our community needed color in their voices and the strengths it brought along. In the first days of our organization, we fought hard to ensure each soul we came to assist knew their worth. Eventually, we realized when you advocate and lead with integrity, you do not have to fight—we stand in solidarity, and our combined voices drown out injustice.

Those first months were just the beginning of this story. There is not one day that has gone by where the plight of the migrants' situations doesn't replay in my mind or the stories they shared are not stuck on repeat in my memory. It could have been so much easier to let the call go unanswered. I cannot explain why I have been chosen to advocate and assist, same as I cannot explain why I was always there at every one of those traffic accidents. I just knew that I could help, even with just saying, "Your mother loves you; you will find your way."

On this journey, we travel with them through their heartache and quest towards freedom. We witness their resiliency, and we find how we fit into their lives and assist in their healing. We did not actively seek out this task. We did not wake up one day and say, "Let's focus on migrants and healing our communities." There was a hole, and we knew it could be filled with kindness. *They are but shadows and words after they leave. We are here to ensure they matter and to share their stories.*

PART III

Asserting Rights and Calling Out Hegemony and Oppression Through a Praxis of Frontera Madre(hood)

TESTIMONIO

I AM His Mother

Challenging Traditional Paradigms of Latina Mothering in the Paso del Norte Region

CLAUDIA YOLANDA CASILLAS
Critical Pedagogue and Mamá Fronteriza

Mi Árbol

We stood together hand in hand and watched as our tree was cut down. She had been sick, infested with bores, who found refuge in her body. This refuge she offered was at her own expense. She was filled with holes, and her outer body was scarred with the memories of small feet finding their way up to the sanctuary of shade, marking her outer bark with the same deep wrinkles I recall from my *abuelita*'s face. Both spent their days laboring in the sun, holding and carrying children, both gone too soon.

This tree, this majestic creature, lived for almost fifty years in our backyard. I tried to be a good caregiver; her demise cut into my memories, my body, my heart, always remembering how my own *árbol* sustained me. *Mijo* took my hand, and as I held his, we wiped each other's tears and turned away.

Soy Mamá

Despite my infertile body, I have a son. I watched as he grew inside the belly, turning, kicking, and always moving. I pondered his name as I pondered mine; what would he call me? Mom, Mami, Mamá? When his time came to enter this world, I could not call on my own mother for advice because this boy came to me and my infertile body through my wife. I tell him he is *mijo* of my spirit and his blood runs through my veins, feeding my heart with his blood.

As I enter this work, reflecting on my mothering, reflecting on my own mother's wisdom, *sabiduría* and *sobrevivencia* (Galván 2015, 131), I know I must enter the space of Nepantla (Anzaldúa 2002b, 2015) to examine and interrogate my positionality as a queer and Brown mamá.[1] My own mother is with me still, as I mourn her still and always, but I am not alone. I am told, "Those of the invisible realm walk with you" (Anzaldúa 2015, 137). My mother is with me. She is still *abuelita* to *mijo*, her true grandson, although she initially rejected him as such. Cindy Cruz (2001) asserts that "our production of knowledge begins in the bodies of our mothers and grandmothers, in the acknowledgement of the critical practices of women of color before us" (12). I carry this knowledge in my cells and in my spirit. So, too, it begins through the music of the *corridos* heard across the way, when you are outside, and the mountains are your haven. I waited days and then I waited weeks for her to come meet him. I imagined her rushing to the hospital, that beautiful smile and her vibrant energy gushing for *mijo*. But I was there without any comfort or wisdom as my wife and I navigated the hospital system, where we had to thoughtfully skirt the space as outsiders, daring to let our gay love bring forth more love and life.

His Birth

The contractions come on heavy; she jumps up and pleads, "What do I do? What do I do?" I try to comfort her and suggest breathing techniques, and I simply stay near her, touch her leg, her shoulder, telling her, "I am with you." I make the physical contact gentle yet firm.

We go to the hospital and return, as she is not quite ready yet.

---

1. Nepantla, the transformative and liminal space of possibilities (Anzaldúa 2002b, 548).

The opening, the tearing of muscles,
The softening,
The widening,
The show
The lightning
The water breaking
The stretching of ligaments and muscles.[2]

I am in awe of what she can do, mesmerized by the hours spent sitting, walking, resting, finding a comfortable position—there just isn't one. My big boy is ready to enter the world and leave the comfort of his *mami's* warm and viscous womb. We wait for hours while his heartbeat, which beats in time with hers, is monitored. My heart is outside my body seeing syncopation. She accepts relief. I watch the needle—it is much, much larger than I expected—and I'm relieved she cannot see it. She is closer. At eight centimeters we are told he is coming soon! But then there is silence on the monitor, his heartbeat no longer detected. Nurses rush in and prepare to roll her bed out to the operating room, as I am directed by another nurse's hands firmly placed on my shoulders, a gentle push to GO NOW!

My hands and arms are scrubbed, my hair and body covered, and even my shoes wrapped with protective gear. I am led and directed with their gentle push to where I see her on the operating table. I stand by her, share some unknown words of strength, and I send my prayers to Mother Tonanztín.

The doctor's arm can be seen only from the elbow up as my wife's body is intensely and forcefully opened at the belly to bring my baby out. I see his head, but there is a silence that is so loud, my head begins to float. Time slows down. Even the beat, beat, beat of the hummingbird's wings breaks. Blue is my favorite color, the color of the sky and of the ocean, the sacred spaces that hold the earth in the middle. There is comfort in shades of blue, the indigos, *azure y la turquesa*. But at this moment, I hate blue. His little face is so blue it is purple, the umbilical cord wrapped around his tiny neck. Breathe, boy. Breathe.

Looking back, you recall seeing the boy with your own heart above his head, the image a reminder of the flame of the Holy Spirit reenvisioned to be your own telling of a twist of fate you always thought would be yours.

---

2. Pregnancy, Birth and Baby 2022.

When we discovered his placenta was separating from him—his safe and viscous space requiring injections of heparin—my scoldings to my wife when work hours were routinely too early and too late finally had merit. Actively loving him, his little body forming and growing in her sacred and queer womb, I envisioned the care I would give him, planning also for my turn to bring forth life.

During his nine months in her body, I nurtured him by preparing the healthiest foods possible for my wife to eat, by kissing her belly, by singing to *mijo* the songs from my own childhood, the *pio, pio, pio* and the *ru ru que ru, y la de allí en la puente las hormiguitas se están lavando sus enaguitas*, and don't forget the silliest of all, *la de, la pulga y el piojo se van a casar*.

These were the silly songs my *abuelita* sang to my mother. I had to recall them and sing them on my own to him by crossing the border of remembrance through my initial sadness of not having *mi madre a mi lado en esos momentos* to share in my joy of becoming. I was becoming a mother, doing the things my sisters, *tías, primas* had all done in preparation for receiving their children. So I crossed again the border made fluid through my tears—the way we borderlanders cross through, back and forth, back and forth, in between, back in the space of Nepantla. I return there as I was in my first breakthrough *testimonio*, with the shards of glass that reflected my broken Self. With Coyolxauhqui to propel, guard, and fight with me, I use my *testimonio* to create mySelf anew.[3]

I go to him, his body clean and new (too clean, as the habit on this side of the border is to wipe all remnants of the birthing process away) and, to me, perfect, with strong cries that are soothed with the first of many songs I would sing to him. He turns his head toward me as I sing, mesmerized by my own sense of connection to all mothers in this moment of comforting my child. I feel the shift in the air. The *colibri* begins to fly again, leaving as his first cries are heard, granting my prayer. *Breathe again, boy, breathe again*, I pray. Heaven doesn't need another angel. After we settle back into our room, the process of paperwork begins.

---

3. Coyolxauhqui is the Aztec goddess of the moon, whose fragmented body serves to guide toward remembering, reconstructing, and healing (Anzaldúa 2002b, 546).

Birth Certificate

"Who is the father?"

We squirm a little, unsure of how to respond to this question. The nurse assumes and states, "Oh, you don't know?" Yes, we do; we just chose to leave it blank. We take a few short minutes to discuss the heaviness of the uninviting and literal space where the name of a parent on his birth certificate belongs. It is assumed we do not know who the father is when, with great intention, we created him first in our minds. We planned our steps across this threshold and with the help of her dear friend from Italy. Our son would know him as his genetic father, relative, and friend. Then, I would carry our next child.

We do not put his name, and it never occurs to me to cross out the word FATHER and to write my name underneath the capitalized words—what would I write, *other* mother? I am othering mySelf; in the span of a few short minutes, my status as his mother is nullified by his birth certificate. We leave it blank, with my wife's name written on the page and mine only written in my heart. I was stunned and still reeling from witnessing my wife's body jerking back and forth. . . . Are those guts I see on the table, and why is the room so quiet? My senses sharp, hyperaware, I hear the tools and body parts being moved until—pop! He is out. I am the Other with no space for me. I birthed him in my head way before his conception by envisioning mySelf as a mother.

Why didn't I cross out the word "father," place the word "mother" there, and write my full name on his birth certificate? I now write my name in the space in between with this *testimonio*. I am not brave enough to do this work, to reveal the ache, to sit with the wounds, to sit on the outside hoping to be invited in. My *testimonio is* the invitation—the hurt, the disappointment in my mother's eyes, *how could you?* It is all still there but wounds me less tightly writing my *testimonio*, bearing witness to it all with its daring magic to reveal a hope that lies in the in-between spaces of my life on the border.

How dare I cross the boundary of family into madrehood? I crossed the border into my own *familia* with disregard to the white, heteronormative gaze that sets its colonial judgmental glare on me. I was told I would never be a mother by my own mother when I came out to her. My coming out meant those doors were closed to me. I had to at that moment continue to assert my *sueños* of mothering for many years.

I think about my own little angel, never really made, just the blood stains of disappointments and the eventual submission to my infertility. I dreamed of tiny feet, wide like mine but strong, strong enough to run, eventually into my arms after coming through my own queer womb. But you were a never baby, a dream baby, the baby of my Nepantlera dreams, living in my in-betweenness, where I eventually blasphemed my way to motherhood. How would I be punished for daring to be me, a queer and Brown mama? Maybe this was it—the shock of infertility, something I never for a moment anticipated. Now, as I continue to surrender to my *testimonio*, I've had to reconnect to that mother's ache that my body never knew but my spirit has always felt.

It was assumed I would never be a parent, relegated only to the *tía* who would help my sisters with their own families. I practiced and thought about my mothering at an early age, envisioning my own children while I cared for my *sobrina-mijas*. I thought about everything: the food, the clothing, the activities. There was so much emphasis in my mind on how I would be as a mother. The expectation placed on me in our collective culture of shared responsibility was that I would never say no to helping. The emphasis on the mother, recalling my own mother's involvement with my fertile sisters and their families, left me with an empty cup of hope in the moment of seeing no space for me on his birth certificate.

Commitment Ceremony—Not a Wedding

We chose the flowers, the colors, and the invitations on our own. I searched for a wedding dress without my mother or my sisters, just the one best friend who graciously cried when seeing me in a wedding gown. I imagined my wedding as so many women do, my life's projections and goals geared toward this walk down the aisle, where I would gleefully surrender to womanhood. I imagined the church, the music, and what the priest would say. Mostly, I imagined my family with me, all of them, including the seventy first cousins, all the *tías* and *tíos*, dancing the dollar dance, the food . . . yes, I envisioned a party like so many of the parties and weddings my family hosted and that we attended so often.

When we had our commitment ceremony, we felt like the outsiders we were/are in this heteronormative world, which we carefully navigate. Enduring the expulsion from the family, I had to find another way to survive. I went inward, tried to find a calm within the storm of my emotions, the rejection driving me to thoughts of unworthiness. My queerness was too much for her to bear. How could I do this to her? My mother would not allow any extended family to attend our commitment ceremony. We didn't even call it a wedding. There were no papers to sign and store safely. We made a promise in front of friends and very limited family: my brother and sister walked me down the aisle; my wife's father and mother were present. Her mother even called me "daughter" in her speech before we cut our cake! I treasure that memory: a mother called me daughter. And my son was there, witness from the womb of our love promise.

Nonparent Conservatorship

What would become of us if something were to happen to my partner? Could *mijo* be taken from me? We seek the advice of a lawyer. No, I cannot adopt him, as we are not legally married. This is prior to 2015, when legal marriage was not an option. We file the paperwork and sign the documents agreeing to the next steps. We are told to make our private lives open for viewing and scrutiny. She explains that we will be required to attend interviews and to just be ourselves, everything will work out. But it is not *we* who will be scrutinized. It is *me*.

I am ready, I think. But my head begins to swirl.

I dared to enter madrehood beyond the type of motherhood that was expected of me. By queering my own desires for motherhood, I countered my mother's statement of assumption: "Well, now you won't be able to have kids!" She knew how much being a parent and having a family had always meant to me. As the youngest of the family, I observed my sister's teenage pregnancies with distinct curiosity. The teenage brides provided me the opportunity of becoming a *tía* at age eleven with the expectation of helping to care for my nieces, my *sobrina-mijas*, throughout my adolescence.

I stare at the document I must complete.

I was not sure about the number of questions that dealt with topics I was too familiar with, but the heaviness of them could not be denied: Ever been a victim of a crime? Ever been the victim of child abuse? How would I explain to a stranger that I am afraid to answer honestly? I feared being truthful. I am a survivor. Yes, it was a crime I endured. If I tell her this, will she think I'm incapable? I am honest. She is kind. Did I have any criminal history? No, but suddenly, I feel like I do. I skirt the edges of acceptance with this act of seeking rights to the boy I am raising. He is a toddler and calls for me for comfort, too. He knows I'm his *mammaaa.*

Over the next few weeks, we wait anxiously for the next steps—the home interview. She looks at our home, our pictures, the Sacred Heart, and the notes of Pride mingling together in the living room. She is warm and generous and tells us not to worry. But it is not my wife who has to worry, it is me, the "other mama" without rights! My wife assures me this will work out. So does the social worker. I began to feel my queerness in a new way, seeing how it complicates the navigation of legal spaces. First, with his birth certificate, and now, with the quest for my *documentos* to *mijo*, I am challenging and crossing the border into madrehood.

The day comes. We park and walk into the courtroom alone with our son. The judge immediately asks, "Where is everyone else? Where is your family? This is a happy day!" I am shocked. I am saddened; I never thought to invite anyone for fear I would not be granted some sort of rights.

But I was granted the rights of nonparent conservatorship with quiet relief and big tears. He is just a little bit more *mine.*

Papers, Please / *Papeles, por Favor*

La Frontera, this metroplex of Ciudad Juárez, El Paso, and Las Cruces, offers reclamation through/with the back-and-forth border crossings and the in-between, *entre mundos*, ways we occupy and reclaim a space and place here. This tumultuous existence, where the colonized re-create and where our daily lived experience is a constant contradiction of the expectations of the rest of the "out there." We borderlanders can feel the *vibra* of our *antepasados*; our Brown bodies carry that knowledge of what we once were, how we became Mexica. There is something so special about the borderland. The space of Nepantla becomes accessible through the constant transformation that occurs here on this land.

Growing up on the border, moving back and forth with the specifics of the logistics, "Papers, please" was the phrase I heard over the years, witnessing the crossings of my *tías, mi abuelita, mis primos*, so much *familia* that came to El Norte. "Papeles, por favor." I learned early in life that papers hold a type of proof necessary for survival. I had my way of survival, which depended on movement. Over time, I realized how vital movement across this international bridge was, the back and forth that was allowed, or the restrictions that often followed. Sometimes, the river would be depended on for safe passage. Whether the coyote swims with them or not, the risk was worthy of trying. Who has papers? Who gets access to *papeles*?

Everyday Moments of Othering

As the grass grew over the mound where our tree once stood, so *mijo* grew, too. Vibrant, the way the grass dares to glitter green with the flash floods the desert carries from the sky, he became even more the sun and moon that lit up our days and nights. The grass remained green only a short time as things do in the desert, but the earth grew over it, while the roots still spread underneath. I imagine the roots reaching across toward a desert animal's tunnels, perhaps even making new tunnels for the desert critters.

His toddler days turned to school days.

"I Have Two Moms"

I squirmed a little every time I heard my son gleefully announce that he had two moms. It is first grade, a new public schooling experience much different from the small home Montessori Early Childhood Education program. His big slate blue eyes take in the sights and sounds of this new world, his socializing prospects magnified much to his delight. Interestingly, in his primary grade years, he demonstrated a keen understanding of the norms of family, and he felt the need to announce that he had two moms. Often. In random grocery store moments, the everyday became a "coming out" for a little boy who just knew that having two moms was worthy of identifying. The announcement was necessary for him. His young mind had received messaging to know that this is a distinction—is this what urged him to proclaim "I have two moms"?

There are always documents, paperwork, family surveys to complete. Once, on the phone with an administrative assistant at the school, I was asked point-blank, "And who are you? You are listed as the other. . . ." Indeed, I had to maneuver this type of question over the years and prove my-Self as his parent. Perhaps the questions will sting less someday. There are only two choices to choose from for paperwork: proof of dependency—biological or adoptive—but the term *nonparent conservator* is not there. My court-ordered document doesn't exist as a choice to select from the various forms I have had to complete over the years.

A Visit to Papi: Passport Needed

We are thrilled about the plans to travel to Italy, home of his father and his family. I begin making the stacks of clothes and various items we would need, the gifts for the family, the *dulces* and special sweet and spicy treats, the *cajetas, mantelitos*, and various *cositas* to share. It is time to go for our passports at the El Paso Passport Agency in the downtown U.S. federal building. I take my documents, my legal proof connecting me to my child. I made the appointment weeks in advance. Flight numbers in place, locations secured, passport picture created. In mine, I try not to smile too brightly, but in my eyes the wander-lust is there, my excitement for the journey, for *mijo* to meet his other grandparents and family of his *papi*. I provide my file with the various required documents, birth certificates, license, forms. I am handed back my conservatorship and asked, "What is this?" I stand my ground in this federal government office, but it crumbles out from under me. "We need his real mother here."

Mijo asks why I look sad *and* angry. I am startled at the knot forming in my throat. I provide my legal documents that do not quite call me parent, but it is what I have: nonparent conservatorship. Poor lady does not know how to handle me, a queer woman demanding my rights with proof of legal rights. "No, what does this mean?" she asks, as she is genuinely unsure, and I notice she glances behind me. I asked mySelf, What is she looking at? Later, I realized it was a federal guard who was standing nearby. I am in a federal office with guns, security cameras, walls for safety, and protocols for entry and exit.

I try to bite back the pleading. "I am his mother," I state clearly again. "I'm sorry, ma'am, his mother—his birth mother—must be here."

The squeezing of a little hand, a little too hard. "Duele, mama." *Cola entre las piernas*, we depart *pero con un coraje*; something has to change!

Where are we safe to be who we are? The border offers this magical in-between potential of fluidity, but this must be found through a mestiza consciousness.[4] The border also does exactly what it is designed to do: stop time, stop moments, stop to prove you have the right to names such as parent or mama, or wife to a wife. My senses are heightened for survival. I will traverse my way through with the memory and strength of my mother's green card, using her status as *residente, ni de aqui ni de alla* to negotiate this space. Although I am a U.S. citizen, I am a resident of El Mundo Zurdo, which will also allow me to see with new eyes.[5]

Queering MySelf to Queer My Familia

Lovers meet poolside while sitting on the edge; legs linger in the water while the other swims about, mermaids singing; why do the sirens sing to me and lull me closer to her? What kind of death will I die? Will it be like the sailors of Greek mythology, boats crushed with crashing waves?

We were so young and so passionately in love; it was love at first sight.

Loving her meant losing part of my family, the rituals that make our *cultura, nuestra*. I had to learn to think about my safety in an additional way; in losing part of my *gente*'s acceptance, I had to learn to carry this extra weight of loving from the fringes. Being queer, Brown, living on

---

4. *Conocimiento*, or insight, is ignited through the mestiza consciousness, which deconstructs colonial patriarchal ideologies via critical Chicana feminist epistemologies (Anzaldúa 2002b, 2012, 2015).

5. El Mundo Zurdo, Anzaldúa's concept of the space inhabited by queer groups (Anzaldúa 2002a).

the U.S. side of the border, losing access to parts of my culture, having the border of my own body crossed, I must acknowledge my survivorship as an asset to guide me as a queer mama, as I employ the deep and heavy work of *testimonio*. As women, our lives hold many intersectionalities that affect each and every one of us (Crenshaw 1991), carrying the burdens in our diaper bags, agendas, laundry baskets, power suits, and pleasant faces, sometimes required for safety, sometimes to avoid the patriarchal punishments doled out in both subtle and blatant ways. I have to ask mySelf, What are the ways I embody this system? What are the ways I use my voice, my body, my gestures, my memories to manifest a way of being that is mine, standing my ground while straddling *dos mundos*?

I run to Nepantla and find *el árbol de la vida* there and ground my feet in this place on the borderland and bring the space alive from the liminal to the magical to real. I come to life in a different way in this realm. The iridescent hues I can almost touch but most certainly feel in this transformative and creative location. Nepantla offers the opportunity to learn from this transitional and transformational site; it is "the overlapping space between different perceptions and belief systems" (Anzaldúa 2002b, 541). Understood as a liminal space, it is full of possibility, where I can embody all the contradictions of who I am. I find strength here.

I'm captivated by the everyday. I'm finally granted permission through my *autohistoria-teoría* (Anzaldúa 2015) to seek, study, and confirm not only the knowledge of my lived experience, but also the knowledge imparted to me from the pedagogies of the home (Delgado Bernal 1998).[6] My mother, a product of her time and her culture, needed time to come to grips with my love for my wife. From the Sierra Madre de Chihuahua, where my *primas* and *tías* had to ask permission of their husbands to run for the simple errands that were part of *las responsibilidades de mujeres*, my mother, *una gran mujer*, as she was called, did not subscribe to these codes of conduct. *Ella quería más*, so she left at fourteen to El Norte, leaving behind the wood-burning stove, the *terreno* that held the possibilities of enough food and enough ground, just enough to claim for one's own.

---

6. *Autohistoria teoría* is the blending of cultural and personal biographies with memoir, history, storytelling, and poetics toward transformation, healing, and personal growth (Anzaldúa 2015).

I have only recently been out, calling my life partner—finally—my wife after being affirmed legal rights with our legal marriage in 2020. She, with the gentle heart, heavy work ethic, and powerful leader in her business, I have loved for so long. I had to unlearn the ways a wife "should" be. No, the table does not need to be set perfectly, and the dishes can now wait. I am not responsible for everything in our home, but I am responsible for unlearning and rebuilding what it means to be a mama and a wife through my *testimonio*. I am teaching *mijo* to listen through the clutter of iPhones, technology, homework, and activities to feel the connections— and yes, to know the pain of the world, too, so that he may gift the world some of his big, beautiful heart. My call is toward a new tribalism with a new language to use toward a spiritual activism that connects all that I am with all that is around me (Anzaldúa 2015).

Queering My Faith

With the wink of her eye, she let me know that perhaps I, too, could partake of this knowledge and sacraments in the way I needed to. I would not call upon that rebellious Nepantlera act my mother demonstrated sometimes while we attended Catholic Mass until much later in life, once I began to harness the power of my *testimonio* and the *autohistoria-teoría* that I would create. I traverse the border of the church; I am not allowed to fully participate, but my beautiful boy is. He could receive the sacraments and savor them as I would like to. Growing up Catholic, you develop an appreciation of drama, tragedy, and setting, the rituals that are part of my *cultura*. I want my son to have these special moments too, despite the church being the main reason my mestiza consciousness had to find its way through my *testimonio*, to decolonize my mind and forge my bodymindspirit cohesion. I still want him to participate.

Conversations and discussions have been extensive. Teaching my *mijo* directly and explicitly about the ideologies that say men are stronger than women makes me wonder, What other rules does he know and follow? I ask him, we talk, we discuss, he wonders aloud. I have to create this space where he can also question and wonder. Alma Itzé Flores (2019) describes the role of religion and spirituality in her work "A Chicana Mother-Daughter Spiritual Praxis," acknowledging and recognizing the role Catholicism has played as "a tool of colonization for our communities, especially for Women of Color and LGBTQ people" (196). I am choosing to merge my Catholicism with Gloria E. Anzaldúa's metaphysics of interconnectedness as I continue to create my Self.[7] I am going to make it work for me and my spiritual journey to question, wonder, recreate, and reimagine what faith is.

I have come to appreciate my spirituality as a journey into the metaphysics of interconnectedness. Knowing my queerness separates me from the hegemonic mainstream, I am charged with creating a new space to live as a queer mama with my *familia*. I continue to learn from Chicana feminist epistemologies (CFE), as "within this framework, Chicanas become agents of knowledge who participate in intellectual discourse that links experience, research, community, and social change" (Delgado Bernal 1998, 560). Attending Mass as a family is in and of itself an act of rebellion; I will still claim this space even though dogma will have me damned. I will teach him these prayers, these virtues, but *also* teach him of the metaphysics of interconnectedness and the lifesaving gift of imagining (Anzaldúa 2012, 2015). Of course, I want my son to partake in the rituals of my life, my history.

As I sit across from the catechism director at the specific church where I felt we could be somewhat safe, I explain how my son was baptized and why my name is not on his baptism certificate. I am asked, "Who are you to the child?" I am the one skirting around the rules, and while the church will damn me, I will still try to access what I *choose* to access. It does not mean I was not shaking with fear and later crying my eyes out, feeling like I had reopened wounds that were sealed shut. He received his first Holy Communion, and my wife and I sat side by side to witness this.

Defense of Marriage Act Repealed

We are in San Francisco and happen to be there on the day the courthouse was lit up all week with rainbow colors. We could not marry yet; my father was terminally ill. Then it was 2016, with my pop having just

---

7. Metaphysics of interconnectedness describes Anzaldúa's holistic understanding and belief in divine energy existing in all forms across all boundaries (Keating 2002).

passed on Christmas Day. In 2015, it would not have been *decente* to marry and party. But this time, instead of my mother's rejection and isolation from the *familia*, she agreed on a celebration *con todos*. "Sure, why not?" she proclaimed and said, "I've come a long way, *que no, mijita*." Indeed, she had. With all the border crossings she had made in her lifetime, with the final one being her earthly crossing, in this moment for me, it was as expansive as time and space itself, the unknown that I finally came to know in that moment.[8]

Bridges and My *Papelitos Guardados*

We walk across the bridge, *el puente*, where so many of us wait to be called, and where so many have waited lifetimes and days, weeks, months to wait to be called. I clutch my *papeles guardados*—the papers that say, "I can be with this child, he's mine, I'm his nonparent conservator, his mamá, his *mammaaaaa* he used to cry for." I told no one of these documents I carried back and forth this time. Am I being extra cautious unnecessarily? But the border holds so many questions and moments of prodding. I play along: "His father is Italian," I say when asked about his name. A look I interpret as, oh, cool, look at this fine Mexican Italian American. And my last name is . . . ? Casillas. Yes, different. Yes, his dad is Italian. I can't say my son's name is my wife's last name and that his second middle name is mine. I thought to blend our names in the Mexa way; one time my mom said we should have put my last name last, like the woman does with the husband's name. I am the girl, right? But I had to put it somewhere, and the second middle name it became. Not only is the question "What's in a name?"; it also became what's in the location of my name on his birth certificate? We panicked, we argued a little, we thought, Who do we ask for help? Neither of our parents could be asked, I thought. His birth *mami* had secured her position, with her name firmly placed and mine second to the middle name. Fuck it, it is there. I put it where it would fit for the time. Where do I fit—where do I fit in?

---

8. *Papelitos guardados*—as described by the Latina Feminist Group, inclusive of de Alba Acevedo et al. (2001)—are part of the meaning making of the process of *testimonio* through the revelation of tucked-away pieces of our lives, memories, and feelings with the connection to significant documents or roles.

As I write, we are active in the adoption process, the claiming of my child under the rules I have to play along with, which requires that the father—he has a name that feels above mine—must complete a Voluntary Relinquishment of Parental Rights and an Affidavit of Interest in Child. I have to sit with this: Why does it make me feel angry? It feels like this unwritten rule that allows him as a man to have a claim to *my son* whom I am raising. I have to go through this whole process to claim *my own son*.

Although I was granted conservatorship with some measure just below what is named parent, I swallow my pride and take what I can get, what is allowed for me, this absurd title of nonparent conservatorship, this document, my own green papers across the border to claim and protect my family. I carry it with me in a folder. I carry it with me stamped on my heart, written on my skin, which feels sweaty, clammy as I stand in a line that curves throughout this building, splitting the land into two. This space is the linking of the two wounds that our land sustains. Is the land also resilient?

We must now address the big detail of the father relinquishing his parental rights. Even he—who agreed to simply help us and, yes, be known as his father and *be* his father—has the title of parent, of father in the necessary documentation of relinquishing his parental rights. The conservatorship is written like a divorce decree, outlining the weeks we would exchange the child we planned for, dreamt of, created in our minds, and brought forth, defying any biological constraints and expectations of who we were supposed to be. We continue to explore how to maintain our son's father as his father while creating the space for me, his mama, to be his legal mama.

Documentos Importantes

I knew where the *documentos importantes* were stored. I witnessed my mother being thoughtful and cautious of the precious items in her care. Birth certificates of her siblings, whose papers she would negotiate over the years, along with ours in the next folder. There were large *sobres* that held titles to property and vehicles and various major life events information, among them the best picture ever of my siblings, in a beautiful Cadillac as part of a parade representing LULAC, my mother with the frosted lips and hair of the late sixties. My sister's horrific car accident. Insurance documents. I found a type of pleasure in the regular flow of information about my parent's busy lives and business endeavors. Information fueled my imagination as I had freedom to peruse *los documentos*. Someday soon, I, too, will have more *papeles* to store: my legal and full rights to my child.

Testimonio as Bridge to Madre(hood)

What has this *testimonio* taught me, and what kind of bridge was created in this process, so that the burden is less heavy, as I bear witness for mySelf and for others; what will my fate be? I create my fate with the embrace of my *testimonio*. I find my sisters and *antepasados* in Nepantla, where time and space fold into each other, and I use my mother's green card, her *papelitos guardados*, which taught me to negotiate *documentos* of my own like magic. I, too, fold in and inward to the beat beat beat of my own queer heart. The ocotillo blooms with summer rains, their fuzzy stalks before then holding the promise of a bloom. Even if the bloom never comes, I know it still in my mind. *Y las raíces de mi árbol, el árbol de mi familia se conecta con todas las raíces de todos los árboles—el árbol de la vida*—all connect underneath the bridge, through the spaces in between, where memories, new imaginings, and *ensueños* reside to take form, whether in our minds, our collective culture, or a reimagined future. I reach through time and space here in Nepantla; I embrace you, my child, my inner child, the girl-woman who grows with me. I have needed to unveil these bits and pieces of my heart and memories to allow the reclamation of my *testimonio* to take place. I ran from this *testimonio*, eyes wild and fangs and soul bared. We battled, she (my earlier Self) and I (my reclaimed Self), finally meeting in Nepantla, where we remembered to reclaim what has been told could not be ours. I can reach Nepantla because of my *testimonio*, because I theorize from the flesh (Moraga and Anzaldúa 2002). I now embrace all that is and has come before me and my time. We clutch each other, our eyes larger than space, falling stars carrying the memories of our *antepasados*. We stop and forgive each other. I see with new eyes my boy. I embrace him, my little love. *I am his mother*.

REFERENCES

Anzaldúa, Gloria E. 2002a. "La Prieta." In *This Bridge Called My Back: Writings by Radical Women of Color*, edited by Cherríe L. Moraga and Gloria E. Anzaldúa, 220–33. Berkeley: Third Woman Press.

Anzaldúa, Gloria E. 2002b. "Now Let Us Shift . . . The Path of Conocimiento . . . Inner Work, Public Acts." In *This Bridge We Call Home*, edited by Gloria E. Anzaldúa and AnaLouise Keating, 540–76. New York: Routledge.

Anzaldúa, Gloria E. 2012. *Borderlands/La Frontera: The New Mestiza*. 25th anniversary ed. San Francisco, Calif.: Aunt Lute.

Anzaldúa, Gloria E. 2015. *Light in the Dark / Luz en lo oscuro: Rewriting Identity, Spirituality, Reality*, edited by AnaLouise Keating. Durham, N.C.: Duke University Press.

Crenshaw, Kimberlé. 1991. "Mapping the Margins: Intersectionality, Identity Politics, and Violence Against Women of Color." *Stanford Law Review* 43 (6): 1241–99.

Cruz, Cindy. 2001. "Toward an Epistemology of a Brown Body." *International Journal of Qualitative Studies in Education* 14 (5): 657–69.

del Alba Acevedo, Luz, Norma Alarcón, Celia Alvarez, Ruth Behar, Rina Benmayor, Norma E. Cantú, Daisy Cocco De Filippis, et al., eds. 2001. *Telling to Live: Latina Feminist Testimonios*. Durham, N.C.: Duke University Press.

Delgado Bernal, Dolores. 1998. "Using a Chicana Feminist Epistemology in Educational Research." *Harvard Educational Review*, 68 (4): 555–83.

Flores, Alma Itzé. 2019. "A Chicana Mother-Daughter Spiritual Praxis." In *The Chicana M(other)work Anthology: Porque Sin Madres No Hay Revolución*, edited by Cecilia Caballero, Yvette Martínez-Vu, Judith Pérez-Torres, Michelle Téllez, and Christine Vega, 195–211. Tucson: University of Arizona Press.

Galván, Ruth Trinidad. 2015. "Campesina Epistemologies and Pedagogies of the Spirit." In *Women Who Stay Behind: Pedagogies of Survival in Rural Transmigrant Mexico*, 131–48. Tucson: University of Arizona Press.

Keating, AnaLouise. 2002. "Forging El Mundo Zurdo: Changing Ourselves, Changing the World." In *This Bridge We Call Home*, edited by Gloria E. Anzaldúa and AnaLouise Keating, 519–30. New York: Routledge.

Moraga, Cherríe, and Gloria E. Anzaldúa, eds. 2002. *This Bridge Called My Back: Writings by Radical Women of Color*. Berkeley, Calif.: Third Woman Press.

Pregnancy, Birth and Baby. 2022. "What Happens to Your Body in Childbirth." Pregnancy, Birth and Baby, Healthdirect Australia. Last modified August 2022. https://www.pregnancybirthbaby.org.au/what-happens-to-your-body-in-childbirth.

CHAPTER 7

On *Fronteriza* Madre(hood)s

Una Plática Entre Mujeres Académicas

JUDITH FLORES CARMONA AND BRENDA RUBIO

New Mexico State University and University of North Texas

Una lucha de fronteras / A Struggle of Borders
Because I, a mestiza,
continually walk out of one culture
and into another. Because I am in all cultures at the same time,
alma entre dos mundos, tres, cuatro,
me zumba la cabeza con lo contradictorio.
Estoy norteada por todas las voces que me hablan
Simultáneamente.

—GLORIA E. ANZALDÚA (1987)

Gloria E. Anzaldúa's powerful poem speaks to us. We are two Mexicanas, navigating borders, who have lived and worked in the U.S.-Mexico borderland region. Both of us were undocumented—brought to this country as children. We have crossed and continue to cross many borders. Employing plática methodology, in this chapter we share our testimonios of how interlocked and overlapping subordinating structures—such as racism and sexism—remain pervasive in academia. Additionally, both of us, with our intersecting identities, experienced dismissiveness from colleagues concerning how our race, class, and gender shaped our experiences with oppression and marginalization in higher education.

Herein, we share how we navigate different borders, including metaphorical borders: Judith with those who prevented her from becoming a biological mother, and Brenda with the continuing expectation of motherhood and scholarly productivity during a pandemic. We start by defining the methodology of pláticas-testimonios. We then share about our madre(hood) (Bejarano and Morales, this volume) experiences based on pláticas that we had together. We conclude by answering the following questions: How is academia complicit in the exploitation of our bodies? How do we enact mothering in other ways—sisterhood, femtorship, collaborations, co-conspiring—to challenge the violence at our border institution?

Pláticas~Testimonios Methodology

Brenda and I have had pláticas for over a year now. Pláticas are "informal conversations that take place in one-on-one or group spaces" (Fierros and Delgado Bernal 2016, 117). As Francisca E. Gonzalez contends, they are a "way to gather family and cultural knowledge through communication of thoughts, memories, ambiguities, and new interpretations" (1998, 647). Testimonio is an anti-imperial and antimilitarist methodology rooted in Latin America. Testimonio is "not the speaking of truth, but rather, the telling of an account from an individual point of view whose conscious[ness] has led to an analysis of the experience as a shared component of oppression" (Reyes and Rodriguez 2012, 528). We bridge both methodologies because, as we had pláticas, our testimonios sprung—hence, pláticas~testimonios. And we contend, "Our pláticas led us to constant reflexión as we divulged our testimonios (pláticas → reflexión → testimonios), thus becoming closer as friends, colleagues and as allies" (Flores Carmona et al. 2018, 35).

Herein we share some of our pláticas~testimonios. Judith starts by sharing three pivotal moments of her madre(hood). The first one addresses her pregnancy loss; the second concerns the bullying she experienced as she underwent several trials of in vitro fertilization (IVF) and intrauterine insemination (IUI). The third transformative madre(hood) moment brings closure to her open wound. Brenda writes about being forced to produce scholarship even as she recovered from pregnancy loss, then having a child and experiencing postpartum depression. The pandemic exacerbated inequitable expectations of her as a mother-scholar through comparison to male counterparts. We conclude by theorizing that our testimonios reveal how interlocking and overlapping identities affected our experiences of/with madre(hood) in academia. Specifically, we explore how we have been susceptible to abuse at a Hispanic-serving institution and academia's lack of response and action against these abuses.

Our pláticas~testimonios shed light on how we understand and experience frontera madre(hood) given our intersecting identities, where we come from, and where we live in proximity to the U.S.-Mexico border. We are both Mexicanas who, at one point, did not have papeles: we were undocumented. Therefore, we are sensitive to the militarization and hypersurveillance of the border and the trauma that creates. We are marked bodies wherever we enter. We are also first-generation students and scholars. Our madre(hood) experiences are inextricably connected to the standards and expectations of being in academia. Both of us are phenotypically Brown, learned English as our second language, and have had to learn to navigate academia as we straddle worlds. For us, familia and community—our personal, political, and professional identities— are all interwoven and intersect like a trenza de identidades (Crenshaw 1991; Delgado Bernal 2008).

Judith's Testimonio of Loss, Trials, and Closing of the Wound

My testimonio is not mine alone, nor is it unique. My testimonio is an open wound that will finally sear a scar. It is a painful reality of many women in academia. At one point in my academic department, I counted eleven of us, mostly women of color, who had no children—but all the men did. On March 15, 2013, during my first year in my tenure-track position, I had a pregnancy loss. I wrote a script for a digital testimonio I produced, titled "Loss." Now, by writing this piece, I am in the wound-closing stage of my loss.

Loss

"I saved your life" were the first words I heard.

I looked at the clock still drowsy—almost two in the afternoon. I had gone into surgery at 10:00 a.m.

Not thirty minutes but almost four hours.

It all began on February 16, 2013.

My body was speaking to me, but I wasn't listening to her.

It all started with an abdominal pain; three days delayed.

I went to see my doctor, a woman who said she cared about her patients.

Dr. Ida. I liked her.

Small cup—urine test.

Crossing my fingers.

Rodrigo is quiet. I am hoping it is positive.

"Inconclusive," Dr. Ida says. "I cannot tell you yes or no. When was the first day of your last period?"

This question was asked many more times. No caffeine, no intercourse, no exercise.

February 22: First lab work. Sangre.

February 26: First ultrasound. Week four since gestation.

"Inconclusive."

An odd look on her young face, the technician sees me cry and calls the doctor. He steps in, y nada más me pregunta, "Are you pregnant ma'am?" He leaves, I cry more, and then the technician blurts out, "I see a growth next to your ovaries. Maybe a cyst, but I'm not sure. . . . Get dressed; we will send the results to your doctor. We are done here."

I left the room—with its white walls and sterile smells—feeling scared. "Tengo miedo," I tell Rodrigo. We drove to my doctor's office, but she was out. No answers. I get no peace of mind, no sleep. I cried for three hours nonstop. When I calmed down, I googled the phrases "cyst next to ovaries" and "growth next to ovaries," and what I read left me feeling more scared.

March 4: I finally see la doctora who says she cares, and again she only has a few words for me. No ayuda a calmarme. Su silencio me pone en alerta, su silencio me ahoga con preocupación.

"Lab work every forty-eight hours."

Sangre, sangre, sangre.

March 12: Second ultrasound. Again, same orders: "Get undressed, spread your legs, it might hurt, relax." I position my body so I can get a glimpse of the screen. Nada.

Another day goes by: más miedo.

March 14: Last appointment with Dr. Ida—2:00 p.m. As we wait in the exam room, I can hear my birth date and name being repeated—once, twice, tres, cuatro . . . ocho veces.

I can hear her say, "I don't know what to tell her. Can I send her to you?"

JUDITH FLORRREZZ CAR-MO-NA . . . I start feeling like an object. She does not care; she *has not* cared.

At around three she finally talks to us, not about us: "I have to send you to the best; he is the best. I don't have answers for you." That was the last time we saw her! Within ten minutes, I was in the emergency room, más sangre taken from me, another ultrasound, and finally a doctor who had answers.

He took one look at the ultrasound and immediately, within thirty seconds, knew something was wrong: "Esa Ida, what was she thinking?"

Within two hours I was scheduled for an emergency surgery.

March 15, 10:00 a.m.: Dr. Duarte explains why. "It was an ectopic pregnancy," he says, "an inevitable miscarriage. You also have a cyst. Once we get in there, I will know exactly what happened; it should take no more than thirty minutes." And then he translates for Rodrigo, "Lo siento. . . ."

The night before the surgery I could not sleep; I was nervous; I had started to mourn. . . . I continue to mourn after *siete* fechas, cinco cicatrices, dos corazones rotos y muchas lágrimas porque nuestro angelito nunca llegó.

Trials

The drive between Las Cruces and Los Angeles is about twelve to thirteen hours. On January 4, 2016, on our way back from visiting my family in L.A., I talked for most of the trip. I had been in different treatments for two and a half years—jolted by multiple tries of IVF and IUI. My body was traumatized by an invasion of hormonal treatments to get pregnant, but I was done trying. I had become someone *irreconocible*: unrecognizable. Mood changes, depression, weight gain, anger. I was spent, literally and figuratively. The reproductive treatments had left us in debt and me in shambles. The hormonal injections had turned me into someone I did not like. Besides, being told when to have intercourse takes out all the fun and spontaneity of intimacy and sharing love with your spouse. That ride was decisive: we were going to adopt. Five years later and still no baby. The trials continue, but now my body is speaking to me, and I have to listen to her.

Closing of the Wound

The year I turned forty, two major events happened: I earned tenure, and I became perimenopausal. I come from matriarchs who had between nine and thirteen children. I have had none. I have had five surgeries: an ectopic pregnancy, a dilation and curettage (D&C), a hysteroscopy to remove the first five polyps that formed inside my uterus, a painful hysterosalpingography, a partial hysterectomy to remove more polyps and a cyst next to my left ovary, and finally a full hysterectomy. Now, there is no hope for bearing children. Nunca.

Finally, I feel like my wound will close. I will stop bleeding. I will stop hurting. The open wound will close; my reproductive system will sear a scar. As for my body, I finally listened to her.

Brenda's Testimonio of Loss, Postpartum, and Being a Tenure-Track Mother-Scholar During a Pandemic

Loss

I lost Stenda December 8, 2017. Steve, my partner, held my hand as I labored through the loss at home while two of my sisters coached us over the phone, sharing the heartbreaking knowledge they had gained through their own experiences with pregnancy loss. Am I really supposed to flush my baby down the toilet? Yes. I begged Steve to retrieve our baby instead so we could have a dignified end, but I changed my mind at the thought of putting him through that.

When it was over, my sisters offered advice for managing the physical pain but had little to say about the pain in my heart. I did not have time to grieve. I had a dissertation to finish in three months and a faculty position waiting for me back home at Borderlands University.

My heart weighed heavily on the day of graduation in May 2018. One week later, I had a positive pregnancy test. Baby Breve. I had received a calendar reminder sent by a close friend a month earlier for Stenda: "Brenda's baby meet and greet," Sunday, July 8, 2018. This prompted a check-in text from her. I responded, "Nine weeks tomorrow. I'm still feeling a little guarded, scared to get too attached. I'm getting better about talking to Breve and letting them know they are just as loved and desired as Stenda was."

Postpartum

After twenty-two hours of labor and an emergency cesarean, I welcomed my son the second week of the spring 2019 semester. Ten hours later, while my son was held for observation at the neonatal intensive care unit, I was responding to a student email. They had a question about the syllabus. This was only my second semester as faculty, and I felt that I had to prove that I was not "that type of woman" who would stop caring about her career, as a department co-director—a white woman—had put it.

That April, I received an invitation from a colleague to submit a chapter proposal for a handbook they were co-editing with my co-director, a woman of generational wealth whose ethnicity is classified as white and identity rooted in whiteness. Ironically, she is often mistaken for being a Latina.

I declined.

I was still healing from the physical and emotional wounds of having my abdomen sliced and spread apart, my child ripped from my womb, exasperated by my desperate ongoing efforts to get my baby to latch for breastfeeding. I was trying to figure out how to mother a newborn while meeting my full-time faculty responsibilities and managing with little sleep.

"Wrong answer," my colleague responded, so I sheepishly accepted the invitation to submit a proposal for a chapter they later claimed to have "gifted" to me.

"At least now I know you can write," the co-director scoffed a few months later, after berating me over the car speakerphone for being late with the submission. I was on my way to the airport for a work trip with my partner and infant in tow. I felt incapable of looking my partner in the eyes. I received the copyedits a few weeks ago and texted Judith:

> I can't bring myself to read it. All I remember about this fucking article is how much I was struggling to heal from the C-section, care for an infant, and to pump every 3 hours so I could breastfeed my baby. . . . Moms don't talk nearly enough about the hell and sacrifice that comes with breastfeeding and pumping. Imagine arranging your entire day into 2-hour intervals, then stopping for an hour because there's prep time, pump time, feed time, and cleanup involved with pumping for feeding every 3 hours, even at night. It's cruel how little we acknowledge and allow for this work. I would still do it again.

That year, 2019, days after my son's first birthday and a month before the pandemic hit our country, I was evaluated as "Failing to make progress towards promotion and tenure." When I questioned their lack of consideration for the tenure clock extension I had been approved for, I was attacked by the leadership, threatened with a nonrenewal of contract, and treated from that day forward as if I were using having a baby as an excuse to get out of doing my work. I became the latest target of ongoing, intentional, and malicious retaliatory acts frequently enacted by the leadership in the college and condoned by the university.

Pandemic

Like millions of women across the globe, when the pandemic hit, I lost access to childcare and had to figure out how to tend to my one-year-old while holding a full-time job. I work in the field of educational leadership, preparing current and future public-school administrators. My teaching/mothering affects not only the students in my courses, but the public schools and communities they serve. The support and guidance I am able or willing to give graduate students has a short distance to travel for it to make an impact on my borderland community. During the pandemic, students wanted additional time to meet weekly to discuss the real-time policy decisions being made on their campus and district; not responding to them was not an option.

When I discussed these growing needs of my students and their school campuses with the new interim co-director, a Latino from the borderland who had not yet earned tenure, he responded, "This is why we need to wait for the university leadership to make decisions." Why would we wait and not offer guidance ourselves when we are the experts in the field? As the year progressed, students in the program were dealing with an increased need for mental health support for the teachers and children from their public-school campuses. Again, I turned to my leadership only to be told there was nothing available to our graduate students because, in their words, "They don't do emotional labor."

Among the student comments that I saw repeated in my teaching evaluations for 2020 were "compassionate," "supportive," and "equity-focused." Preparing materials for my annual performance review made my stomach turn. If there was one thing I knew my institution would not appreciate, it was my mothering. I received a single negative critique from a white male student that said I was "A bit heavy-handed on the anti-white stuff." *This is what they'll focus on*, I thought.

Surrender

In midspring 2021, shortly after receiving a good 2020 annual performance review, I was emailed a "rationale letter" submitted three months prior to the latest interim leadership—a white man—by a doctoral student who had dropped me as their chair. The co-director, in a carefully crafted email likely written by the legal department, was requesting a meeting so I could respond through a recorded interview. The student accused me of trying to organize a "coup" against my department because I suggested collective action in reporting violence that he and a couple of his peers were experiencing in the program.

The student also questioned my integrity and commitment to students because his proposed dissertation research was not methodologically sound. Rather than trusting and valuing my expertise and following my guidance, he claimed I simply did not like his work. His unfounded questioning of my professionalism was the result of my disagreement with him on changing his dissertation research away from focusing on Indigenous communities—communities to which he, an educator recruited from abroad/international teacher recruit, does not belong. The student explained that he wanted to switch his focus because the panelist at a graduate student symposium he attended told him focusing on Indigenous communities would make him more appealing to a potential university employer. I responded by recommending readings on Indigenous research methodology and asking him to take time to reflect on his positionality and what it would mean to conduct research with/in Indigenous communities. In his letter, the student went on to accuse me of trying to create systemic change in our public schools through my teaching. In his words, it was "a system that is fair and equal for all of the students." To his argument, I *am* unapologetically guilty for teaching students about inequality, systemic violence, and their responsibility as school leaders to be responsive and disruptive to injustice.

In closing, the student's letter questioned my mental stability. The department's email request for a recorded meeting feigned concern for my well-being. The absurdity of this student's letter along with my department's attempt to grasp at straws by entertaining this attack on my character, the way each claim and their response stood in clear opposition to the department's espoused social justice mission, left me feeling confused and, at times, laughing hysterically. Unbeknownst to them, I was being recruited by a different university—a move I had not committed to, since it meant leaving my mother and sisters, leaving the borderland. It meant taking my son away from our safe and loving community amid a deadly pandemic. To support myself and my family, I took medical leave after this final attack, ya que estoy loca. I felt unable to open my email those weeks and focused instead on healing old and new spiritual wounds and strengthening my bonds with my baby and partner. I submitted my resignation when I returned.

Testimonio Theorizing: Our Bodies Speak

Being madres in academia is hard and not understood by many academics or university leadership. Madre(hood) is also complex. It is not only about those who are able to have children—it is also about loss, trials, and tribulations, giving up, surrendering, and sacrifice. The way the system is set up does not help. Universities have historically served faculty who are primarily men. That is the very foundation of U.S. universities. Both Brenda and I have had a difficult time writing this chapter. Our madre(hood) testimonios need to be told, however, porque hay que compartir para sanar; telling is healing. Indeed, mujeres in academia have been sharing their madre(hood) testimonios for a long time. In 2001, Gloria Holguín Cuádraz wrote a piece titled, "Diary of *La Llorona* with a PhD"—more than twenty years later, many of us with PhDs continue to cry and mourn.

The Educated *Llorona*

llora
en silencio
dropping *lagrimas*
onto the beautiful
brown curvature of her belly
no por los niños que perdió
pero
por los niños
que nunca tuvo
And for the children
she consciously gave up.

—GLORIA HOLGUÍN CUÁDRAZ (2001, 212)

In *Telling to Live*, in the section titled, "The Body Re/members," the Latina Feminist Group remind us, "Our bodies document how women's bodies are damaged," metaphorically fractured, broken, dismembered. Our bodies re/member what we have endured and survived (del Alba Acevedo et al. 2001, 263). Both of us first-generation students and scholars, both of us border crossers. As Mexicana university professors, the institution has not been able to fully understand or nuance our experiences, not as scholars, not as mothers. Our intersectional identities have not been acknowledged, recognized, or valued.

Kimberlé Crenshaw (1991), a critical legal scholar, coined the concept of intersectionality. Intersectionality allows us to see how women of color, especially first-generation students and scholars, experience higher education within interlocked systems of oppression and overlapping subordination structures, such as racism, sexism, and classism (Crenshaw 1991, 1241). Yet, "the university is seldom held accountable for the institutional violence and exploitation faced by first-generation, low-income, and working-class Mother-Scholars of Color" (Caballero et al. 2019, 6).

Conclusion: Searing the Scars and Our Ongoing Pláticas

We won't dare to share consejos/advice about our distinct madre(hood) experiences because we hope the readers are moved to also share their papelitos guardados and become testimonialistas—bear witness to their own experiences (Delgado Bernal 2008). We do, however, share about our embarking on a healing path. We hope our chapter inspires others, especially other m(other) scholars and pretenured faculty, to share their testimonios—to divulge the injustices they have experienced. Many of us stay silent. Perhaps we have been told that sharing our vulnerabilities is not professional or that this discloses our vulnerabilities, but for us, our trenza de identidades weaves our personal, professional, and political identities (Delgado Bernal 2008). As we have shared, we believe that telling is healing.

Try to find allies at your campus. Take account of how many of your colleagues, male or female, have children. Create spaces where you can let out/release the weight of oppression. Release and speak of the pain and trauma, the violence experienced, and then create spaces of healing. Know that some people have experienced similar oppressions and will create relationships of compassion and solidarity with you. Such praxis requires courage for us to come together and bear our wounds, to trust, and to find ways to push back against the structures that replicate these silences.

Indeed, Mara Chavez-Diaz (2019) reminds us that we are "living proof of the centrality of strong, powerful muxeres who redefine mothering from an Indigenous perspective, one that simultaneously disrupts the colonization of our bodies" (282). Brenda's strength is demonstrated in her reflection, and I reflect on different ways in which I enact madre(-hood) in academia.

Brenda: The decision whether to have more children is an ongoing struggle I am actively battling. It is what my heart desires, but it does not seem realistic or within reach. Now I constantly wonder about the support and resources available to Latinx mother-scholars. I'm at another institution, and while their responses seem promising, I am not naïve. I expect to experience similar institutional violence and struggles. This change has also forced me to move away from my biological and spirit/academic sisters, those that I have leaned on and have carried me through when I felt I could not. Now I am physically alone, scared of repeating history, and dealing with the additional layers of uncertainty. I also fear a future where I might wake up feeling regret that I did not complete my family. I attempt to embrace this liminal space, knowing that as much as I want certainty and a conclusion, I do not have one—just faith.

Judith: I have many nieces and nephews. I am *that* tía that has become the madrina/godmother to many. At the university, I femtor students and junior colleagues. I embrace the womb that did not bear children. I do the emotional labor that other faculty refuse to engage in. I purposefully connect and develop reciprocal relationships with others. I create and reinvent the concept of familia. After all, as some say, skin folk aren't always kinfolk. I write to heal; I share to denounce. That is what testimonialistas do!

REFERENCES

Anzaldúa, Gloria. 1987. *Borderlands/La Frontera: The New Mestiza*. San Francisco, Calif.: Aunt Lute.

Caballero, Cecilia, Yvette Martínez-Vu, Judith Pérez-Torres, Michelle Téllez, and Christine Vega, eds. 2019. *The Chicana M(other)work Anthology: Porque Sin Madres No Hay Revolución*. Tucson: University of Arizona Press.

Chavez-Diaz, Mara. 2019. "Birthing Healing Justice: My Journey Through Miscarriage, Healing Conocimientos, and Decolonizing my Womb." In *The Chicana M(other)work Anthology: Porque Sin Madres No Hay Revolución*, edited by Cecilia Caballero, Yvette Martínez-Vu, Judith Pérez-Torres, Michelle Téllez, and Christine Vega, 272–87. Tucson: University of Arizona Press.

Crenshaw, Kimberlé. 1991. "Mapping the Margins: Intersectionality, Identity Politics, and Violence Against Women of Color." *Stanford Law Review* 43 (6): 1241–99.

del Alba Acevedo, Luz, Norma Alarcón, Celia Alvarez, Ruth Behar, Rina Benmayor, Norma E. Cantú, Daisy Cocco De Filippis, et al., eds. 2001. *Telling to Live: Latina Feminist Testimonios*. Durham, N.C.: Duke University Press.

Delgado Bernal, Dolores. 2008. "La Trenza de Identidades: Weaving Together My Personal, Professional, and Communal Identities." In *Doing the Public Good: Latina/o Scholars Engage Civic Participation*, edited by Kenneth P. Gonzalez and Raymond V. Padilla, 134–48. Sterling: Stylus.

Fierros, Cindy, and Dolores Delgado Bernal. 2016. "Vamos a platicar: The Contours of Pláticas as Chicana/Latina Feminist Methodology." *Chicana/Latina Studies: The Journal of Mujeres Activas en Letras y Cambio Social* 15 (2): 98–121.

Flores Carmona, Judith, Manal Hamzeh, Cynthia Bejarano, Ma. Eugenia Hernández Sánchez, and Yvonne Pilar El Ashmawi. 2018. "*Pláticas~Testimonios*: Practicing Methodological Borderlands for Solidarity and Resilience in Academia." *Chicana/Latina Studies: The Journal of MALCS* 18 (1): 30–53.

Gonzalez, Francisca E. 1998. "The Formations of Mexicananess: *Trenzas de identidades multiples*; The Development of Womanhood Among Young Mexicans: Braids of Multiple Identities." PhD diss., University of California, Davis.

Holguín Cuádraz, Gloria. 2001. "Diary of *La Llorona* with a PhD." In *Telling to Live: Latina Feminist Testimonios*, edited by Luz del Alba Acevedo, Norma Alarcón, Celia Alvarez, Ruth Behar, Rina Benmayor, Norma E. Cantú, Daisy Cocco De Filippis, et al., 212–17. Durham, N.C.: Duke University Press.

CHAPTER 8

Ma'ala Meecha, Watch Over Me

A Hiaki Interpretation of Frontera Mother+hood

MARISA ELENA DUARTE
Arizona State University

This chapter is about loss and renewal. It is about a kind of traumatic loss that is pervasive but often unaddressed: the loss of infants. Many times, mothers who suffer miscarriage or reproductive complications, mothers whose infants are stillborn, mothers who experience fatal complications during labor and delivery, or whose child passes away due to sudden infant death syndrome are left to manage interrelated traumas and long-term complex grief on their own. Few physicians are trained in managing maternal and postpartum physiological responses to grief and emotional trauma, and infant deaths are still relatively mysterious. Few physicians and pathologists are in a position to offer adequate and complete medical explanations to the mother in mourning. Thus, mothers who endure loss enter into a period of spiritual, emotional, and relational change that often has profound effects on their sense of self, family, work life, well-being, and system of faith.

In this chapter, I share insights from an intense period of transformative grief that I experienced during and after my second pregnancy. I offer these insights from a very private, vulnerable, recent period in my life and in the life of my family because I think it is important to express the significance of maternal grief and how it shapes the compassion fundamental to motherwork and the role of *comadres*—mothers devoted to each other through kin, faith, and affection—across the borderlands. *Inepo*

Marisa Elena Duarte *ti teak*. My name is Marisa Elena Duarte. *Inepo hiak hamut into* Chicana *hamut*. I am a Hiaki woman and also Chicana. *In hapchi* Marco Antonio Duarte *ti teak into in maala* Angelita Molina Duarte *ti teak*. *In hapchi* Mexican American *o'ou into in maala hiak hamut*. *In Finikapo hoak*. My father Marco Antonio is Mexican American, and my mother Angelita Molina Duarte is Hiaki. I live in Phoenix, Arizona.

I grew up in a large Hiaki and Mexican American family with many influential aunts and grandparents, in a household immersed in Chicano history and politics and in devotion to Hiaki religion, ancestral political truth, and spirituality: *itom hiak luturia into itom herensia yo'owe yo'owe*. In this chapter I italicize Hiaki and Spanish words and offer in-text translations. I am an enrolled member of the Pascua Yaqui Tribe, but in this chapter I spell the word Hiaki in the modern orthography of our binational—U.S. and Mexican—tribal nation. I hope that my words bring comfort and validation to mothers who have also experienced similar trials.

Grief Is Unexpected, Yet Its Effects Are Pervasive

In December 2021, my husband, Jake, drove me to the Mexican Art Import shop on 24th Street in Phoenix so that he could buy me a Christmas present. I chose a two-foot-tall statue of La Virgen de Guadalupe, and I asked him to build a *nicho* outside where she could watch over us.

First appearing to a Chichimec man named Juan Diego and his uncle Juan Bernadino in the sixteenth century at the Hill of Tepeyac, the apparition of a young Indigenous woman offered Juan and his uncle, two men from distant northern tribes experiencing the traumas of an apocalypse, spiritual consolation and hope. The Catholic Church sought veneration, characterizing the encounter as a vision of Jesus Christ's mother, Mary, hence the name Our Lady of Guadalupe; yet Indigenous Meso-American thinkers and believers also perceive the encounter as a visit from Indigenous spiritual feminine forces. Many venerate her as a faceted representation of the Nahuatl beings Tonántzin, Ometecuhtli, and Omecihuatl. Chicana scholar Irene Lara (2008) refers to this epistemic faceting as *tonanlupanisma*.

In my own Hiaki belief system, over the years I have come to see Her as the sacred doe that escapes the hunt, and a manifestation of the sacred celestial rhythm of Ma'ala Meecha, Mother Moon. Upon identifying petroglyphs in Mexico indicating moon cycle timekeeping with deer antlers, contemporary non-Indigenous anthropologists expressed surprise at the eco-spiritual insights of our ancestors: "[Deer] antlers are exclusively male and grow larger with the waxing summer sun. The females are impregnated under the light of the moon and later give birth to the new generation," writes William Breen Murray (2013, 202). The sacred pull of the moon on one of our most nourishing Indigenous wild foods bears spiritual significance for attentive hunters and their families, as well as, according to *hitevi*, Hiaki healer, Micaela Estrella, for women: "La luna es como una almanaque para las que no saben nada, que no saben ni una letra, así saben de eso, así se dirigen, 'no, que está la luna acá, entonces, ya me va a venir la regla,' conocen ellos y ya la toman, es su calendario" (Olavarría, Aguilar, and Merino 2009, 33).[1]

In Mesilla, New Mexico, where I grew up, *nichos* are indentations built into mud or brick walls that can serve as a home within a home for meaningful spiritual and ancestral belongings. When my mother and father built their adobe home in New Mexico, they constructed several *nichos* where, over the years, my mother has placed a rotation of candles, *santos*, baskets, crosses, bundles of sage, small plants, and, ever present in our lives, the open-armed figure of La Virgen soothing and blessing the family.[2]

---

1. "The moon is like an almanac for those who have no other, for those who do not know how to read, they do know this, what the moon indicates, 'ah, the moon is in that position there, therefore the cycle governing my body's flows will come,' this they understand as their calendar" (my translation).

2. In English, *santos* means saints. For many Indigenous peoples of North America, basket making is an art through which the weaver expresses an ancestral relationship to a lush ecosystem, reflecting symbols of nests, butterflies, rainclouds, whirlwinds, mountain ranges, water, and other natural phenomena in the meditative pattern of weft-and-weave and coil. Sage is a plant that, once harvested and bundled, is either burnt or ingested as a tea to alleviate spiritual sickness, emotionally tumultuous spirit apparitions, long-term illness, and sorrow. Various varieties have antibiotic and aromatherapeutic effects.

My husband and I had been living in our downtown Phoenix home for four years, and I had slowly been designating spaces to reflect my needs as a mother. Jake planted a summer vegetable garden and flower gardens. I chose creosote and pitaya to sweeten the air and revive the soil, as well as to reclaim the hardy and nourishing desert from the arid concrete grasp of the city. The pitaya reminds me of the Rio Yaqui territory in Sonora, and the creosote, of the Chihuahua desert life around the Rio Grande in southern New Mexico. I began watering the flowering *tronadora* by the bedroom window and the mesquite by the sidewalk, and Jake trimmed both so they would grow tall and sturdy.[3] He planted grass and desert oak where our toddler could play, with the oak yielding the acorn medicine of his people, the Mechoopda Rancheria Band of Chico, California. He constructed a mini-ramada in a nod to the Hiaki-style ramadas, where the *ma'aso, paskolas,* and *musikom*—the deer dancer, musicians, and ancient desert spirits—play deer songs, and where the women and children rest and pray in the company of our little brother Jesus (Itom Saila Jesus) when He traverses to the peaceful and graceful flowering world (*sea ania*).[4]

As my mother once did as a child, I have favorite memories of sitting as a child beside my cousins and aunts while watching the deer dance in the flower-laden ramada during Hiaki Easter celebrations.[5] I also have

---

3. The *tronadora* is *Tecoma stans*, or Arizona yellow bells.

4. In ancestral Hiaki philosophy, there are at least five interrelated domains, or ways of perceiving: *huya ania* (wilderness), *tuku ania* (night), *tenku ania* (dreaming), *yo ania* (spirit domain), and *sea ania* (flowery paradise or blossoming). American anthropologists Edward Spicer and Muriel Thayer Painter characterize these domains as "worlds." Nowadays, some Hiaki-language speakers translate the Hiaki word *aniam* to signify *worlds* as in facets of a worldview, while others refer to the five ways of perceiving as *itom mamni hiak luturiam*, which means, roughly, our five Haiki truths, or realities. To read more about these, see Painter (1986).

5. At least since the eighteenth century, Hiaki people have merged aspects of Meso-American Catholicism with our own ancestral land-based spirituality, including veneration of the deer and respect for the hunt, and attentiveness to ancestral and spirit messengers as well as to ecological rhythms around the Rio Yaqui and in the monte, or desert mountain ranges. Modern celebrations of the Easter pageant take place each year at the end of Lent, or Cuaresma, in Hiaki pueblos and villages in the United States and in Mexico, integrating these belief systems along with a striking

memories of keeping vigil in the ramada during wakes and listening to the long minor-chord *alabanzas,* or hymns of the *cantoras,* the devotional singers intrinsic to many of our tribe's religious rites.

In our Phoenix home, I selected the location for the outside *nicho* with the intention of also using the space to hold the table, the mesa, I set each November for our immediate family during *animam mikwam,* our Day of the Dead, concurrent to the mesa my *tía* sets for our extended family in Pascua, the Hiaki village in Tucson. In the heart of a city that prides itself on real estate speculation and urban reinvention—the phoenix: the mythical bird consumed by fire who rises again—my husband and I create a place to live rooted in honoring our ancestral ways of relating despite the temptation of sparkling swimming pools, HOA xeriscaping, and Astroturf.

Resolved by Tragedy: Walking the Boundary Between Life and Afterlife

Just before Christmas my husband finished constructing the *nicho,* and I set La Virgen inside. A week passed, and I woke one night feeling a great stillness. I held my sleeping son in my arms. I did not know it yet, but our new baby had died in my womb. He was nearly thirty-five weeks along. I had been dreaming of visiting with Paiute and Hupa friends, watching our young children play in a clear pool near the Pacific Ocean, waves glittering beneath the late afternoon sun. In the dream, one of our babies slipped into the pool, and I panicked. A friend told me, "Don't worry, he went with his father," and I was soothed. The dream was my body's way of telling me our baby boy Seyewailo had silently slipped away in the salty sea within my womb. It was my mind's way of beginning a long and painful period of intense grief. I had just come up with his name a few days before; *seyewailo* is a Hiaki word for an oasis or place of rest in the arid desert.

---

critique of the evils that trouble our communities in the present as expressed through the antics and *mandas,* or devotional acts, of the *chapayekam* and *pahkolam.* Muriel Thayer Painter's 1986 book *With Good Heart: Yaqui Beliefs and Ceremonies in Pascua Village* describes Hiaki Easter and is based on the village where my grandparents participated in Cuaresma and included their children in the celebrations.

I went into labor a few days later, and while I recovered in the hospital, my husband commenced stoking a four-day fire beside the *nicho*, following his tribe's tradition of a wake. Every day for months I prayed our infant would live, grow, and be born into my arms, but truthfully, I had a feeling early in the pregnancy, a mother's intuition, that our blessed baby might not fully breathe on his own. At sixteen weeks, in a moment of despair, I shared this worry via text message with a dear friend who, like me, is also Hiaki and Xicanx. My doctor, a young Mexican American obstetrician and mother herself, confirmed for me early on some of the challenges I was physically feeling throughout the pregnancy: high likelihood of Down syndrome and all that entails; a slowly developing heart and bowels; and my own inability to gain enough weight. The morning after a physically easy labor, my doctor sat on the edge of my hospital bed, told me that I had experienced a traumatic labor, and asked how I was doing, remarking that I seemed very calm. My baby was a little over three pounds; he had lost almost a pound in the few days since the spirit left the flesh. He was long-limbed with beautiful hands, feet, and toes like mine and eyebrows arched like rainbows to frame a serene gaze much like that of his brother. The nurse dressed him for us in a white dress with a rainbow knit cap.

I was outwardly calm and felt still, as though I were resting under the moon's midnight gaze, but the grief was and is extraordinary. Some Hiaki women and Mexican women are taught at a very young age not to go into the light of the full moon, as it supposedly can result in fetal abnormalities and other reproductive challenges during pregnancy and even during later pregnancies. Lunar eclipses bring their own challenges: "Durante el eclipse de la luna, el gestante puede ser dañado o comido, por ejemplo, nacer sin una oreja, con el labio comido, esponer de más, el bebé puede nacer con seis dedos en cada mano y en cada pie."[6] Years before, my mother had given me an amulet of the evil eye braided into a red thread: a bracelet for protection during the full moon. I see those bracelets sold at the markets at Magdalena, the site of an ancestral pil-

----

6. "During the lunar eclipse, the gestating fetus can be hurt or eaten, for example, by being born without an ear, with a chewed lip, or by receiving extra body parts such as six fingers on each hand and foot" (Olavarría, Aguilar, and Merino 2009, 96, my translation).

grimage for Hiaki, Mayo, and O'odham people, and at the Mexican markets in Tucson and Phoenix. My mother gave it to me as fashion mostly. But growing up Hiaki—our religious, spiritual, and political inheritance nested in the sensations of the night world, dawn world, dream world, flower world, ocean world, desert and sierra, and spirit world—affects my emotions, dispositions, and perspective on other modern constructs. The birth of one son and the loss of another gave me the space to walk through a profound contemplation of the temporality of reproduction; the spiritual spatiality of birth, loss, grief, and growth; the limitations of Western obstetrics; and likewise, the capacity to grieve alongside other mothers in a way I hadn't before.

The morning that my doctor sat on the edge of my hospital bed at St. Joseph's, a Catholic hospital in the heart of Phoenix, I did not have the words to express that I was at the beginning of that long walk. I mostly felt shock, tempered by a low keening sorrow born from a cellular familiarity with mother-child loss. For weeks to come, when I dreamed, I would see seas and rivers of tears, and hear my own voice howling in despair. I am not alone in that experience; many mothers who lose infants hear themselves howl in the isolation of their sorrow.

Finding the Spiritual Strength in Ancestral Memory

Where I grew up in Mesilla, New Mexico, families pass along stories of La Llorona, the ancestral ghost of a crying mother haunting the banks of the Rio Grande looking for her lost children, children she may have drowned in a moment of emotional vulnerability. Like many children, at nightfall, I would run inside feeling as though I were being chased by a dangerous spirit.

When I was older, studying Mexican American history in college, I began to learn more about the political wars and gender oppression shaping the myth of La Llorona (Carbonell 1999). I also learned that La Llorona was not a weeping woman who haunted only the banks of the Rio Grande; she was, and is, the ghost of matriarchal sorrow who haunts many Latinx families who have experienced family separations, domestic violence, sexual assault, and the loss of children amid political and national upheavals (Delgado and Stefancic 2019). In my collegiate reading, the river was a symbol of a political boundary. Why would it not be? As a teenager in the 1990s, I watched the Ciudad Juárez news stations' footage of people drowning in desperate attempts to cross the Río Bravo/ Rio Grande. Alarmed by President Donald Trump's genocidal treatment of immigrant children and families, legal scholars Richard Delgado and Jean Stefancic (2019) assert that "rejecting the wisdom and identity that immigrants from Mexico and the Northern Triangle countries bring to the United States merely allows spirits like la Llorona (in the form of President Trump) to enter our national house and wreak havoc (i.e., steal children)" (313).

My maternal ancestors fought for centuries to protect the ecology and safe haven of their sacred homeland along the Río Yaqui in Sonora. But only after hearing my own screaming in my head did I realize that the symbol of the river could be a metaphor for grief *and* spilled amniotic fluid. The river thus transcends the boundaries of the gendered myths of Latinidad and political border crossing. The river is an experience of birth and death transformations in motherhood.

There have been many losses in my mother's family. She has many sis-ters, and each of them have endured the loss of children at different times in their lives. Their daughters and sons have also endured those types of losses. Losses occurred through miscarriages, childhood illness and acci-dents, suicide, separations and divorces, adoptions, and unnatural deaths in adulthood. There have also been the losses that occur when a parent watches a child slip into despair, or vice versa, and relationships fracture, inducing a great anxiety and years of grieving. Thankfully, some of those relationships have repaired and transformed over time with great prayer, effort, and often, degrees of sobriety. Others have not, and the family is sensitive to ways of relating through periodic fracture and tentative reconciliation.

Before that, there were the losses of wartime. The years of the Mexi-can Revolution, from roughly 1910 to 1920, were preceded by the Yaqui Wars in Sonora (Hernández-Silva 1996; Hu-DeHart 1981, 1984; Taibo 2013; Padilla Ramos and Trejo Contreras 2012; Donjuan Espinoza et al. 2010; Padilla Ramos 1995, 2011, 2018; Spicer 1967). For five centuries my ancestors were entangled in and leading a cycle of wars of territo-rial defense against various forms of brutal colonial invasion, from the Spanish land grabs of 1533 to the mid-eighteenth century; through the

nineteenth-century period of Mexican Independence, when Hiaki people faced unjust taxation, Mexican settlement, and land allotments; and
through the twentieth-century anti-Yaqui dictatorship of Porfirio Díaz.
The modern consciousness of this intergenerational anticolonial struggle
is printed in the colors and symbols of our tribal flag and memorized in
the footfalls and prayers of our ceremonial people when they carry out
their annual *mandas* in service to our communal religion.[7] A crescent
moon, sun, and cross are situated on a field of white bordered by yellow stars and red and blue panels; the black cross signifies the deaths of
Hiaki warriors; the white signifies the blessed and pure spiritual state of
our children, while our ancestral predecessors observe our continuation
in their form as stars, *chokim*. I am certain that when I am in my final
days—if the passing takes time—it will be those ritual songs, *alabanzas*,
and footfalls of spiritual determination that march through my thoughts.

My oldest aunts pass on the stories of my great-grandmother Juana,
who as a girl lost her father, Rosario, likely to *peones*, Mexican men
hired by constitutionalist military leaders to deter potential revolutionary threats in a mercenary fashion. In her early twenties, she witnessed
soldiers and *peones* carrying out genocidal orders. A story that is passed
down through the women in my family and by women in other Hiaki
families is about how soldiers with the Mexican military bashed babies
against rocks until their brains fell out (Valdes et al. 2022; León 1998).
Others tell of soldiers who, while transporting Hiaki prisoners of war
to the sugar cane and hemp plantations of Yucatán and Quintana Roo,
threw babies in the sea (León 1998). My great-grandmother Juana Mal-
donado was a *pariente* of General Tetabiate, also known as Juan Mal-
donado, the influential Hiaki lieutenant who took command after the
death of Hiaki general Cajeme. Juana was captured and sent to the Catmis plantation in 1900, which was known to be a location for punishing
Hiaki and Mayo prisoners of war (Avilez 2014; Padilla Ramos 2011; Wells
and Joseph 1996). She escaped perhaps five or six years later with her

---

7. *Mandas* are devotions or offerings in which an individual takes on a responsibility to their religious community as a form of repentance or prayer for others. In Pascua, *mandas* are often long term, occurring in cycles of several years or more, and can
mean involvement in many years of ceremonial service, hosting masses, preparing
food for community gatherings, or doing other spiritually responsible forms of work.

young son Eulogio, slowly traversing central Mexico all the way back to Sonora and into the United States. She would have witnessed, if not heard, stories of proud, defiant, and utterly devoted Hiaki mothers who, during the January 1900 Battle of Mazocoba, jumped from cliffs holding their babies and small children close in order to prevent Mexican bullets from touching the bodies of their children (León 1998). That was a story I also heard from my aunts growing up, one that was shared with them when they were girls.

Another story my aunts shared was about *torocoyoris*, Hiaki people, mostly soldiers working for the state, who informed Mexican soldiers as to the location of Hiaki families in flight, and who helped sell Hiaki children off to upper-caste Mexican households as housemaids and farmhands. When my aunts were children in the 1930s and '40s, my grandparents hid them under beds or in other secret places whenever strangers—white, Mexican, or Hiaki—approached their homes in the refugee Hiaki communities north of Tucson.

The trauma of those losses is incalculable and palpable in the foundation of our spiritual truth and in the specifically anticolonial parts of our religion and willpower. They form the backbone of our spiritual strength as *hiak hamuchim*, as women who are taught not to cry out during intense labor pains, who are taught to work hard because life is hard, who co-parent many children other than our own, and who persist through the long cycles of prayer, pilgrimage, and observation that culminate in our various forms of spiritual renewal concurrent to the tribe's annual Lenten spiritual renewal (Erickson 2008; León 1998; PACMYC 1994; Gomez Quintana 2020; Kelley 1978, 1989; Valdes et al. 2022). As Hiaki professor Dulce Aurelia Felix Valdes asserted in a 2022 presentation on Hiaki womanhood, "El ser hiaki es el querer ser y el que quiere seguir haciendo" (Valdes et al. 2022).[8]

My father is Mexican American, and unlike my Hiaki family, his family's births, baptismals, marriages, and deaths were neatly registered with the Mexican Civil Registry during Mexico's Independence and Revolutionary years. Their records indicate many maternal-child losses as well. My great-grandmother Manuela died in childbirth in Nogales just after

---

8. "A Hiaki way of being is in the desire to exist and the actions of persistence" (my translation).

the 1918 Battle of Nogales, when U.S. border agents allowed married Mexican women and their children to seek refuge from crossfire in the U.S. city. Her son, my paternal grandfather Augustín, was soon given into the care of a Tohono O'odham family at Pozo Verde near Arivaca, Arizona, but Augustín would return to his Mexican family at the age of four, only to experience the shadow of his mother's absence. After she died, his father, a Mexican constitutionalist soldier, was captured as a U.S. prisoner of war and sent to Fort Rosencrantz in San Diego. When he returned to Arivaca after that ordeal, he was not inclined to paternal warmth toward his first son. Desert ranch labor was difficult and demanding, and Revolutionary soldiers turned bandits were a frequent threat (Wilbur-Cruce 1987).[9]

My grandfather shared with my father a story illustrating the impact of his mother's loss. When he was around eleven years old, a group of bandits threatened to blow up the nearby pueblo of Sasabe, Sonora, with a bomb if the townspeople did not hand over their valuables. My great-uncles and other vaqueros—Mexican cowboys—and ranch hands were not impressed; they took up rifle posts and fired a volley of bullets at the thieves filing into town, one of whom, poor soul, carried over his head a big bomb. My great-uncles shouted at Augustín to run into the crossfire and bring back unused cartridges and rifles from the bodies in the street. My father tells me that Augustín described the sound of *abejas*—bees— whizzing by his head: speeding bullets. After that incident, a desperate sadness loomed over my grandfather. He knew that no mother or father who loved their son would ever send their child into such brutality. He told his son, my father, that story when my father was a young man worrying over the war in Vietnam. My father complained, "They are killing innocent people with bombs over there." My grandfather told my dad, darkly, "Mijo, there is always a man with a bomb."

The night after I delivered my Seyewailo's body, I lay awake at night in the bleached hospital bed and heard the strong cries of other infants in the maternity ward. A nurse entered my room close to midnight and offered to move me to another room, where I would not be troubled by those miraculous first cries. But I was not troubled. The stories of ma-

---

9. Arivaca rancher Eva Antonia Wilbur-Cruce (1987) offers insights from these difficult years in her memoir, *A Beautiful Cruel Country*.

ternal courage in my family soothed me. My Hiaki great-grandmother Juana hid her young son Eulogio in her skirts so that ruthless Mexican soldiers would not sell him into slavery. My Hiaki grandmother Maria grabbed a wandering bull from the yard so it would not harm her eight children. I imagined my Mexican great-grandmother Manuela cuddling her infant son Augustín, though she knew she was hemorrhaging with no apt midwifery care. My Mexican American grandmother Margarita dared to become pregnant again and to love her surviving children—to continue her motherwork—even as she mourned the loss of her infant son Luis to a heart defect. I told the nurse that I was not troubled. I was very happy for those mothers and their new babies. In my heart, I knew that my baby was not meant for this world, and that I am. Through the long threads that connect us to our ancestors' affection—the fact that those stories emerge and continue through the hearts, words, and hands of my relatives—I rely on the mother-child love that transcends the flesh, rivers flooded and dry, border wars, and occasional periods of peace. My son's dying made me mother myself in a long tradition of women and girls mothering under duress. Those moments make us who we are.

Serenity Through Lunar Devotion

For Hiaki people, the moon is a powerful cosmic force (Olavarría, Aguilar, and Merino 2009). The moon is feminine: Mother Moon, Ma'ala Meecha. Her counterpart, the masculine Sun, our ancient Father Sun, Itom O'ola Achai Ta'a, chases Her as a lover chases his desire through Her seasons of change, darkness, and renewal (Giddings 1959). He asks Her to marry Him, to be by His side for eternity, but She agrees only on the condition that He make Her a dress that will fit Her perfectly. He measures Her and makes the dress, only to find that it does not fit. He tries again and again but cannot get it right. He does not cease His celestial pursuit and affection. In our Hiaki language, words are not feminine or masculine, and verbs sit beside subjects and objects in a statement of relatedness rather than a description of an object's action over a subject. These two celestial beings, Mother Moon and Father Sun, stabilize the field of values illustrated in our tribal flag. Mother Moon watches over us while we work with devotion and intention under the light of Father Sun. The Mother is the mythical reason for the Father's motion.

When I was a child living in my mother's house in Mesilla, New Mexico, we experienced a total lunar eclipse, *maala mecha muuke*: the dying of Mother Moon. My mother opened the kitchen windows and blasted the stereo speakers—James Brown and Motown hits—and sent all of us kids outside to bang pots and pans and shout so that the darkness eating Ma'ala Meecha would flee, and She could come out again, a big gold and silver coin shining radiantly in the soothing deep blue night sky. Years later, as a teenager, I lay in the back of my father's pickup truck beneath a full moon with my best friend and told her that my aunt said that there was a rabbit in the moon.[10] My friend, who is from Thailand, remarked, "Oh, we have that belief too!" Was the rabbit in the moon—or of girls who, at the beginning of their reproductive years, are first learning how the moon draws their blood, thirst, and moods within the body's capacity for fertility and renewal—the rabbit who kindles a litter each spring?

Though I had grown up attending Catholic Mass each Sunday, I took for granted the image of La Virgen resting in the cradle of a crescent moon and warmed in a *rebozo* of stars.[11] I did not interpret the archetypal meaning of her shawl. As a brave young woman, I walked alone on many nights through the moonlit streets of D.C., Seattle, and Tucson, or drove hundreds of miles at night to be with loved ones in San Pedro, Seattle, Austin, and Las Cruces, peering up at stars for comfort and direction. When I was frightened or was being followed by strange men, I called on my grandfather Augustín and my grandmother Maria to walk beside me, as I knew them to be most protective and unafraid to apply physical force.

Many nights I accompanied my aunts wrapped in *rebozos*, silently weeping or observing tranquility, when, during the Easter ceremony, the *cantoras* keep vigil beside the figure of Jesus hiding in fear of the treacherous Roman soldiers in the Garden of Gethsemane, soldiers as treach-

---

10. This is a common belief among Indigenous peoples in Meso-America (López Austin 1996).

11. Contemporary Catholic believers note that the forty-six stars on her shawl represent the constellations shining over Mexico City in the days of her appearance before Juan Diego. For some it is a tradition to recite forty-six rosaries in her honor.

erous as the Mexican soldiers who hunted Hiaki sons, uncles, brothers, and fathers in the Sierra of Bacatete (Hernández Silva 1996; Hu-DeHart 1984). One time my aunt asked me to think with her what Mary must have felt that night when she knew her son was a fugitive in flight, his heart broken by the betrayal of those closest to him.[12]

In my thirties, so much travel, work, and distance from my family left me experiencing anxiety attacks in airports, on trains and buses, and at other points of departure. A mentor who is also Eastern Band Cherokee and who adheres to the teachings of Saint Kateri Tekakwitha recommended the novena Mary Undoer of Knots, which I turned to, using my fingers to keep count of the decades of the rosary and adding the small phrases particular to Hiaki recitations of the *rosario*.[13] For me, Ma'ala Meecha, Mother Mary, Tonántzin, and La Virgen de Guadalupe had merged to become a collective ever-present expression of compassion, courage, and maternal guard.

The loss of Seyewailo evoked a grief threaded with layers of preexisting unaddressed losses, some stemming from experiences with other relatives. The grief combined with the secondary losses associated with the pandemic, as well as with compassion fatigue for the years of attending to the needs of those greatly affected by COVID-19. In 2020, COVID swept through reservation communities like the grim reaper cutting down wheat. In the spring and summer of 2020, many of my Native American students lost two or three close relatives within days of each other, and I silently prayed for them as they plodded through their coursework in a state of shock laced with depressive lows. I was furious at how our

---

12. For believers, in a meditation about Mary, who suffers in prayer as her son Jesus Christ sweats blood while hiding from Roman soldiers in the garden, Mary is also sleepless and her heart beats in unison with her son, indicating the feeling of oneness or physiological intimacy that many mothers experience through their bond with their children. The experience of maternal sleeplessness and worry is certainly relatable. The meditation is known as "Mary and the Agony in the Garden."

13. Kateri Tekakwitha is a well-known saint based on the historical actions and disposition of a Mohawk woman in the seventeenth century. Her life story is filled with examples of Indigenous spirituality during colonial encounters (Arac 2020). Elders say that the contemporary recitations of the rosary in the Hiaki language are created by *maehtom*, Hiaki religious leaders supported by the local diocese, who pass along over generations the particular translations they use, including specific phrases and emphases.

university offered little to no relief for Native students and others from highly affected social groups. Once again, as Native American faculty, we were expected to alternatively ignore, compartmentalize, or deal with student trauma on our own with what few tools we had personally picked up through our own life circumstances.

I had to threaten to obtain a labor lawyer when my college first refused to allow me to work from home due to complications associated with pregnancy during the pandemic. The federal Genetic Information Nondiscrimination Act protects employees from discrimination due to genetic conditions. My baby had a genetic condition, and so the university administration recommendation was that I apply for disability leave. I had read other mothers' accounts of similar scenarios, how carrying and raising a baby with Down syndrome means standing up for your rights and their rights even during the period of gestation. I had to insist that being pregnant was not a disability, noting the slippery slope toward indicating female reproduction as a kind of "incapacity to work," and pointing out the needs of my students and colleagues, whose rights as (dis)abled people were also greatly affected by COVID-19. I noted many instances demonstrating the university administration's determination to avoid responsibility associated with the fatal reality of COVID-19 and its effects on students, employees, and their families, particularly regarding its effect on the extraordinary increase in unpaid emotional, reproductive, and caregiving labor of women and mothers.[14]

True to the saying that death comes in threes, two first cousins unexpectedly died in the same couple of weeks as my son, and I heard news of two other distant relatives who had also passed. In spring 2022, Vladimir Putin ordered the Russian invasion of Ukraine in an obviously colonial and genocidal effort to seize the country as a so-called Russian territory. I burst into tears at newscasts showing the expressions of shock and sorrow in the faces of families fleeing Ukraine and Russia. I recognized the expressions in their faces: loss and the shock of trauma sits around the eyes and jaw in a certain way. After months of intense grieving and a mind that felt scattered and fogged with trauma, I was advised by an Anishinaabe friend and writing partner to try a Midewin medicine: to leave a jar of water under the light of the full moon and to apply it as an

---

14. Women scholars have noted the reality of unpaid labor in academia made most striking by the pandemic (Minello 2020; Seedat and Rondon 2021).

ameliorative.[15] My heart lit up at her kind recommendation, affirming the sensations of interconnected Indigenous ancestral motherwork alive beneath the gaze of colonial Western proscriptives, the shared knowledge of how to soothe the pain of disconnections, of how to ground oneself in our reality as humble beings of this earth, nourished by that particular gentle reflective light, the light that has certainly carried me safely from one homeplace to another, from one transformation to the next. I knew in my heart what she was advising. I had already made the epistemic and spiritual place for it. I needed to be reminded by another mother who had also experienced the long walk through loss.

The Power of *Comadres*: Grief as Motherwork

Multiple facets of a Hiaki family have endured the disruptions of war and revolution while sustaining the ancestral traditions of our *herensia*. These include informal and formal adoption, coparenting, godparenting, grandparenting, and motherwork by aunts and elder sisters. My mother has many sisters and cousins, and her mother also grew up surrounded by women and girls who were related by blood, marriage, and the elaborate *komae* and *kompae* system, which is roughly comparable to the Mexican Catholic *comadre* and *compadre* system and somewhat similar to the Roman Catholic godparent system. As a child, I was fortunate to have many examples of what Hiaki womanhood, sisterhood, and motherwork look like. When I was a teenager, many of my cousins were beginning to have their own children, some of them while they were still in high school. In a tradition wherein the eldest daughter is expected to behave as a secondary mother, my mother raised me to be responsible and attentive to the needs of my younger brother and sister. To me, caring for children was a normal everyday matter. I took care of babies. My cousins took care of babies. My aunts were teaching in the tribal Head Start programs and counseling Native youth. Now grandmothers and great-grandmothers, many of them are still taking care of babies.

---

15. Midewin beliefs are rooted in Indigenous healing practices of peoples of the Northeast and upper Midwest United States and in southeast Canada. For an Indigenous view, see Battiste (2000).

When I went away to college, I grieved the loss of caring for and seeing my younger brother and sister every day, especially as I became swept up in the highly individualistic experience of an American co-ed liberal arts college lifestyle. While in that new experience, though, I learned about the ways race and caste shape experiences of sexuality, abortion, and bodily autonomy. I listened to beloved girlfriends—white, Native, Black, and Mexican—struggling with new experiences related to sexual harassment, assault, sexually transmitted diseases, body dysmorphia, pornography, same-sex desire, colonial desire, choices about clothing and self-expression, painful menstruation, unexpected pregnancies, and unwanted pregnancies.

There were times when I stood in my dorm room closet and cried with the gravity of some of those experiences. I traveled to Ciudad Juárez one time with some white dorm mates who described hungry Mexican children as "cute." Once I sat with a white dorm mate whose relationship had turned abusive. She was a dancer, and when we went dancing together, she was so filled with energy and light. But by sophomore year, she was preparing to drop out of college; the controlling voice of her boyfriend resounded so completely in her heart and mind, and I could see it in the ways her eyes would wander up to the sky and she would lose her train of thought. I was witnessing a dangerously submissive aspect of her forming in her heart. Another time, one of our friends, a Black and Choctaw woman, became pregnant, raised her baby with the father for a short time in a lovely Tucson apartment, and then quite unexpectedly returned with the baby to the southern town where she had grown up. We did not hear from her again, and neither did her boyfriend. There was the time I asked around for a ride to South Tucson. "Oh, don't go there," said my roommate's openly racist boyfriend. "You will get shot," he said. "My grandmother lives there," I said, "and my grandfather just passed away." A line had been drawn across the tiny dorm room: Mexicans (me) on one side, and whites and obedient Brown girls (not me) on the other. A question for my roommate's boyfriend: Should a good Brown girl break a class boundary to travel across town to comfort her Mexican grandmother? And another question for my roommate: Should a good Brown girl tell her white boyfriend to stop being rude to her bad Brown roommate? Her answer was no. She should not.

After finishing college, I sustained close relationships with a few of those women and allowed other friendships to lapse in a season of emotional maturation. I enjoyed another season of intimate sisterly bonding with other women while I was in my late twenties and thirties in graduate school. When my baby died, I turned to the women in my family and to my sister-friends—*hermanas* and *comadres*—for comfort and prayer. They showed up in person and via text by sending gifts, food, candles, plants and flowers, warm embraces, and by sending up prayers for months after. They shared their experiences of acute grief and loss: miscarriages, infertility, terminations, abortions, suicides, death by illness, accidents, and separations. All those years of deep listening, keeping company, acceptance, and *comadreando*—a manner I had learned from my cousins and aunts—now emerged with a new meaning for me. My *comadres* held me up during a season when I had just enough energy to get my toddler to school and feed and cuddle him through the bedtime routine. I needed to live, but like many mothers who lose a child, I felt like a part of me had died.

Thanks to a referral by a counselor who is a mother and woman of color, I became a client in a mental health practice that specializes in treating Native American and Latinx women struggling with reproductive challenges. My first counselor was from Spain, and so we spoke in Spanish through those first few months of shock and emotional pain. I speak mostly in English at work, that is to say, I speak English professionally, and so the switch in language was a balm to my heart, as I could express my emotions in the metaphors and associations of a gentle language I had grown up with. In those days, I was caught in what is commonly known as the bargaining stage of grief. To shut off the emotional pain, I emphasized the orderly power of my doctoral training, and I was poring over peer-reviewed articles and lab results looking for evidence of why my son had died, how he had died, correlations between various conditions and trisomy 21, and the likelihood of my being able to carry another baby to term. I made an appointment with a genetic counselor but never showed up. I had spent months learning how to be an effective mother for a child with Down syndrome, and I was reading everything I could about how other mothers of children with Down syndrome managed loss and health challenges in their mother-child relationship. My counselor said to me, plainly, "Mira, la ciencia le esta creando en ti una angustia. No te conforta."[16] She challenged me to put it all aside—my tools of scientific negotiation and futile prediction—and pursue the spiritual truths of my tribal philosophy and religion. It was the first time a counselor acknowledged the strength of my reality as a Hiaki woman and the practical value of Indigenous healing.

I called my *comadre* Ramona, and she shared with me the tragic details of a loss that was quite fresh for her. Meanwhile, a few weeks before, in summer 2022 through the *Dobbs v. Jackson* decision, the U.S. Supreme Court had stripped women and anybody with a female reproductive system of their inherent right to bodily autonomy, reproductive privacy, and abortion. We cursed Supreme Court Justice Samuel Alito for his misogyny. I thought of my physician, who was also shocked and saddened by the unexpected loss of my baby, especially as it occurred during a season when her medical staff was suffering the tragic deaths of several young healthy mothers, all pregnant Mexican and Mexican American women who, believing the disinformation about the COVID-19 vaccine and refusing vaccination, became victims of the virus. Ramona and I transformed our curse into a poem we intend to publish so that one day our children can turn to it when they need the life-giving comfort of a Hiaki/Xicanx curse against the absurdity of masculine violence. My friends, counselors, and relatives reminded me of perhaps the most important ancestral medicine we have: listening well and listening deeply to the self and each other, so that the heart becomes tender with compassion, including compassion for the self.

Indigenous, Chicanx, and Mexican feminist scholars have written about the border as a scar, a wound, a source of grief, and of relational and ecological destruction (Moraga and Anzaldúa 1981; Anzaldúa 1987; Fregoso and Bejarano 2010; Rivera Garza 2020; Speed 2019). In the winter of 2020, during some of the most isolating months of the COVID-19 pandemic, I began researching the effects on my family of various battles during the Mexican Revolution, both in my mother's

---

16. "Look, the science is causing you to anguish. It brings you no comfort" (my translation).

Hiaki lineage and in my father's Mexican lineage. Though I suppose I should have recognized this before, for the first time in my life, I realized the impact of being only the second English-speaking generation of two families who for hundreds of years spoke primarily Spanish or Hiaki, and who worked very close to the land, either as farmers and ranch hands or through subsistence hunting, fishing, and wild food gathering. I felt the distance, the roads traveled, the lives lost, and the hope cultivated: the gravity of suppressed ways of relating and the density of dispossession.

My sister-in-law Ali, who is Mechoopda Maidu, Wintu, and Nomlaki, and a mother of four who experienced the challenges of childbirth, knew precisely what to do when she heard of our sad news; she drove with my brother-in-law to see us in Phoenix, bringing with her a deer antler green with moss that she had found beside a creek in sacred Mechoopda territory shortly after Seyewailo had crossed into the spirit world. Ali knew exactly the significance of what that would mean for me as a mother and a Hiaki woman, for herself as an auntie and mother and Mechoopda woman, and for our baby in the spirit world—all of our babies who die young and traverse the flower world and sacred mountains, where they join the circle of our ancestors willing to be born again in flesh and blood through our sacred wombs. My scientific training and obstetrician's advice could not offer the relief that my sisters could. I told Ramona, "I think as Brown women, we know death before we know birth." Though it sounds dark and despairing to someone not yet spiritually and physically transformed by grief, for those of us who grew up primarily loved by parents and grandparents cycling through periods of irrevocable losses, serenity, and joy—witnesses to an ancestry of spiritual nourishment fueled by forced dispossession—it feels like truth. Before I gave birth to my first child, before I parented, my mother, father, and aunts had already prepared me for the naturalness of death and dying. All around me, I observed the subtle transformations of grief as a kind of motherwork, of attending to those who are dying as a kind of friendship, the kind that brings us closer to whom and what we love, the kind that brings us closer to the renewal that helps us to continue caring for ourselves and others. In the spirit of this renewal, in spring 2022, my husband planted for me a garden of sunflowers.

Motherwork as Renewal

My baby Seyewailo knew no life outside that of my body, and yet it was an active life. He kicked and elbowed me quite a lot and enjoyed our family's early evening ritual of resting in the "big bed" together and watching cartoons. He responded to his father's voice and his brother's laughter with kicks and rapid thrums, as if he were reaching out to wrestle with them as they would tickle and roll around while laughing at each other and the characters on TV. I communicated with him constantly through touch, songs, dreams, and light massage. I embraced his lightness alongside the physical discomforts and passing sensations of grief. There is quite a lot of grief that a family first experiences when they learn early on that their child likely has Down syndrome. Much of it pertains to letting go of ableist expectations and learning to embrace the creativity of disability. There is also quite a lot of joy. Mothers of babies with Down syndrome describe the sparkling eyes of their babies, their warm hugs, joyful learning, and celebrations of developmental milestones that ableist-oriented parents often take for granted. I safeguarded my own physical health throughout the pregnancy and so was very mentally, emotionally, and physically present for those moments of prenatal joy.

Some mothers who lose babies describe a sensation of aching, heavy arms, arms wishing for a baby or a child to hold. I experienced that for quite a long time. It felt like a phantom climbing on my lap and hanging on my chest, tugging at my heart, and pulling the hair at the base of my neck. But I did not want to associate my baby Seyewailo with loss. I knew that sensation of heavy pain was not him. I wanted to find a way to detach from those painful physical sensations, to experience them as passing discomfort. I wanted to find a way to remember my baby boy for the joy that he brought me. And it did happen. It does happen, periodically, when I am in a half-dream state, exercising and in the flow, or happy with my living family. Then the gentle baby sensations of him, his presence and being, return, and I am reminded of the vibrancy of renewal and living through change.

Six months after he passed, I began to be able to offer comfort to other mothers who had experienced similar losses. I learned that those losses are situated in a field of precarious conditions, and that those conditions are heightened for Black and Brown women. I listened to a hairdresser describe how she lost a baby that, had he been born, would have entered the abusive dynamic of the relationship she was in at the time with her boyfriend. She believes that it changed her way of life. Not only did she leave her boyfriend, but she became an intuitive healer within her family. I listened to young mothers describe miscarriages that their families ignored and how it caused them to reflect on their self-worth and significance in domineering families, and how little their sorrow mattered in the pressure to reproduce. I listened to a woman in her seventies describe how she believes her baby's little spirit left many decades before because it was a time for her to accept that she, as a young woman back then, needed to escape a violent relationship. She realized how new relational horizons emerged in the wake of that initial internal physical stillness, a stillness I imagine as similar to the stillness I experienced.

I listened to many women describe how they lost their jobs in the wake of the tragedy, as their employers offered neither bereavement nor postpartum recovery. My neighbors—Mexican and Salvadorean women in their fifties, sixties, and eighties—came to greet me and offer condolences, holding my hands over the fence, crying with me, and sharing their own experiences: doctors' curt explanations; subsequent pregnancies; acceptance of the absence; and making room for a newly emerged anxious or melancholy facet of their emotional dispositions.

I listened to so many women: Native, Chicanx, white, Black, Latinx, Brown mothers of all ages who vividly remembered details of their losses and who reflected on how those losses changed their ways of caring for themselves, relating to their partners and parents, and committing their physical labor to unrelenting workplaces and employers, and sometimes led them down unexpected spiritual paths and cross-country moves. One grandmother shared with me how when her granddaughter died after struggling with a long infant illness, blood streamed from her grandbaby's eyes and nose. I kept a bracelet to remember her baby by, a baby whom I never met but for whom I could pray. The Black women I listened to described their connections to the motherwork inherent to the Black Lives Matter movement and, for some, Black queer and womanist work. In all the women I listened to, I sensed the gentle tug of acceptance tempering remaining sorrows, a quality of generosity with their selves and their bodies, of forgiveness, and a spiritual submission to the mystery of what is beyond our control.

Mother Moon Watch Over Us: A Hiaki Interpretation of Frontera Madre(hood)

When Cynthia Bejarano and Cristina Morales invited me to contribute to the volume on motherwork in the borderlands, I eagerly accepted because, post-tenure, in a scholarly turn, I had decided to begin writing much more about the family memory work I had been doing for a long time with my relatives and other Hiaki women about the political, and therefore spiritual, willpower of contemporary Hiaki women. Professor Bejarano and Professor Morales are scholars who are fearless about researching topics related to violence against women. Through their writing, they narrate the path toward our dignity as women of the border. I submitted for their review a rather lengthy essay—over sixty pages—that seemed to emerge quite easily through divine literary guidance during the same season that I was reading extensively about how to mother a baby with Down syndrome. In that essay, I wrote about the lateral violence we experience in the tribe, hypermasculinity, and how the politics of empowered Indigenous matriarchy emerge in distinctive ways through, respectively, Chicanismx and Hiaki political and spiritual life.

But then I changed. My son Seyewailo's life changed me. I can write about the Yaqui Wars and how those shaped political turbulence and separations among families during the Mexican Revolution and thereafter. I can write about how the Yaqui Wars have, in fact, continued, and about how Hiaki women in the United States and Mexico continue making tough choices about how to raise their children, including choosing not to become pregnant, as they face life-changing decisions about where to live, how to work, schooling, illness, environmental degradation, care for elders, and romantic intimacy. My hope is to make those contributions in time, but for now, I think it is most important to indicate the centrality of grief and transformative grieving as a common unspoken and unexpressed space that many mothers experience in the U.S.-Mexico borderlands.

I agree that border enforcement is a scar, a fresh wound, a wall, a spy, a government agent in charge of family separation, a lack of medical care, an excuse for cruelty, a system of assault, and a pathway to imprisonment. I have also found the multiple spiritual places across the borderlands that are, for mothers who believe in transformative experience, the places to practice lunar devotion, to share sacred Indigenous knowledges about how to defend, respect, and heal our feminine bodies, those of our children, and, fundamentally, the lands where we are born and where we honor the physical and spiritual crossings of our ancestors.

I understand the profound peace of resting on the bank of a river winding its way through a desert. I understand why it is important to make fresh paper flowers for wooden crosses. I bear a volcanic fury for politicians who cage and sicken our children and look the other way when the police shoot them down as if they are no more than political targets. Yet, I am not consumed by anger or despair. As Lorena Pronsky (2020) asserts, "En cada entierro de relaciones perdidas usé, hasta exprimirlas, cada uno de las emociones que tuve a flor de piel. Siempre vale todo en materia de latidos. . . . Eso no quiere decir que lo que tenga que morir lo someta a sobrevivir" (36).[17] For me, there is another reason why La Virgen Tonántzin blankets Herself in stars: they are Her ancestors, including the son She lost—the one we know about—and the names of all the others whom She has kept to Herself. She shines in their grace, roses and *nopal* at Her feet.

REFERENCES

Anzaldúa, Gloria. 1987. *Borderlands/La Frontera: The New Mestiza*. San Francisco, Calif.: Aunt Lute.

Arac, Katelyn. 2020. "From Hagiography to Historiography: Reclaiming Kateri Tekakwitha." *Historical Studies* 86:51–70.

Avilez, Gilberto. 2014. "Los fantasmas de la guerra de castas, o 'la quema de las cañaverales' Parte II: Catmis, 1911." *Desde la Península . . . y las inmediaciones*

---

17. "With every burial of lost loved ones I expressed, until they left my body, each of the emotions rippling beneath my skin. Everything matters in the heat of the flesh. . . . This does not mean to say that what has to die does so as a means of my survival" (my translation).

de mi hamaca (blog), September 12, 2014. http://gilbertoavilez.blogspot.com /2014/09/los-fantasmas-de-la-guerra-de-castas-o.html.

Battiste, Marie, ed. 2000. *Reclaiming Indigenous Voice and Vision.* Vancouver: University of British Columbia Press.

Carbonell, Ana María. 1999. "From Llorona to Gritona: Coatlicue in Feminist Tales by Viramontes and Cisneros." *MELUS* 24 (2): 53–74.

Delgado, Richard, and Jean Stefancic. 2019. "Lessons from Mexican Folklore: An Essay on U.S. Immigration Policy, Child Separation, and La Llorona." *University of Pittsburgh Law Review* 81 (2): 287–314.

Donjuan Espinoza, Esperanza, Raquel Padilla Ramos, Dora Elvia Enríquez Licón, and Zulema Trejo Contreras, eds. 2010. *Religión, nación y territorio en los imaginarios sociales indígenas de Sonora, 1767–1940.* Hermosillo: El Colegio de Sonora.

Erickson, Kirstin C. 2008. *Yaqui Homeland and Homeplace: The Everyday Production of Ethnic Identity.* Tucson: University of Arizona Press.

Fregoso, Rosa-Linda, and Cynthia Bejarano, eds. 2010. *Terrorizing Women: Feminicide in the Américas.* Durham, N.C.: Duke University Press.

Giddings, Ruth Warner. 1959. *Yaqui Myths and Legends.* Tucson: University of Arizona Press.

Gomez Quintana, Thalia. 2020. "Infrastructure Gender Based Violence and Yaqui Refusal." UCLA Thinking Gender Papers, Center for the Study of Women. https://escholarship.org/uc/item/8db4r6vj.

Hernández Silva, Héctor Cuauhtémoc. 1996. *Insurgencia y autonomía: Historia de los pueblos yaquis, 1821–1910.* Mexico City: Centro de Investigación y Estudios Superiores de Antropología Social, Instituto Nacional Indigenista.

Hu-DeHart, Evelyn. 1981. *Missionaries, Miners, and Indians: Spanish Contact with the Yaqui Nation of Northwestern New Spain, 1533–1830.* Tucson: University of Arizona Press.

Hu-DeHart, Evelyn. 1984. *Yaqui Resistance and Survival: Struggle for Land and Autonomy, 1821–1910.* Madison: University of Wisconsin Press.

Kelley, Jane Holden. 1978. *Yaqui Women: Contemporary Life Histories.* Lincoln: University of Nebraska Press.

Kelley, Jane Holden. 1989. "'Law-Talk,' Mobilization Procedures, and Dispute Management in Yaqui Society." *KIVA* 54 (2): 79–104.

Lara, Irene. 2008. "Tonanlupanisma: Re-Membering Tonantzin-Guadalupe in Chicana Visual Art." *Aztlán* 33 (2): 61–90.

León, Juan Silverio Jaime. 1998. *Testimonios de una mujer yaqui.* Mexico City: Conaculta.

López Austin, Alfredo. 1996. *The Rabbit on the Face of the Moon: Mythology in Mesoamerican Tradition*. Salt Lake City: University of Utah Press.

Minello, Alessandra. 2020. "The Pandemic and the Female Academic." *Nature* blog, April 17, 2020. https://www.nature.com/articles/d41586-020-01135-9.

Moraga, Cherríe, and Gloria Anzaldúa. 1981. *This Bridge Called My Back: Writings by Radical Women of Color*. Watertown, Mass.: Persephone Press.

Murray, William Breen. 2013. "Deer: Sacred and Profane." In *Rock Art and Sacred Landscapes*, edited by Donna Gillette, Mavis Greer, Michele Helene Hayward, and William Breen Murray, 195–206. New York: Springer.

Olavarría, María Eugenia, Cristina Aguilar, and Érica Merino. 2009. *El Cuerpo Flor: Etnografía de una Noción Yoeme*. Mexico City: Universidad Autónoma Metropolitana.

PACMYC. 1994. *Tres procesos de lucha por la sobrevivencia de la tribu yaqui: Testimonios*. Colección Etnias. Hermosillo: Patronato Centro Cultural Cócorit, Museo de los Yaquis, Instituto Sonorense de Cultura.

Padilla Ramos, Raquel. 1995. *Yucatán, fin del sueño yaqui: El tráfico de los yaquis y el otro triunvirato*. Hermosillo: Gobierno del Estado de Sonora, Secretaría de Educación y Cultura, Instituto Sonorense de Cultura.

Padilla Ramos, Raquel. 2011. *Los irredentos parias: Los yaquis, Madero y Pino Suárez en las elecciones de Yucatán, 1911*. Colección Historia. Mexico City: Instituto Nacional de Antropología e Historia.

Padilla Ramos, Raquel. 2018. *Los partes fragmentados: Narrativas de la guerra y deportación yaquis*. Mexico City: Secretaría de Cultura, Instituto Nacional de Antropología e Historia.

Padilla Ramos, Raquel, and Zulema Trejo Contreras. 2012. "Guerra secular del Yaqui y significaciones imaginario sociales." *Historia Mexicana* 62 (1): 59–103.

Painter, Muriel Thayer. 1986. *With Good Heart: Yaqui Beliefs and Ceremonies in Pascua Village*. Tucson: University of Arizona Press.

Pronsky, Lorena. 2019. *Cúrame*. Barcelona: Penguin Random House.

Rivera Garza, Cristina. 2020. *Grieving: Dispatches from a Wounded Country*. Translated by Sarah Booker. New York: Feminist Press at CUNY.

Seedat, Soraya, and Marta Rondon. 2021. "Women's Wellbeing and the Burden of Unpaid Work." *British Medical Journal* 374:n1972. https://doi.org/10.1136/bmj.n1972.

Speed, Shannon. 2019. *Incarcerated Stories: Indigenous Women Migrants and Violence in the Settler-Capitalist State*. Chapel Hill: University of North Carolina Press.

Spicer, Edward. 1967. *Cycles of Conquest: The Impact of Spain, Mexico, and the United States on Indians of the Southwest, 1533–1960*. Tucson: University of Arizona Press.

Taibo, Paco Ignacio, II. 2013. *Yaquis: Historia de una guerra popular y de un genocidio en México*. Mexico City: Planeta.

Valdes, Dulce Aurelia Felix, Maria Luisa Sopomea Bacasewa, Maria Leon Buitimea, and Reyna Buitimea. 2022. "Mujer yaqui en la historia y voces de distintas generaciones." Proyecto Goj Naiki Sewam, Museo de los Yaquis, Cócorit, Sonora, Mexico, April 6.

Wells, Allen, and Gilbert M. Joseph. 1996. "Primeras Chispas." In *Summer of Discontent, Seasons of Upheaval: Elite Politics and Rural Insurgency in Yucatán, 1876–1915*, 187–215. Stanford, Calif.: Stanford University Press.

Wilbur-Cruce, Eva Antonia. 1987. *A Beautiful, Cruel Country*. Tucson: University of Arizona Press.

CHAPTER 9

Indigenous Women and Motherhood Within a Border Context

The Case of the Nan davi in Ciudad Juárez, Chihuahua

MARIELA VÁSQUEZ TOBON

Lawyer and Human Rights Defender

My name is Mariela Vásquez Tobon, Nan davi, originally from the Oaxacan Mixteca region.[1] I am also a lawyer by profession. I have been living permanently on the border of Ciudad Juárez, Chihuahua, Mexico, for just over twenty years. My childhood was very unstable until the age of eight because we were nomadic families until we settled permanently in this northern city, Ciudad Juárez. The Mixtec community to which I belong is originally from San Andrés Montaña, a municipality of Silacayoapam in the state of Oaxaca. We were some of the first families to migrate in the late eighties to the border of Ciudad Juárez, taking advantage of the networks of family and countrymen there. We now form a community of just over forty families that mainly settled in two of the peripheral colonies of the border: Rancho Anapra and Plutarco Elías Calles Extension.

From an early age, I experienced multiple acts of discrimination due to my ethnicity, gender, and age. These situations aroused an interest in me to give voice to forgotten communities, which continue to suffer discrimination, gender violence, stigmatization, and the violation of their

---

1. This chapter was originally written in Spanish and translated by GMR Transcription Services, Inc. Nan davi is a word in the Mixtec language to identify Indigenous people.

fundamental rights. The field of healthcare, for example—particularly as it relates to Indigenous motherhood—is the focus of this chapter.

Motherhood is an uncommon topic for Indigenous women, especially those who are in border contexts, as they often face other problems outside their communities. As a result, motherhood is left aside as a topic for reflection. This text tries to summarize the opinions and concerns of the Nan davi, or Indigenous, women concerning motherhood in general or motherhood from their particular worldviews. The following generative questions guide this work: What does motherhood mean from the Indigenous worldview? How do the Nan davi experience motherhood on the border of Ciudad Juárez, Chihuahua? What are the challenges that Indigenous women face when giving birth in urban contexts outside their communities? Are the Nan davi informed by healthcare providers about the stages of motherhood from conception, pregnancy, childbirth, and puerperium? Among other questions. Broadly speaking, this text highlights the cultural and linguistic difficulties faced by Indigenous women who settle in border contexts, especially the case of the Nan davi, or Mixtec and Chinantec women, in Ciudad Juárez, Chihuahua, in relation to their cultural conditions and worldview perspectives on motherhood, as well as their experiences in these urban spaces.

Finally, my interest in the topic of Indigenous women and motherhood in border contexts is a result of the work I have developed in defense of the rights of Indigenous peoples and communities, especially in the promotion and defense of the rights of Indigenous women in urban contexts, since I am from the Mixtec community and have faced challenges as an Indigenous migrant woman at the border. Despite my academic preparation, I have been the victim of discriminatory acts because of my gender and ethnicity, which are further aggravated for monolingual or illiterate migrant Indigenous women.

Methodology

I used a qualitative approach for this work by conducting a series of interviews with Indigenous women who shared with me their maternity experiences and the challenges they faced when settling in this border context outside their communities of origin. I conducted a total of seven interviews consisting of ten reflective questions with women belonging to the Mixteca, Chinanteca, Nahua, and Purépecha communities that settled in the peripheral colonias of Ciudad Juárez. I have worked on and off with these women for several years on numerous Indigenous community projects. I also worked with some of these women on various projects while I attended the Autonomous University of Ciudad Juárez. Each interview lasted between a half hour to an hour, and they were conducted in their homes or by phone if they were not able to meet in person.

Nan davi and the Border Context

In Ciudad Juárez, Chihuahua, just over eighteen thousand people self-identify as Indigenous, men, and women who have left their places of origin in search of better living conditions and who have settled permanently on the border of Ciudad Juárez. In Mexico, Indigenous populations are considered groups in conditions of vulnerability due to poverty, exclusion, and discrimination because of how they have historically remained oppressed within the Mexican political structure. Even more so, migrant Indigenous populations have suffered a triple process of discrimination because of linguistic and cultural barriers that are not accepted or understood in the urban spaces where they come to settle.

The issue of access to healthcare for Indigenous women is an overlooked topic, and even more so is migrant Indigenous women's access to culturally relevant information concerning maternity stages. This compilation of *testimonios* from Indigenous mothers who settled on the border of Ciudad Juárez shows the difficulties and challenges they have experienced during their pregnancies, especially their medical care and the right to relevant and culturally appropriate information, since they are from unique populations with their own languages. This chapter is an analysis of an important but little examined issue through the voices of Indigenous mothers who settled in Ciudad Juárez, including the difficulties and challenges they experienced as first-time mothers.

Creation of Indigenous

The border of Ciudad Juárez, Chihuahua, has become a city emblematic of high levels of insecurity. It is especially known as a dangerous city for women, so some issues have been elevated because of their high levels of violence, but others have gone unnoticed by public authorities and civil society organizations. Indigenous issues specifically have not figured prominently in the political agenda of government authorities. According to the National Institute of Statistics, Geography, and Informatics (Instituto Nacional de Estadística, Geografía e Informática; INEGI 2020), and as mentioned earlier, in Ciudad Juárez, just over eighteen thousand people self-identify as Indigenous, highlighting the growing presence of the Ralamuli, Mixteca, Chinantec, Purépecha, Mazahua, and Nahua communities.[2] Most of these populations have migrated to this city in search of better living conditions because in their places of origin, there is no access to even the most basic services such as food, water, or healthcare (INEGI 2020).

According to data from the State Commission for Indigenous Peoples of Chihuahua, more than 90 percent of the Indigenous population is distributed in fourteen municipalities across the state. Ciudad Juárez holds third place as one of the municipalities with the greatest Indigenous presence, since large numbers of Indigenous migrants from central or southern Mexico settle there. Despite the multiculturalism and multilingualism that characterizes this border as a result of the high migratory flow of Indigenous populations, to date no adequate public policies have been created aimed at protecting and guaranteeing the fundamental rights of these communities (Comisión Estatal para los Pueblos Indígenas 2021).

In the case of the Mixteca and Chinantec communities from the state of Oaxaca, where many of the women who shared their *testimonios* are from—women who are the reason for this research—there was a massive migration during the eighties and early nineties, so that now three generations of Indigenous families live in Ciudad Juárez. Data provided by the state of Chihuahua reveal that Mixtec families mainly settle in the peripheral colonias of Rancho Anapra, Ampliación Plutarco Elías Calles, and Las Gladiolas (Comisión Estatal 2021). Meanwhile, the Chinantec community occupies suburban colonias such as Boulevard Zaragoza, Riveras Etapa 9, Parajes del Sur and El Valle, and Terrenos Nacionales and Lomas del Valle in Ciudad Juárez (Comisión Estatal 2021). The men of these communities were the first to arrive at the border, since their

---

2. The Rarámuri also refer to themselves as Ralamuli.

intention was to emigrate to the United States. In addition, the development of U.S. factories meant an important source of employment for those who could no longer fulfill "the American dream" in the United States, so gradually, a large number of Mixtec and Chinantec families (men and women) began arriving to the city, settling in these borderlands, and self-identifying as Indigenous Juarenses (Comisión Estatal para los Pueblos Indígenas 2020).

Lack of Access to Maternal Healthcare and Mistreatment

The issue of Indigenous motherhood is little commented on because other topics, such as access to work, education, justice, security, and so forth, are prioritized. Access to maternal health and antenatal, perinatal, and neonatal information is neglected. The testimonies of Indigenous women in this chapter show that it is common for them to go through a series of obstetric violence and complexities when they become mothers in urban contexts, caring for their families far from their communities of origin. We observe not only linguistic and cultural barriers, but also the mistreatment they receive from medical personnel and the little to no information that the state provides them with. This ensures that they do not achieve substantive equality of access to health for themselves or their babies.

The health system in Ciudad Juárez turns out to be inaccessible and apathetic to the needs and specificities of Indigenous people, especially in the case of Indigenous mothers, who face dehumanizing and insensitive medical care. They are treated with disrespect and violence, resulting in negative health effects (low self-esteem, fear, and stress) and even human losses (miscarriages). Even though national and international laws on Indigenous matters, such as Convention 169 of the International Labour Organisation (ILO), recognize and prioritize the fundamental rights of Indigenous women to live a dignified life and to safeguard their full exercise of their human rights (ILO 1989), the fact is that Indigenous women have been treated as second-class individuals by being denied the opportunity to have dignified motherhoods. Therefore, it is necessary to give voice to Indigenous women from different backgrounds, to express and show their concerns, including the experiences they have had as mothers.

Indigenous Women Living in Ciudad Juárez

The following experiences of Mashi, Lux, Mar, and Ena, Indigenous women from the Mixteca and Chinantec communities living in Ciudad Juárez for more than twenty years, show us the adversities they endured during their maternities. Indigenous women on the border of Ciudad Juárez share the same problems arising from the discriminatory policies they experience because of their gender, ethnicity, age, monolingualism, illiteracy, poverty, and other factors. These women describe the challenges they experienced during the early stages of their motherhood, since they do not know how to use, or the effects of, contraceptive methods, and they do not have the support of a medical specialist (gynecologist). They also do not know the prevailing language (Spanish), so they could not explain to doctors what they were experiencing during their births and were humiliated and verbally violated during their visits to the doctor. They receive differential treatment without adequate cultural relevance during their medical checkups and other care. Therefore, through their testimonies, they give an account of the multiple types of violence and racial discrimination they suffer as Indigenous mothers on the border of Ciudad Juárez.

I begin with Mashi, a forty-six-year-old Mixtec woman, who reports having four children and having had two abortions. She shared her experiences with miscarriage:

> I had two miscarriages, because of the injections or pills [contraceptives] I took to keep from getting pregnant. I bought it by myself at the pharmacy. I never went to a gynecologist. I didn't know about that. Since I got pregnant, I never went to a doctor to supervise my pregnancy. I [did not] go to the doctor until I had a miscarriage, and they told me that my miscarriage was caused by the contraceptive medication I had taken before pregnancy. I spent five years taking birth control. In my second miscarriage, I didn't ask because I assumed it was because of the same thing that happened with the first miscarriage. (Mashi, October 2022)

Similarly, Lux, a thirty-five-year-old Nahua mother of three children, who also underwent an abortion, shares her story of pregnancy loss:

In my first pregnancy, I had a loss. My pregnancy was high risk, but those days I had arguments with my partner that I did not pay attention and that maybe was the reason. I only know that it was spontaneous. I did not see when I passed it in the bathroom. I had a lot of bleeding, but I never observed what I was passing. When I arrived at the hospital, my baby was no longer there. In my births, the first time was very complicated, because my delivery lasted eight hours, and with intense pain for three days, and they had to induce me due to a lack of liquid. Being from an Indigenous community, I had no knowledge to turn to and ask for help because my life was at risk, and nobody told me anything. (Lux, October 2022)

With these statements, we can see that Indigenous women have been victims of miscarriages because they do not know the effects of contraceptive methods or because they have not had timely medical attention, which has also placed their lives at risk. Indigenous women have also experienced episodes of discrimination, stigmatization, and obstetric violence. This is evident in the testimony of Mar, a Chinantec woman, who is a thirty-one-year-old nurse:

While giving birth, they were surprised when they asked me if I was an Indigenous person and I confirmed it. I speak Spanish, so in that matter I had no problems. I am a nurse, and I know what had to happen, but maybe when you do not know and do not understand what they say, there is unprofessional treatment from the medical staff. But there are many challenges just being a mother, and to that, we must add being an Indigenous woman. In isolated communities, there is no information on family planning methods nor prenatal control; therefore, there is a deficiency in health services, even more so in rural populations. (Mar, October 2022)

Ena, a forty-seven-year-old Mixtec woman and mother of three children, points out that one of the most complex challenges she faced was the language barrier; since she did not understand Spanish, she preferred to remain silent. She explained:

Maybe the language—I spoke very little Spanish; I didn't understand much; that's why I didn't say anything. I didn't ask anything. I kept quiet.

The good thing was that they didn't ask me either. My belly hurt, but when I saw that the nurses were bad and insulting the other pregnant women who were screaming, I forgot about the pain. I didn't feel anything anymore because I was afraid that they would insult me anyway. I didn't know the sex of my first baby until I gave birth. (Ena, October 2022)

Another of the maternal health challenges that mostly Indigenous migrant women face is the lack of family or community support. When a woman gives birth, Indigenous peoples usually receive visits from relatives, neighbors, and so forth. When they are outside the community, however, these traditional practices are not followed. So the lack of emotional accompaniment—because of forced migration or because of their partners' machismo, considering motherhood and the care of children as tasks assigned only to women—causes these women to experience worry, loneliness, and anxiety, among other emotions, which translates into psychological violence surrounding them and preventing them from enjoying their motherhood to the fullest. This is noted by Mashi and Lux, respectively:

It was difficult because I was alone and did not know what to do with my daughter. Nobody explained to me what to do with a baby, how to change diapers, feed it, etc. I suffered, the first time; I cried and did not know what to do. I cried a lot and didn't know what to do. I felt lonely because there was no one with me. My partner didn't care, because that's how the men of the community are. They were macho. They thought it was a women's activity. They thought they were women's things. That's why my partner was like that back then. That's why I didn't know what to do. I didn't know what to buy and about the needs of my first daughter, or what to give her if she got sick.

Lux described a similar circumstance:

[It was] very complicated being so used to the attention of your family in your community and starting again in a completely different place, with medical care but where your obstetric rights are violated, and you do not know how to defend yourself. When your baby grows up not having the same attention, for example, not having health checkups because you do not have health insurance, or you do not have enough money to pay for it. Without reliable people to support you in their care while you work. It is a very difficult challenge, since without money, you honestly feel very vulnerable. Children may have the best opportunities in terms of a better quality of life, but always the level of discrimination in an urban area will be the greatest obstacle to overcome.

Finally, with the lack of cultural relevance and awareness among medical personnel, as well as the lack of care protocols or dissemination campaigns on the subject of maternal health aimed at the Indigenous population, Indigenous women on the border are excluded and fall behind in access to appropriate and timely services. They do not have relevant information about the earliest stages of motherhood (conception, pregnancy, childbirth, and puerperium). Mashi speaks to this:

No, I never took my kids to a professional like a pediatrician or something. I never went to a gynecologist. When I was about to give birth, I went to the doctor. I was not afraid because I did not even know what they were going to do to me, and when I was there and I heard the other women crying I was more afraid when I heard the nurses shout, "shut up you old asshole" to the others. I was very scared. I thought they were going to do something to me. I was afraid and since there was no one with me to tell them, I was more scared (Mashi, October 2022).

Lux had similar thoughts:

The first time, I did not have any information, but in the following pregnancies I did. In the first one, it was not until a week before losing my baby, but as I did not have insurance when I lost it, [it] was very difficult because I did not receive the same attention in the IMSS [general hospital]. I spent a long time on a stretcher to have the curettage [procedure]. After they attended me, they asked me to try to [physically] move myself, alone, to another stretcher because there were other patients who needed attention. I was waking up from an anesthetic and didn't even know how to act. The nurses were always despots, always. (Lux, October 2022)

As Indigenous women, when we are attended to by doctors with high levels of bias against Indigenous women, the challenges we experience are much greater, since they do not clear our doubts or respond to our answers as they should. If we have any doubt about what they say, we do not know how to express it, and they laugh and answer sarcastically, making us feel naïve and ashamed to ask again. That affects us, and by not clarifying our doubts, we make many mistakes in how we practice our motherhood.

Conclusion

The difficulties and challenges that migrant Indigenous mothers face when living in border contexts during their motherhood are aggravated by various factors of intersectionality—that is, discrimination not only because they are women, but also because they are Indigenous, migrant, monolingual, and often mothers at an early age. In this chapter, I highlight the predominant difficulties for Indigenous mothers in border contexts: (1) ignorance of the side effects of contraceptive methods; (2) linguistic and cultural barriers, including the lack of cultural relevance and awareness among medical personnel; (3) discrimination and stigmatization for being Indigenous; (4) obstetric and psychological violence for arriving alone without any support; and (5) the lack of community and family support from mothers, sisters, neighbors, and others because of distance from their communities of origin.

Despite the prevalent legal recognition of the rights of Indigenous peoples and women, the truth is that for Indigenous women in urban contexts, the disrespect for their human rights is rampant, especially in the field of maternal health, which is a subject little regarded or respected by government authorities and civil society organizations. Access to health is a fundamental right that has rarely been guaranteed to Indigenous people, especially not to women in terms of their maternal health. Indigenous mothers in border contexts, as this research shows, continue to face a series of challenges and difficulties throughout their maternities, because of absent or failing public policies aimed at caring for them.

REFERENCES

Comisión Estatal para los Pueblos Indígenas. 2020. *Directorio de comunidades Indígenas de Ciudad Juárez*. Chihuahua: Gobierno del Estado de Chihuahua. https://chihuahua.gob.mx/sites/default/atach2/directorio_final.pdf.

Comisión Estatal para los Pueblos Indígenas. 2021. *Programa Sectorial para los Pueblos Indígenas 2017–2021*. Chihuahua: Gobierno del Estado de Chihuahua. https://chihuahua.gob.mx/atach2/programa_sectorial_2017-2021.pdf.

INEGI (Instituto Nacional de Estadística, Geografía e Informática). 2020. *Censo de Población y Vivienda 2020*. INEGI, Subsistema de Información Demográfica y Social. https://www.inegi.org.mx/programas/ccpv/2020/.

ILO (International Labour Organisation). 1989. *C169—Indigenous and Tribal Peoples Convention, 1989 (No. 169)*. Geneva: ILO. https://www.ilo.org/dyn/normlex/en/f?p=NORMLEXPUB:55:0::NO::P55_TYPE,P55_LANG,P55_DOCUMENT,P55_NODE:REV,en,C169,/Document.

Interviews

Ena, October 2022

Lux, October 2022

Mar, October 2022

Mashi, October 2022

CHAPTER 10

Border Walls and Barriers to Care

Latina Mothers and Access to Care During the COVID-19 Pandemic

MARISA S. TORRES

Joint Doctoral Program at San Diego State University and the University of California, San Diego

VICTORIA M. TELLES

Joint Doctoral Program at San Diego State University and the University of California, San Diego

ELVA M. ARREDONDO

San Diego State University

Conceptualizing Health Predictors at the U.S.-Mexico Border

This chapter examines the multilevel impact of the pandemic on residents from the California U.S.-Mexico border, with a focus on Latinas living in San Diego and Imperial Counties. To assess the pandemic's effects on health outcomes for Latinas in the border region, we begin with a conceptualization of health predictors at the U.S.-Mexico border. This includes identifying structural and systemic factors, as well as intermediary influences on health outcomes. Our analysis of these factors relies on regional census data spanning nineteen jurisdictions, which we examine for variables related to employment, housing and utilities, nutrition, incidence of COVID-19, and parent-child information, analyzing how these variables affect Latinas and how their experiences reflect the idea of frontera madre(hood). We then contextualize cultural considerations with reference to health risks and factors among Latinas. Our findings

offer an objective description of the challenges experienced and characteristics exhibited by Latinas and their families during this tumultuous
time in history. We end this chapter with our commentary on the fragility of frontera madre(hood), future trends in motherhood for women
of color, and what is needed to sustain the essence of Latina frontera
madre(hood).

Despite being one of the fastest-growing regions in the country, the
U.S.-Mexico border is also one of the most medically disadvantaged. The
region has high rates of uninsured, high rates of chronic and infectious
disease, and inadequate access to dependable medical services (United
States–Mexico Border Health Commission 2014). Living near the two-
thousand-mile-long U.S.-Mexico border presents challenges and disparities not observed in other regions, as communities and neighborhoods
are often overlooked and facing constrained environments. Coupled with
high rates of violence, detainment and deportation, racial discrimination, and limited opportunities for steady employment, it is an extremely
difficult time to maintain a basic quality of life in a border community.
Negative political rhetoric from politicians and the media regarding immigration and funding for physical barriers at the U.S.-Mexico border
distracts attention from the limited resources, such as healthcare, allo-
cated to this area. The inequitable distribution of healthcare resources in
border communities is determined by larger systemic factors.

We propose a conceptual model, shown in figure 10.1, to illustrate the
complex systemic, structural, and intermediary influences predictive of
health outcomes for Latinas living at the U.S.-Mexico border. The top tier
of our model considers structural and systematic factors at the *frontera*,
such as sociopolitical forces and one's physical environment and social
structures—that is, the hood (Bejarano and Morales, this volume). These
upstream mechanisms often exert influence beyond the means of an individual and can determine risk exposure while contributing to social
disadvantage and social inequities (Bharmal et al. 2015). The lower tier
of the model outlines predictors that have an intermediary influence on
health outcomes for *madres* (Bejarano and Morales, this volume). These
factors include characteristics specific to an individual and elements that
determine access to care. Some predictors outlined in the lower tier are
modifiable middle or downstream mechanisms, while other predictors

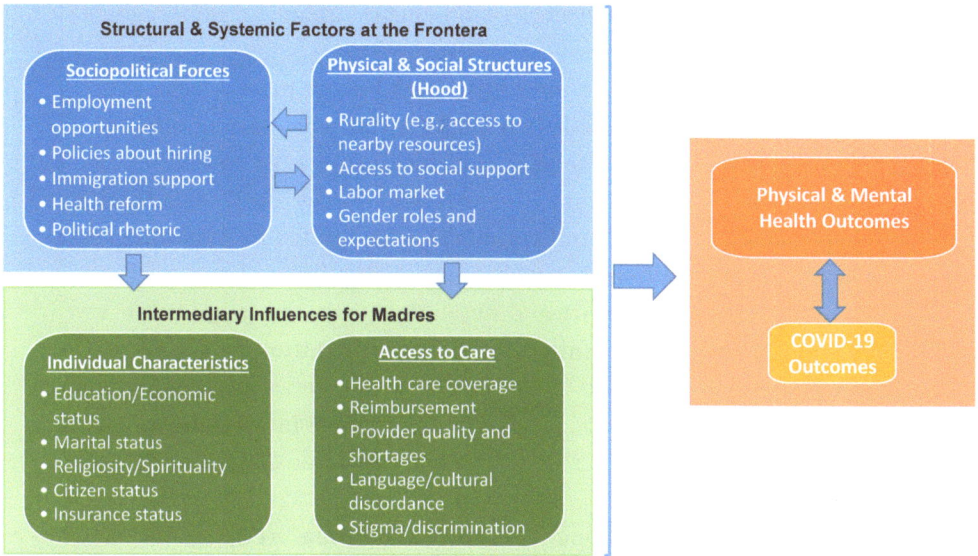

Structural & Systemic Factors at the Frontera

Sociopolitical Forces
- Employment opportunities
- Policies about hiring
- Immigration support
- Health reform
- Political rhetoric

Physical & Social Structures (Hood)
- Rurality (e.g., access to nearby resources)
- Access to social support
- Labor market
- Gender roles and expectations

Intermediary Influences for Madres

Individual Characteristics
- Education/Economic status
- Marital status
- Religiosity/Spirituality
- Citizen status
- Insurance status

Access to Care
- Health care coverage
- Reimbursement
- Provider quality and shortages
- Language/cultural discordance
- Stigma/discrimination

Physical & Mental Health Outcomes

COVID-19 Outcomes

FIGURE 10.1 Health predictors for Latinas living at the U.S.-Mexico border.

are areas where new and emergent public health partnerships and advocacy are needed to achieve optimal health outcomes (Ndumbe-Eyoh and Moffatt 2013). Collectively, these concepts can inform our understanding of the experiences of Latinas at the border and the directionality between predictors of health, physical and mental health outcomes, and COVID-19 outcomes. In the following text, we expand on these structural, systemic, and intermediary influences on health and offer evidence of how they have augmented health trajectories within the COVID-19 health context.

Structural and Systemic Factors at the *Frontera*

Nearly 30 percent (29.5 percent) of residents living in the U.S.-Mexico border region reside in rural areas, which is higher than the U.S. average (Lady, Henning-Smith, and Kunz 2017). Urban and rural geographic contexts in this region determine the availability of resources such as job opportunities, social support, and health services. As such, there may be some advantages and disadvantages to living in urban and rural regions for Latina mothers.

In urban regions, Latina mothers report having more access to information about opportunities for work, social services, and other resources essential to their families' well-being compared to their counterparts living in rural regions (Cerrutti and Massey 2001). As a result, Latina mothers living in rural regions may be limited in economic independence. In addition, Latina mothers living in rural regions have less access to social support and networks, given the large distances between domiciles and limited public transportation in rural areas (Abrego and Schmalzbauer 2018). Furthermore, Latina mothers living in rural regions have less access to health services including specialty care services (e.g., cancer treatment, etc.) compared to those living in urban regions.

For rural residents of Imperial County, California, access to specialty care can be up to seventy miles away (Kemper 2015). Public transportation is extremely limited in this region; the base rate for nonemergency medical transportation begins around twenty dollars, with an additional fee per mile (Nelson and Nygaard Consulting Associates 2008). These estimates are conservative and do not factor in rates of inflation. As such, many Latinas without reliable transportation forgo necessary medical appointments and preventive health screenings because they are unable to afford transportation expenses (Sharp Mesa Vista Hospital 2019). The cost of living in rural regions is lower, however, which allows Latina mothers living in these regions to spend more time with their family and children (Kurre 2003). Latina mothers living in rural areas may also be less concerned about crime, drugs, and gangs, and they report more tranquility compared to Latina mothers living in urban regions (Abrego and Schmalzbauer 2018).

Lack of healthcare coverage has large-scale consequences for health and healthcare in the U.S.-Mexico border region. While the United States and Mexico both focus on expanding access to healthcare for vulnerable border populations, the neighboring countries' unique healthcare systems often have stark differences in policies, priorities, and available resources in response to major health problems (Ramos et al. 2009). Though the Affordable Care Act (ACA) has withstood opposition efforts by U.S. government officials and through legislative reforms, Mexico's national health system (formerly existing under Seguro Popular) is undergoing massive restructuring by the current government administration (Reich 2020). When Andrés Manuel López Obrador (AMLO) came into office, he criticized Seguro Popular for its lack of complete coverage of services and populations, poor reduction of out-of-pocket spending, widespread corruption, and poor improvement of health outcomes (Reich 2020). The new system under the Instituto de Salud para el Bienestar (INSABI), which began on January 1, 2020, purported to provide healthcare that was universal, free, and anticorrupt. The registration system under Seguro Popular was abandoned, and access to healthcare under INSABI required only proof of citizenship (Fellowship for International Services and Health, n.d.).

Additionally, INSABI required no out-of-pocket expenses for covered services and supplies, unlike Seguro Popular, which required income-adjusted fees for registered members (Fellowship for International Services and Health, n.d.). Although INSABI provided free coverage of primary and secondary care, more complex tertiary services, such as chemotherapy/radiotherapy, organ transplants, and dialysis, would not be covered, leaving many individuals paying out-of-pocket costs for necessary specialty services and prescriptions (Mexico Business Publications 2021). This was different than the wider-spread coverage of Seguro Popular, which included first-, second-, and third-tier services (Fellowship for International Services and Health, n.d.). Implementing new healthcare systems like INSABI dismantles policies that have been established for nearly two decades, and the consequences of these changes will take some time to manifest and evaluate (Reich 2020).

Polarized health reforms in Mexico that are constructed, dismantled, and restructured through politics have widespread implications for people residing in the U.S.-Mexico border region, who may pay the cost with their health, well-being, or lives (Reich 2020). In addition to challenges regarding insurance coverage and high costs of healthcare services, the U.S.-Mexico border region is characterized by high unemployment, lower educational status, and high poverty rates, which are all associated with inadequate access to care and subsequent poor health outcomes (Bastida, Brown, and Pagán 2008). These structural and systemic factors at the *frontera* are the upstream mechanisms that can influence intermediary factors on *madres* and their families.

Intermediary Influences on Health Outcomes

Mothers' documentation status is a factor that intersects legal contexts and frontera madre(hood). Regardless of living in a rural or an urban region, undocumented Latina mothers encounter myriad barriers compared to their documented counterparts (De Genova 2002). Undocumented Latinas may have more difficulty developing trusting relationships and may tend to be on guard as they navigate their environment. If a child gets hurt and a mother is undocumented, the mother may be hesitant to call for services, regardless of the region she lives in. Undocumented women are less likely to have desirable jobs and more likely to have limited employment opportunities and work at the bottom of the income hierarchy in domestic and other low-end services that keep them away from their children much of the time (Abrego and Schmalzbauer 2018). During the pandemic, these challenges were compounded, as many Latinas found themselves with increased caregiver expectations and limited social support (Ornelas et al. 2021). The research on Latina mental health and well-being during the pandemic is limited but suggests a negative long-term impact as a result of COVID-19 stay-at-home orders, which resulted in social isolation (Hibel et al. 2021). Globally, rates of stress, anxiety, depressive symptoms, fear, and other psychological disturbances rose during the pandemic (Hibel et al. 2021). We expect these trends were also present among marginalized Latinas grappling with the intersections of racism, sexism, and survival (Hibel et al. 2021).

Citizenship status and lack of documentation is a major barrier to care with most undocumented individuals, who often avoid healthcare systems for fear of deportation (Cha and McConville 2021). Current provisions under the ACA require health insurance coverage for all documented immigrants and their children; however, recently arrived documented immigrants (less than five years of residence in the United States) are often excluded from Medicaid expanded coverage, and undocumented immigrants are excluded from all ACA provisions (González Block et al. 2014). As a result, about 45 percent of undocumented individuals in the United States are completely uninsured; the rate of uninsured undocumented individuals rises to 87 percent after excluding Medicaid coverage (Cha and McConville 2021). The high rate of uninsured Latinxs is especially problematic for older undocumented individuals who are ineligible for Medicare and may need additional health services as they age (Cha and McConville 2021).

Individuals living in the U.S.-Mexico border region have historically had limited access to comprehensive health services and medical professionals. Most U.S.-Mexico border counties are medically underserved and are designated by the U.S. Health Resources and Services Administration (HRSA) as health professional shortage areas (HPSAs) (Rural Health Information Hub 2023). Both California counties that share a border with Mexico, San Diego and Imperial, are designated as HPSAs for healthcare services related to primary care, dental care, and mental health (U.S. HRSA, n.d.). In 2019, approximately 3.5 million people resided in San Diego and Imperial Counties (Southern Border Communities Coalition 2023). In the same year, 34 percent of residents in San Diego County and 85 percent of residents in Imperial County were Latinx (U.S. Census Bureau 2023). By sex, both counties were approximately 50 percent female (U.S. Census Bureau 2023). Despite half of the county's residents reporting as female, regular preventive health services, such as those provided by obstetricians/gynecologists, were scarce. In 2019, San Diego was ranked 11 of 50 in the U.S. index for highest risk of OB-GYN shortages (Doximity 2019). These compounding barriers of health professional staffing shortages, geographic location, and inadequate or absent insurance coverage threaten the potential for any woman to thrive and achieve an average quality of life (Doximity 2019).

It is common for U.S.-Mexico border residents to seek binational care—healthcare from both countries—because of myriad systemic, structural, and intermediary challenges that influence access to quality healthcare services. First, the U.S. border economy is largely supported by Mexican nationals who are employed in service, manufacturing, and agricultural business industries, which offer low wages (Bastida, Brown, and Pagán 2008). These sectors typically force employees to pay the high cost of insurance premiums, rendering the U.S. healthcare system unaffordable for most border residents. Second, language and cultural discordance between patients and providers contributes to access issues, with language discordance and cultural incompetency further exacerbating health disparities (Fernandez et al. 2011). Immigrant Latina mothers, in particular, report limited access to language services, stigma, and discrimination in healthcare settings as a result of language barriers

(Steinberg et al. 2016). Third, accessibility to U.S. healthcare is limited not only by a lack of health insurance coverage but also by the region's large uninsured population, which has been shown to limit the quantity of providers and the quality of healthcare services available to all residents (Bastida, Brown, and Pagán 2008). Last, limited knowledge of the U.S. healthcare system places many Latinxs at a disadvantage and often leads to individuals seeking binational care in Mexico because of the inability to obtain care in the United States (Wallace, Mendez-Luck, and Castañeda 2009).

These challenges have resulted in a long-standing pattern of U.S. residents crossing over to obtain healthcare services in Mexico. Some Latinxs with transborder mobility travel to Mexico to use health services and procure pharmaceuticals, even with access to comprehensive care in the United States (Gorman 2014). Many individuals who are underinsured or uninsured also rely on international healthcare provided by Mexico to fulfill unmet needs from the U.S. healthcare system, whether due to lack of insurance coverage or affordability (Su et al. 2014). For example, if cost, coverage, or long wait times limit access to care in the United States, those with transborder mobility will seek care across the border. While this option may be beneficial for some individuals, those with chronic illness, inability to pay, or immigration restrictions are limited to services provided by the U.S. healthcare system (Bastida, Brown, and Pagán 2008). Without the resources to pay for healthcare, many people continue to face significant barriers accessing and using healthcare services (González Block et al. 2014). Collectively, these barriers perpetuate disparate health outcomes for residents of the border region, many of whom are Latinx and disproportionately represented among the uninsured.

Health Risks and Protective Factors Among Latinas

Research suggests that Latinxs living in the United States live longer and have lower mortality rates from heart disease, cancer, and many other leading causes of death than other racial/ethnic groups, including non-Hispanic whites, despite a range of psychosocial and physical health challenges, as well as poor access to care (Hostetter and Klein 2018; Salinas, Su, and Al Snih 2013), an epidemiological finding known as the Hispanic or Latino health paradox (Lancet 2015). Latinxs living along the U.S.-Mexico border, however, have been shown to suffer from an increased burden of diseases, contradicting this paradox (Salinas, Su, and Al Snih 2013). Systemic challenges and socioeconomic disparities have a bidirectional relationship with preventable chronic and communicable diseases that affect residents in border communities. For example, a rural border resident with low income has an increased likelihood of chronic disease, which can also increase the likelihood of being low income as a result of healthcare expenditures. Border populations experience some of the highest rates of tuberculosis in both the United States and Mexico; childhood obesity of epidemic proportions; pervasive diabetes, more than twice the prevalence among non-Hispanic whites; emerging threats of dengue; increased rates of diagnosed mental health conditions; and long-known challenges associated with HIV/AIDS (Oren et al. 2015). Latina adults in particular tend to suffer from hypertension at significantly younger ages and are at elevated risk for related health outcomes, such as heart failure, stroke, and diabetes (Lisabeth et al. 2008). These health disparities and deep-rooted inequities were further exposed by the COVID-19 pandemic.

Positive physical health outcomes are critical to maintaining a high quality of life, but overall health for Latinas extends beyond physical health and the mere absence of disease to encompass mental and emotional stability and spirituality (Garcés, Scarinci, and Harrison 2006). While Latinx culture values happiness, interpersonal relationships, and family, a national sample of mental health services used among Latinxs found that Latinas are almost twice as likely to be diagnosed with a mood or anxiety disorder compared to Latinos (Hochhausen, Le, and Perry 2011). Some predictors of depressive symptomology include levels of educational attainment, health status, and living with a partner (De Oliveira et al. 2017). Despite the high prevalence of mood affective disorders, Latinas in general are less likely than other racial/ethnic women to use mental health services, even after controlling for the same level of access (Hochhausen, Le, and Perry 2011). Public health and clinical efforts are still needed to achieve the balance between mental and physical health for Latinas, as both are required to achieve overall wellness and prevent premature morbidity and mortality (De Oliveira et al. 2017). Spiritual health and religiosity may be one outlet to improve mental health outcomes, as the effects of religion have been demonstrated to be inversely related to stress and depression among Latinas (Kirchner and Patiño 2010). In a nationally representative sample of N = 3,814 Latinx adults, 59 percent reported the importance of religion in one's life as very important, and 63 percent had a feeling of spiritual peace and well-being at least once a week (Pew Research Center 2014). This indicates the significance of spiritual health for this population.

Cultural considerations specific to Latinx communities may also include gender influences on health (Marshall et al. 2005). Prescribed gender roles in Latinx culture can influence psychological and physical health for Latinas when it comes to critical health and clinical issues such as pregnancy, intimate partner violence, and chronic or terminal illness (Miville, Mendez, and Louie 2017). Social determinants driving health inequalities related to gender for Latina women include unfair paid labor, violence, and limited education (Velasco-Mondragon et al. 2016). Latina women are more vulnerable to abuse and mistreatment and may suffer from low self-esteem (Velasco-Mondragon et al. 2016). Cultural expectations related to the management of multiple familial and domestic responsibilities among Latinas can also interfere with positive health behaviors, such as physical activity, which can lead to increased risk for cardiovascular disease and overweight/obesity (Arredondo et al. 2015; Koniak-Griffin et al. 2015). The cumulative intersectionality of social identities for Latinas in regard to gender, ethnicity, and social class can influence overall quality of life and risk for morbidity and mortality (Ramírez García 2019).

Surviving the Pandemic as a Latina in a Border Community

To better understand the influence of COVID-19 on health behaviors and emotional well-being for Latinas in San Diego, California, we examined data from nineteen local regions to assess the impact of COVID-19 and associated stressors. These data provided insight into effects of COVID-19 on employment, housing instability, unmet food and utility needs, number of cases per region, and parent/caregiver challenges.

The pandemic adversely affected the economy of San Diego, with heightened effects on Latinx residents. An estimated 430,000 San Diegans lost their jobs as a result of the pandemic; this increased the rate of unemployment to nearly 30 percent (SANDAG 2020a). Over 70 percent of Latinxs resided in zip codes with higher-than-average unemployment rates and 50 percent of all Latinxs in the county lived in neighborhoods with higher-than-average rates of COVID-19 (SANDAG 2020a). Service-oriented employees, such as those who work in hospitality, food service, transportation, or as in-home caregivers or medical support staff, were among the hardest hit by the pandemic. A geographic analysis by zip code revealed those most affected were residents who lived in the southern portion of the county, including along the U.S.-Mexico border (SANDAG 2020a). San Ysidro, the highest ranked neighborhood in the San Diego region for percentage of COVID-19 cases per capita, has a demographic profile of approximately 94 percent Latinx (SANDAG 2020a). This demonstrates the disproportionate impact of the pandemic on Latinxs in the border region.

COVID-19 will likely have long-term negative emotional, physical, and financial consequences on Latinx communities. Latinxs have the second highest number of confirmed COVID-19 cases by race/ethnicity in San Diego County ($N = 30,306$) and have experienced the most deaths ($N = 2,376$) in comparison to other racial/ethnic groups (County of San Diego HHSA 2022). This disparity has created compounding health effects, with Latinx individuals reporting high rates of mental health conditions due to COVID-19-related morbidity, mortality, and stay-at-home orders. Large financial burdens due to job losses and decreased work hours have created additional constraints with the limited availability of affordable housing and increased food costs. Further, societal attitudes, discrimination, and political rhetoric that have been heightened during the era of COVID-19 have far-reaching consequences on the health and quality of life for those residing along the U.S.-Mexico border.

Data collected across various counties in California confirm that the highest rates of COVID-19 exposure have been among essential workers in high-contact service roles (Garfield et al. 2020). An estimated 50 percent of Latinxs who experienced job loss were in the tourism sector (SANDAG 2020a). While the majority of middle- to upper-class employees were safeguarded from high exposure to COVID-19 as a result of the ability to work from home, essential and service-sector employees were required to attend work in person. As many service jobs are labor based, tasks cannot be completed remotely. Many of these roles are filled by females (58 percent), and the majority are Latinas (Garfield et al. 2020).

The COVID-19 pandemic was a public health crisis that disproportionately affected communities of color, exacerbating the long-standing barriers to care for Latina women living in the U.S.-Mexico border region. As a result of the pandemic, Latinx communities have faced increased restrictions to medical resources and to basic needs to survive. Many of the Latinxs and immigrants in this region who are underinsured or uninsured must rely on federally qualified health centers (FQHCs) or community clinics, which are often underfunded, limiting their ability to provide testing, management, and follow-up services to their patients (Clark et al. 2020). Furthermore, restricted access to preventive care increases risk and morbidity of underlying comorbidities associated with more severe COVID-19 manifestations (Clark et al. 2020). Regarding COVID-19 exposure, Latinxs living in border regions are at an elevated risk because of socioeconomic circumstances that require continuing in-person work, often in service-related jobs that require high contact with the general public. Those that continue working are also more likely to use public transportation, thus increasing exposure. At home, multigenerational housing situations are very common among Latinxs and immigrants, increasing risk of elderly or immunosuppressed family members coming in contact with others in the home, as well as creating undue stress to keep older family members safe.

In a survey conducted among N = 3,500 respondents from each of the seven major statistical areas in San Diego County, seven out of ten San Diego residents reported immediate unmet needs related to housing, food, and utilities (SANDAG 2020c). Over half of respondents (52 percent) reported the pandemic as the cause for their housing instability and inability to pay rent or mortgage (SANDAG 2020c). Previous research has linked housing instability to poor health outcomes in both children and caregivers (Ramirez 2019).

Maternal caregivers experiencing housing insecurity are also more prone to depressive symptoms (Ramirez 2019). The pandemic has presented multiple challenges for parents and caregivers, with a high burden placed on mothers. Three out of five parents from the San Diego region reported challenges with their school-aged children and distance learning for the 2019/20 school year (SANDAG 2020c). Approximately 14 percent of parents/caregivers had to stop working or reduce their hours because of difficulties with childcare (SANDAG 2020c). Working mothers were more likely to take on childcare responsibilities or leave their jobs entirely, at three times the rate of fathers, widening existing gender inequities (Henderson 2020).

Frontera Madre(hood) in the Time of a Pandemic

Latinas manage multiple dynamic roles, functioning as employees, partners, mothers, and caregivers to elderly and extended family members. Performing each of these roles under "normal" circumstances can involve great physical effort and be mentally taxing. The pandemic amplified the responsibilities typically carried out by all women, including but not exclusive to Latinas. Not all women, however, had the capital or familial resources available to withstand the conditions of the pandemic as well as others. More than half of Latinas (64 percent) work in low-paying jobs earning on average $10.93 per hour (Bateman and Ross 2020). For nonpartnered Latinas, maintaining a household in San Diego County on a low wage can be extremely challenging given the high cost of living. According to a cost-of-living index in which 100 represents the national average, the overall cost of living in California is 149.9, and the overall cost of living in San Diego is 160.1 (Best Places, n.d.). This cost transcends borders. For example, the major northern Mexican border communities of Tijuana (bordering San Diego), Ciudad Juárez (bordering El Paso, Texas), and Matamoros (bordering Brownsville, Texas) ranked 4th, 13th, and 112th in average cost of living in Mexico (Livingcost 2022).

Latinas represent a bulk of working poor employees who hold jobs as domestic workers and home health aides (Bateman and Ross 2020). In 2016, the median annual salary for a direct care employee of Mexican descent was only $14,900, lower in comparison to other Latinx workers of Caribbean or Central/South American descent (Campbell 2018). In addition to not receiving adequate compensation for these roles, home health aides are excluded from federal protections by not receiving a guaranteed minimum wage or overtime pay (Bateman and Ross 2020).

To be a mother in a border community who is caring for others of non-biological descent requires certain characteristics and compassion for others. This raises the question, however, of who is taking care of these women while they are busy taking care of (i.e., mothering) others?

During the height of the pandemic when most of the world was in isolation, many women who became new mothers or continued to parent children did not receive the social support typically extended by other family members or close friends (Steger Strong et al. 2021). In many regions, the risk of postpartum depression in Latina mothers is up to 40 percent greater compared to white mothers (Ceballos, Wallace, and Goodwin 2017). Socioeconomic status, family life, community of residence, and immigration status contribute to postpartum depression; many Latinas who lived in isolation as a result of the pandemic were more likely to experience depressive symptoms because of these factors (Ceballos, Wallace, and Goodwin 2017). Approximately 70 percent of households in the San Diego region have school-aged children (SAN-DAG 2020c). For many parents, the pandemic required a transition to virtual education and the need to guide offspring through periods of disappointment as they missed schoolmates, teachers, and traditional rite of passage milestones, such as prom and graduation ceremonies (Steger Strong et al. 2021). This transition to virtual education had many Latinx parents (42%) very concerned that their children have fallen behind in school because of disruptions caused by the pandemic. In one study, this feeling was exacerbated among Latinx immigrant parents compared to their U.S.-born counterparts (46% vs. 34%) (Noe-Bustamante, Krogstad, and Lopez 2021). The pandemic required mothers to be emotionally available and resilient for their families (Jefferson Center, n.d.). Maintaining constant composure during difficult times can be draining, cause prolonged fatigue, incite feelings of burnout, and contribute to mental exhaustion, especially when respite becomes impossible (Collins Bernier 2021).

For many, the pandemic has provided a time to pause, reflect, and reevaluate one's trajectory in life and responsibilities. Frontera madre-(hood) in the time of a pandemic is a delicate dance—oscillating between strength and fragility. As COVID-19 persists, it will be essential to consider the state of mind for mothers, quality of parenting, and condition of self. Latinx culture, while rich in many qualities including resiliency and strong work ethic, minimally encourages acts of self-love and respite. Traditional cultural values instead place greater worth on the advancement and subsistence of the family unit (*familismo*), female self-sacrifice and moral strength (*marianismo*), amicability, conflict avoidance, and politeness toward others (*simpatía*) (Ortiz 2020; Mendez-Luck and Anthony 2016). While these cultural values carry some strengths, collectively, they may be hindering Latinas' ability to achieve catharsis by silencing the challenges women are experiencing. Reenvisioning cultural expectations for Latinas will help women to heal and move forward from the traumas of the pandemic.

Conclusion

This chapter illustrates the challenges affecting health outcomes for Latinas from border communities across San Diego and Imperial Counties. Regional data from these counties have informed our understanding of the effects of the pandemic on high-risk families from low-income, migratory backgrounds, with increased risk for COVID-19. Barriers to accessing healthcare in the border region were heightened during the pandemic. The importance of surveillance for infectious disease was also demonstrated, as we were able to see the true, disproportionate impact on Latinxs across the United States. Disease surveillance continues to be pivotal in detecting binational exposures from transborder migration and contributes to the maintenance of domestic and international health standards. The lessons learned from the global health response to COVID-19 can be applied to future prevention efforts, including those targeting chronic conditions.

The juxtaposition of health outcomes for those who live at the southern border of the United States as opposed to those at the northern border, and for residents of urban versus rural locations, needs considerable attention. Disparate health outcomes among Latinxs should not be dictated by urban or rural residency, but require improved health infrastructure to achieve minimal health standards. Border health initiatives should continue to recruit physicians for HPSAs and implement health resources that have demonstrated effectiveness for improving health outcomes, including the self-management of chronic conditions.

For Latinas, the complexity of motherhood often includes transitions and negotiations, while looking out for the best interests of others. With recent declines in and delaying of childbirth among women of color, the concept of mothering is transforming to include caring for others and caring for oneself. Border walls may represent barriers to care, but they also symbolize the opportunity to attain a basic standard of care, quality of life, and improved future.

REFERENCES

Abrego, Leisy J., and Leah Schmalzbauer. 2018. "Illegality, Motherhood, and Place: Undocumented Latinas Making Meaning and Negotiating Daily Life." *Women's Studies International Forum* 67:10–17. https://doi.org/10.1016/j.wsif .2017.12.004.

Arredondo, Elva M., Jessica Haughton, Guadalupe X. Ayala, Donald J. Slymen, James F. Sallis, Kari Burke, Christina Holub, et al. 2015. "Fe en Accion/Faith in Action: Design and Implementation of a Church-Based Randomized Trial to Promote Physical Activity and Cancer Screening Among Churchgoing Latinas." *Contemporary Clinical Trials* 45 (B): 404–15. https://doi.org/10.1016/j .cct.2015.09.008.

Bastida, Elena, H. Shelton Brown, and José A. Pagán. 2008. "Persistent Disparities in the Use of Health Care Along the US–Mexico Border: An Ecological Perspective." *American Journal of Public Health* 98 (11): 1987–95. https://doi .org/10.2105/AJPH.2007.114447.

Bateman, Nicole, and Martha Ross. 2020. "Why Has COVID-19 Been Especially Harmful for Working Women?" Brookings, October. https://www.brookings .edu/essay/why-has-covid-19-been-especially-harmful-for-working-women/.

Best Places. n.d. "Cost of Living in San Diego, California." Best Places. Accessed August 7, 2021. https://www.bestplaces.net/cost_of_living/city/california/san _diego.

Bharmal, Nazleen, Kathryn Pitkin Derose, Melissa Felician, and Margaret M. Weden. 2015. "Understanding the Upstream Social Determinants of Health." Working paper, RAND Health, May. https://www.rand.org/content/dam /rand/pubs/working_papers/WR1000/WR1096/RAND_WR1096.pdf.

Campbell, Stephen. 2018. "Racial Disparities in the Direct Care Workforce: Spotlight on Hispanic/Latino Workers." Research Brief, PHI, February. https:// phinational.org/wp-content/uploads/2018/02/Latino-Direct-Care-Workers -PHI-2018.pdf.

Ceballos, Miguel, Gail Wallace, and Glenda Goodwin. 2017. "Postpartum Depression Among African-American and Latina Mothers Living in Small Cities, Towns, and Rural Communities." *Journal of Racial and Ethnic Health Disparities* 4 (5): 916–27. https://doi.org/10.1007/s40615-016-0295-z.

Cerrutti, Marcela, and Douglas S. Massey. 2001. "On the Auspices of Female Migration from Mexico to the United States." *Demography* 38 (2): 187–200. https://doi.org/10.1353/dem.2001.0013.

Cha, Paulette, and Shannon McConville. 2021. "Health Coverage and Care for Undocumented Immigrants in California: An Update." Public Policy Institute of California, June. https://www.ppic.org/wp-content/uploads/health-coverage-and-care-for-undocumented-immigrants-in-california-june-2021.pdf.

Clark, Eva, Karla Fredricks, Laila Woc-Colburn, Maria Elena Bottazzi, and Jill Weatherhead. 2020. "Disproportionate Impact of the COVID-19 Pandemic on Immigrant Communities in the United States." *PLOS Neglected Tropical Diseases* 14 (7): e0008484. https://doi.org/10.1371/journal.pntd.0008484.

Collins Bernier, Amanda. 2021. "The Burnout Is Real: Coping with Pandemic Parenting and Redefining Self-Care." *Bay State Parent*, January 14. https://www.baystateparent.com/story/news/2021/01/14/parenting-burnout-coping-pandemic-self-care/4164826001/.

County of San Diego HHSA (Health and Human Services Agency). 2022. "COVID-19 WATCH: Weekly Coronavirus Disease 2019 (COVID-19) Surveillance Report." County of San Diego HHSA, October 13. https://www.sandiegocounty.gov/content/dam/sdc/hhsa/programs/phs/Epidemiology/COVID-19%20Watch.pdf.

De Genova, Nicholas P. 2002. "Migrant 'Illegality' and Deportability in Everyday Life." *Annual Review of Anthropology* 31 (1): 419–47. https://doi.org/10.1146/annurev.anthro.31.040402.085432.

De Oliveira, Giovanna, Rosina Cianelli, Karina Gattamorta, Norma Kowalski, and Nilda Peragallo. 2017. "Social Determinants of Depression Among Hispanic Women." *Journal of the American Psychiatric Nurses Association* 23 (1): 28–36. https://doi.org/10.1177/1078390316669230.

Doximity. 2019. *2019 OB-GYN Workforce Study: Physician Shortages Contribute to Women's Health Crisis.* Doximity, September. https://s3.amazonaws.com/s3.doximity.com/press/2019_ob_gyn_workforce_study.pdf.

Fellowship for International Service and Health. n.d. "INSABI vs. Seguro Popular." Accessed August 20, 2022. https://www.orangefish.org/insabi.

Fernandez, Alicia, Dean Schillinger, E. Margaret Warton, Nancy Adler, Howard H. Moffet, Yael Schenker, M. Victoria Salgado, Ameena Ahmed, and An-

drew J. Karter. 2011. "Language Barriers, Physician-Patient Language Con-
cordance, and Glycemic Control Among Insured Latinos with Diabetes: The
Diabetes Study of Northern California (DISTANCE)." *Journal of General Internal Medicine* 26 (2): 170–76. https://doi.org/10.1007/s11606-010-1507-6.

Garcés, Isabel C., Isabel C. Scarinci, and Lynda Harrison. 2006. "An Examination
of Sociocultural Factors Associated with Health and Health Care Seeking
Among Latina Immigrants." *Journal of Immigrant and Minority Health* 8 (4):
377–85. https://doi.org/10.1007/s10903-006-9008-8.

Garfield, Rachel, Matthew Rae, Gary Claxton, and Kendal Orgera. 2020. "Double
Jeopardy: Low Wage Workers at Risk for Health and Financial Implications of
COVID-19." Kaiser Family Foundation, April 29. https://www.kff.org/corona
virus-covid-19/issue-brief/double-jeopardy-low-wage-workers-at-risk-for
-health-and-financial-implications-of-covid-19/.

González Block, Miguel Angel, Arturo Vargas Bustamante, Luz Angélica de la Sierra, and Aresha Martínez Cardoso. 2014. "Redressing the Limitations of the
Affordable Care Act for Mexican Immigrants Through Bi-National Health Insurance: A Willingness to Pay Study in Los Angeles." *Journal of Immigrant and
Minority Health* 16 (2): 179–88. https://doi.org/10.1007/s10903-012-9712-5.

Gorman, Anna. 2014. "Many Insured U.S. Latinos Prefer to See Doctors in Mexico." *PBS News Hour*, May 5. https://www.pbs.org/newshour/health/many-u
-s-latinos-find-better-health-care-mexico.

Henderson, Tim. 2020. "Mothers Are 3 Times More Likely Than Fathers to Have
Lost Jobs in Pandemic." *Stateline*, September 28. https://www.pewtrusts.org
/en/research-and-analysis/blogs/stateline/2020/09/28/mothers-are-3-times
-more-likely-than-fathers-to-have-lost-jobs-in-pandemic.

Hibel, Leah C., Chase J. Boyer, Andrea C. Buhler-Wassmann, and Blake J. Shaw.
2021. "The Psychological and Economic Toll of the COVID-19 Pandemic on
Latina Mothers in Primarily Low-Income Essential Worker Families." *Trau-
matology* 27 (1): 40–47. https://doi.org/10.1037/trm0000293.

Hochhausen, Laila, Huynh-Nhu Le, and Deborah F. Perry. 2011. "Community-
Based Mental Health Service Utilization Among Low-Income Latina Immigrants." *Community Mental Health Journal* 47 (1): 14–23. https://doi.org/10
.1007/s10597-009-9253-0.

Hostetter, Martha, and Sarah Klein. 2018. "In Focus: Identifying and Addressing Health Disparities Among Hispanics." Commonwealth Fund, December 27. https://www.commonwealthfund.org/publications/2018/dec/focus
-identifying-and-addressing-health-disparities-among-hispanics.

Jefferson Center. n.d. "Mom Burnout Is Real: Here's How to Take Care of Your
Mental Health and Your New Baby." Jefferson Center. Accessed November 13,

2023. https://www.jcmh.org/mom-burnout-is-real-heres-how-to-take-care -of-your-mental-health-and-your-new-baby/.

Kemper, Lee D. 2015. *On the Frontier: Medi-Cal Brings Managed Care to California's Rural Counties.* California Healthcare Foundation, March. https:// www.chcf.org/wp-content/uploads/2017/12/PDF-FrontierMediCalMgdCare Rural.pdf.

Kirchner, T., and C. Patiño. 2010. "Stress and Depression in Latin American Immigrants: The Mediating Role of Religiosity." *European Psychiatry* 25 (8): 479–84. https://doi.org/10.1016/j.eurpsy.2010.04.003.

Koniak-Griffin, Deborah, Mary-Lynn Brecht, Sumiko Takayanagi, Juan Villegas, Marylee Melendrez, and Héctor Balcázar. 2015. "A Community Health Worker-Led Lifestyle Behavior Intervention for Latina (Hispanic) Women: Feasibility and Outcomes of a Randomized Controlled Trial." *International Journal of Nursing Studies* 52 (1): 75–87. https://doi.org/10.1016/j.ijnurstu .2014.09.005.

Kurre, James A. 2003. "Is the Cost of Living Less in Rural Areas?" *International Regional Science Review* 26 (1): 86–116. https://doi.org/10.1177/0160017602 238987.

Lady, Brian, Carrie Henning-Smith, and Susan Kunz. 2017. "Addressing Health and Health Care Needs in the United States-México Border Region." National Rural Health Association Policy Brief. https://www.ruralhealthweb.org /NRHA/media/Emerge_NRHA/Advocacy/Policy%20documents/05-11-18 -NRHA-Policy-Border-Health.pdf.

Lancet. 2015. "The Hispanic Paradox." Editorial. *Lancet* 385 (9981): 1918. https:// doi.org/10.1016/S0140-6736(15)60945-X.

Lisabeth, Lynda D., Melinda A. Smith, Brisa N. Sánchez, and Devin L. Brown. 2008. "Ethnic Disparities in Stroke and Hypertension Among Women: The BASIC Project." *American Journal of Hypertension* 21 (7): 778–83. https://doi .org/10.1038/ajh.2008.161.

Livingcost. 2022. "Cost of Living in Mexico." Livingcost. Updated November 2022. https://livingcost.org/cost/mexico.

Marshall, Khiya J., Ximena Urrutia-Rojas, Francisco Soto Mas, and Claudia Coggin. 2005. "Health Status and Access to Health Care of Documented and Undocumented Immigrant Latino Women." *Health Care for Women International* 26 (10): 916–36. https://doi.org/10.1080/07399330500301846.

Mendez-Luck, Carolyn A., and Katherine P. Anthony. 2016. "*Marianismo* and Caregiving Role Beliefs Among U.S.-Born and Immigrant Mexican Women." *Journals of Gerontology Series B: Psychological Sciences and Social Sciences* 71 (5): 926–35. https://doi.org/10.1093/geronb/gbv083.

Mexico Business Publications. 2021. *Mexico Health Review 2020/21*. Mexico City: Mexico Business Publications. https://issuu.com/mexicobusiness publishing/docs/mhr2020-21_no_password_design_only_/1.

Miville, Marie L., Narolyn Mendez, and Mark Louie. 2017. "Latina/o Gender Roles: A Content Analysis of Empirical Research from 1982 to 2013." *Journal of Latina/o Psychology* 5 (3): 173–94. https://doi.org/10.1037/lat0000072.

Ndumbe-Eyoh, Sume, and Hannah Moffatt. 2013. "Intersectoral Action for Health Equity: A Rapid Systematic Review." *BMC Public Health* 13:art1056. https://doi.org/10.1186/1471-2458-13-1056.

Nelson and Nygaard Consulting Associates. 2008. *Imperial County Coordinated Public Transit—Human Services Transportation Plan*. Final Plan Submitted to the Imperial Valley Association of Governments. Nelson and Nygaard Consulting Associates, October. https://www.transitwiki.org/TransitWiki /images/3/3f/IMPERIAL_Coordinated_Plan_Oct._2008.pdf.

Noe-Bustamante, Luis, Jens Manuel Krogstad, and Mark Hugo Lopez. 2021. "For Latino Parents, Pandemic Has Brought Challenges in Child Care and Worries About Kids' Academic Progress." In *For U.S. Latinos, COVID-19 Has Taken a Personal and Financial Toll*. Pew Research Center, July 15. https://www.pew research.org/race-ethnicity/2021/07/15/for-latino-parents-pandemic-has -brought-challenges-in-child-care-and-worries-about-kids-academic-progress/.

Oren, Eyal, Gabriela Alatorre-Izaguirre, Javier Vargas-Villarreal, Maria Guadalupe Moreno-Treviño, Javier Garcialuna-Martinez, and Francisco Gonzalez-Salazar. 2015. "Interferon Gamma-Based Detection of Latent Tuberculosis Infection in the Border States of Nuevo Leon and Tamaulipas, Mexico." *Frontiers in Public Health* 3:220. https://doi.org/10.3389/fpubh.2015.00220.

Ornelas, India J., Stephanie Tornberg-Belanger, Jennifer E. Balkus, Perla Bravo, S. Adriana Perez Solorio, Georgina E. Perez, and Anh N. Tran. 2021. "Coping with COVID-19: The Impact of the Pandemic on Latina Immigrant Women's Mental Health and Well-Being." *Health Education and Behavior* 48 (6): 733–38. https://doi.org/10.1177/10901981211050638.

Ortiz, Fernando A. 2020. "Self-Actualization in the Latino/Hispanic Culture." *Journal of Humanistic Psychology* 60 (3): 418–35. https://doi.org/10.1177/00 22167817741785.

Pew Research Center. 2014. "Latinos." *Religious Landscape Study*, May 30. https:// www.pewforum.org/religious-landscape-study/racial-and-ethnic-composition /latino/.

Ramirez, Amelie. 2019. "Research: Latino Families Burdened by Housing Costs, Eviction." *Salud America!* (blog), May 10. https://salud-america.org/research -latino-families-burdened-by-housing-costs-eviction/.

Ramírez García, Jorge I. 2019. "Integrating Latina/o Ethnic Determinants of Health in Research to Promote Population Health and Reduce Health Disparities." *Cultural Diversity and Ethnic Minority Psychology* 25 (1): 21–31. https://doi.org/10.1037/cdp0000265.

Ramos, Rebeca, João B. Ferreira-Pinto, Kimberly C. Brouwer, Maria Elena Ramos, Remedios M. Lozada, Michelle Firestone-Cruz, and Steffanie A. Strathdee. 2009. "A Tale of Two Cities: Social and Environmental Influences Shaping Risk Factors and Protective Behaviors in Two Mexico–US Border Cities." *Health and Place* 15 (4): 999–1005. https://doi.org/10.1016/j.healthplace.2009.04.004.

Reich, Michael R. 2020. "Restructuring Health Reform, Mexican Style." *Health Systems and Reform* 6 (1): e1763114. https://doi.org/10.1080/23288604.2020.1763114.

Rural Health Information Hub. 2023. "Rural Border Health." RHIhub. Last updated August 30. https://www.ruralhealthinfo.org/topics/border-health.

Salinas, Jennifer J., Dejun Su, and Soham Al Snih. 2013. "Border Health in the Shadow of the Hispanic Paradox: Issues in the Conceptualization of Health Disparities in Older Mexican Americans Living in the Southwest." *Journal of Cross-Cultural Gerontology* 28 (3): 251–66. https://doi.org/10.1007/s10823-013-9202-9.

SANDAG (San Diego Association of Governments). 2020a. "COVID-19 Impact on the San Diego Regional Economy." San Diego Association of Governments, June 16. https://www.sandag.org/uploads/publicationid/publicationid_4679_27578.pdf.

SANDAG. 2020b. "COVID-19 Impacts on the San Diego Regional Economy: Six-Months of Economic Analysis Since Statewide Stay Home Order Began." San Diego, CA: SANDAG, October 15, 2020. https://www.sandag.org/uploads/publicationid/publicationid_4712_28193.pdf.

SANDAG. 2020c. "The Hardest Hit: Community Members Share COVID-19 Impacts." SANDAG, September 2020. https://www.sandag.org/uploads/publicationid/publicationid_4705_27996.pdf.

Sharp Mesa Vista Hospital. 2019. *Sharp Mesa Vista Hospital Community Health Needs Assessment Fiscal Year 2019*. San Diego, Calif.: Sharp Mesa Vista Hospital. https://www.sharp.com/about/community/community-benefits/upload/Sharp-Mesa-Vista-2019-CHNA.pdf.

Southern Border Communities Coalition. 2023. "The Southern Border Region at a Glance." SBCC. Last updated June 28, 2023. https://www.southernborder.org/border_lens_southern_border_region_at_a_glance.

Steger Strong, Lynn, Miriam Valdovinos, Sheree Thompson, and Sacha Pfeiffer. 2021. "Isolation, Acrobatics, 'Mommy Networks': Motherhood During the

Pandemic." *All Things Considered*, transcript, NPR, May 9. https://www
.npr.org/2021/05/09/995264976/isolation-acrobatics-mommy-networks
-motherhood-during-the-pandemic.

Steinberg, Emma M., Doris Valenzuela-Araujo, Joseph S. Zickafoose, Edith Kief-
fer, and Lisa Ross DeCamp. 2016. "The 'Battle' of Managing Language Barriers
in Health Care." *Clinical Pediatrics* 55 (14): 1318–27. https://doi.org/10.1177
/0009922816629760.

Su, Dejun, William Pratt, Jim P. Stimpson, Rebeca Wong, and José A. Pagán.
2014. "Uninsurance, Underinsurance, and Health Care Utilization in Mexico
by US Border Residents." *Journal of Immigrant and Minority Health* 16 (4):
607–12. https://doi.org/10.1007/s10903-013-9828-2.

United States–Mexico Border Health Commission. 2014. "Access to Health Care
in the U.S.-México Border Region: Challenges and Opportunities." White paper, November. https://www.ruralhealthinfo.org/assets/939-3103/access-to
-health-care-u.s.-mexico-border.pdf.

U.S. Census Bureau. 2023. "QuickFacts: California." U.S. Census Bureau, July 1,
2023. https://www.census.gov/quickfacts/CA.

U.S. HRSA (Health Resources and Services Administration). n.d. "HPSA Find."
Data.HRSA.gov. Accessed November 13, 2023. https://data.hrsa.gov/tools
/shortage-area/hpsa-find.

Velasco-Mondragon, Eduardo, Angela Jimenez, Anna G. Palladino-Davis, Dawn
Davis, and Jose A. Escamilla-Cejudo. 2016. "Hispanic Health in the USA:
A Scoping Review of the Literature." *Public Health Reviews* 37 (1): art. 31.
https://doi.org/10.1186/s40985-016-0043-2.

Wallace, Steven P., Carolyn Mendez-Luck, and Xóchitl Castañeda. 2009. "Heading South: Why Mexican Immigrants in California Seek Health Services in
Mexico." *Medical Care* 47 (6): 662–69. https://doi.org/10.1097/MLR.0b013e
318190cc95.

CHAPTER 11

"Ya Vámonos Que Va a Ver Mucha Fila en el Puente"

*A Mother–Daughter's Reflection on Crossing Borders
Using a* Transfronteriza *Intersectional Consciousness*

SYLVIA FERNÁNDEZ QUINTANILLA AND SILVIA QUINTANILLA MORENO
The University of Texas at San Antonio and Mamá Fronteriza

n the border area of Ciudad Juárez, Chihuahua, and El Paso, Texas, mothers and daughters experience the intersectionality of gender, age, and citizenship as divisions and fragmentations.[1] They also experience the complexities that generational bonds across mother-daughter relationships manifest. In this chapter, I (Sylvia) analyze these complexities using a *transfronteriza* intersectional consciousness, which allows us to understand how the geopolitical division of the border imposes a series of dynamics that make women experience difference through the intersections of language, cultural-religious beliefs, and generational struggles as they navigate the border using their different national citizenships. This framework derives from W. E. B. Du Bois's (1903) "double consciousness" and the postcolonial transnational feminist work of Chandra Talpade Mohanty (2003), Gloria Anzaldúa ([1987] 2012; Moraga and Anzaldúa [1981] 2015) and Cherríe Moraga (Moraga and Anzaldúa [1981] 2015), who push for understanding and bridging between transnational women of color and queer spaces. In this work, I use their teachings by centering both sides of the border in how I navigate both worlds using the tenets of intersectionality proposed by Kimberlé Cren-

---

1. The chapter title translates to "Let's Go Now or There Will Be a Big Line at the Bridge."

shaw (1991). Together, these scholars contribute to comprehending the *testimonios* presented here as fluid forms of citizenship that explain the systems of violence and oppression that women confront at the U.S.-Mexico border.

This chapter focuses on two *testimonios*, my mother's and my own. *Mi mamá*, a Mexican citizen, and me, her U.S. citizen daughter, and our transborder experiences are grounded in Moraga and Anzaldúa's theory in the flesh ([1981] 2015), Anzaldúa's mestiza consciousness ([1987] 2012), and Cynthia Bejarano and Cristina Morales's representations of frontera madre(hood) in this volume. Although this chapter concentrates on our lived experiences, our *testimonios* also represent the challenges and tensions caused within mixed-status families by the differences created by the colonial, patriarchal, and surveillance systems established at U.S.-Mexico international ports of entry, which border families cross each day. *Mi mamá* and I would cross daily, I as a transborder commuter student attending school in the United States while living on the Mexican side of the border, and my mother navigating Mexican and U.S. systems with aims of securing a better future for her daughter.[2] Our "theory in the flesh" (Moraga and Anzaldúa [1981] 2015) is marked on our bodies and in our memories of daily crossings, "where the physical realities of our lives—our skin color, the land or concrete we grew up on, our sexual longings—all fuse to create a politic born out of necessity. Here, we attempt to bridge the contradictions in our experience" ([1981] 2015, 19).

Mi mamá is a monolingual Spanish speaker with a U.S. tourist visa. She set her life aside as the first professional woman in her family to become completely dependent on her husband so that she could dedicate herself to her three children, driving them back and forth across the border to receive an education in El Paso. My parents felt that having an

---

2. Transborder, or cross-border, students are young people who cross international ports of entry to attend school. According to Estefania Castañeda Peréz (2022), "Transborder commuters are a heterogeneous population that includes U.S. citizens, lawful permanent residents, and Mexican nationals who have the legal documentation to cross the Mexico–U.S. border regularly for a variety of reasons. However, in order to engage in transborder mobility, transborder commuters must navigate land ports of entry and undergo extensive scrutiny from U.S. Customs and Border Protection (CBP) officers, who are afforded ample discretion to conduct their day-to-day policing operations" (1).

education in the United States and learning English would provide more opportunities for my siblings and me. My mother adjusted her life to constantly moving across the border, relying mostly on the income that her spouse generated as a maquiladora worker in Mexico. I was raised in a traditional household, where women were expected to be the primary caregivers, so in the logic of a culturally hetero-patriarchal societal structure, my mother was mainly responsible for our care and everyday well-being.

As a teenager, I started to cross the border every day to attend middle and high school in El Paso, since I was a U.S. citizen and had the right and entitlement to study in the United States, but I had to attend private schools because I did not have "legal proof" of living in El Paso, a requirement for attending public schools in Texas. Representing two generations living in Ciudad Juárez but traveling daily to El Paso, our mother-daughter *testimonios* offer a theoretical and personal reflection on the challenges and lessons of many people living in constant movement across the Río Bravo and on how we learn to live in these international liminal spaces. Our mother-daughter *testimonios* reflect what Bejarano and Morales call "frontera madre(hood)": "a state of being and a condition of Brown mothering, specifically at the U.S.-Mexico border, that is unique, complex, and a departure from other locations" (this volume).

Ciudad Juárez, Chihuahua, and El Paso, Texas, where I was born and raised, have taught *mi mamá* and me to turn imposed divisions into lessons of transgression and solidarity between us and others. Living in both places has been a process of learning how to find ways to strengthen the connections among border women and across our intersectional differences, as well as how to navigate and contest systems of micro and macro violence. *Termina siendo*

> a reality that results very subjectively, since it allows us to approach a complex and paradoxical social imaginary in which many border residents, especially Mexicans, suppose they live in a space where they can enjoy the best of two worlds—Mexico and the United States—but they also suffer the worst. The cost to access the benefits of the other side is having to wait in long and tedious lines, which prolong the wait to cross for up to two hours; to play the game of cops and robbers over and over again during inspection time; to expose yourself to the possibility of receiving

discriminatory treatment; and to feel firsthand the inequality between Mexico and the United States. (Padilla Delgado 2011, 16, translated by Sylvia Fernández)[3]

Basically, our everyday lives are a symbol of resisting an oppressive culture of surveillance that has made us live in fear and in a state of constant obedience.

My sixty-nine-year-old mother, who has lived in Juárez since she was born, and I, her thirty-two-year-old daughter, who was born in El Paso but raised in Juárez and visits the city often, will share aspects of our *transfronteriza* story that will resonate with thousands of other border families, who made the same sacrifices and movements to better secure their families' future. It personifies the "mothering practices at the U.S.-Mexico border" (Bejarano and Morales, this volume) that are prevalent across the nearly two thousand miles of the international border.

While *mi mamá* and I wrote our *testimonios* in 2022, we took care of *mi papá*, who had suffered a stroke, and while he recovered, we were able to spend time together and reflect on our experiences crossing the border as *transfronterizas*, and the struggles my parents had to secure a stable future for my siblings and me. *Mi mamá* had three U.S.-born children. She is a Mexican citizen with a U.S. tourist visa and is married to *mi papá*, who is also a Mexican citizen. For ten years, my mother would cross the border to El Paso to take her children to school. As her daughter, I witnessed the many efforts my parents made to allow my siblings and me, as U.S.-born citizens, to benefit from experiencing life on both sides. Our experiences as *transfronterizas* who crossed each weekday from Juárez to El Paso are illustrated in our mother-daughter *testimonios*, including what it was like to live in a region heavily affected

---

3. Original quotation in Spanish: "Una realidad que resulta muy subjectiva, ya que permite aproximarnos a un complejo y paradójico imaginario social en el que muchos residentes fronterizos, especialmente los mexicanos, suponen vivir en un espacio donde se puede disfrutar lo mejor de dos mundos—México y Estados Unidos—pero, también, sufrir lo peor. El costo para acceder largas y tediosas filas, que prolongan la espera para cruzar hasta por dos horas; representar una y otra vez el juego de policías y ladrones en el momento de las revisiones; exponerse a la posibilidad de recibir tratos discriminatorios; y sentir en carne propia la desigualdad entre México y los Estados Unidos."

by violence, both narco violence and imposed violence by binational governments (before and after the 2006–present Mexican war on drugs). The liminality of border living is reflected in our daily engagement with authorities and with institutional structures and protocols, as well as in the intersectional differences we negotiate, even still.

Testimonio de mi Mamá

We were seven siblings in my family, three brothers and three sisters, and my dad and mom. We grew up with economic difficulties, since as a young man, my dad was a campesino, who migrated from San Buenaventura, Chihuahua, an agricultural town that currently has been drastically affected by cartel violence, to Ciudad Juárez, to work in whatever he could, which were low-income jobs. I was the youngest, the one who longed to study and to have a career, since my brothers had to work from a very young age to help at home, and my sisters got married and had kids at a very young age. Gratefully, I was very much supported by my brothers, my sisters, my dad, and my mom to attend school and to finish my career. Thank God—I also started working from a very young age and went to school in the afternoons, which helped me continue my studies.

After graduating and obtaining a degree as a public accountant from the National Technical Institute of Mexico campus in Ciudad Juárez, I practiced my career in some jobs in Ciudad Juárez, and then moved to Guadalajara, Mexico, to work for a car agency. At that time, I was presented with the opportunity to earn a specialization in business administration. I was the first and only one in the family who graduated from the university, so this gave me the opportunity to do things that in my family were not common for the women of the house. I was able to travel to different parts of Mexico with my college friends, to purchase a car, clothes, and to become independent from my parents, but also from the impositions my sisters and mom had as women. Nonetheless, I always felt the pressure from my mother to marry. She would tell me that she could pass away at any moment, and she did not want me to be single. After two years of living by myself in Guadalajara, my mother traveled with two of my sisters there to bring me back home. She did not want me to be living alone and so far away from the family.

Several years later, I got married and continued to work for many years while I was married. When my children—one girl and two boys—were born, the situation began to get a little complicated since my husband and I worked, and I had to work and take care of the house and my family (children and husband). When my children were in Ciudad Juárez, I took them to school and then to daycare so I could work full time. My husband and I met at the Toshiba maquiladora near the Zaragoza International Bridge in Ciudad Juárez. I worked in the Finance Department as an accountant, and my husband worked in Material Resources as head of that department. My husband studied metallurgical engineering at the Autonomous University of San Luis Potosí and was born and raised in Santo Domingo, a mining town near the capital city of Chihuahua.

We worked together [from] 1985 in the same maquiladora and were married in 1990. We lived in my parents' house while we saved money for a down payment to buy a house. At that time, the general manager of the maquiladora lent us money, and that allowed us to give the down payment and start building our house in a year. We paid back the loan between the two of us. At thirty-five years old, I became pregnant with my daughter, and three years later, my middle child was born, and a year later, the youngest one, both boys. The birth of each of the children cost us about three thousand U.S. dollars at that time, plus pre- and postpartum doctors' appointments. With both of us working, we were able to achieve this. Then, they grew up, and I was in charge of taking them to school and everything that entails (meetings, festivals, trips, etc.), and my husband was in charge of taking them to afterschool sports (cycling, swimming, soccer). I [had] placed the three of them in daycare since they were little in order for me to keep working. At first, they all attended kindergarten and then elementary school in Ciudad Juárez, although we wanted each of them to study in El Paso, Texas, from the beginning, since all three were born there. That way, they would have two opportunities, in Mexico and in the United States.

During that time, the three of them were in private schools in Juárez, until my daughter finished elementary school, and then we decided that it was time for them to begin studying in El Paso. Although we were Mexican citizens and worked in Mexico, we frequently crossed into the United States on a tourist visa. We began looking for a school in El Paso that would accept us living on the Mexican side of the border without any problems. Private schools were very expensive, and it was a huge effort to get the three children into St. Patrick's Cathedral School. This border-crossing routine began with me taking them to school every day. We would usually cross at six in the morning and sometimes earlier. I would return to Juárez to work and cross again at three in the afternoon to pick them up after my work departure time. Back then, I was still working from 8 a.m. to 3 p.m., at a more flexible job and not at the maquiladora, since it was the only way I could accommodate my schedule to my children's school schedule. After two years with that routine, my daughter graduated from eighth grade and entered high school, and we were deciding whether to place her in a public school, Coronado or Franklin, by renting an apartment or house in El Paso, so she could attend school, or continue crossing back and forth from El Paso to Juárez and attend private school. At that time, the options were Loretto, a very expensive parochial school just for girls, or to have her attend Father Yermo, a much less expensive school that is near the international "free bridge/*puente libre*" (Bridge of the Americas). Attending Father Yermo was ideal for her, as she would be able to cross the international bridge walking, and I would continue crossing by car, since the younger children were still in elementary school. My daughter started crossing *el puente* back and forth by herself [when] she turned fifteen years old and until she was nineteen years old. At that time, my husband would pick her up once she crossed, since that was the time when there were multiple executions during daytime hours in the most concurrent streets of Juárez. Once she graduated from high school, she would then cross the border driving to attend New Mexico State University during the week, and then return home on the weekends.

Things were getting more complicated, since we had triple expenses by having to pay tuition and school expenses in dollars, not pesos, and all the meals the children had were twice the price in El Paso, much more than they were in Juárez; plus the car maintenance, gasoline costs, and other expenses added up. Taking them to school and going back for them was very difficult and time consuming. Sometimes, we had to wait at least three hours in the line every day, and that was for over ten years, without me knowing that I could get a permit to live on the U.S. side of the border legally, since I had my children in a U.S. school because they were U.S. citizens (according to Silvia's perception of the law). When my children entered school in the United States, after two years it became increasingly difficult for me to fulfill my work responsibilities one hundred percent, and I decided to stop working. Since we had a lower income, we had to find a way for my children to continue studying in El Paso, and we managed to get the two boys transferred to a public school.

My two sons were able to enter a public school since my older sister lived in east El Paso, first as a resident and then as a U.S. citizen after working at Farah's, the jeans factory in El Paso, during the 1960s, and later working for a family cleaning as a maid and taking care of children in a mansion in Oklahoma City. We asked her son if we could arrange for him to have temporary custody of my two sons so that my children could attend school using my sister and nephew's home address. At that time, we stayed a few days with my sister, who lived with my mother, who was already a ninety-year-old woman.

During that time of our lives, I lived in fear. I was even afraid of interacting with the mothers [at] the school of my kids, thinking they could report me. My sister had moved into my nephew's wife's house, and they offered me the house that belonged to my sister to rent it, so we moved to that house, and on the weekends, we would go back home to Juárez. At first, we paid rent but with the purpose of buying it, giving him a deposit of ten thousand dollars. This money was my husband's savings from the sale of his parents' home. [With us] not knowing the laws, my nephew, a U.S. citizen, took advantage of the situation, especially knowing the need for my children to go to school in the United States, and on the other hand, our immigration status and not being able to pay what he asked. As a result, he sent the police to the house, ran us out of the house, and never returned the deposit, making us feel as if we were criminals. We never fought anything because we did not know about U.S. immigration laws, and we feared losing what we had already achieved.

To this day, despite our difficulties, I think that despite everything, there are rewards. My children have managed to get ahead in their studies and have done very well in their professional careers. My oldest daughter is a professor at a university; my middle child graduated from UTEP and currently serves as a pilot for the government; and my youngest son is about to graduate with his electrical engineering degree from UTEP.[4] We struggled a lot, but being tenacious allowed everything that

---

4. University of Texas at El Paso

we envisioned to be achieved. Maybe I did not stand out as a professional, but the truth is that I am more interested in the future of my children. *Gracias a Dios*, and even though the border divides us since we, my husband and I, continue living in Ciudad Juárez, the five of us are united, and many things have been achieved, struggling or not—we have learned how to move forward together. Perhaps, in aspects of health, it has not all been pleasant. My husband suffers from diabetes and receives dialysis and has gone through very difficult times, since he never paid attention to his illness due to the demanding work of the maquiladora and because of his age, family history, and culture. But everything was with the intention to give the best opportunities to our children in this border region, which was an education and living in Mexico and the United States and allowing them to have a good job and life as bilingual citizens.

When our children were born, our intention was to at some point live in the United States, and one of my sisters who lives in Oklahoma City made the petition with the U.S. immigration service for us to become U.S. residents. This process took twenty-two years. It was at the same time that my daughter turned twenty-one, and it was either her submitting our papers to the U.S. immigration system or going through my sister's petition. We went through my sister's petition, and the [application] was processed faster, since during that time, my husband's maquiladora job had factories in Ciudad Juárez and in El Paso. His work proved that he would have a stable job and income once we became residents of the U.S. through a work visa [green card]. However, working and living in El Paso was no longer possible due to my husband's illness, since he received a disability retirement, and because he receives all his medical services in Mexico with his social security, since we never settled in the United States or received services from there, even though much of our time and salary was invested on the U.S. side.

My kids live in the United States in different states. The youngest one is the one who lives closest to us now, but my three children come to the house often. I still cross to El Paso but only to do some shopping or visit relatives there, and only when my children come to visit, since my husband was the one who was most familiar with driving throughout the city. Even though I used to cross every day and drive from downtown El Paso all the way to Horizon City, I never got used to driving on the freeway, so now I don't cross very often. I still get very nervous when I have to cross and show my papers. I get very afraid of the CBP and the border patrol. I don't know much English to defend myself, and I do not want to affect my children's jobs or lives in the United States.

Mi Testimonio as a *Transfronteriza*

As a border woman born in the early nineties, the border/*la frontera* has given me a lot and has taken other things from me. Being born on the U.S. side of the border in El Paso, Texas, being raised on the Mexican side of the border in the city of Juárez, and being able to cross from one side to the other without much difficulty to carry out different activities in my daily life have made my life experiences uniquely *transfronterizo*. Having specialized in border studies and its intersection with gender studies at New Mexico State University, I wanted to write this border *testimonio* to shed light on the complexity and humanity of this region—which is full of contradictions and a lot of frustration—but with my utmost respect for it. These feelings make me identify with people of color in the borderlands, as border scholar Gloria Anzaldúa (2015) once said: "I see Third World peoples and women not as oppressors but as accomplices to oppression by our unwittingly passing on to our children and our friends the oppressor's ideologies. I cannot discount the role I play as an accomplice, that we all play as accomplices, for we are not screaming loud enough in protest" (207).

I speak as a border woman who is part of and at the same time resists a patriarchal system embedded on both sides of the border. This system represents a culture and society on the Mexican and U.S. sides that have made us believe we must be dependent on patriarchal colonial violence, which simply cannot be recognized or fought against, because it has become part of our everyday lives and is intertwined throughout numerous generations.

I refuse, however, to resent *la frontera*. On the contrary, I have immense respect, gratitude, and affection for everything that implies being born and raised at the border, with its multiple intersectional communities from the past and present time. It is because of the border and these experiences that I have been able to develop a *transfronteriza* intersectional consciousness, which is embodied in personal experiences while understanding and expressing solidarity with the experiences of others on both sides of the border.

I can say that I am a product of what NAFTA (the North American Free Trade Agreement) created in this border region—in a positive way—since *mi mamá* and *mi papá* met in a maquiladora in the late eighties. Both of my parents' families migrated to northern Mexico in search of better opportunities than those offered at that time in other parts of Mexico. My grandfather's work from my dad's side was in the mining industry for foreign companies such as Asarco.[5] This allowed *mi papá* and his sisters and brothers to receive an education in English since they were children. From my mother's side, *mi abuelo*'s work was as a bracero in Artesia, New Mexico, where he worked in the vast cotton fields that existed at that time. My dad and mom, both the youngest of six and seven children, were of the generation who had university studies in accounting and engineering.

For them, and at that time, the border symbolized work opportunities and progress in the maquiladora industry. The fact that both worked in maquiladoras allowed my brothers and I to attend private schools on both sides of the border, and to be involved in extracurricular activities, such as participating in sports like swimming, athletics, cycling, and soccer from an early age. During kindergarten and the six years of elementary school when I studied in Juárez, my classes were half in English and half in Spanish, which has given me the tools to be a bilingual citizen, student, and now a professor. I keep learning how to navigate both the oral and the written worlds. Those skills have been essential in my life, and I think these are some of the things the border offers *transfronterizos* like me. My mom and dad had a vision for us to have a better life as border citizens, so they did everything possible to make this happen.

Throughout my education in Mexico, I was always one of the outstanding academic students. I really liked my school, and I loved to learn what my teachers taught me. I loved competing for the spelling bee, writing fiction stories, reading a lot to be in the honor roll, and competing in athletics. I really liked my Juárez elementary school because of the support the teachers gave to us and the familiarity with everyone around us. When I was about to graduate from elementary school, my parents decided it was time to move us to El Paso schools. They started looking at different options in El Paso. They thought we needed to practice our

---

5. Asarco is a transnational business that has been located in Ciudad Juárez, El Paso, and other towns in Chihuahua since the 1960s.

English more and start to have an official record within the U.S. system for when it was time to apply for college.

I remember crying so much over the news that they were going to transfer me and my brothers to a school in El Paso. I was very afraid of losing the friends I had known since I was little. I felt so insecure about having to speak English at that moment and of going to a new country that I did not feel part of—in essence, to know that our lives were going to change. Some of my fears came from the cultural shock I felt when watching television shows and movies like *Thirteen* and *Mean Girls*, or when listening to music like Pink and Britney Spears. My crying and begging my parents to not change our school didn't work, and in the summer of 2003, our paperwork was completed to enter St. Patrick's Cathedral School, close to downtown El Paso. Neither my father nor my mother told me what having my brothers and I in that school would involve. As Mexican citizens with U.S. tourist visas, my parents had to open a bank account in the United States, pay tuition fees in dollars, and apply for the expensive Express Line to cross the international port of entry from Juárez to El Paso. All of this involved sharing information about our lives, records, and identities through intensive investigative background checks that U.S. private and government institutions require, which, in the end, meant giving them more control of our external individual data.

My mom once told me that during those years, my parents forgot about any social life or purchasing anything extra for any reason, as the expenses they allowed were strictly to eat, go to school, or support us in some sporting activity. For my parents, education and sports were the perfect combination for us to learn values that would serve us for the rest of our lives. For a few months after school at St. Patrick's, my mom would bring food, and we would eat it at a park, and from there, we would go to the YMCA to exercise. My dad would cross the international bridge after work and meet us to do workout drills with us.

The years when I was at St. Patrick's seem like a time when we were living in a bubble that was not part of our reality. For instance, most of the students in that school were from families with an income in dollars, yet in some cases, they lived in Juárez. Others had already lived in El Paso for a long time, while others were from well-known wealthy border families, and still others had families whose income was unknown, such as coming from businesses related to drug trafficking.

During my adolescent years, I became *una rebelde*. I went against everything my parents told me to do. *Mi mamá* became my worst enemy because I felt that instead of being my ally and supporting me in the changes I was facing, she gave *mi papá* all the authority and responsibility over me. Without understanding much, I was very angry that neither my mom nor dad would let me go out, especially with the boys from my class or with those who were at Cathedral, which was the all-boys high school next to my school. In those years, some of the young people who attended the private schools in El Paso were among the children who lost their fathers during some of the first executions that took place in public places by organized crime groups in Ciudad Juárez.

I later realized that my never-ending fight with *mi mamá* was because I would ask for money or clothes to go out with some of the girls who invited me to go eat, or to go to parties and quinceañeras. Some of these events were in the nightclubs of the Pronaf Zone, a metropolitan zone with popular restaurants and night life in Ciudad Juárez, across the international Bridge of the Americas. All of this caused strong tensions between my mom and me because at the time, I didn't understand that my parents' budget was just enough to pay for school fees, food, and monthly bills. Growing up middle class in Juárez is not the same as growing up middle class in the United States. I also did not understand the generational and social class differences we experienced, so my parents could never afford the comfort and lifestyle that some of my peers had. At the time, I did not grasp the dangers across the border region, and in my parents' wisdom, they feared for my and my siblings' safety. I did not comprehend these concerns, and I never spoke with my mom about them. I am now very grateful with *mi mamá* and *mi papá* for keeping us in sports.

As I reflect on the past, I can see that my parents protected us from the violence in Ciudad Juárez, where during the day, when going to school or coming back home, we saw some of the people who were hanged from the bridge, shootings happening in the middle of the street, and bodies after a shootout. Most of the places where my generation used to hang out, like Juárez nightclubs and restaurants, were burned or sites of several killings by the narcos. The Pronaf Zone is now abandoned, and many places and stories that I am remembering are just in our memories; few traces are left.

As I am writing this *testimonio*, I am reflecting on how the demands of capitalism in border regions are tied to drug trafficking, and they often intertwine. I remember demanding that my parents buy me clothes from Abercombie & Fitch or Guess and to get me a Nextel because at that time, having a Nextel was the trend, a subtle trend imposed by the narco culture at the border without us even noticing it.[6] Sometimes without realizing it, our everyday lives and the people, places, and experiences we have are related to systems of violence. My *testimonio* of my cross-border education reveals some of the reasons that my mother and I fought all the time. Mother-daughter arguments are common generational rites of passage, but at the border, they were influenced by two cultures, two nation-states, and a complexity that is unique to border regions.

During my last semester at St. Patrick's, the dynamics of crossing to El Paso and returning to Juárez changed a bit, since at that time, my mother was still working. One of the neighbors who had placed her daughters in the same school as us formed a carpool with my mom. *Mi mamá* would take us in the morning, and the neighbor would pick us up in the afternoon. At that time, we had the Express Line to cross the international border quickly, which was supposed to be faster to cross, but in the mornings, because of so many people crossing into El Paso, we had to be in line at six in the morning to be at school by eight. Crossing the Express Line was extremely intimidating, since U.S. Customs and Border Protection (CBP) extensively investigated us before we could have access to the Express Line.

My parents would tell us that we should always obey the officials, that we should never cross something prohibited because CBP could take away the Express Line from all of us, or they could even take away my parents' visas to cross. *Mi mamá* and *papá* were always so obedient, trying to do everything the correct way, and being very cautious about who crossed with us because they were always afraid of being punished. This was stressful and frustrating because to have the privilege of crossing quickly to go to school or work, you could not question rules and policies, and you must be obedient and beholden to the protocols of surveillance and punishment when crossing. I remember *mi mamá* being very stressed when she wanted to bring us food from Juárez so that we would

---

6. A popular phone at the time that had walkie talkie capabilities.

not spend so much time without eating while in school, because eating at school was expensive, and buying food in El Paso was even more expensive. Crossing certain foods was always prohibited, and the foods one could cross were limited, and sometimes it was uncertain what could or could not be crossed and what would be confiscated by CBP, even leading to punitive charges. Many times, it depended on the mood of the officer in charge at that moment.

With the neighbor that my mom would take turns carpooling with, we would cross to Juárez through the free bridge, since they did not have the Express Line.[7] As time passed, we began to notice that she changed trucks to a more luxurious one every month, and from one day to the next, that family lived surrounded by luxury, which began to alarm my parents. One day when our neighbor picked us up, we were sitting in the seats in the last row of their SUV, and we were playing, and one of the boys knocked the other one down and fell onto the trunk. When he sat down again, his eyes were wide open, and he had a surprised and scared look on his face. When we arrived home, we were talking about what we saw in the trunk, which was filled with many packages of fifty- and one-hundred-dollar bills. My parents were so scared that they told us we should not accept nor touch anything from them or from whoever else might be with them. At the end of that semester, we stopped carpooling. Years later, we learned that they grew *amapola* in the Sierra Tarahumara of Chihuahua, and that a family member had been killed in an ambush.[8] We never found out what happened to them, since they later divorced and went to live elsewhere.

Border crossing when there was a lot of fear that you could be associated somehow with drug trafficking, directly or indirectly, affected everyone, everywhere, on both sides of the border wall. I think about how at the border, a mother can talk with her daughter about these issues to understand the seriousness of things and make decisions about who should be your boyfriend or friend, who to go to eat with, or go to parties with, or establish groups with, and to know which places to go to or not to go to. As a mother and daughter with different citizenships at the border, *mi mamá* and I learned how to navigate these difficult worlds,

---

7. The Bridge of the Americas is locally known as the free bridge.

8. *Amapola* is opium poppy.

where the rules are contradicted on a day-to-day basis, and where the bad and the good become so confusing that learning to question adolescent defiance is trumped over reinforcing silence, obedience, and fear, which becomes a form of generational trauma.

After I graduated from middle school at St. Patrick's, my mom stopped working, and my parents decided to enroll my siblings in a public school near my aunt's house. I went to Father Yermo, a private school near the Bridge of the Americas, where most of the students would cross the bridge to attend. In my second year of high school, my mom transferred me to a public school, Americas High School, where I saw many classmates smoke marijuana during recess hours and consume cocaine during English literature class. Now, it seems ironic to me that El Paso was where I saw the two worlds of drug trafficking: one, where some financially benefited but were affected emotionally by that system, and two, those who bought and consumed it in El Paso yet were afraid to go to Juárez because of the violence. These views also perpetuated the notions that all violence existed on the Mexican side of the border, but not on the U.S. side.

When my mother stopped working, it was no longer possible to continue paying for the Express Line. We began to cross the bridge that does not charge, the Bridge of the Americas. This involved getting up at five in the morning so my mom could drop me off at the bridge, where I would then walk to school, and she would drive to the other side of town to drop off my brothers, who went to school in the eastside of El Paso. In the ten years my mom and I crossed the border almost daily, we were exposed to state militarized and narco violence, but we resisted this violence so my siblings and I could be educated in the United States. I would say this is a kind of frontera madre(hood). I saw how *mi mamá*'s hands would sweat when crossing and while driving because of the fear imposed by the CBP, when the only thing she was doing was taking us to school in the United States. I heard my mom begging to God that nothing bad happen to us when crossing to school and back home. I would get so frustrated seeing my mom's reactions of fear, crying, and screaming to my brothers and me to be serious, to sit down and buckle up, to not say anything other than "U.S. citizen," with our passports in hand and ready to cross. I felt my mom worried and frustrated with having to remain silent and not being able to defend herself in an environment that made her dependent on *mi papa*'s income, her tourist visa, and the geopolitical division that the border represents.

I witnessed so many injustices that have become normalized at the border by family members and private and governmental institutions, and nobody says anything or does anything out of fear, because they have made us believe that all these forms of micro and macro violence are normal, and it is ingrained in us not to defend ourselves. It taught us that if we want a better future, we must forget, keep obeying, and not question anything. The division of the border causes these weaknesses in its communities, and it is up to the individuals living there to preserve these memories, to learn ways to navigate this violence, and to defend ourselves and fight against these injustices and divisions on the border.

In our two *testimonios*, the maquiladora industry, the army of CBP agents, and the drug-trafficking industry are systems founded by the ideals of patriarchy that produce mass legal and illegal goods and impose power, control, and hierarchies within geopolitical divisions. They are three enemies that directly and indirectly work to control and surveil the border by allowing business, every kind of business, to take place. We know of people and families on both sides of the border who are part of these industries as sources of primary income, and they operate on fear mongering, control, and power. In the middle of it all are families and mothers like *mi mamá*, who confronted her fear and sacrificed for her children as so many other women did. Within all that fear that my mother experienced when crossing each day without speaking English and armed with only her tourist visa to cross, as the car idled in long lines during the hot months when she sweated and was nervous, or when it was cold and freezing, *mi mamá* taught me several things. Reflecting on our memories and understanding our experiences as border women deeply from our body and through a *transfronteriza* intersectional consciousness allow us to keep pushing back to "name, archive, and dismantle the violence we see, feel, or hear about, and the daily violent affronts against everyday border people, immigrant people, migrant people, species, and any being crossing through our homelands" (Hernández Sánchez and Bejarano 2022, 104). My mother taught me to navigate the border and take the warrior's torch to keep fighting as a border woman who hopes for a life on the border that is not divided, and who protects the lives of women, children, and communities.

REFERENCES

Anzaldúa, Gloria. (1987) 2012. *Borderlands/La Frontera: The New Mestiza.* 4th ed. San Francisco, Calif.: Aunt Lute.

Castañeda Pérez, Estefania. 2022. "Transborder (In)securities: Transborder Commuters' Perceptions of U.S. Customs and Border Protection Policing at the Mexico–U.S. Border." *Politics, Groups, and Identities* 10 (1): 1–20. https://doi.org/10.1080/21565503.2020.1748066.

Crenshaw, Kimberlé. 1991. "Mapping the Margins: Intersectionality, Identity Politics, and Violence Against Women of Color." *Stanford Law Review* 43 (6): 1241–99. https://doi.org/10.2307/1229039.

Du Bois, W. E. B. 1903. *The Souls of Black Folk.* New York: Bantam Classic.

Hernández Sánchez, Ma. Eugenia, and Cynthia Bejarano. 2022. "A Feminist Border Manifesto for Unsettling Times: Shouting 'Basta' at the US-Mexico Border." *Chiricú Journal: Latina/o Literatures, Arts, and Cultures* 6 (2): 96–105.

Mohanty, Chandra Talpade. 2003. *Feminism Without Borders: Decolonizing Theory, Practicing Solidarity.* Durham, N.C.: Duke University Press.

Moraga, Cherríe, and Gloria Anzaldúa. (1981) 2015. "Entering the Lives of Others: Theory in the Flesh." *This Bridge Called My Back: Writing by Radical Women of Color,* 19–59. 4th ed. New York: SUNY Press.

Padilla Delgado, Héctor Antonio. 2011. "Reflexiones surgidas de la vida cotidiana." In *En el puente con la migra: Anecdotario de la vida fronteriza,* edited by Héctor Antonio Padilla Delgado, 25–36. Juárez: Universidad Autónoma de Cuidad Juárez.

TESTIMONIO

Changing the Narrative on How Our Mexican Immigrant Communities Should Be Served Along the Border

HILDA VILLEGAS
La Mujer Obrera and Las Familias de Chamizal

M y name is Hilda, and I am part of La Mujer Obrera in El Paso, Texas, and I have been with this organization for over twenty years.[1] I am very fortunate to have come across La Mujer Obrera at a young age. I was twenty-three years old and a single mom of a three-year-old and a three-month-old. I call myself fortunate because I had to come to La Mujer Obrera to learn about my history, the history of my community—the Chamizal—and the struggle of Mexican immigrant women in the factories for better working conditions and to fight against NAFTA [North American Free Trade Agreement] displacement.[2] I had to come to La Mujer Obrera to learn and understand my own oppression as a woman and as a child from a Mexican immigrant household, and that of my community.

---

1. "La Mujer Obrera is a local independent organization dedicated to creating communities defined by women. Our organization was founded in 1981 by women who were both garment workers and Chicana activists. Our experience showed us that as women we must implement our own ideas and strategies for our community. La Mujer Obrera has developed its organizing strategies based on the following basic human rights: employment, housing, education, nutrition, health, peace, and political liberty" ("About," La Mujer Obrera website, accessed November 23, 2023, http://www.mujerobrera.org/about).

2. The Chamizal is an important and a historically contested area of El Paso located directly between the United States and Mexico.

I am a product of the barrio schools in a predominantly Mexican immigrant community. Their curriculum focused on Americanizing us and making us "productive members" of society by taking away our language and our identity, and by imposing upon us another culture that totally goes against our own practices and culture. I could not help but grow up with a sense of either helplessness, shame, or fear of being identified as Mexican, as an immigrant, and feeling an urgency to disassociate from who you are. I call it a forced separation from your family, your mother—a total isolation; and when you are isolated, then it is easier for others to dictate what your place in El Paso is and how your community is supposed to be served. This continues to exist within our community, and it is very detrimental to the relationships that exist between families and children, and between residents of the Chamizal.

For us to discuss this change in narrative, we would have to understand past narratives. One narrative that was very dominant was that Mexican families and Mexican children present a threat to the livelihood of white supremacy in El Paso. It is a narrative that identified a Mexican woman as fertile and a problem, which led to massive incarcerations by border patrol of women and children during the 1940s, making us look like inferior Mexican peons, and redlining our communities as hazardous areas. This ensured El Paso's labor force, which kept us as working poor with little to no investment in the infrastructure of our communities, leading to the intentional segregation of Mexican families.

And even in recent efforts to change narratives, we see how the Glass Beach Study portrayed Mexican immigrant families and border regions.[3] The City of El Paso commissioned this 2006 study to implement economic development projects. Information from this study was leaked to the public, where the old El Paso was pictured with an elderly campesino (farmworker) and the new El Paso, with a picture of Penelope Cruz and Matthew McConaughey. The study claimed they could turn poor, old El Paso into the image of tourism and celebrities.

When city leaders or decision makers talk about the community of El Paso, we hear them portray a certain image, but they do not ask in-

---

3. The Glass Beach Study was a controversial and racist study from 2006 to "de-Mexicanize El Paso" and demolish parts of El Segundo Barrio. See Paredes (2015).

dividuals from El Paso barrios for their opinion. For us, the women of the Chamizal and the Mujer Obrera, we know and see our people, the residents, the women and children of our barrios, our schools, and our homes. When asked—if they ever ask us—What are your needs?, we say the basic needs that humans should be entitled to, which are health, safety, education, housing, political freedom, food, and jobs. Then we hear them say we stand strong with the immigrant community, we support migrants, yet we see them closing our elementary schools, closing our housing projects, and moving families to the outskirts of the city, displacing women and children to make room for private investment, and placing a massive school bus hub in our neighborhood high school, Bowie High School, that serves our community. They do not fool us. It concerns us when they have these talks about what the El Paso community needs and wants because we know that their progress only leads to the destruction of our Chamizal community and the massive displacement of our communities. We say that progress cannot be at the cost of others.

The change in narrative will have to come from us, the residents in the Chamizal, the women and children defending their schools, advocating for equity, and preserving their community. The shift will have to be of who is telling our story, who is telling our history, who is controlling our narrative as people, and who defines who[m] our community is supposed to serve. Because our work as *mujeres en la lucha* is convincing ourselves and other women that we have what it takes to do that, to build our community and to defend it.

In the Chamizal area, we identify ourselves by the major streets that we live on. Looking back to my childhood and growing up in the Frutas barrio of the Chamizal, I can tell you that most of the families shared similar struggles, financial shortfalls, hurdles, barriers, and some conditions that are not favorable. Yet, a lot of these circumstances in which we find ourselves have not been by choice but imposed on us.

La Mujer Obrera understands that to help our community and to change outcomes and these circumstances, we need to heal ourselves as people and women, as well as to help our community heal. We need to repair the relationships between one another and the relationship with mother earth, and we must learn to work together using our knowledge and our collective practice, our creativity. If we look back to what we inherited from our ancestors and what they left us, it is the ability to be creative, the relationship with the earth, the practice of community, and all the generational knowledge that has been preserved and that we still see in our barrio and in our people.

REFERENCES

Paredes, Martin. 2015. "Further Proof of the De-Mexicanization of El Paso." *El Paso (Tex.) News*, April 13. https://elpasonews.org/2015/04/13/further-proof-of-the-de-mexicanization-of-el-paso/.

AFTERWORD

Frontera Madre(hood) and the Path of *Conocimiento*

IRENE LARA

San Diego State University, California

> As keepers of the fire of transformation we invite awareness of soul into our daily acts, call richness and beauty into our lives; bid spirit to stir our blood, dissolve the rigid walls between us, and gather us in.
>
> —GLORIA ANZALDÚA, "FOREWORD 2001,"
> *THIS BRIDGE CALLED MY BACK*

Frontera madre(hood)—as a geopolitical *sitio*, as a Coatlicue borderlands, as a gathering of knowledge, as a call to action—is generative and destructive. It is where *monstruos* named empire, cisheteropatriarchy, militarization, racism, and economic greed, who feed on constructed divisions and fears, are called out. It is also where freedom seeds take root and grow. It is a place of/for "survivance," of/for "la sobrevivencia."[1] Where we "measure our actions against [the question], 'Will

---

1. Gerald Vizenor and other Native thinkers use "survivance" to recognize the history of Native peoples as actively surviving and resisting settler colonialism and its impact rather than passively surviving day by day. Recent struggles for sovereignty at *la frontera* include protesting the building of the border wall, which desecrates Native sacred lands. See, for example, Rivlin-Nadler (2020), "Young Kumeyaay Women Lead Protests Against Border." Citing Vizenor, Ana Castillo, and campesina organizers in Sierra Linda, Guanajuato, whose spiritual epistemologies were the source of their "sobrevivencia," Ruth Trinidad Galván theorizes *la sobrevivencia* as beyond survival; it "is what lies ahead and beneath plain victimry, our ability to *saciar* (satiate) our hopes and dreams in creative and joyful ways" (2006, 163).

this help the people survive?'"[2] It is a place for dreaming into being "otro modo de ser humano[a][x] y libre."[3] Where we can cultivate critical consciousness and awareness of s/Spirit(s) and embody the indigenous principle that "we are related to all that lives" (Hernández-Ávila 2002, 532).[4]

The afterword. This is the part where you ask "¿y ahora qué?" *Mi comadre* Angelita Bórbon, who has been traversing frontera madre(hood) since the sixties as a midwife, public health practitioner, Indigenous thought leader and dialogue facilitator, mother, grandmother, and community activist, reminds me of that central question, "Now what?" "We were praying for you" at the protests, at the kitchen table *pláticas*, at the ceremonies, she says. Praying for us: students, educators, writers, scholar-activists, community activists, researchers, survivors of the "educational survivor complex" (Love 2019). Us, right now, armed with the privileges to write, read, research, teach, and learn from this text. So what is next?

To continue to seed and water the Land for the cultural shift work that is needed for radical change—one grounded in love, care, justice, respect for self-autonomy, and our relationality to all of Life—on this frontera madre(hood) "path of *conocimiento*," as Gloria Anzaldúa theorized, we need to devote ourselves to doing both "inner work" and "public acts" (Anzaldúa 2002b, 540–78). This "internal work coupled with commitment to struggle for social transformation" (Anzaldúa 2002b, 574) includes activities that focus on self-reflection and contemplation, creativity, intellectual and spiritual development, self-care, and healing our personal wounds and intergenerational traumas, as well as activities that focus on sharing knowledge and resources, politically mobilizing, community organizing, protesting, collaborating, publishing, public speaking, mothering/caretaking, teaching, and healing in community (Rendón [2009] 2023; Medina and Gonzales 2019).

The tremendous resistance and transformational work of frontera madre(hood) deserves to be recognized and adapted. I wonder, however, how we can intentionally practice frontera madre(hood) in ways that further sustain well-being? As evidenced by the experiences of oppres-

---

2. These were Angelita Borbón's opening words during our interview in Tucson on April 7, 2001.

3. These are Mexican novelist's Rosario Castellanos's poetic words.

4. I learned to write "s/Spirit(s)" from Laura E. Pérez. See her *Chicana Art: The Politics of Spiritual and Aesthetic Altarities* (2007).

sion and violence documented in *Frontera Madre(hood)*, the need to be a guerrera against harm and injustice is undeniable. Just as important is our need to cultivate our ability to do curandera work, to help heal and sustain our selves and our communities. Can we listen to the curandera/x-guerrera/x within, who with fierce tenderness says "cuidate"? Community health worker and researcher, herbalist, and birth attendant Patrisia Gonzales discusses how the first *promotora* program on Mexican/Indigenous traditional medicine in the United States, in 1998, worked to revitalize "*curando*, or healing our own bodies and that of our families," adopting the phrase "Curandera de yo misma" from ceremonial leader Sylvia Ledesma. This was a politically and epistemologically meaningful and necessary step in paving a path for the resurgence of *curanderismo* (Gonzales 2012, 20). We all deserve wellness and the opportunity to rest when we are feeling tired, sick, or sad. "You must be as dedicated to your spiritual self-care as you are to your families and communities," *nos recuerda* practitioner of *curanderismo* and cultural educator Grace Alvarez Sesma (2019, 173). Black feminist writer Toni Cade Bambara emphasized the same message in the visionary *This Bridge Called My Back: Writings by Radical Women of Color* when she wrote in her foreword, "It is the Afterword that'll count," including "the contracts we creative combatants will make to mutually care and cure each other into wholesomeness" (Moraga and Anzaldúa [1981] 2002, xlii).

Creative combatants who care and cure, YES.

Conocimiento as not only knowledge and awareness, but also "that aspect of consciousness urging you to act on the knowledge gained" (Anzaldúa 2002b, 577), can take many forms. To be effective curandera-guerreras/xs, we need to connect with "inner work" and "public act" practices that feel authentic for us. Given the impact of the living legacy of colonialism, capitalism, and other systems of dominance on our whole selves, our "bodymindspirit[s]" (Lara 2002, 435), our environment, and our whole social structure, doing healing work must be a priority. With decades of disability and environmental justice work to build on, Aurora Levins Morales testifies: "The only sustainable way to heal human society is if we all stay rooted in who we are and what we bring, connected with each other, and find the works our body-heart-minds are called to" (2023, xviii–xix).[5]

---

5. For further inspiration, see the whole *Healing Justice* (2023) book.

Luz Alvarez Martínez, a past director of the National Latina Health Organization (NLHO), located in Fruitvale, California, a Latinx immigrant community, would always say, "We all have to do our own work." By this she meant that if we want to effectively work with others toward liberation and justice and transform systems of oppression, we need to be vigilant about engaging in ongoing critical consciousness, emotional, and healing work. How have *we* been hurt by systems of power? How can working on our internalized sexism, racism, colorism, classism, ableism, ageism, queerphobia, and transphobia help to liberate us and keep us from perpetuating oppression, conceivably freeing energy to dream of and create a new world? In all of our collaborations and healing circles, we always worked from the presupposition that we all have the capacity to heal our selves and society.[6]

Frontera Madre(hood) unapologetically highlights *madres'* lives and ways of knowing and being, expansively defined, and *madre* co-conspirators engaged in survivance and social justice praxis, as educators, caretakers of children, maquiladora workers, activists working to end gender violence and violence at the hands of the state, health researchers, directors of shelters, weavers, and more. The potential for frontera madre(hood) collaboration, innovation, persistence, and resiliency in the face of multiple experiences of individual and systemic violence is well documented throughout the book. I hope this strengthens our s/Spirits while we continue to confront and work to transform the unnatural disasters affecting *frontera* lives in the context of globalization, profit-driven policies, political corruption, and inequities based on race, ethnicity, color, sexuality, sex, gender identity and expression, socioeconomic status, citizenship status, religion, language, ability, size, age, and other categories of social inequality.

We do not all have to lead our own organizations or earn professional degrees to contribute to social justice. We do need to meaningfully show up and align our actions with the values of frontera madre(hood) and *transfronteriza* solidarity as demonstrated throughout the narratives in the book. As you consider how you want to practice *conocimiento* and "act on the knowledge gained," I invite us to collectively think about

---

6. On the NLHO's holistic approach to Latina health and community-engaged partnerships with universities, see Ayala et al. (2006).

ways to address the daily need for accessible and culturally responsive social supports that will indeed "help the people survive" *and* the need for completely new ways to structure society. On a personal level and on a community level, how do we dismantle oppressive structures while creating new ways or refashioning old ways of being and relating built on values that assume all peoples are worthy and deserving of dignity, well-being, and self-autonomy, and have the right to live, raise families, play, and work in healthy and safe hoods?

Let's continue to intentionally integrate knowledge about and by community activists and scholar-activists, strengthening our relationships with one another. Let's commit to self-care and communal care, *cuidarnos y cuidar*, compassionately listen to our bodies and s/Spirits and respond. Let's respectfully seek out healers and cocreate healing circles in our hoods. Through our "inner work" and "public acts," let's continue to contribute to frontera madre(hood).

contigo,
Irene

REFERENCES

Anzaldúa, Gloria E. 2002a. "Foreword 2001: Counsels from the Firing . . . Past, Present, Future." In *This Bridge Called My Back: Writings by Radical Women of Color*, edited by Cherríe Moraga and Gloria Anzaldúa, xxiv–xxxix. 3rd ed. Berkeley, Calif.: Third Woman Press.

Anzaldúa, Gloria E. 2002b. "Now Let Us Shift . . . The Path of *Conocimiento* . . . Inner Work, Public Acts." In *This Bridge We Call Home: Radical Visions for Transformation*, edited by Gloria E. Anzaldúa and AnaLouise Keating, 540–78. New York: Routledge.

Ayala, Jennifer, Patricia Herrera, Laura Jiménez, and Irene Lara. 2006. "Fiera, Guambra, y Karichina! Transgressing the Borders of Community and Academy." In *Chicana/Latina Education in Everyday Life: Feminista Perspectives on Pedagogy and Epistemology*, edited by Dolores Delgado Bernal, C. Alejandra Elenes, Francisca E. Godinez, and Sofia A. Villenas, 261–80. Albany: State University of New York Press.

Gonzales, Patrisia. 2012. *Red Medicine: Traditional Indigenous Rites of Birthing and Healing*. Tucson: University of Arizona Press.

Hernández-Ávila, Inés. 2002. "In the Presence of Spirit(s): A Meditation on the Politics of Solidarity and Transformation." In *This Bridge We Call Home: Rad-*

ical Visions for Transformation, edited by Gloria E. Anzaldúa and AnaLouise Keating, 530–37. New York: Routledge.

Lara, Irene. 2002. "Healing *Sueños* for Academia." In *This Bridge We Call Home: Radical Visions for Transformation*, edited by Gloria E. Anzaldúa and Ana-Louise Keating, 433–38. New York: Routledge.

Levins Morales, Aurora. 2023. Foreword to *Healing Justice Lineages: Dreaming at the Crossroads of Liberation, Collective Care, and Safety*, by Cara Page and Erica Woodland, xvii–xx. Berkeley, Calif.: North Atlantic Books.

Love, Bettina L. 2019. *We Want to Do More than Survive: Abolitionist Teaching and the Pursuit of Educational Freedom*. Boston: Beacon Press.

Medina, Lara, and Martha R. Gonzales, eds. 2019. *Voices from the Ancestors: Xicanx and Latinx Spiritual Expressions and Healing Practices*. Tucson: University of Arizona Press.

Moraga, Cherríe, and Gloria Anzaldúa, eds. (1981) 2002. *This Bridge Called My Back: Writings by Radical Women of Color*. 3rd ed. Berkeley, Calif.: Third Woman Press.

Rendón, Laura I. (2009) 2023. *Sentipensante (Sensing/Thinking) Pedagogy: Educating for Wholeness, Social Justice, and Liberation*. 2nd ed. New York: Routledge.

Rivlin-Nadler, Max. 2020. "Young Kumeyaay Women Lead Protests Against Border Wall." *KPBS*, August 6. https://www.kpbs.org/news/border-immigration/2020/08/06/young-kumeyaay-women-lead-protests-against-border.

Sesma, Grace Alvarez. 2019. "Womxn Caring for Womxn Is Ceremony." In *Voices from the Ancestors: Xicanx and Latinx Spiritual Expressions and Healing Practices*, edited by Lara Medina and Martha R. Gonzales, 172–76. Tucson: University of Arizona Press.

Trinidad Galván, Ruth. 2006. "Campesina Epistemologies and Pedagogies of the Spirit." In *Chicana/Latina Education in Everyday Life: Feminista Perspectives on Pedagogy and Epistemology*, edited by Dolores Delgado Bernal, C. Alejandra Elenes, Francisca E. Godinez, and Sofia Villenas, 161–79. Albany: State University of New York Press.

CONTRIBUTORS

Elva M. Arredondo is a professor in the Department of Psychology and core investigator at the Institute of Behavior and Community Health at San Diego State University. Dr. Arredondo graduated from the University of Washington with a degree in psychology and attained her PhD in clinical psychology from Duke University.

Cynthia Bejarano is a Regents Professor in gender and sexuality studies and the College of Arts and Sciences Stan Fulton Chair at New Mexico State University. Her scholarship and advocacy center on the U.S.-Mexico border. She authored *Qué Onda: Urban Youth Culture and Border Identity* and co-edited *Terrorizing Women: Feminicide in the Américas*.

Bertha A. Bermúdez Tapia is an assistant professor of sociology at New Mexico State University. Her research focuses on the impacts of state power on migrant and border lives, as well as the production of violence on the U.S.-Mexico border. She specializes in ethnographic photography and drone images to create interacting mappings of migrant camps.

Margaret Brown Vega is an anthropologist and activist who dedicates time to supporting immigrants. A native *tejana*, with deep family roots in southern New Mexico, she focuses her time and energy on the betterment of her community and working on pressing social issues such as displacement, migration, and mass incarceration.

Macrina Cárdenas Montaño has a master's degree in theological studies from the Franciscan School of Theology in Berkeley, California. She
was the director of the Ministry of Hispanic Migrants for the Dioceses of
Rochester and Buffalo in New York. Currently, she is a volunteer at Casa
del Migrante de Tijuana and loves to knit.

Claudia Yolanda Casillas is from El Paso del Norte, and her work is
centered on Chicana feminist epistemologies using borderland theory to
deconstruct and reframe deficit ideologies in school systems. Through
the power of *testimonio* and *autohistoria teoría*, she remains steadfast in
employing these as instruments toward decolonizing praxis.

Luz Estela (Lucha) Castro is a human rights defender, theologian, and
feminist lawyer. She is cofounder of El Barzon, CEDEHM, Justicia Para
Nuestras Hijas, Mujeres de Negro de Chihuahua, and the Observatorio
Nacional Femicidio. Since the 1990s, she has represented victims of trafficking, feminicide, forced disappearances, rape, and domestic violence.
Her contribution to making femicides visible is recognized across the
world.

Marisa Elena Duarte (Pascua Yaqui/Chicanx) is an associate professor
in the School of Social Transformation at Arizona State University. She
teaches courses in justice theory, digital studies, and American Indian
education. She writes about Indigenous responses to digital technolo-
gies. She lives in Phoenix with her son, husband, and dog.

Taide Elena is the founding member of the Border Patrol Victims Network (BPVN), a solidarity network working with others to fight the culture of violence and impunity in the U.S. Border Patrol. She is the grandmother of José Antonio Elena Rodríguez, a teen killed by a border patrol
agent in Nogales, Arizona, in 2012.

Sylvia Fernández Quintanilla is a transborder woman and a transborder
interdisciplinary public and digital scholar. She is an assistant professor
at the University of Texas at San Antonio in public and digital humanities. Her research, teaching, and service focus is on transnational, intersectional, and translingual humanities studies and digital humanities.

Paula Flores Bonilla, from Durango, Mexico, was married to Jesús González Hernández and had six daughters and one son. In 1995, Paula and her family emigrated to Ciudad Juárez, Chihuahua, where her daughter María Sagrario was a femicide victim. Paula initiated Voces sin Eco, a group of mothers seeking justice to end femicides. In 1999, Paula was also instrumental in bringing basic services to her community.

Judith Flores Carmona is a professor in the Honors College and the College of Health, Education and Social Transformation at New Mexico State University. She is a Faculty Fellow for the Office of the Vice President for Equity, Inclusion and Diversity. Her scholarship includes critical race feminism, critical multicultural education, and *testimonio* methodology and pedagogy.

Sandra Gutiérrez has her doctorate in clinical sexology and is a first-generation college graduate and College Assistance Migrant Program alumna. Her professional history includes clinical social work, graduate school instructorship, clinical supervision, and mentorship. Most of her clinical work revolves around psychological trauma treatment within the Latinx community.

Ma. Eugenia Hernández Sánchez is a professor at the Autonomous University of Ciudad Juárez. Her research interests are feminist theory, forced migration, creative research methods, and radical friendship. She teaches in the UACJ departments of art, creative processes in design and art, and the doctoral program in urban studies.

Irene Lara is a professor at San Diego State University and a Xicana teacher, femtor, and spiritual activist in the Borderlands. Focusing on healing, spirituality, pedagogy, and mothering, her scholarship furthers decolonial feminism, curandera/x praxis, and women of color, queer, and Anzaldúan theory. She is the co-editor of *Fleshing the Spirit: Spirituality and Activism in Chicana, Latina, and Indigenous Women's Lives.*

Leticia López Manzano was born in Juárez on March 29, 1956, and lived with her seven siblings and parents (†). She went to the university and finished her studies in social work, which helped her to develop ideas and actions to improve the lives of those most in need. She has a daughter and a granddaughter.

Mariana Martinez studies visual arts at the Autonomous University of Ciudad Juárez. Their research interests include spatial segregation and identities in relation to urban space and belonging. Their theoretical and creative work include *The City that Fractures* (2023), which produces comics that address spaces both familiar and foreign in Ciudad Juárez.

Maria Cristina Morales is a professor of sociology at the University of Texas at El Paso. Her research focuses on social inequality among Latinxs, the U.S.-Mexico border, and structural violence. She co-authored *Latinos in the United States* and publishes on Latina migrants' exposure to inequality and their resiliency.

Paola Isabel Nava González, granddaughter of Paula Flores Bonilla, is a college student majoring in psychology in Mexico. Throughout her high school years, she cultivated her love for art by drawing portraits, mainly of her grandmother, who is a great inspiration to her due to her years of activism in the community.

Olga Odgers-Ortiz is a researcher at El Colegio de la Frontera Norte. Among her publications are the book *Making Los Angeles Home: The Integration of Mexican Immigrants in the United States* (2016). She participates as a volunteer in migrant shelters in Tijuana and likes to knit.

Priscilla Pérez was born and raised in Ciudad Juárez, Chihuahua, Mexico, and is an architect. Growing up in a border city showed her the unique dynamic of border cultures in Ciudad Juárez and El Paso, Texas. She is studying for her master's in architecture and urban development at the Autonomous University of Ciudad Juárez.

Silvia Quintanilla Moreno is from Ciudad Juárez, Chihuahua, and the daughter of working-class Mexican citizens, Angelina Moreno and Manuel Quintanilla. She received a degree in public accounting from the Technological Institute and a postgraduate degree in administration from the University of Guadalajara. For thirty years, she pursued her career and is the mother of three.

Cirila Quintero Ramírez is a sociologist in the Colegio de México, and a professor and researcher at El Colegio de la Frontera Norte, Campus Matamoros. Her areas of research are labor unions, maquiladoras, and gender and migration. She has been a visiting professor across universities in Canada, Spain, Sweden, and the United States.

Felicia Rangel-Samponaro is a border activist devoted to defending migrant lives and the co-director of the Sidewalk School for Children Asylum Seekers, which provides quality education, medical care, employment, housing, and food assistance to those who would go without as they experience displacement on the Mexico border.

Coda Rayo-Garza is a PhD candidate in applied demography at the University of Texas at San Antonio. She is a policy advocate and researcher. She is a co-author of *Latinos in the U.S.* and mother to Carlitos and Grace.

Shamma Rayo-Gutierrez was born in Nuevo Laredo, Tamaulipas, and currently resides in Laredo, Texas. Shamma is a real estate professional who helps families navigate the home-buying process. She is the mother to three children—Madison, Ellah, and Matthew.

Marisol Rodríguez Sosa is an architect with a PhD in urban planning from the Federal University of Rio de Janeiro, Brazil. She is a research professor at the Institute of Architecture, Design and Art, at the Autonomous University of Ciudad Juárez, and member of the National System of Researchers in Mexico.

Brenda Rubio is an assistant professor in educational leadership, teacher education, and administration at the University of North Texas. Her action research focuses on creating educational spaces where culturally and linguistically sustaining materials can be co-created with/in community and critically conscious educational leadership praxis can develop.

Ariana Saludares began volunteering with community service programs and organizations as a little girl. She is the executive director of Mariposa Ranch, a migrant shelter in Deming, New Mexico, and a cofounder of Colores United, a nonprofit that connects people in need with resources to help them heal and grow.

Victoria M. Telles is a PhD student in the Joint Doctoral Program in Public Health at the University of California, San Diego, and San Diego State University. She received her bachelor's in sociology from the University of California, Riverside, and her master's in public health from Claremont Graduate University.

Michelle Téllez is an associate professor in the Department of Mexican American Studies at the University of Arizona. She co-edited *The Chicana M(other)work Anthology: Porque Sin Madres No Hay Revolución* (2019). Her book *Border Women and the Community of Maclovio Rojas: Autonomy in the Spaces of Neoliberal Neglect* (2021) won the 2023 National Association of Chicana/o Studies Book of the Year Award.

Marisa S. Torres is a doctoral student in public health at San Diego State University and the University of California at San Diego. She received degrees in biological sciences from Bakersfield College, Chicana/o studies from the University of California, Santa Barbara, and public health from George Washington University.

Edith Treviño Espinosa is a passionate educator who lives and teaches in La Frontera. Dr. Treviño Espinosa's research is grounded on the lived experiences of people in La Frontera, with a focus on displacement and historical trauma, and how people's lived experiences at the border affect and intertwine with educational systems.

Mariela Vásquez Tobon, Ña'a 'ndavi (Juarense Mixteca), is a lawyer and promoter of Indigenous rights and national languages. She is an interpreter-translator, workshop leader, and university professor. She graduated in law from the Autonomous University of Ciudad Juárez and has a master's in law from the National Autonomous University of México.

Hilda Villegas is a community organizer in El Paso, Texas. She is a co-leader of Familias Unidas del Chamizal, a grassroots organization in a barrio next to the international Bridge of the Americas, which works for educational equality and to alleviate exposure to environmental hazards.

INDEX